Performance Banking and Rural Development

Performance Banking and Rural Development

Dr. R.P. Sharma

RANDOM

RANDOM PUBLICATIONS

NEW DELHI (INDIA)

Performance Banking and Rural Development

ISBN 978-93-5111-807-7

Published in 2016 in India by

RANDOM PUBLICATIONS

4376-A/4B, Gali Murari Lal, Ansari Road
New Delhi-110 002
Phone : +9111-43580356, 011-23289044, 011-43142548
e-mail: sales@randompublications.com,
info@randompublications.com, randomexports@gmail.com

Reprinted 2026

Type Setting by : Friends Media, Delhi-110089

Preface

Development of the rural areas has been the major focus of growth in the third world countries since long and India is no exception to this. However, owing to varied development approaches the aim of achieving a speedier growth in rural sector has been beset with many a bottleneck. Rural development is basically a micro approach, which has to be entwined with macro objective depending on the micro perspectives.

Regional Rural Banks plays a key role as an important vehicle of credit delivery in rural areas with the objective of credit dispersal to small, marginal farmers & socio economically weaker section of population for the development of agriculture, trade and industry .But still its commercial viability has been questioned due to its limited business flexibility, smaller size of loan & high risk in loan & advances. Rural banks need to remove lack of transparency in their operation which leads to unequal relationship between banker and customer. Banking staff should interact more with their customers to overcome this problem. Banks should open their branches in areas where customers are not able to avail banking facilities. In this competitive era, RRBs have to concentrate on speedy, qualitative and secure banking services to retain existing customers and attract potential customers.

Co-operatives were first formal institution to address credit needs of rural people in the country like India in the early twenties. State Co-operative agricultural and rural development banks are playing a key role in meeting credit requirement of rural population at Taluka level as apex Bank with Primary co-operative agricultural and rural development banks as its members.

This book will be of special interest to bankers and policy makers in delineating the relative contribution of various commercial and cooperative banks at the local level and how branch specification as to the policy prescription.

– Author

Contents

Preface .... *v-vi*

1. Rural Financial Institutions **1**

WHO is the Money Lender? 1
Disbursement of Farm Credit 4
Rural Debt 4
Service Area and Recovery of Credit 6
Rural Infrastructure Development Fund 10
Financial Institution in the Euro Era 15

2. Rural Banking **19**

Objectives of Rural Banking 20
Initiatives towards Rural Banking 21
Micro Finance Sector and Rural Banking 26

3. Cooperative Banking **28**

Financial Sector Reforms 30
Urban Cooperative Banks (UCB's) 33
Need for sustainable Long Term Agricultural Credit System 34
Cooperatives In India 37
Cooperative Marketing 39

4. Rural Development **43**

Integrated Rural Development Programme (IRDP) 43
Strategy for Rural Development 48
Prime Goal of Rural Development 53
Rural Services and Resources 54
Structural Change 56
Theoretical Framework for Industrialization 62
Agro based activities for Income Generation 66
Essential Aspects of Rural Development 70
Integrated Wastelands Development Project (IWDP) Scheme 72
Comprehensive Integrated Development in Rural India 73

5. **Trends in Rural Credit** **91**
Agency-wise credit flow 91
Recent Initiatives 94
Reduction in Rural Bank Branches 100
Cooperative Credit in India 103
Health of Rural Credit Cooperatives 109

6. **Development of Rural Economy** **116**
Introduction 116
Role of Regional Rural Banks 118
Reconstruction of the Rural Economy 124
Urbanization and Rural Economy 137
Integrated Rural Development Programme 143

7. **Bank Performance** **146**
Data and Methodology 147
Form of Government Regulation 149
Instruments and Requirements of Bank Regulation 151

8. **Role of Commercial Banking Industry** **155**
Strategic Implications from a US Perspective 155
Technological Change and the Industrial Organisation of US Banking Markets . 158
An Internet Banking World and the Role of Local Banks 164
Pervasive Computing: Really Getting to Know Your Toaster 165

9. **Central Banking** **174**
the meaning of Central Bank 174
Functions of the Central Bank of India 175
Central Bank as Banker to Commercial Banks 181
Central Bank as Controller of Credit 182
Main points aboutCommercial Banking 184

10. **Development of Banking Operations** **187**
Salient Features of Deposit Schemes 187
Customer Identification and Introduction: Opening of Accounts 189
Opening of Accounts 191
Opening and operating of Accounts Under Different Categories 197
Nomination of Account Holder 206

11. **Capital Control and Banking Policy** **274**
Capital Control 274
Reformation of Banking System 277
Tasks of the Monetary Policy 282
The Banking System Reform 284

Bibliography **310**

Index **312**

1

Rural Financial Institutions

Improved rural infrastructure and technology have all contributed to agricultural growth, but their impacts have varied by settings. Government expenditure on roads and R&D have by far the largest impact on poverty reduction and growth in agricultural productivity. Government spending on education has the third largest impact on rural poverty and productivity growth in agricultural products on growth in agricultural productivity and rural poverty reduction, even after allowing for trickle-down benefits.

WHO IS THE MONEY LENDER?

Since Independence India increased wheat output from five/six million tones in 1947 to 72.5 million tones in 2007; per capita power consumption from 15.5 kW to 606 kW; telephones from 1.1 million to 218 million; national highways from 19,634 Km to 65,569 Km; exports from ₹. 403.4 crore to 5.64 lakh crore; Government revenue from ₹. 171 crore to ₹ 4.03 lakh crore; doctors from 0.5 lakh to 5.54 lakh and reduced infant mortality from 145.6 per 1000 live births to 58 per 1000 live births.

Rural areas have also witnessed varying rates of development, growth and progress. More importantly, Rural Financial Institutions [RFIs] during 60 years have touched the lives of millions and supported, through efficient resource mobilization and credit deployment, banks' own as well as Government's programmes aimed at accelerating process of integrated rural development, stepping up farm output, creating self-employment opportunities, minimizing incidence of poverty and regional imbalances. It is against this background that an attempt is made here to appreciate the role and effectiveness of RFIs in their efforts to disburse credit for the development of farrm and allied sector, small scale industries, rural and cottage industries including handloom and handicrafts and service and business sector, empowerment of women through forming Self-Help-Groups and linking them with banks, development of scheduled castes and tribes and creating most essential rural infrastructure in villages. A buoyant agricultural sector is necessary to ensure food security, provide livelihood to a large proportion of the workforce, contribute to the growth of the economy by producing wage goods, raw material for industry, goods for export, generate surpluses and provide markets for non-agricultural goods. Comparative advantages in several agriculture products add to its significance as an important contributor to foreign exchange earning.

RURAL FINANCIAL INSTITUTIONS

Institutional rural credit in India was put in place during the 1570s, when the Government began the practice of extending loans to farmers in drought years. Later, it was decided to experiment with rural credit cooperative on the lines of the Raiffeisen models in Germany [based on the principles of materialism, solidarity, participation of management, and one-person-one-vote democracy] and since the beginning of the 1900s, when the first cooperative credit institution was established, these continued to be the primary lending institutions, catering to the short-term and long-term credit needs of farmers for their agricultural operations. Their system was subjected to a major review in 1950s by the All India Rural Credit Survey Committee, which observed that a large share of the credit requirements of rural households, particularly the poor, came from traditional sources such as relatives, landlords, traders and money lenders.

India's rural credit system is unique in its reach and diversity. Besides, the basic role of financial intermediation, the RFIs play a unique role in accelerating agricultural growth. They have contributed substantially to the country's continuing efforts to reduce poverty and regional imbalances. To make the rural credit delivery system, vibrant and dynamic and the functioning of the RFIs proactive, the RFIs have been under periodic examination over the years. The pioneering All India Rural Credit Survey [1954] was followed by the All India Rural Credit Review Committee [1969], the Committee to Review Arrangements for Institutional Credit for Agriculture and Rural Development [1981] and the Agricultural Review Committee [1989] which had comprehensively investigated various emerging issues in rural credit and made recommendations. In addition, a number of issue-specific and institution-specific studies have also been made from time to time by various agencies. The recommendations of these committees/studies and the actions thereon have brought about momentous changes in the rural credit scenario of the country.

Multi-agency Approach

By the mid-sixties the credit requirements of agricultural sector grew multi-fold with the realization that cooperatives alone would not be able to fulfill the burgeoning demand of rural credit. Therefore, the concepts of a multi-agency approach to rural credit and the social control measures were adopted. The major commercial banks that were privately owned [with the exception of the State Bank of India] were brought under "social control" and within a few years thereafter nationalized., The nationalized commercial banks were called upon to extend credit to rural areas on a priority basis and they were directed to expand the network of their branches in rural areas to serve rural masses especially the poor.

In 1972 the Banking Commission observed in their report that despite the massive expansion of network of commercial banks, there would still be the need and possibility of having a specialized network of bank branches to cater to the needs of rural poor. Thus, originated the concept of "Rural Bank". By 1975 when the structure of rural moneylenders was regulated under the Government's efforts to eradicate rural indebtedness as a part of its "20-Point Economic Programme" an urgent need was felt for an alternative institutional mechanism to reach the rural poor particularly the small and marginal farmers, artisans and agricultural labourers. Consequently, Government of India constituted the Working Group on Rural Banks in July 1975.

The Working Group recommended setting up of State sponsored, region based, rural oriented commercial banks, which would blend the rural touch, local feel, the professional discipline, ability to mobilize deposits and access to central money markets and the modernized outlook of commercial banks. In a sense it was an experiment to hybridize commercial banking culture with the rural ethos. The role as perceived for this new institution was to supplement and not supplant the existing financial institutions in the rural sector. It was envisaged that this institution would help in reducing regional imbalances by mobilizing and simultaneously deploying resources in the same region. It was asserted that these banks would cover primarily the small and marginal farmers, landless labourers, rural artisans, small traders and other weaker sections of rural society for their productive credit needs and to a limited extent, the consumption credit needs.

The institutional credit delivery system in rural India comprises the cooperative credit institutions, commercial banks, and the Regional Rural Banks. The cooperative credit system is a century old primary rural credit delivery system in the country and is organized into its short-term and long-term arms at primary/glass-root level, central level and State / apex level that operates through more than one lakh window covering about 4.5 crore borrowing members. There are 28 public sector commercial banks and 32 banks in private sector operating in villages through their more than 32,000 branches in rural and semi-urban areas. Similarly, 196 RRBs provide their financial services to rural masses through 14,311 branches.

It is discernible that the cooperative credit institutions were virtually the only institutions providing credit for agricultural activities till 1970-71, when the commercial banks made a beginning in this area. With the spread of their branches, the commercial banks moved fast and by 1988-89, when they adopted the Service Area Approach, they claimed more than 41 per cent of the share in disbursement of agricultural credit and about 54 per cent share in the outstanding agricultural credit.

The market share of the RRBs in agricultural credit by this time was mere 5 per cent but the credit had gone entirely to the rural poor. The demand for credit had risen faster from year to year and the figures of annual disbursements for agricultural purposes moved from ₹ 7,438 million in 1970-71 to ₹ 91,062 million 1988-89 until the concept of Service Area Approach was implemented.

And now the disbursements shoot up to ₹ 1,574,800 million in 2005-06. Following table exhibits the phenomenal contribution made by the RFIs during the period from 1970-71 to 1999-2000 and the resultant impact on informal sources of credit from 1951 to 1991.

DISBURSEMENT OF FARM CREDIT

With the induction of public sector and nationalized banks and RRBs credit disbursement has increased significantly from year to year since 1970-71. Total disbursement rose from ₹ 7,438 million in 1970-71 to ₹ 3,005,182 million at the end of 1999-2000. Annual growth in the disbursements of all banks had not been progressively rising as it varied from 42 per cent to 131 per cent. Annual disbursement on an average was ₹ 49,688.2 million by Co-operatives followed by commercial banks at ₹ 42,911.6 million and RRBs at ₹ 6,826.8 million. Share of co-operatives was as high as 51.25 per cent followed by commercial banks at 42.84 per cent where as its was 5.91 per cent in case of RRBs.

RURAL DEBT

Dependence of rural households on non-institutional sources of credit were as high as 92.8 per cent in the year 1951, just four years after India's independence which declined to 82.7 per cent in 1961 and further to 70.8 per cent in 1971 when cooperative credit institutions made their presence felt on the rural scene after acceptance and implementation of recommendations of the All India Rural Credit Survey Committee in 1954 and entry of major private sector banks after their nationalization in the year 1969.

Access of rural households to formal credit institutions sharply increased to 61.2 per cent in 1981 partly because of enabling measures initiated by the Reserve Bank to direct public sector banks towards rural lending and partly because of the establishment of Regional Rural Banks from the year 1975 onwards specifically to cater to the credit needs of rural poor households.

However, in the year 1991 there was only marginal increase in the institutional sources of credit from 61.2 per cent in 1981 to 64 per cent in 1991. While dependence of rural households on professional moneylenders in particular declined very significantly from 46.4 per cent in 1951 to 8.3 per cent in 1981, it again increased to 10.5 per cent in 1991. The role of agricultural money lenders had also declined progressively from 47 per cent in 1961 to 7.1 per cent in 1991. Commercial banks' performance was very spectacular between 1971 and 1981 but it showed little improvement in 1991. Cooperatives had shown good performance from 1961 to 1981 but its performance declined in 1991.

Doubling Farm Credit

The goal of Union Government, as announced by the Finance Minister in his Budget speech in 2004, to double the flow of farm credit in three years [2004-07] was achieved in two years. Actual flow of credit during the year 2006-07 is expected to exceed the target of ₹ 1,750,000 million set for the year by ₹ 150,000 million. During April to December 2006, around 5,337,000 new farmers, as against target of five million, were linked with the institutional credit system. For the year 2007-08, target of farm credit disbursement has been fixed at ₹ 2,250,000 million [28.6 per cent over target of 2006-07] and an addition of five million new farmer-borrowers. Following table exhibits banks' commitment, particularly of commercial banks and RRBs, to respond to Finance Minister's call to double the credit disbursements during 2004-07.

Total disbursements progressively increased from ₹ 620,450 million in 2001-02 to ₹ 1,574,800 million in the year 2005-06 reflecting rise by 153.8 per cent. Commercial banks and RRBs recorded phenomenal rise by 216 per cent and 189 per cent respectively as compared to 58 per cent by co-operatives. While there has been progressive rise in each successive year in case of cooperatives, commercial and regional rural banks, there has been spectacular increase during 2004-05 and 2005-06 in respect of commercial in the total disbursements of short-term and long-term credit progressively declined from 37.9 per cent in 2001-02 to 23.65 per cent in 2005-06 whereas that of commercial banks recorded progressive increase from 54.13 per cent to 67.41 per cent during the corresponding years. RRBs accounted for 7.82 per cent in 2001-02 which progressively rose to 9.91 per cent in 2004-05 but declined by one percentage point in the following year. Agriculture credit flow for the banking system as a whole during 2005-06 has surged to ₹ 1,804,860 million, reflecting 128 per cent of the target of ₹ 1,410,000 million that was set for that year data further revealed that proportion of short-term credit to enable farmers to conduct seasonal agricultural operations was around 63 per cent as against 37 per cent of long-term credit for investment purposes. Following table exhibits comparative performance among banks and within banks during nine months of 2005 and 2006.

Agriculture credit flow target for 2006-07 had been pegged at ₹ 1,750,000 million. However, for the fiscal year 2006-07, agriculture credit up to December

2006 stood at ₹ 1,493,430 million which represented a 25.38 per cent increase over the achievement of ₹ 1,191,150 million recorded in the same nine-month period in the previous year. Agriculture credit flow during April to December 2006 from public sector banks grew by 25.91 per cent to ₹ 868,650 million from ₹ 689,910 million during the corresponding period in the previous year. In case of private sector banks, it increased by 40.90 per cent to ₹ 141,340 million from ₹ 100,310 million. While cooperative banks recorded increase by 14.60 per cent from ₹ 289,470 million to ₹ 151,700 million. Share of public sector banks in the total disbursement during April-December'06 accounted for as high as 58 per cent followed by cooperative banks at 22 per cent where as RRBs and private sector banks had almost equal share of 10 per cent and 9 per cent respectively.

SERVICE AREA AND RECOVERY OF CREDIT

Rural and Semi-Urban branches of each of the public sector banks have been allotted Service Area comprising specified number of villages, since April, 1989. This has facilitated all villages, [around 700,000] of the country easy and dependable access to banks to meet rural households financial services [savings, credit and remittances]. Each branch is expected to formulate Service Area Credit Plan every year for the purpose of providing credit to the rural households. This micro level credit planning exercise should help the bank to progressively bring within its fold all eligible households for receiving credit and related services. In the ultimate process this exercise should prove to improve quality and productivity of lending.

RBI has since the year 1994-95 has advised public sector banks to ensure 25 per cent annual growth rate in the matter of disbursement of credit in their Service Area. Accordingly, the data presented in the above Table showe4d that annual growth was between 12.5 per cent and 24. per cent during 2000-2001 to 2003-04. The growth was spectacularly high at 54.5 per cent during 2004-05 which, however, declined to 44.6 per cent in the following year. Disbursements of credit as against targets ranged from 92.1 per cent to 117.3 per cent during the six-year period. Achievements were higher than 100 per cent only in the last two years.

Public sector banks recovery to demand under direct agricultural advance was 69.3 per cent during the year 2001 which gradually increased during following three years. It, however, phenomenally rose to 84.1 per cent in the year 2005. During the five year period, the demand, [loan amount to be recovered] and percentage of recovery to demand have progressively increased in the successive years whereas overdue amount has increased until the year 2004 and then it steeply declined by ₹ 29,620 million in the following year. Following table exhibits the impact of formulating and implementing the Service Area Credit Plans by Banks.

PRIORITY SECTOR LENDING

Commercial banks and RRBs have been providing credit for small scale industries, rural and cottage industries, tiny sector, Khadi and village industries, handloom, handicrafts, coir and silk units under secondary sector as well as for a wide variety of purposes under service and business sector. Thus, priority sector advances include agriculture, small-scale industries and service and business sector. The credit support to priority sector not only stimulates increased farm and non-farm sector output, but also creates large scale self-employment opportunities. Following table exhibits commercial banks' comparative performance on outstanding credit to agriculture as well as to priority sectors.

During the seven year period from 2000-2006 public sector banks' outstanding credit to priority sectors increased by 221.9 per cent from ₹ 1,274,780 million as on 31st March, 2000 to ₹ 4,103,790 million as on 31st March'06, whereas that of private sector banks shot up by 480.2 per cent from ₹ 183,680 million to ₹ 1,065,660 million during the corresponding period. Priority sector advances of public sector banks as group accounted for over 43 per cent of net bank credit in four years as against the target of 40 per cent which, however, declined from 42.8 per cent to 40.3 per cent in three years. In this respect, private sector banks as a group had less than that of targeted 40 per cent during initial three years but they showed impressive performance [42.8 per cent to 47.3 per cent] in the following four years.

Agricultural advances of public sector banks during the period rose by 242 per cent from ₹ 452,960 million to ₹ 1,549,000 million whereas that of private sector banks increased significantly by 799 per cent from ₹ 40,230 million to ₹ 361,850 million during the period. Share of agricultural advances in the net bank credit by public sector banks ranged between 14.3 per cent and 15.7 per cent whereas that of private sector banks varied from 8.3 per cent to 14.2 per cent during the period. Neither public sector banks nor private sector banks as a group could achieve targeted agricultural credit of 18 per cent of net bank credit.

During 2005-06, all public sector banks [except State Bank of India (SBI) and State Bank of Patiala] were able to meet the priority sector target of 40 per cent of net bank credit in 2005-06 and only 10 public sector banks met the 18 per cent sub-target for agriculture. None of the private sector banks could meet sub-target for lending to agriculture.

KISAN CREDIT CARD

Kisan [Farmers] Credit Card scheme was introduced in August, 1998 to facilitate farmers easy and timely access to short term credit for purchasing farm inputs while conducting seasonal agricultural operations for raising crops. Now the scheme has been extended to cover tenant farmers, oral lessees, farmers to redeem debt from informal sources, besides providing long term as well as consumption credit. During the period from 2001-02 to 2005-06 banks provided 59,093,000 kisan credit cards to farmers to facilitate them to purchase farm inputs and other requirements. Share of commercial banks was 37 per cent as against co-operatives and RRBs at 51 per cent and 12 per cent respectively.

Refinance Facilities

NABARD has been providing refinance facilities at reduced interest rates [6-6.5 per cent] to cooperative banks and RRBs for their short and long term credit and to commercial banks for long term credit in order to augment their loan able resources and enable them to on-end to farmers at reduced interest rate.

The refinance provided by NABARD to banks has significantly increased from ₹ 45,210 million in 1998-99 to ₹ 86,223.7 million in 2005-06. Only commercial banks availed significantly increased amount of refinance in successive years. Share of refinance in the total agricultural loans disbursed by cooperatives, PSCARDBs and SCBs] were as high as 50.3 per cent followed by commercial banks at 31.4 per cent whereas RRBs accounted for 18 per cent.

SELF-HELP-GROUPS/MICRO/FINANCE

The late 1980s and early 1990s witnessed the beginning of what was to usher in the Self-Help-Group [SHG] Bank-Linkage movement in India, a movement that has been described as the largest micro-finance intervention in the world. At present the major involvement of commercial banks in India micro-finance is through SHGs. Self-Help affinity groups were started by NGOs which were donor-funded and established for a range of community purposes.

With increasing skepticism about the ability of commercial banks and RRBs to lend directly to the rural poor, NABARD proposed that if these SHGs could be linked to wholesale suppliers of credit, then this could be a way to channel institutional credit to the poor. This led to a pilot project in 1992 and subsequent mainstreaming of the approach. The SHG model is a financial delivery model which has as its objective reaching out to the unreached poor in conjunction with achieving cost-effectiveness for the participating financial institutions. It involves three partners viz, [1] the SHGs [2} the Banks as wholesale suppliers of credit and [3] NGOs, Government agencies and individual as agencies to organize the poor, build their capacity and facilitate empowerment. SHGs have been described as a unique for of Community Level Financial System, sharing a number of characteristics with Credit Unions, though lacking even a minimal legal structure. SHGs, as compared to Grameen Bank Groups pioneered by Grameen Bank in Bangladesh, are more independent, flexible and democratic in character.

As on 31st March'06, the number of SHGs stood at just over two and quarter million of which over one and a half million had outstanding bank loans. Even with this huge number of SHGs it is estimated by the Committee on Financial Inclusion that the number of SHGs will have to e doubled to cover all the 50 million poor households in the country.

As reported under the NABARD-GTZ Rural Finance Programme, at around 98 per cent on time repayment to the SHGs is reported to be very high.

Other Programmes

Commercial banks and RRBs have been actively involved in providing credit support to Government sponsored programmes that have specified aims and objectives viz, alleviating poverty, improving socio-economic status of scheduled castes/tribes and weaker sections of the society etc.

Year	SCARDBs	SCBs	Com. Banks	RRBs	PUCBs/ ADFCs	Total
1998-99	21,680	4,300	12,060	7,140	30	45,210
1999-00	23,460	5,400	15,470	7.750	70	52,150
2000-01	23,400	7,230	22,010	8,680	260	61,580
2001-02	27,320	10,890	16,080	11,780	760	66,830
2003-04	25,441.4	17,365	17,136	15,893.5	217	76,052.9
2004-05	27,099.8	12,49.2	25,695.6	20,491.1	48.9	85,774.6
2005-06	20,824.7	11,737.2	40,277.4	13,324	60.4	86,223.74
Total	169,225.9	69,414.4	148,729	850,586	1,446.3	73,821.2
Share	35.7%	14,6%	31.4%	18.0%	0.3%	100%

- The Integrated Rural Development Programme was one of several programmes under which bank credit was linked with capital subsidy provided by the Government to the beneficiaries, amount of credit and subsidy provided during the period from 1980 to 1988 were not available, total amount of credit and capital subsidy provided to 25,906,000 beneficiaries was ₹ 153,166.5 million and ₹ 83,529.2 Million respectively. The recovery percentage to demand varied from 29 per cent in 1993-94 and 1994-95 to 41.4 per cent in 1990-91. As on 31st June'96 overdue amount was as high as ₹ 12,100 million as compared to ₹5,310 million recovered out of demand of ₹17,140 million.
- Under Differential Interest Rate scheme [at 4 per cent] loan outstanding as on 31st March'05 was of the order of ₹4,900 million outstanding with 389,000 borrowers accounting for 0.07 per cent as of previous year's outstanding credit as against stipulation of one per cent.
- As on 3st March'06 outstanding with weaker sections of the society was as high as ₹ 1,045,768.9 million.
- Outstanding credit to tribal increased from ₹ 14,851,330 million in 1993-94 to ₹ 39,620,390 million in 2000-01 reflecting the share of commercial banks as high as 57 per cent followed by 29 per cent of cooperative banks and 14 per cent of RRBs.
- During the year 2005-06 banks have lent ₹6,440 million accompanied with Government's subsidy of ₹2,380 million to 755,969 beneficiaries

of Swarna jayanti Gram Rozgar Yojana and under Prime Minister's Rozgar Yojana sum of ₹ 7,610 million was provided to 131,290 beneficiaries.

- Commercial banks, RRBs and Cooperative banks have disbursed sum of ₹ 21.4 million, ₹ 22.2 million and ₹ 70.5 million to 5,173 farmers, 283 farmers and 2,826 farmers respectively to redeem their past debt with informal sources during the year 2005-06.

Table 9 : Number of Self-Help-Groups and Credit Disbursed by banks During 2004-06

[₹ Million]

Banks	2004 No. of SHGs	2005 No. of SHGs	2006 No of SHGs	2004 Credit Rs.	2005 Credit Rs.	2006 Credit Rs.
Commercial	538,422 [50]	843,473 [52]	118,807 [53]	22,548.3 [58]	41,590.2 [60]	69,877.0 [61]
RRBs	405,998 [38]	563,846 [35]	740,024 [32]	12,782.5 [33]	20,995.5 [31]	38,221.5 [29]
Cooperative	134,671 [12]	211,137 [13]	310,194 [14]	3,711.2 [9]	6,398.9 [9]	10,871.8 [10]
Others	00	00	271	00	00	5.2
Total	1,079,091 [100]	1,618,456 [100]	2,238,565 [100]	39,042.0 [100]	68,984.6 [100]	113,975.5 [100]

Figures in brackets indicate per cent share in the total

RURAL INFRASTRUCTURE DEVELOPMENT FUND

Rural infrastructure [both physical and institutional] such as irrigation, watershed development, rural electrification, roads, markets, credit institutions, rural literacy, agricultural research and extension etc. together play a key role in determining the agricultural output in India. For instance, irrigation infrastructure increases the land use intensity and cropping intensity, and provides incentives to farmers to use yield increasing inputs, and thus results in higher agricultural output. Rural electrification increases the energisation of pump-sets, which helps to increase the irrigated area using groundwater; the output of crops under groundwater irrigation is always higher than those under canal or tank irrigation, because of its better reliability and controllability. Rural road increase the diffusion of agricultural technology by improving access to markets, enhances more efficient allocation of resources, reduces the transaction costs as well as helps the farmers to realize better input and output prices. Improved road infrastructure also increases the transparent facility through which the rural farm households are able to get better health care, education, and credit facility. Rural-urban linkages are developed through road development, which also helps strengthening the backward and forward linkages in agricultural sector. A classic study by Bhatia [1999] shows that, Indian states with highest rural infrastructure index [a composite measure for rural electrification, roads, transport, health, irrigation, farm credit, fertilizer, agricultural marketing, research and extension] such as Punjab, Haryana and Tamil Nadu have the highest food grain productivity per hectare and the states with lowest index such as Rajasthan, Bihar and Madhya Pradesh have lowest food grains productivity per hectare; the rural infrastructure explains about 68 per cent of the variability in the yield in different states; and 10 per cent improvement in rural infrastructure index in states with lower score would increase their food grains productivity by about 470 kg per hectare on an average. This study establishes a strong relationship between the level of rural infrastructure development and the level of agricultural output.

Using Indian state-level time-series data for 1957 to 1991, show that states with better initial endowments of physical and human infrastructure [towards the early 1960s] achieved higher rates of agricultural output growth than poorly endowed states; higher initial irrigation, higher initial literacy, and lower initial infant mortality, all contributed to higher long-term growth rates.

Using state level data for 1970-93 in Inida researches studied the relationship between government expenditure on agricultural research and development, irrigation, roads, education, power, soil and water conservation, rural development spending on agricultural growth and rural poverty. The study concludes that improved rural infrastructure and technology have all contribute3d to agricultural growth, but their impacts have varied by settings. Government expenditure on roads and R&D have by far the largest impact on poverty reduction and growth in agricultural productivity. Government spending on education has the third largest impact on rural poverty and productivity growth. Irrigation investment has had only modest impacts on growth in agricultural productivity and rural poverty reduction, even after allowing for trickle-down benefits.

The linkages between the Green Revolution technology package [irrigation, research and extension, improved varieties and fertilizer] and other rural infrastructure and agricultural output / growth are well established by several researchers at All India level, state level, project / scheme level, taluka / sub-district level and village level. Likewise, studies using agro-ecological zones [AEZs] typology also provide further evidence on varied contribution of infrastructure to agricultural output growth in India.

A recent comprehensive study to better understand the linkages between rural infrastructure development and agricultural output using cross-sectional data for 256 districts in India drawn from 13 states at three time points [1970-71, 1980-81 and 1990-91] shows that the districts having value of agricultural output above the average are better placed in terms of rural infrastructure development [irrigation, road, literacy, school facility, rural electrification and fertilizer] than the other districts.

NABARD in its annual exercise of preparing district-wise Potential Linked Credit Plans has been sharply focusing on the immediate needs for creating rural infrastructure having direct impact on increasing farm output and the sustainable development of farm sector. In order to supplement the efforts of the State Governments, at NABARD level Union Government has established Rural Infrastructure Development Fund [RIDF] which has yielded rich dividends. Following table exhibits the use of the fund in creating rural infrastructure from 1995-96 to 2005-06.

Commercial banks falling short of achieving priority sector/agricultural lending targets have since 1995-96 till 2005-06 deposited sum of ₹287,499.5 million with NABARD under Rural Infrastructure Development Fund at very reduced interest rate. NABARD has so far disbursed sum of ₹313,373.4 million to support 244,651 projects in various parts of the country. Types of projects supported relate to irrigation development, construction of rural bridges and roads, social sector and power generation etc. Share of irrigation development projects in terms of number was the highest at 36.7 per cent followed by social sector and rural roads, whereas in terms of amount disbursed irrigation development also accounted for as high as 34.3 per cent share followed by rural roads, rural bridge and social sector.

AREAS OF CONCERN

Rising Informal Debt

With the progressive institutionalization of rural credit system through adoption of multi-agency approach farmers' dependence on informal sources of credit sharply declined from 92.8 per cent in 1951 to 36 per cent in 1991. More importantly role of moneylenders [agricultural and professional] declined from 71.6 per cent to 17.1 per cent and that of banks [cooperatives and commercial] increased from 3.5 per cent to 55.3 per cent during the period. However, According to All India Debt and Investment Survey, the share of institutional credit appreciably declined to 57 per cent in 2001 from 64 per cent in 1991. Moreover, debt sourced from moneylenders [the very informal agents the institutionalization of credit was designed to replace] sharply increased in overall share of rural debt from nearly 18 per cent in 1991 to nearly 30 per cent in 2001.

According to recent Survey, a formal institutional credit provision in India now accounts for just 27 per cent of total cultivator debt, and that this reduces to just 20 per cent if data from the five States reporting the highest proportion of formal rural debt are removed. Moreover, nearly 90 per cent of households reporting no debt, either formal or informal are headed by small and marginal farmers. Intriguingly, Andhra Pradesh, the State with the highest concentration of SHGs, MFIs and banks, reports the highest proportion of rural non-institutional debt [nearly 73 per cent] and the highest proportion of rural moneylender debt [nearly 57 per cent] for all the States in India.

Table 10: Number of Projects and Amount Disbursed under RIDF during 1995-96 to 2005-06

Year	No. of Projects	Amount	Type of Projects	Number [%]	Amount [%]
1995-96	4,168	17,608.7	Irrigation	78,442	146,841.5
1996-97	8,334	23,979.5		[36.7%]	[34.3%]
1997-98	14,346	24,536	Rural Bridge	9,285	47,608.4
1998-99	6,172	24,280.0		(4.3%)	(11.1%)
1999-00	12,254	30,326.6	Rural Roads	43,857	144,935.7
2000-01	43.354	38.568.2		(20.5%)	(33.9%)
2001-02	24,987	37,568.2	Social Sector	67,995	38,718.4
2002-03	21,012	44.403.4		(31.7%)	(9.1%)
2003-04	19,605	33,874.8	Power Sector	717	12,943.7
2004-05	59,979	29,678.1		(0.3%)	(3.0%)
2005-06	30,440	8,070.8	Others	13,915(6.5%)	36,639.1 (8.6%)
Total	**244,651**	**313,373.4**	**Total**	**214,211 (100%)**	**427,686.8 (100%)**

NSSO'S FINDINGS

Findings of the National Sample Survery Organization revealed following.

1. At the All India level estimated number of rural households were 147.90 million of which 60.4 [89.35 million] were farmer households.
2. Of these farmer households 48.60 per cent [43.42 million] were reported to be indebted to either formal or informal or both sources of credit.
3. This implied that 51,4 per cent [45.93 million] farmer households were not indebted at all and 88 per cent of these excluded farmer households were either marginal farmers [less than one hectare] or small farmers [between 1-2 hectares.]
4. The incidence of indebtedness was 60 per cent in four States viz, Andhra Pradesh [82 per cent], Tamil Nadu [74.5 per cent], Pubjab [65.4 per cent] and Kerala [64.4 per cent]. However, Incidence of indebtedness was laower in States of Meghalaya [4.1 per cent], Arunchal Pradesh [5.9 per cent], Uttarakhand [7.2 per cent], Mizoram [23.6 per cent], Mnaipur [24.8 per cent] Jammu and Kashmir [31.8 per cent].
5. This indicated that incidence of indebtedness was relatively higher n agriculturally advanced States than that in agriculturally less developed States.

6. Ouit of 43.2 million indebted farmers 54 per cent [23.3 million] were indebted to formal sources.
7. Of the total farmer households [83.95million] coverage to formal sources.
8. More than 50 per cent of the indebted farmer households took loans for capital and current expenditure in farm business. Such loans accounted for 58.4 per cent of the outstanding loans.
9. The extent of farmer households not indebted to formal or informal sources of credit was more in the case of farmers with land holding of less than one hectare [55 per cent] than farmers with land holding of four hectares *and more [33 per cent].

WORLD BANK AND NCAER STUDY

The findings of the World Bank and the National Council of Applied Economic Research under the "Rural Financial Access Survey" conducted in States of Andhra Pradesh and Uttar Pradesh in 2003 also paints a very disheartening picture. The data reveal that

1. Only 21 per cent rural households had access to formal credit.
2. Small and Marginal farmers were in a relatively disadvantaged position as only 11.8 per cent of marginal farmers in Andhra Pradesh and 13.5 per cent in Uttar Pradesh secured loans from banks.
3. The time taken for loan clearance ranged from 24 to 33 weeks and loans were generally collateralized.

According to NSSO, rural poverty declined from 27.1 per cent to 21.1 per cent in 1999-2000 as against urban poverty at 23.6 per cent to 15.1 per cent respectively. This shows that rural areas have still very large number of households Below Poverty Line.

While these shocking finding are engaging the attention of the Government and Reserve Bank and further need immediate comprehensive research, broadly the factors contributing to this development are [i] percentage share of agriculture and allied sectors in the total Plan Outlay of Annual Budgets has sharply declined to below 6.0 during the 6th FYP [1980-85] and onwards from 11.3 and 16.4 in earlier FYPs. [ii] while total investment in agriculture has been continuously declining to around 1.3 per cent and 2.2 per cent of the GDP, share of public sector investment has also declined from 33 per cent to 17.8 per cent during the period frm 1993-94 to 2004-05. [iii]rural infrastructure as pointed out in Annual District PLPs by NABARD has grossly been inadequate [iv] while commercial banks have financial resources which they have been deploying and their own limitation [v] Cooperative banks being leaders in the field of rural lending are very weak in all respects and are in the process of restructuring and being reapitalised.

FINANCIAL INSTITUTION IN THE EURO ERA

The euro has been transforming and will continue to transform the financial industry in Europe. It has had the impact of a tidal wave hitting the shore: forex margins in the euro-zone are gone, lending margins are under pressure and so on.

FIRST IMPERATIVE: MANAGE YOUR COSTS

The challenges and opportunities brought by the euro are in general the same as those brought by any market-broadening event. To some degree, the gradual removal of the Glass-Steagall Act will have similar effects in the US. Consolidation will accelerate, customers will become more demanding, distribution channels will proliferate.

All these effects will increase the pressure significantly to lower costs. The need to manage costs in general and the cost income ratio in particular is the first imperative observed here: the need for cost reduction in order to keep pace as an incumbent financial institution. New attackers from within the industry, Internet-related such as ConSors and DAB or not, or from outside the industry, such as retailers and telecom operators, often enter the industry with tailored propositions at very low cost.

The existing financial institutions are faced with matching the new offering while maintaining the existing offering. This matching does not imply the same value at the same price, but the essence of a competitive offering should be present in terms of cost/benefit. This is the core of the multichannel strategy, and the resulting complexity makes a low-cost position very difficult to achieve.

It represents a new development compared with previous years' when there was a trend to make better use of IT and to move to bigger branches to deliver a full service at acceptable costs. Besides the tidal wave of the euro there are less visible but more powerful forces at work in the financial industry: technological change, regulatory issues, globalisation and demographics.

SECOND IMPERATIVE: OFFER YOUR CUSTOMERS A GLOBAL WINDOW

One particular implication of globalisation is that financial institutions will increasingly concentrate certain activities in 'hot spot' financial centres such as London or New York because they offer access to a larger pool of talent, and there are no hurdles in the Internet age against serving customers from these centres. This is what happens in advisory investment banking, in custody and increasingly in brokerage. This implies that all financial institutions will be forced to rely upon the talent pool of those centres and to open shop there. These centres are very competitive markets, and it may take years to establish a good position for newcomers, given the risks of trying to move forward.

On a more general note, globalisation will increasingly change the financial industry because technology and deregulation facilitate trade. For years the total value of international trade has been growing at a multiple of the growth rate of world GDP, and the advent of e-commerce will only accelerate this trend.

Increased global trade, the growth of business and personal travel, and the seamless information flow through classical and new media such as the Internet are causing a paradigm shift. The typical local banking customer-even a small business or a well-experienced individual-will increasin-gly demand a window on the world within the local banking relationship. Financial institutions therefore need to offer this to virtually all customers.

Offering a global service with a local rooting is a new paradigm for the industry and those who can deliver this have the best chance of retaining their customers. At this point disintermediation can stop: if customers receive cost-effective, quality advice the financial institution can claim the relationship. The question facing all financial institutions is how to implement this global/local strategy.

THIRD IMPERATIVE: DEVELOP THE SKILLS OF YOUR PEOPLE

Demographics are a second powerful current of change. There will not only be a much older population, which traditionally owns the majority of all savings, but lower birth rates will concentrate wealth over generations through the mechanism of inheritance.

So customers will be fewer, more affluent and in need of advice. Retaining customers, who will be faced with a seamingly endless choice of financial institutions, will be the key for growth. Hence the increasing power of brand as a vehicle to inspire and maintain customer attention and loyalty. Secondly, these customers will be very sensitive to the quality of service and advice, including a clear appreciation of the risks they are facing.

But qualified advisors will be scarcer: not only will the proportion of the working population shrink, but all industries will compete with the financial industries for the talent available. The pressure on financial institutions to engage in productivity improvement and skill development will be tremendous.

Financial institutions will be forced to invest even more in the quality of their people, because these people will be the key advisors to customers, and therefore their quality will be the institution's quality.

The case of Almanij: In Belgium, Almanij and its group companies have been relentlessly striving to meet these imperatives. The creation of KBC is a good example of this.

- The creation of KBC has met the first imperative of cost reduction, because the merger of the former Kredietbank with CERA Bank allows it to rationalise its distribution network in Belgium without losing coverage. This is a tedious process, since the net present value of merger benefits can only be captured after meeting the costs of integration. Secondly, such a merger needs to be well prepared, manage the organisational culture and maintain the growth momentum of the initial positive goodwill from the public's reaction. Fifty per cent of all mergers fail on one or more of these criteria. However Almanij is confident that it can successfully conclude this integration, given the track record of the former Kredietbank.

- The creation of KBC has also significantly strengthened Almanij's capital base, creating options for international expansion. This is helping the Almanij Group to meet the second imperative: to create a window on the world in a local relationship. Needless to say, many things still need to be done. The merger enabled the Almanij Group to strengthen its position in Belgium (its home market), to finance its expansion into Central Europe, and to maintain or improve its position in certain niche markets, such as trade finance. The concept of a second home market is still under investigation. The key challenge is to preserve its focus in its growth process.
- Finally: embracing the bancinsurance concept is helping the Almanij Group to develop new skills in product development and marketing.

INNOVATION AND GROWTH

There is a common theme at the core of meeting these three imperatives. It has to do with growth and innovation. The importance of innovation is well known, and meeting the three imperatives only stresses its importance:

- Reducing costs while expanding the availability and quality of customer service requires innovation.
- Opening a window on the world and making it available to all local customers requires new ways of leveraging technology and alliances.
- Achieving new standards of productivity and skills for bank personnel requires innovations in working methods, the use of computers and the training of employees. Growth is essential to offer these people a career, to retain them and to preserve the investment made in them.

The importance of growth is equally clear. Growth is necessary to broaden the earnings base and to motivate good people. However, organic growth opportunities in traditional markets are limited.

Capital markets' expectations for earnings growth are exceeding the business growth rate. Consequently growth raises the issue of size in the financial industry. Almanij's decision to create KBC is a good illustration of how it thinks about this issue.Almanij believes that shareholder value is the result of many factors, of which scale is only one.

But it recognises that scale and size make a huge difference in certain lines of business, for example in most activities in investment banking and custody. In other lines of business, the jury is still out. An example here is asset management, where some players prosper by going after scale, while others specialise and equally prosper.

Other businesses are much more skill- and reputation-driven. Private banking is an example.Almanij believes in the importance of scale in any line of business, influenced by factors such as regulation and technology.

Constant evaluation of position in terms of size is necessary in any line of business, as is assessment of the potential of business unit leaders and the quality of customer service.

Almanij and its group companies realise that growth and innovation lie at the core of competition. Not all innovations, though, have the nature of a breakthrough: some are small and even barely visible, but can help to meet the imperatives described above.

The following are a few examples:

- Almanij developed a strong position in the ECU trading market, a market that has now gone but gave Almanij some quality business over a number of years.
- Almanij pioneered new mutual funds with embedded options for its affluent customers and gained a significant market share.
- It expanded into new markets, including Eastern Europe, for their growth potential. Such expansion takes time, although there is a limited opportunity to enter such markets and it can soon be too late, as in China. Almanij's initial hesitation to enter unknown territory has been compensated by a pace of development that time exceeded expectations.
- It developed new types of collaboration between employees in bank branches and independent specialist exclusive agents in insurance in order to increase service quality.
- It was the ambition of one of the founders of IBOS, an international network for cash management and payment services, to start building more international service line.

Of course growth and innovation have no limits. Therefore Almanij must aggressively seek all growth opportunities and explore all ways to innovate. However the reality is that any advantage will be short-lived, and that there is a price to pay for innovation, which occasionally makes coming in second just fine.

2

Rural Banking

Amongst developing economics, India has a relatively deep financial system. Its financial depth is attributable in large to India's vast network of financial institution, particularly those focused on rural customers. The need to improve financial access to India's poor, the overwhelming majority of whom are concentrated in rural areas, motivated the establishment of a vast network of rural banks. Financial tools help entrepreneurs start and expand small businesses which are a source of local job creation, growth and poverty reduction. Rural banking has become a national and a government imperative in the last few years.

The process of economic growth, especially when it is on high growth trajectory, must strive to encompass participation from all sections of society. Lack of access to finance for small farmers and weaker sections of the society has been recognized as a serious threat to economic progress especially in developing countries. Moreover, prolonged and persistent deprivation of banking services to a large segment of the population leads to a decline in investment and has the potential to fuel social tensions causing social exclusion. Access to finance, especially by the poor and vulnerable groups is a prerequisite for employment, economic growth, poverty reduction and social cohesion. This will be providing them an opportunity to have a bank account for saving as well as investment purposes and thereby facilitating them to break the chain of poverty.

However, while there is a growing awareness and agreement on the importance of rural banking, it is also important to appreciate that the objective of providing affordable access of suitable financial services to the financially excluded is to ensure 'economic development and progress of the financially excluded and that inclusion of the excluded' is only a means to an end and not the end in itself. Banks could play a major role in inclusive growth through financing of MSMEs, especially in rural and semi-urban centres in a big way.

Recognizing the contributory impact of the rural banking for achieving the inclusive growth, a series of efforts are being undertaken by the Government of India and Reserve Bank of India during the last few decades for greater inclusion. However, the seriousness of financial exclusion of poor was brought out in the report of National Sample Survey Organization (NSSO, 2005) based on which greater attention was focused on this aspect. While assessing the contributory factor for such exclusion, it was recognized that in spite of a large network of the institutional credit system, it has not been able to adequately penetrate the informal rural financial markets and the non-institutional sources continue to play a dominant role in purveying the credit needs of the people residing in rural areas. As a complementary persons have access to credit bears the fact that the exclusion is not only large, there is also a wide variation across regions, social groups and asset holdings. The poorer the group, the greater is the exclusion. The estimates of rural banking index revealed the wide variation in the status of rural banking was observed among the regions and districts with the regions and inadequate branch networking was observed to be one of the contributing factors for the greater exclusion. This situation called for appropriate institutional arrangements to bridge the gap between the existing bank branches and poor clients. Though several initiatives were undertaken for deepening and widening the process of providing financial services to the poor and vulnerable groups, in the recent periods, still there exists greater potential for qualitative and quantitative additions in the ongoing efforts.

OBJECTIVES OF RURAL BANKING

Rural Banking ensuring access to financial services and timely and adequate credit as needed by vulnerable groups such as weaker sections and low income groups at an affordable cost.

- Extending formal banking system among rural sector.
- Weaning them away from unorganized money markets and moneylenders.
- Equipping them with the confidence to make informed financial decisions.

WHY IS RURAL BANKING IMPORTANT?

- Equitable growth is achievable only through the rural banking. There are hardly any instances of an economy transiting from an agrarian system in a post-industrial modern society without broad-based rural banking.
- Accessibility of public goods and services is a necessary condition of an open and efficient society. Banking services are like public goods, it is essential that the availability of banking services to the entire population is ensured.
- Financial access is essentially meant for the economically backward as it provides them opportunities to build savings, make investments and avail credit. Importantly, access to financial services also helps

the poor insure themselves against income shocks and equips them to meet emergencies such as illness, death in the family or loss of employment. Needless to add, rural banking protects the poor from the clutches of the usurious moneylenders.

- It is now well understood with the experiences of FMCG companies, LIC, Microfinance companies that commerce with the poor is more viable and profitable, provided there is ability to do business with them. The availability of uncomplicated, small, affordable products can help bring low-income families into the formal financial sector. Taking into account their seasonal inflow of income from agricultural operations, migration from one place to another, and seasonal and irregular work availability and income, the existing financial system needs to be designed to suit their requirements. Mainstream financial institutions such as banks have an important role to play in this effort.
- Rural banking benefits banking sector in two ways. First, rural banking provides an avenue for bringing the savings of the poor into the formal financial intermediation system and channels them into investment. Second, the large amount of low- cost deposits offer banks an opportunity to reduce their dependence on bulk deposits and help them to better manage both liquidity risks and asset-liability mismatch.

INITIATIVES TOWARDS RURAL BANKING

The elements of rural banking focused in the recent initiatives by RBI includes, saving cum overdraft account, remittance facility, an access to credit through instruments like a general credit card. Performance of providing these services depends on the institutional network coverage of bank branches in the remote areas.

The RBI had pursued the rural banking agenda more closely and now the banks have prepared plans in each and every State targeting 72,800 villages with the population of more than 2000 that are not covered by main stream financial institutions. Progress and issues in the implementation of the selected initiatives towards rural banking which are having direct bearing on micro finance sector progress.

Today, the banking has become imperative to all the households irrespective of their social and financial status and expects minimum financial services from the banking system. The recent rural banking initiatives of the Government, *i.e.* provide access to banking services at all villages through branch banking or business correspondent at affordable cost is going to transform the banking landscape to greater extent and it is an important business segment for banks. However, providing financial services to the poor, especially in rural areas, is both challenging and costly. The transaction costs have become one of the deterring factors to reach the un-banked by the banks. The stupendous task can be achieved by adopting following Initiatives:

ALTERNATE DELIVERY CHANNELS

The residents of far-flung areas are unable to pay visit to branches located at distant places on account of resource constraints *viz.*, time, cost and opportunity. Thus, it has become imperative for banks to reach out customers through a variety of technology driven delivery channels such as Micro ATMs, Bio-metric ATMs, Mobile ATMs, and Smart Cards etc., which are most cost effective compared to Brick and Mortar model. ATM has brought sea change in Indian banking space with significant qualitative improvement in delivery of banking services and within short span the presence of ATMs is outnumbered the physical branch network.

(i) *Micro ATMs*: Though there is considerable improvement in ATM network, the presence of ATMs in rural areas is very limited. Banks are not keen to install ATMs at Rural/Semi Urban centers on account of high investment and low transaction volume. In order to make the ATMs viable at these centers, there is a need to deploy low cost ATMs with basic features such as cash withdrawal and balance enquiry etc. It is convenient and cost effective to the customers compared to pay a visit to the bank branch located at nearby center.

(ii) *Biometric ATMs*: The penetration of ATMs in Rural areas may not serve the envisaged purpose unless it is put to use by illiterate/semi-literate whose presence is predominant in unbanked areas. The existing ATMs are not put to use optimally by rural folk on account of PIN/Password related issues. Introduction of Biometric ATMs enable them to avail hassle-free services as these devices function on thumb print and recognize voice commands in vernacular language.

(iii) *Mobile ATMs*: In this model, ATM is installed in a vehicle, which would move to the pre-determined places at regular intervals to provide doorstep banking. These new breeds of ATMs also have biometric authentication mechanisms like fingerprint verification and voice guided animated screens with touch enabled transactions. Mobile ATMs can undertake opening of accounts, which has immense benefit of the residents of unbanked centers.

(iv) *White Label ATMs*: The recent initiatives of the RBI and the Government is to allow white-label ATMs, permitting third-party service providers to set up more ATMs in off-premises areas, which include residential complexes, hospitals, tourist destinations, bus stops and railway stations. These ATMs would not belong to any bank in particular but will be owned as well as maintained by independent service providers. This initiative will enable the excluded segments to avail ATM services as at present majority ATMs are confined to

Urban/Metro areas only. However, service provider levies charges which are to be either bear by the Bank or the customer.

(v) *Smart Cards*: State Governments are actively looking at making pension payments and disbursals under rural employment generation programme using smart cards linked bank accounts. Smart card provides biometric authentication, which would help in reducing frauds and ensure identity of customers. In order to popularize smart cards, all agriculture short term loans and payment of social security schemes are to be dispensed through Smart Cards.

All the above initiatives warrant the banks to invest substantial amounts in infrastructure besides recurring expenditure which adds cost to the customer whereas the distribution of financial products and services at the lowest rung of the pyramid requires a low-cost model. High Operating Costs and Low Business Volume are the major constraints of the banks in extending banking services especially in remote rural and inaccessible areas through Branch Banking Model. To address this issue, RBI permitted the banks to make use the services of Business Correspondents to take banking to un-banked areas in a most cost effective manner.

BUSINESS CORRESPONDENT (BC) MODEL

Business Correspondent model using smart card and mobile technology is also an effective tool to reach the remote rural areas where alternate delivery channel mechanism is not feasible. This model enables greater rural outreach to improve the business volumes. RBI has permitted the BCs to undertake basic banking services *viz.*, Collection/payment of small value deposits, disbursal of small value loan amounts, collection of loan installments, receipt and delivery of small value remittances and sale of micro insurance/mutual fund products/ pension products/other third party products. Though, BC model has been gaining momentum since last two years, still desired results are not coming as the model is confronting the following issues and challenges, which need to be addressed on priority.

(i) *Operational Issues*: Cash management is the biggest challenge as the major operations of BCs pertains to cash transactions. It entails interest costs as well as operational risks. Further, the beneficiaries of BC services are mostly illiterate and are susceptible to misguidance. At times, customers tend to perceive the BCs as banks. The success of the model crucially depend on the trust levels among customers, banks and BCs, which is possible through spread of financial awareness by conducting financial literacy programmes on an ongoing basis.

(ii) *Viability*: The viability of the BC model is the most critical issue which probably is one of the main reasons for not taking-off the model as envisaged. The transaction volume is not encouraging since many of the accounts opened are in dormant stage. Absence of sufficient business is causing concern to both BCs as well as banks; and in turn it is becoming difficult for BCs to continue operations on account of mismatch of revenues earned and costs incurred. Banks need to tweak the products and work with the BCs to design products that are suitable to the target market to make the model profitable. Further, to make the BC model viable, the funds pertaining to various government schemes are to be routed directly through the beneficiaries' bank accounts only.

BRANCH EXPANSION

(i) *Physical Branches*: The penetration of banking in India is low compared to developed nations, which is evident from the presence of 5.40 lakh unbanked villages across the country. Branch banking continues to play significant role in business development despite increased adoption of Alternate Delivery Channels in the recent years. The road map of Indian banks clearly indicates that BC model is going to be used in a big way to achieve the rural banking objective. However, banks need to open more number of brick and mortar branches especially in unbanked centers to cover the large population on one hand and branch network acts as service branch to route the transactions undertaken by BCs. Hence, branch network continued to grow in the ensuing years also.

(ii) *Ultra Small Branches (Mobile Branches)*: As part of the liberalized branch authorisation policy, RBI has granted general permission to domestic scheduled commercial banks to open satellite branches in unbanked areas where the population is under 50,000. It envisages the extension of banking facilities through one or two dedicated staff members who visit the identified village location on specified days. It is a cost effective model compared to physical branch model. A designated officer of the link branch shall visit the village on a prefixed date and time every week with a laptop with Virtual Private Network (VPS) connectivity to Core Banking Platform. The role of the visiting official is authorization of the accounts, balance enquiry, printing of account statements and recovery. However, the normal cash transactions will be done by the BC agent only.

(iii) *Branch-in-a-Box*: It is primarily a cost-effective, relocatable and pre-fabricated bank branch. It uses modern, broadband satellite technology for communication. This enhances customer convenience as it provides speedy access. It can also be used to test new markets, especially in areas with limited infrastructure where banking services are not readily available. It provides full transaction facilities to customers, including cash withdrawals and deposits, sales and service.

MOBILE BANKING

Till recent years, Mobile/Cell phone used to be a status symbol or lifestyle product, and now it has become a necessity and inseparable with day-to-day life of the individuals irrespective of age, education and financial background. India accounts for about $1/4^{th}$ of world's mobile market with 965 million and making inroads in to remote rural areas. The share of rural subscribers is around 35 per cent speaks growing potential of this segment. The reach of mobile to the remote areas and its usage by the common man has become order of the day. The swift growth in number of Mobile users and wider coverage of mobile phone networks has made this channel an important platform for extending banking services to customers. Mobile banking runs on Interbank Mobile Payment Service (IMPS) mode which enables the bank customers to have access to their bank accounts and carryout banking transactions including funds transfers across the banks using mobile phones independent of Branch/Business Correspondents.

M-wallet is the further extension of Mobile Banking and it acts like a pre-paid account operated through a mobile phone which can be used for small purchases, remittances, bill payments and cash withdrawals. Telecom players are playing significant role in taking this concept forward with strategic tie-ups with banks as service provider as well as business correspondents. As per the recent study, the cost effectiveness is one of the major advantages of the Mobile Banking, as the mobile based transaction cost is about 2 per cent of branch banking, 10 per cent of ATM and 50 per cent of the Internet banking.

NO FRILLS ACCOUNTS

Taking the view that access to a bank account can be considered a public good, in 2005, RBI directed all banks to offer at all branches the facility of 'No Frills' Account (NFA) to any person desirous of opening such an account. These accounts have nil or low minimum balances and charges and have limited facilities. As at the end of the year 2009-10, 74.4 million NFAs had been opened by the banking system. The impressive performance in terms of growth in number of NFA may not be contributory unless and otherwise, these accounts are considered to be active in operation. At the ground level, it was observed that most of the NFAs were non-operative and clients were not even aware of the terms of use of these accounts. There are certain barriers that inhibit the active operation of such accounts like the time and cost involved in reaching the nearest branch where the accounts have been opened. Concerted efforts by the implementing authorities by providing appropriate financial literacy with the innovations in use of technology will certainly improve the impact of these efforts to a greater extent.

MICRO FINANCE SECTOR AND RURAL BANKING

The Micro Finance Sector over the period has evolved two different delivery models, one focused on Self Help Group (SHG) and its federations based on community participation and other one based on commercially oriented market driven Micro Finance Institutions (MFIs). The former one (SHG channel) is termed as non profit and non commercial with perfect integration of the existing financial structure where as the latter one (MFIs) has emerged as a profit oriented entity as a consequence of slow progress of SHG bank linkage model. The issues on rural banking for the above two channels in Micro Finance sector is discussed in this section.

MICRO FINANCE INSTITUTIONS

The rapid growth of MFIs and the consequent changes in regulatory environment in Andhra Pradesh led to a serious crisis in the sector which has the client outreach of 3,104 million. The direct group lending methodology, under which MFIs borrows bulk loans from banks and in turn lend to small loans to people in the lower income segment, has its own demerits. The MFIs were, until recently, a highly profitable as the demand from the low income groups are price inelastic. Accordingly, the MFIs could charge reasonably high interest rates and generate return of 25 per cent and above on their equity. This situation of a sellers market with limitless possibility of growth was hampered due to nonpayment of dues by the clients and rising defaults. This will be aggravated further when the defaults are soon loaded to banks by the MFIs. The regulatory initiatives by RBI in the recent time on NBFC - MFIs are aiming to have corrective measures in streamlining the credit delivery through MFIs. MFIs are also in the process of adopting self regulated code of conduct. Assuming that these initiatives adopted in true spirit by all the stakeholders, the MFIs must have another opportunity to emerge as renewed model in micro finance. In this context, banks having MFIs as agents of banks operating as Business Correspondents (BCs) may be considered as an alternative approach for greater rural banking. In this model, the banks can make use of the extensive MFI network established in remote areas as their extended arms. Further, as an off-shoot of banks, the model can be used to offer a much wider range of products - savings, credit, insurance, pension and remittances. From the MFI's perspective, acting as BC to a greater extent insulate from political and operational risk and brought under regulation of RBI. At the same time, MFIs as agents of banks will be able to offer clients with a wider range of products. In a multi-product environment, it will be difficult for any section of the stakeholders to suddenly put brakes on the operations of MFIs. The MFIs would not only be offering credit but would also be the front end for savings deposits and withdrawals, as well as for pension and for insurance services - thus broad-basing their relationships with clients.

SHG BANK LINKAGE MODEL

An important regulatory dispensation that facilitated rural banking was given in the early 90s, when banks were allowed to open savings accounts for SHGs, which were neither registered nor regulated. The impressive progress of SHG bank linkage programmes in reaching the poor clients by providing financial services led to greater rural banking. At the end of March 2010, 7.52 million groups had been linked to the banking system. Commercial banks had a share of 60 per cent of the amount saved by SHGs and 64 per cent of all the groups with outstanding loans. Further, the federation of SHGs is emerging as an intermediary institutional set up between the groups and bank branches and varying degree of success is being observed in several states. Under National Rural Livelihoods Mission (NRLM) Programme being implemented by Government of India, many States are in the process of setting up higher tier institutions of SHGs. These federation structures are expected to play mainly non financial role such as training, auditing, etc. However, there is greater potential for banks to use the matured and well trained federations as financial intermediaries as this model may be cost effective and wider coverage of clients with minimum efforts. Ownership of the institutions by the members is the strength of this model from client perspectives.

The design feature of NRLM emphasises the active role of federation of SHGs and hence the banks need to recognize it as potential intermediary in extending financial service to poor clients. Selecting the well established and matured federation of SHGs and using them as Business Correspondent may be a viable proposal for ensuring speedy rural banking. However, cautious approach is essential while entrusting BCs role to federations in terms of its selection based on clear and rigid standards to have greater sustainability.

3

Cooperative Banking

The cooperative banking system accounts for the largest proportion of total institutional Credit to Agriculture and allied activities in rural Sector. Globalization has unquestionably opened up new challenges, prospects, opportunities and potentialities in the economic system. The author suggests that the cooperative Banking system must approach "Globalization of Cooperative Banking Systems" phenomenon with courage and determination to ensure good quality of banking products and services, use of the latest knowledge and skills in Financial Engineering, Information and Communication Technologies, maintenance of the interest of the consumers, and users of Cooperative banking system. The Cooperative Banking System must respond and strengthen its infrastructural facilities to complete in the globalized financial system.

In India, the Cooperative Banking System is comprised of Rural Co-operative Credit Institutions, Central Cooperative banks (CCB's), Primary Agricultural Cooperative Societies [PACS], Urban Cooperative Banks [UCB's], State apex level federations for short-term credit and medium-term credit [loans] and state level federation for long-term [credit] loans known as the State Cooperative Agriculture and Rural Development Bank. All these banks are nowadays facing very stiff competition and the question arises: Who will survive in this harsh Liberalized economic Environment? The answer is obvious, namely those who are fit and ready to change with the changed environment shall survive.

The Cooperative Banking System aims at mobilization of savings of the middle-income groups and provides credit requirements in the middle and economically weaker sections of the society. Thus, it occupies an important position in the financial system of the Economy. It accounts for the largest proportion {55 per cent} of total Institutional Credit to Agriculture and allied activities in the rural sector. The Rural Credit Cooperative Institutions play a vital role in the rural credit delivery system with credit cooperatives forming almost 70 per cent of the rural credit outlets. The Cooperatives credit Institutions provide 55 per cent of Agriculture sector loans. The Rural

Cooperative Banks accounts for around 30 per cent of rural deposit and 44 per cent of outstanding loans and advances of the banking system for Agriculture and Rural development.

In fact, states such as Tamil Nadu, Andhra Pradesh, Karnataka, Punjab, Himachal Pradesh, Maharashtra and Gujarat account for over 80 per cent of UCB's presence with 75 per cent of Deposits. The economic liberalization was officially adopted in July 1991 in consonant with the changing Global market trends. The New Economic Policy (NEP) was started with high hope that it would prove a panacea for all economic problems. The Cooperative Banking Sector couldn't take full advantage of the first and second-generation economic reforms. There was no level playing field for various sectors of the economy and cooperative sector was particularly affected due to unfavourable impact of economic liberalization. The economic reform packages were not planned properly; therefore, its benefits did not percolate to the real members of Cooperative Banking Sector.

Globalization has unquestionably opened up new challenges, threats, prospects, opportunities and potentialities in the economic system. It means adoption and presentation of global outlook for business strategies enhancing global reach, facing competitiveness, incorporating worldwide manufacturing systems, marketing practices, financial flows and adoption of global logistics systems/approach. Globalization of Banking System calls for the globalization of POSDCORB and having an organization as interdependent system operating many overseas countries, collaboration with an effective communication network in both the directions. The Cooperative Banking System must approach "Globalization of Cooperative Banking Systems" phenomenon with courage and determination to ensure good quality of banking products and services, use of the latest knowledge and skills in Financial Engineering, Information and Communication Technologies, maintenance of the interest of the consumers, and users of the cooperative banking system. The Cooperative Banking System must respond and strengthen its infrastructural facilities to compete in the globalized financial system.

The Cooperative Banking Systems are facing Internal and External problems in the era of Economic Liberalization and Globalization. A few of the problems can be understood through, more and more cut throat competition, lack of autonomy and independence, absence of democratic management control (in the case of Tamil Nadu state there was no elections for over 20 years), untrained employees and inadequate human resource programmes, huge arrears in audit administration, the restrictive policies of State and Central Government , weak infrastructural facilities, insufficient diversification of economic ventures, no freedom of enterprises and business operation, insufficient computerization process and no proper management planning information system{MPIS}, inadequate modernization, no sufficient Data Base Management System

(DBMS), inability to manage funds and cash leading to excess funds, high cost of management and transaction cost, bureaucratization, declining trend in productivity and profitability, regional imbalances, legislative and policy constraints, resource constraints, heavy overdues and NPA's, mis-management and mal-administration, appointment of special officers (SO), excessive politicizations, embezzlement of funds (financial losses and mismanagement), inability to meet the international standards and quality, requires constant vigilance and supervision existence of unscrupulous members who are selfish, self-interest, ineffective and inefficient management committee members who cannot cope up with emerging economic liberalization and globalization, entry of low cost foreign competitive firms and their poor quality of services. All these problems have really affected the operations of the cooperative banking institutions in India.

Introduction of New reforms packages through financial sector liberalization paved way for the introduction of prudential norms, the balance sheet and income statements of banks are made transparent, the deregulation of interest in the banking system, the up gradation of technology in banking system, creation of strong system of supervision and competitive environment. All these factors are affecting cooperative banking system.

FINANCIAL SECTOR REFORMS

There is an urgent need in the era of liberalization and globalization to fully exploit available natural, material and human resources in the most efficient and effective manner. In order to exploit, all these resources, it is essential to have sound financial or banking system at the macro-level and micro-level. Even after nationalization of banks (1969), the spread of banking culture among the poor is still dismal, regional banking imbalance is not yet fully reduced, and inadequate growth in all levels of trade and industries. In fact, in the rural areas, the rural oriented banks such as PACBs, RRBs, lead banks, etc., are not effectively responding to the problems of rural clients, rural industries and customers.

It is well known that, the Narasimhan committee (August 14, 1991) submitted a report and recommended improving the profitability of banking institutions operations and enhancing the operations flexibility and autonomy in decision-making process of all banks and also the financial sector reform. The reforms must encompass both at the banking sector and capital market sector. In order, to fulfill these reforms, the Chakravarthy committee (1985) and Narasimhan committee (1991) aimed at improving the efficiency and effectiveness of Indian banking and financial system. They recommended bringing down the minimum lending rate of sizeable portion and fixed deposits was freed from interest rate control, further more that establishment of the nation wide assets reconstruction fund (ARF) to recover doubtful and bad loans through medium of special tribunals give greater scope for private sector in banking and financial activity. They also stressed the need for operational flexibility, and internal autonomy in the banks and financial institutions.

Further, introduction of new reforms packages through financial sector liberalization paved way for the introduction of prudential norms, the balance sheet and income statements of banks are made transparent, the deregulation of interest in the banking system, creation of strong system of supervision and competitive environment. All these factors are affecting cooperative banking system. One area of neglect is the deterioration in the quality of the loan portfolios which in turn has directly affected the income generation and enhancement of capital funds of the cooperative banking system.

When the quality of loan portfolio is poor, it leads to deterioration of business performance of the cooperative banking system, which can be directly or indirectly be felt by Cooperative Banking Institutions. It leads to increasing the quantum of non-performing assets/ advances which would ultimately affect the financial health of the Banks. It affects the depositors and investor confidence on the business performance and services offered by the Cooperative Banks.

PRIMARY AGRICULTURAL COOPERATIVE SOCIETIES (PAC'S)

Primary Agricultural Cooperative Societies are village level cooperative organizations. A large number are generally multi-purpose and multi-functional. It is a member's own organization and managed for the betterment of their socio-economic conditions. In the era of LPG's it is essential for the PACS to undertake, profitable businesses to fulfill member's objective and survive in the open and free market economy. The PAC's members must show active member economic participation in the overall management and business transactions.

All primary cooperative societies are affiliated to the District central Cooperative Banks and made up of several villages as their area of operation. They admit different types of agricultural and render Banking and Non-Banking services. They provide service to Agricultural Labourers and artisans. They carry out all managerial and financial transactions expected from Banking Institution. They provide Agricultural Production credit (ST and MT), sell fertilizers, consumer goods and provide storage facilities and procurement of agricultural commodities.

The Indian Cooperative Credit System is the largest with a network of 93,816 primary Cooperative Agricultural Credit Societies of which 65.7 per cent are viable, 27 per cent are potentially viable with coverage of 100 per cent of villages having 67 per cent of the farm families. They have deposit base of ₹ 196036 crores with membership strength of ₹ Ten crore. Therefore, they play significant role in the direct lending to agricultural production and development of agricultural sector at large.

Strategies for Successful Operation of PAC's

The following are the basic initiatives to enable successful operations of PAC's.

1. Sensitive leadership style : Even though, they have been honest, innovative, risk taking, sensitive to member needs, they must have open mind and effective developmental approach in the new era. They must improve their work systems, management and administrative process, business operational system then only they can cope with LPG's.
2. Education and Training facilities to be offered to the PAC's members and Management Committee members on the LPG's.
3. Recovery of loans must be made more efficient and effective.
4. PACS must aim at higher business turnover with good margin of surplus.
5. Active participation of all members in the business transactions must be enhanced.
6. Active participation of members in the management and administration of cooperative efforts.
7. Degasification of business activities in the light of profitability and viability.
8. Use of proper information and MI system.
9. Improvement of lending policies and procedures.
10. Appointment of professional managers to run the business affairs of PAC's.
11. PAC's must develop viable business development plans.

District Central Cooperative Banks (DCCB's)

The District Central Cooperative Banks, are generally located at the District HQ's in the state. The Banking Regulation Act of RBI governs these Banks. They have branches located in the rural areas. The membership of DCCB's consists of PAC's and individuals. The major portfolios of these banks include current and saving deposits, term deposits, borrowings from National Banks, Apex Bank, Government, Collect deposits from cooperative societies and individuals. The loan advanced are composed of short term, medium term and long-term loans. The DCCB's compete with commercial Banks in mobilizing deposits by opening branches in the rural areas. There are 367 district Central Cooperative Banks affiliated to 30 state level Cooperative Banks.

The role of cooperative credit delivery systems is significant in economic development, especially for the development of agriculture and rural areas. In fact, it is more significant than ever before, because commercial banks are slowly withdrawing their participation in financing agricultural sector and couldn't fulfill the Government priority sector target of direct financing in agriculture and allied activities fixed at 18 per cent of their net lending. However, it was 17.4 in 1990 and declines further in consequent years.

URBAN COOPERATIVE BANKS (UCB'S)

The Urban Cooperative Banks (UCB's) have made tremendous strides in the last decade. The Urban Cooperative Banks have come along way to occupy a distinctive place in the cooperative credit movement and being described as non-agricultural credit societies. It supplies credit needs of people residing in the urban areas having limited resources. They advance loans mostly to the small traders, artisans, salary earners and others on personal security.

Under the Banking Registration Act, the Urban Cooperative Banks' main purpose is banking, similar to other commercial banks. Their major activities are collection of deposits from members and non-members, to provide loans to members and weaker sections of the society, to provide lockers for safe custody of valuables, collection of endorsed bills, to provide facilities for training and education for employees, directors and to offer consultancy services to the customers.

Only recently, the RBI has classified the Urban Cooperative Banks as weak, sick and strong in terms of its growth and function, because they are not performing well now-a-days. The objective of UCB's is primarily to inculcate the habit of thrift, savings, mutual help, and aid leading to better socio-economic conditions of those joining it. Several Urban Cooperative Banks have been authorized to deal with the foreign exchange and maintain Non-Resident Indian (NRI) accounts.

PRIMARY AGRICULTURE AND RURAL DEVELOPMENT BANKS (PARDB'S)

The organizational structure of long-term cooperative Agricultural credit structure is not uniform all over the country. They have primary level organizations known as PARDB's. The primary level organizations advance loans to the borrowers for long-term purposes. The NABARD has come forward to render refinance assistance to PARDB's and State Cooperative Agriculture and Rural Development banks for financing different rural instrument transactions.

They provide farm and non-farm loans to the borrower and they deal mainly with (i) Granting loans for improvement of loan and introduction of better methods of cultivation (ii) provide loans for minor irrigation schemes like small tube well, canals etc (ii) for land consolidation to secure efficient and economic cultivation (iv) loan for horticulture and social forestry (v) purchase of agricultural tools (vi) develop carts, biogas plants (viii) provide loan for other productive purposes as approved by NABARD.

DIVERSIFICATION OF LENDING OPERATIONS BY PARDB'S

There has been quantum increase of loan advance to the members during the past decade because members have shown interest in modern farming methods and techniques, therefore the demand for greater delivery of Agricultural farm loans and non-farm loans (Rural Non-farm sector). The PARDB's are diversifying their business operations considering the push factors and pull factors of lending operations. They have their diversification measures and policies tuned to the free market economy, hence their strategies and policies must be market-driven market-based *i.e.* oriented towards small scale Agro-Industries, Agro-Processing. Business Services, Marketing, Trade, Financial Services, Small Scale Business; In other words, there should be a paradigm shift from traditional sectoral approach to face the challenges posed by LPG's. A liberalized economic policy environment shall be a pre-condition for promoting intensification and extensification of banking business operations.

NEED FOR SUSTAINABLE LONG TERM AGRICULTURAL CREDIT SYSTEM

Long term agricultural credit strategy and policy option is the determination of the basic long-term goals and objectives of the ARDB's and adoption of the course of action, lending, allocation of resources, and efficient utilization of natural resources. Efficient recovery process of agricultural loans would help to carry out the goals into the future.

In the long run, the ripple effects of the formulated modern strategies and policy options can be in all the areas of long-term agricultural credit system such as:

(a) Identifying specific roles suitable for the ARDB's in the open market economy.

(b) Appropriate integration of various roles with other banks in the era of LPG's.

(c) Sustained effort to obtain combine effects of strength and opportunities.

(d) Expressing the plans in terms of targets and achievements.

(e) Setting up long-term agricultural credit loaning sequences and timing of environmental (internal and External) changes.

(f) Developing modern strategy and transplanting it into managerial action, which requires quick decision making at each stage.

(g) Determination of sustainability of modern strategy and options through;

- Continuous assessment of ARDB's goods and services
- Competitive coordination in the Banking Industry/system in the Era of LPG's
- Enumeration and Exploitation of key success factor (KSF)

- Assessment of Growth Potentials and profit prospects of ARDB's in the era of LPG's.
- Determination of Market strength and weakness to face future Challenges.
- Building Financial capacity of long-term management and Administration of ARDB's to strengthen its financial structure.

COMPONENTS OF THE MODERN MULTI-LINK APPROACH IN LENDING AND RECOVERY PROCESS

Modern pre-Sanction Strategies and its Salient Features : In this state strategic model an attempt is made to reclassify the new components and modern strategies and salient features of realistic strategies for enhancing the growth and development of long-term agriculture credit system, with reference to lending and recovery process. The reclassified new strategies at the pre-sanction stage are:

- Proper identification of the borrowers
- Proper appraisal skills, - appraisal of borrowers attitude and their repaying behaviour
- Adequate credit decision gestation period of loan or investment
- More careful scrutiny and verification of application
- Proper realization in fixing the repayment schedule
- Adequacy of credit disbursement
- More details about the borrowers and family Background
- Installing the MIS system on the borrowers perspective
- Developing an early warning system for identifying potential weakness
- Investigation of the title, value, etc. before disbursement of loan
- Preparation of realistic loan recovery policy, and fixation of targets.

COMPONENTS OF POST-SANCTION MODERN STRATEGIES

- Regular and effective follow up action with borrowers
- Execute timely action on suspected defaulter
- Dispatching demand advice and notice in time
- Approaching borrowers at the time of harvest or cash inflow
- Proper credit rating of clientele
- Adequate and timely extension of period of limitation, debt acknowledgement, partial payment, renewal of documents
- Timely replacement and rescheduling of loan in the event of natural calamity.
- Exercise pressure on the guarantors
- Adjustment of collateral security
- Rehabilitation of potentially viable sectors
- Effective and efficient supervision of loan

- Repayment must come from the earning capacity of the business
- Classification of borrowers as willful, non willful, doubtful, regular and issuing ID cards for each specific category

Modern Integrated Recovery Strategies

- Suitable change in recovery policy environment
- Proper understanding of the rural and semi urban clientele
- More thrust in recovery operation
- Adequate MIS system
- Tackling the issue of misutilisation, misapplication and underutilization of loans
- Strengthening the internal control system of recovery units
- Proper maintenance of assets
- Congenial discussion with willful defaulter
- Application of timely corrective methods
- Motivation of the Bank staff to carry out recovery operations efficiently
- Constitution of special recovery cells and monitoring with
- Out of court settlement of loan account and compromise proposals for recovery
- Application of preventive measures
- Conducting periodic recovery camps in the village
- Regular notices given to the borrowers to remind about overdue
- List of defaulters displayed on the notice board to draw attention of defaulter (as they did in Pakistan last year)
- Direct involvement of Government Agencies in recovery network, *i.e.* revenue authorities, Tehsildars, Joint recovery teas.
- Create special recovery cell at rural village levels or micro-level
- Monitoring the implementation of time bound action plans for the recovery system
- Partial write off
- Approaching debt recovery tribunals
- Recovery through legal process
- Application and use of collaterals and collateral substitute
- Linkage of credit with marketing and processing societies
- Arrangements and introduction of regular savings bank account maintained by the borrowers
- The socio-economic implication of efficient lending and recovery practices would be great if all these strategies are earnestly followed by the banking institutions

Recycling of fund mix strategies

The recycling of fund mix strategies encompasses the salient features of modern pre-sanction, modern post-sanction and modern integrated recovery strategies. The right combination of these strategies would produce suitable results to enable the ARDB's to rotate its funds after cent per cent recovery operation leading to better socio-economic well being of the borrowers. It would determine the growth and development of the long-term agricultural credit in the years to come.

IMPACT OF MODERN STRATEGIES ON SOCIO-ECONOMIC PROGRESS AND LONG-TERM DEVELOPMENT OF BORROWERS

The socio-economic well being of borrower can be fully realized in the advent of adopting better recovery practices and methods by the ARDB's. Similarly, the borrowing community will experience higher social values, higher social status, better confidence, development of personal integrity and identity, acquisition of local and National empowerment, promotion of self confidence. The leadership pattern of the cooperative bank would, acquire better recognition on account of implementing better recovery practices and methods. Ultimately, it would enhance democratic values, uphold political neutrality and pep up social participation in the cooperative banking sector. Moreover, enlightened cooperative members are an asset to the organization.

COOPERATIVES IN INDIA

The cooperative movement in India has its origin in agriculture and allied sectors. The first Cooperative Credit Societies Act was enacted in 1904.Subsequently a more comprehensive legislation called the Cooperative Societies Act was enacted. This Act provided for the creation of the post of registrar of cooperative societies and registration of cooperative societies for various purposes and audit. Under the Montague- Chelmsford Reforms of 1919 cooperation became a provincial subject and provinces were authorized to make their own cooperative laws. Under the Government of India Act 1935 cooperatives were treated as a provincial subject. The 'Cooperative Societies' is a state subject under entry No 32 of the State List of the Constitution of India.

In order to cover cooperative societies with membership from more than one province, the Government of India enacted the Multi-Unit Cooperative Societies Act 1942.This Act dealt with incorporation and winding up of cooperative societies having jurisdiction in more than one province. A need was felt for a comprehensive Central legislation to consolidate laws governing cooperative societies. This led to the enactment of Multi-State Cooperative Societies Act 1984 by the Parliament under Entry No 44 of the Union List of the Constitution of India. After Independence, cooperatives assumed a great significance in poverty removal and faster socio-economic growth. They became an integral part of the Five Year Plans. As a result they emerged as a distinct segment in Indian economy. In the First Year Plan it was specifically stated that the success of the Plan would be judged among other things, by the extent it was implemented through cooperative organisations.

In 1958 the National Development Council (NDC) had recommended a national policy on cooperatives. The cooperative sector has been playing a distinct and significant role in the country's process of socio-economic development. There has been a substantial growth of this sector in diverse areas of the economy during the past few decades. The number of all types of cooperatives increased from 1.81 lakh in 1950-51 to 4.53 lakh in 1996-97.

The total membership of cooperative societies increased from 1.55 crore to 20.45 crore in the same period. The cooperatives have been operating in various areas of the economy such as credit, production, processing, marketing, input distribution, housing, dairying and textiles. In some of the areas of their activities like dairying, urban banking and housing, sugar and handlooms, the cooperatives have achieved success to an extent but there are larger areas where they have not been so successful.

The failure of cooperatives can be attributed to dormant membership and lack of active participation of members in the management of cooperatives. Mounting over dues in cooperative credit institutions, lack of mobilization of internal resources and over dependence on government assistance, lack of professional management, bureaucratic control and interference in the management, political interference and over-politicization have proved harmful to their growth. These are the areas which need to be attended to by evolving suitable legislative and policy support.

For the success of any developmental effort in the agricultural sector is to synergize with the efforts in the cooperative sector. Development of cooperative sector has many benefits. It will involve all sections of the society in development efforts. Cooperative sector of Indian economy has a spiritual content too when it was led by Vinoba Bhave.Cooperative sector has inbuilt democracy and only those who can demonstrate their commitment and efficiency can survive in the cooperative elections. Nowadays most of the financial institutions in the cooperative sector are also run on purely commercial basis. It is here that the State intervention can make the difference. The grant, subsidies and aid meant for the poor farmers must be channeled through the cooperative sector. Once there are enough resources in the sector in terms of money there will be increased participation by the people and will result in the all round development of the village.

Panchayat Raj institutions and cooperative sector can bring about positive change in the rural areas. Cooperatives have extended across the entire country and there are currently estimated 230 million members nationwide. The cooperative credit system has the largest network in the world and cooperatives have advanced more credit in the Indian agricultural sector than commercial banks. In fertilizer production and distribution the Indian Fertilizer Cooperative commands over 35per cent of the market. In the production of sugar the cooperative share of the market is over 58per cent and in cotton they have share of 60per cent.The cooperative sector accounts for 55per cent of the looms in the hand-weaving sector.

Cooperative process, market and distribute 50per cent of the edible oil. Dairy cooperative operating under the leadership of the National Dairy Development Board and through 15 state cooperative milk marketing federations as now become the largest producer of milk. With the rapid growth of the cooperative sector a supportive climate has been created for the development of cooperatives with the opportunities for diversification.

With the efforts of National Cooperative Union of India the Central Government passed the Multi State Cooperatives Societies Act and also formulated a national cooperative policy that provides greater autonomy to cooperatives. With the passage of the Insurance Act, cooperatives have been allowed to enter into the insurance business. Insurance is a field where the immense potential of cooperatives still remains untapped.

In the new economic environment cooperatives at all levels are making efforts to reorient their functions according to the market demands.

Cooperatives are also considered to have immense potential to deliver goods and services in areas where both the state and the private sector have failed.

COOPERATIVE MARKETING

Another major improvement for rural producers is the formation of cooperative societies. Farmer's common interest helped to increase the incomes of the farmers and avoid exploitation of the middlemen. There are about five lack cooperatives working but very few cooperative societies in selected areas like Dairy, sugar, oilseeds, mahagrape in maharastra, tomato growers in Punjab etc. succeeded in cooperative processing industry.

PROBLEMS RELATING TO RURAL MARKETING

The rural market offers a vast untapped potential; it should also be recognized that it is not that easy to operate in rural market because of several problems. Rural marketing is thus a time consuming affair and requires considerable investments in terms of evolving appropriate strategies with a view to tackle the problems.

The problems are:

- *Underdeveloped people and underdeveloped markets* The agricultural technology has tried to develop the people and market in rural areas. Unfortunately, the impact of the technology is not felt uniformly through out the country. Some districts in Punjab, Haryana or Western

Uttar Pradesh where rural consumer is somewhat comparable to his urban counterpart, there are large areas and groups of people who have remained beyond the technological breakthrough. In addition, the farmers with small agricultural land holdings have also been unable to take advantage of the new technology.

- *Lack of proper physical communication facilities* Nearly 50 per cent of the villages in the country do not have all weather roads. Physical communication to these villages is highly expensive. Even today, most villages in eastern part of the country are inaccessible during monsoon season.
- *Inadequate Media coverage for rural communication* A large number of rural families in own radios and television sets there were also community radio and T.V sets. These have been used to diffuse agricultural technology to rural areas. However the coverage relating to marketing is inadequate
- *Many language and Dialects* The number of languages and dialects vary from state to state region to region. This type of distribution of population warrants appropriate strategies to decide the extent of coverage of rural market.

Market Organization and Staff

The size of the market organization and staff is very important, to manage market system effective control. However the existing organizational setup particularly at district and block level needs to be strengthened in order make the services on various accepts available to the farmers timely and also easily accessible to them.

Other Factors Influencing Marketing

Natural calamities and Market conditions (demand, supply and price). Pests and diseases, Drought or too much rains, Primitive methods of cultivation, lack of proper storage facilities which exposes grain to rain and rats, Grading, Transport, Market Intelligence (up to date market prices to villagers), Long chain of middlemen (Large no. of intermediaries between cultivator and consumer, wholesalers and retailers, Fundamental practices (Market Dealers and Commission Agents get good part of sale of receipts).

Major Losers

Small and marginal formers, 75 per cent villagers are illiterates or semiliterate, they facing difficulties like proper paper procedures for getting loans and insurance. The farmers facing high interest rates for their credits (Local money lending system). Most of the credit needed for agricultural inputs like seeds, pesticides, and fertilizers.

The Major Weakness and Challenges

- Traditional mind not to react new ideas.
- Agricultural income mostly invested in gold ornaments and weddings.
- Low rural literature.
- Not persuading new thinking and improved products.

EMERGING TRENDS IN MARKETS

Rural people can use the two-way communication through on – line service for crop information, purchases of Agri-inputs, consumer durable and sale of rural produce online at reasonable price. Farm information online marketing easily accessible in rural areas because of spread of telecommunication facilities all over India. Agricultural information can get through the Internet if each village have small information office.

LOCAL AGRICULTURE INPUT DEALERS

Most of the dealers have direct touch with the local farmers; these farmers need awareness about pests, decease, fertilizers, seeds, technology and recent developments for these information farmers mostly depends on local dealers. For development of rural farmers the government may consider effective channel and keep information at dealers, for farmer education hang notice board and also train the dealer recent changes and developments in agriculture.

COST BENEFIT ANALYSIS

Cost benefit can be achieved through development of information technology at the doorsteps of villagers, most of the rural farmers needs price information of agri-produce and inputs. If the information is available farmers can take quick decision where to sell their produce, if the price matches with local market farmer no need to go near by the city and waste of money & time it means farmers can enrich their financial strength.

NEED BASED PRODUCTION

Supply plays major role in price of the rural produce, most of the farmers grow crops in particular seasons not through out the year, it causes oversupply in the market and drastic price cut in the agricultural produce. Now the information technology has been improving if the rural people enable to access the rural communication, farmers awareness can be created about crops and forecasting of future demand, market taste. Farmers can equates their produce to demand and supply, they can create farmers driven market rather than supply driven market. If the need based production system developed not only prices but also storage cost can be saved. It is possible now a days the concept of global village.

MARKET DRIVEN EXTENSION

Agricultural extension is continuously going through renewal process where the focus includes a whole range of dimensions varying from institutional arrangements, privatization, decentralization, partnership, efficiency and participation. The most important change that influences the extension system is market forces. There is a need for the present extension system to think of the market driven approach, which would cater the demands of farmers.

PROCESSING INDUSTRY

India is the second largest producer of fruits and vegetables in the world with an annual production of more than 110 million tonnes of fruit and vegetable only 1.3 per cent of the output is processed by the organised sector commercially, the reason higher consumption in fresh form. However, as the packaging, transportation and processing capacities increase, the market for processed fruits and vegetables is projected to grow at the rate of about 20 per cent per annum. 100 per cent export oriented units (EOU) and Joint venture units required improving the processing industry.

APANAMANDI / KISAN MANDI / RYTHUBAZAAR

There is a need to promote direct agricultural marketing model through retail outlets of farmer's co-operatives in urban areas. The direct link between producers and consumers would work in two ways: one, by enabling farmers to take advantage of the high price and secondly, by putting downward pressure on the retail prices.

RURAL AGRI- EXPORT

Rural produce, raw fruits and vegetable, processing goods, have the potential market in Asian, Europe and western countries. Particularly some countries have commendable potential for Indian rural produce.

4

Rural Development

The Government of India has designed and implemented a large number of schemes for creation of employment, eradication of poverty and for ensuring overall development in rural areas. Commercial Banks are the main players in the implementation of these schemes.

INTEGRATED RURAL DEVELOPMENT PROGRAMME (IRDP)

IRDP was implemented in 1980 for increasing production and productivity in agriculture and other sectors in rural areas, creation of substantial employment opportunities and making the rural families viable and self-sufficient. The programme seeks in particular to improve the lot of poorest of the poor – small and marginal farmers, sharecroppers, agricultural labourers, rural artisans, scheduled caste/ tribes and other weaker section. The government provided subsidy ranging from 25 percent to 50 percent of the total capital investment depending upon the category of beneficiaries (Srivasthava 2000).

Service Area Approach (SAA)

The RBI started SAA for rural lending in 1988. It refers to a system of assigning special areas to each bank branch in which it can concentrate for productive lending and thus contribute to the development of the area. The SAA is intended to bring about a major change in the quality and productivity of rural lending. It aims at making available adequate and timely credit for meaningful activities and ensuring effective recycling of bank funds.

Lead Bank Scheme (LBS)

The LBS was introduced by the RBI in 1969 with the objective of enabling the commercial banks to assume the role of leadership for the development of banking and credit facilities throughout the country on the basis of area approach. Under this scheme, all the districts in the country have been allotted to different banks. A lead bank is assigned the role of a catalytic agent of economic development through the expansion of bank branches and diversification of credit facilities in the district allotted to it. It is made responsible for surveying the resources and potential for banking development in the district.

Differential Interest Rate (DIR)

The DIR scheme was introduced in 1972 with a view to provide bank credit to the weaker sections of the society at a concessional rate by PSBs. The banks identify beneficiaries who will be eligible for loans under the scheme and conditions under which loans should be given. Different interest rates are charged by CBs on advances to different categories of borrowers on the basis of income and repayment capacity.

Small Farmers Development Agency (SFDA)

The SFDAs have been established to help those cultivators who have small, yet potentially economically viable holdings. The small farmers have always been neglected by both the organised and unorganised sectors of banking. Therefore, the establishment SFDA is a significant development in the field of rural finance, for it forms an important link in the chain of organised financial institutions through which money flows into the rural sector of the economy.

Marginal Farmers and Agricultural Labourers Development Agencies (MFAL)

The MFALs have been established to help sub-marginal farmers and agricultural labourers. Marginal farmers with holdings up to one hectare and agricultural labourers who earn more than 50 percent of their income from agriculture receive subsidised credit support for agriculture and subsidiary occupations under this scheme. The subsidised credit support is given for dairy farming, poultry, fishery, piggery, sheep rearing, horticulture *etc.*

Farmers Service Societies (FSS)

On the basis of the recommendations of the National Commission on Agriculture, Farmers societies have been organised by CBs in SFDA and MFAL areas from 1973-74. The basic objectives of the scheme of FSS have been to offer to small farmers a full package of services and technical guidance instead of just credit (Srivasthava 2000).

Swarnajayanthi Gram Swarozgar Yojana (SGSY)

The SGSY has been launched as an integrated programme for self employment of the rural poor on 1st April 1999 by merging hither to self employment programme of DWCRA, TRYSEM, SITRA, GKY and MWS. The objective of the scheme is to bring the assisted poor families above the poverty line by organizing them into self help groups (SHGs), through the process of social mobilization, training, capacity building and provision of income generating assets through a mix of bank credit and government subsidy. The SGSY will be funded by the central and state governments in the ratio of 75:25 (Government of India 2005).

The focus of the programme is on establishing a large number of micro enterprises in rural areas based on the ability of the poor and potential of each area for a sustainable income generation. Due emphasis is being laid on different components such as capacity building of the poor, skill development, training, technology transfer, marketing and infrastructure. The subsidy allowed is 30 percent of project cost; subject to maximum of ₹ 7500/-. For SC / ST and disabled persons subsidy limit is 50 percent of project cost or maximum of ₹ 10,000/-. For SHGs subsidy is maximum 1.25 lakhs or 50 percent of project cost. There is no monetary ceiling on subsidy for minor irrigation projects (Government of India 2005).

Indira Awas Yojana (IAY)

IAY is a rural housing programme launched by the Government of India. Under this scheme nearly 114.78 lakh houses have been constructed at a cost of ₹ 20022.89 crores by March 2004(Theodore 2005).

Prime Minister's Rozgar Yojana (PMRY)

This scheme was introduced in 1993-94 in selected centres of the country and later to all areas. It is an important credit linked employment generation scheme for the youth which is implemented by District Industries Centres (DICs) and CBs. The scheme provide assistance to educated unemployed youth in the age group of 18-35, with upper age relaxation provided to women, SC/ST and physically handicapped persons whose annual income is below ₹ 40,000/-. Subsidy assistance is at the rate of 50 percent subject to maximum of ₹ 7500/-.

Margin will range between 5 to 16.25 percent such that the subsidy together with margin money will be equal to 20 percent of the project cost. For project with cost up to ₹ 1 lakh no collateral security is to be insisted in the case of business and service sectors whereas ₹ 2 lakhs in the case of SSIs.

Pradhan Manthri's Gram Sadak Yojana (PMGSY)

The PMGSY, 100 percent centrally sponsored scheme was launched on 25th December 2000. The main objective of PMGSY is to develop rural roads connectivity. This scheme seeks to provide connectivity to about 1.70 lakh unconnected habitations besides upgradation of some existing rural roads, to prescribed standards by the end of the 10th plan. A cumulative expenditure of ₹ 6559 crore was incurred till March 2004 (Government of India 2005).

Central Rural Sanitation Programme (CRSP)

Rural sanitation is a state subject. The efforts of the state are supplemented by the Central Government through technical assistance under the CRSP. It was launched in 1986 with the objective of improving the quality of life of rural people and providing privacy and dignity to women. The concept of sanitation was expanded in 1993 to include personal hygiene, home sanitation, safe water, disposal of garbage and waste water (Government of India 2005).

Sampoorna Grameen Rozgar Yojana (SGRY)

It was launched on 25th September 2001 by merging the ongoing scheme of Employment Assurance Scheme (EAS) and the Jawahar Grama Samridhi Yojana (JGSY) with the objective of providing additional wage employment in the rural areas as also food security, along with the creation of durable community assets in the rural areas (Government of India, 2005). An amount of ₹ 9825 crores were provided for rural infrastructure development in 2003-04 as budgetary support and 19,637 number of road works have been completed. In addition 8419 number of road works has been completed during 2003-04 (Theodore 2005)

Swajal Dhara Scheme (SDS)

It was flagged off in December 2002 as a new initiative empowering Panchayaths to formulate, implement, operate and maintain drinking water projects (Theodore 2005).

Watershed Development Programme

The Department of Land Resource is implementing three area based watershed programmes for development of wastelands / degraded lands namely Drought Prone Areas Programmes (DPAP), Desert Development Programme (DDP) and Integrated Wastelands Development Programme (IWDP). DPAP was launched in 1973, DDP was launched in 1977 and IWDP was launched in 1989. Since, 1st April 1995, the three programmes are being implemented on the basis of common guidelines for watershed development (Government of India 2005).

Hariyali Programme

The Department of Land Resources launched a new initiative called Hariyali in 2003 with the objective of empowering Panchayath Raj Institutions (PRIs) both financially and administratively in implementation of watershed development programme. Under this initiative all the ongoing programmes like DPAP, DDP and IWDP would be implemented through the PRIs (Government of India 2005).

People's Planning Programme (PPP)

It was introduced on 17th August 1996. 'Janakeeyasoothranam' contemplates full participation of people in both formulating, planning and implementation of the so planned activities on a time bound basis. Out of the states annual action plan, 35 to 40 percent are deployed for implementation through Janakeeyasoothranam, for which people from different categories are involved. In this, projects are prepared by giving due weightage to local needs etc; and they are subject to scrutiny and discussion before finalization.

Self Help Groups (SHGs)

The SHG linkage programme initiated by NABARD during 1991-92 as a pilot project has taken the shape of a movement and has size pitched up the desired movement. Under this concept, the poor, particularly women are organised into small homogenous groups for taking their own decisions about the saving and credit operations. External lending like bank credit is infused into the groups only after proper evaluation of the functioning of the groups and ascertaining their maturity. The concept has been found to be an effective and successful approach in reaching the unreached and for empowerment of women and poverty alleviation. On cumulative basis, the number of SHGs receiving financial support from commercial banks increased to 538,422 in 2003-04 from 361,061 in 2002-03 with an increase of 49 percent (RBI 2004).

Vikas Volunteer Vahini Clubs (VVVs)

The VVV programme introduced by NABARD in the year 1982, offers a forum in the rural areas for banks and borrowers / rural poor to come together, to have a continuous and positive dialogue for initiating appropriate measures to achieve the desired development. The core objective of the programme is propagation of revival of repayment ethics. Promotion of people's participation is the essence of the programme.

Kisan Credit Card (KCC)

Ensuring timeliness and adequacy of credit to farmers is the most serious challenge faced by the banks while financing this sector. The Financial Sector Reforms (FSRs) ushered in as part of the liberalization of the Indian economy have infused a spirit of competitiveness among the banks in their endeavor for sharpening customer orientation.

KCC is an innovative key product designed and introduced to expand and simplify the credit delivery system of banks by the NABARD. As the pioneering credit delivery innovation, the KCC scheme aims at provision of adequate and timely credit support from the banking system to the farmers for their cultivation needs. It was introduced in 1998 and it was revised in October 2004 to cover term loans for agriculture and allied activities. As on 31st March 2004, CBs, RRBs and Co-operative banks issued KCCs at the tune of 132.43 lakhs, 38.99 lakhs and 242.68 lakhs respectively. So total KCCs issued upto 31st March 2004 came to 414 lakhs (RBI 2004).

STRATEGY FOR RURAL DEVELOPMENT

Despite significant advancement in industrial development, Indian economy is dependent on agrobased activities. Over 70per cent of the population living in rural areas is dependent on agriculture for livelihood. A majority of these families spend over 90per cent of their earnings on basic needs such as food, fuel and health care. Over 50per cent of the rural families who are not able to meet even these essential needs fall under the category of the poor. Thus, in an agrarian country like India, for improving the economic status of the population it is not enough to enhance the per capita GNP, but it is also necessary to ensure prosperity among the poor. Industrial development and adoption of modern technologies are likely to generate additional employment in urban areas and pay rich dividend to elite and rich investors. This in turn might widen the gap between the urban and rural as well as the rich and the poor, with respect to wealth accumulation, resulting in further hardship to the poor. Therefore, we need to address the problems of the poor to ensure social justice and better quality of life. Rural development also deserves priority for maintaining self sufficiency in food supply. Our food security is under severe threat because of the growing population. No doubt, India has tripled her food production over the last four decades, to reach the present level of 195 million tons/year. However, with over 1.8per cent annual birth rate, our growing population is bound to raise the annual demand for food to 250 million tons by 2010 A.D. As food security is a pre requisite for economic progress, agro based rural development deserves attention.

Fortunately, the Government of India has been giving top priority to rural development. However, in the absence of well planned development programmes and efficient delivery systems, most of these resources do not benefit the target groups. It has been reported that only 18per cent of the rural development budget reaches the target families, while the rest is wasted due to inefficient delivery systems or drained out. In the process of assisting the poor, a significant portion of the budget is spent on relief and subsidies. Poor families have received sympathy instead of motivation which has resulted in a dependency syndrome. As a result, most of the poor have lost confidence, initiative and entrepreneurship. The inputs and cash distributed for investment in development are being diverted for household consumption. In such a situation, free distribution of inputs may not help the rural poor any more.

The time is now ripe for a change in the strategy. The rural development programme should identify the problems of the poor and address the local needs, instead of forcing them to accept pre conceived plans. The participating families should take active part in the programme. There should be equal opportunity for the weaker sections of the society and women. The programme should facilitate sustainable management of natural resources and environmental protection and lead to better quality of life.

PROBLEMS OF THE POOR

Rural poor pass through series of problems which affect their survival and quality of life. These problems can be grouped into four broad categories namely livelihood, health, education and social development. These four components can be referred to as 4 A's 'Anna', 'Arogya', 'Akshar' and 'Acharan'. Problems such as scarcity of food, fodder, fuel, shelter, small holdings, poor crop yields, poor quality livestock, lack of irrigation, unemployment and underemployment affect the income generation and hence, fall in the category of livelihood problems. Problems of livelihood are more serious and need immediate attention of the development agencies. The other problems are also serious and interrelated, but can be handled by the villagers, simultaneously with the livelihood programme. Health and education problems can be solved at a greater pace when the villagers start improving their livelihood. In the absence of assured livelihood, other development programmes may not sustain in the long run. Good moral values and commitment for upliftment of the community are also essential to ensure better quality of life.

SETTING THE PRIORITY

The problems of the rural poor throughout the country appear to be common. But the intensity of these problems vary widely and a few of them need to be addressed on priority. The cause of these problems also vary, due to the family size, employment status, ownership of various resources, socio economic background and religious beliefs. These restrictions need to be taken into consideration, while proposing suitable solutions for tackling the problems of rural development. Hence, basic data on the target community will be useful for planning the programme.

Baseline Data

The information needed for preparing a development plan are the nature of problems and their causes, resources available, type of technologies presently adopted and their capacity to absorb new activities for generating income.

Village level information on the following aspects will be useful for project formulation.

- Social background of the families: SC, ST, BC and poor and their employment status (men and women);
- Literacy status (men, women and children). Anganwadis, balwadis and school facilities;
- Land holding pattern with water resources, type of crops and levels of production (average yields) and inventory of livestock;
- Demand and supply of essential commodities such as fodder, fuel, food, agricultural commodities and per capita consumption;
- Prevailing diseases and community health problems, social problems, if any.

It is not feasible to conduct house to house survey in the initial stage as it is time consuming. Any survey without concrete project support may also demoralise the local population, who in turn may not cooperate in the future. Apart from the collection of secondary data, it is also advisable to conduct Rapid Rural Appraisal (RRA) and Participatory Rural Appraisal (PRA).

RRA can be carried out by a team of multidisciplinary specialists who can discuss with prominent people and office bearers of various organisations, local health officials, village sarpanch, school teachers, members of Youth and Women's clubs and cooperatives.

PRA involves discussion with various socio economic groups who can come up with their problems and possible solutions. It is an effective tool for identifying local problems and setting a priority for implementation.

DEVELOPMENT OF PROJECT PROPOSALS

Based on the local needs and available opportunities, it is preferable to prepare a project proposal for raising financial resources and implementation. The proposal should cover various aspects such as infrastructural needs, identification of the target groups and the activities to be undertaken. All these details can be systematically presented in the proposal.

Local Infrastructure

It is necessary to plan for various activities, identify the resources and manpower for proper management with time schedule and budgetary control. The community should be involved in project implementation right from the beginning. The domination of the implementing agencies may result in loss of initiatives among the beneficiaries. Subsequently, at the termination of the project, even the most successful projects may fail to sustain the programme due to inability of the local people. To avoid such a situation, formation of local organisations to implement the programme is helpful. It is not necessary in the initial stage to determine the type of the organisation to be established for implementing the project. The community can be mobilised through Self Help Groups (SHGs) to initiate the development activity. Subsequently, a formal organisation can be registered to manage the programme.

Apart from mobilising people, infrastructure is also necessary to organise input supply, finance, post production processing and marketing of the produce. In livelihood projects, realisation of benefits in the form of cash and kind is the indicator of success. Hence, market plays a very crucial role in sustaining the development programme. Marketing is a dynamic process which is influenced by demand and supply as well as information on new products and processes. Hence, the proposed infrastructure should also provide market information services required to enhance profits. For the success of any rural development programme, there is a need for a strong local organisation having a strong linkage with technology centres, financial institutions and marketing network. An ideal linkage of the local organisation with various institutions at various levels. Close relation with the Gram Panchayat and Gram Sabha is necessary, as most of the government sponsored development projects are implemented through the Gram Panchayat.

Target Groups

The development inputs in general consist of technology and resources. As there is no constraint in acquiring technology from various sources, it is neither feasible nor necessary to restrict the dissemination of technology. However, the poor who cannot mobilise adequate resources to adopt appropriate technologies need financial assistance as well.

It has been observed that the programmes focussed on the development of common properties and local infrastructures have mostly benefited the rich families. In the absence of assured support to weaker sections, the advantages of infrastructural development and technology transfer are enjoyed by the well to do and elite members of the society, while the illiterate and poor families lag behind. Hence, special attention on family based development programme can ensure the participation of the poor in development programmes.

Empowerment of women should cut across all these development activities, as women play a significant role in building the community. Although the women represent 50per cent of the population, they share an additional responsibility of bringing up their children. With empowerment of women, their drudgery will be reduced and they will be able to utilise their time effectively in shaping their children and family.

Programme Components

Establishing a good rapport with the local community before launching the development programme is helpful. However, livelihood programme may not be the correct entry point even among the poor communities.

The entry point activity should be such that a majority of the local population will be able to take part. In certain situations like post calamities, relief measures can be the best entry point. Health camps and drinking water resource development can also be considered for entry point activity.

Water is the lifeline of all human activities. Water is not only needed for survival but also for generating employment in rural areas. Therefore rural development projects involving water resources development may primarily aim at providing drinking water and subsequently for livestock and crop production.

The selection of villages for development can cover the entire area under a watershed. With the development of water resources, various income generation activities can be initiated. The strategy should be to conserve and make sustainable use of the denuded natural resources through appropriate technologies. Activities which provide employment at the doorsteps of local families particularly the women, deserve priority.

For successful economic development, the programme should focus on the following aspects:

- Equal distribution of natural resources, particularly water.
- Good extension network for transfer of technology.
- Infrastructure for timely distribution of inputs.
- Marketing network to procure, process and distribute the produce.

The development programme during the past few decades included free distribution of inputs to the poor. This however did not succeed in motivating the poor to take active part in development. Subsequently in 90's, many donor agencies changed their strategy and provided critical inputs in the form of loan. The response again was poor as the farmers were hesitant to avail loan, due to lack of confidence to generate adequate income and repay the loan. Therefore it is better to initiate the development programme with an aid component and subsequently encourage the families to avail of loans.

INCOME GENERATION ACTIVITIES

The opportunity for employment generation in rural areas can be grouped into on farm and off farm activities. Initially, the agro based activities cannot provide adequate opportunities for the landless. Subsequently, with optimum use of resources and enhanced productivity, demand for labour will rise and even the landless will have increased employment opportunities.

With improvement in agricultural production, job opportunities for ancillary services will also increase and the landless can take advantage of this situation. Nevertheless, land based activities have a serious limitation of maintaining the carrying capacity beyond a certain period. Hence, it is advisable to initiate the development programme through on farm and off farm activities, simultaneously.

While implementing the programme through a particular sector such as crop production, cattle breeding, forestry or kitchen garden or any such activities, it is necessary to estimate the expected benefits. The objective behind this analysis is to ensure that the families can earn adequate income to come out of poverty. If the development programme under implementation is not able to provide sufficient income to meet their basic needs, the beneficiaries may keep on looking for other opportunities, while ignoring the trickling benefits, from the project being implemented.

Therefore, the development strategy should aim at helping the rural families to come out of poverty by making use of the available resources and idle labour force.

However, as the quality and quantity of natural resources owned by families within the community vary widely, their priorities also vary among the families. Therefore, it is preferable to undertake a micro level planning before undertaking various development activities. This planning should address all the problems of the families and the community.

CRITERIA FOR SELECTION OF LIVELIHOOD ACTIVITIES

In the absence of assured jobs in industries, self employment is the best alternative in rural areas. To enhance people's participation in rural development through self employment, priority should be given to the activities having the following criteria:

- Social acceptability of the participants;
- Easy availability of natural resources and external inputs;
- Local skill to operate the programme without depending on external technology;
- Ability of the participants to operate at low risk;
- Easy marketability of the produce;
- Economic viability and higher profitability;
- Short gestation period;
- Year round employment.

PRIME GOAL OF RURAL DEVELOPMENT

The prime goal of rural development is to improve the quality of life of the rural people by alleviating poverty through the instrument of selfemployment and wage employment programmes, by providing community infrastructure facilities such as drinking water, electricity, road connectivity, health facilities, rural housing and education and promoting decentralization of powers to strengthen the Panchayat raj institutions. The Chief Minister's 15 Point Programme is a visionary programme which seeks to make Tamil Nadu the best State in the country by way of creating growth opportunities in rural areas and eradicating rural poverty.

To achieve the above objectives, the following priorities and thrust areas have been identified during the Tenth Five Year Plan period:

- The goal is reduction of poverty from 21.12% in 1999- 2000 to 10% by 2006-07 and near elimination by 2012. Poverty reduction will be attempted
  - By organizing the rural masses into self-help groups and the establishment of micro-enterprises, training, credit linkages, market support, etc.
  - By substantial flow of investment in physical infrastructure like roads, water supply and social infrastructure like health, education and nutrition.
- Special efforts for generation of adequate employment and creation of durable community assets to improve the rural people especially the small farmers, marginal farmers, rural artisans etc., through programmes like Sampoorna Grameen Rozgar Yojana (SGRY).
- Decentralization of the process of planning by entrusting major role to the Panchayat raj bodies in the preparation of local level planning.
- Improving the efficiency and capacity of the officials and elected local body representatives.

- Providing all weather roads to all rural habitations having a population above 500 by 2004.
- Strengthening of Grama Sabha the governing body of village assembly as an agency of social audit and to review the implementation of programmes.
- Special efforts will be made to converge various schemes and programmes for accelerating the development process through special schemes like Village Self-sufficiency scheme etc.
- Emphasis will be given for the maintenance of the assets created under various schemes.

RURAL SERVICES AND RESOURCES

A review of the working of Panchayati Raj shows that it has not come up to the expectations of the people. There are many problems that have made Panchayati Raj Institutions ineffective in accomplishing their basic purpose. It is generally the view that part of the inability of these institutions in performing their functions satisfactorily lay in their weak financial resources. The problems of Panchayati Raj finance are of varied character. In the first place, it has been noticed that in spite of wide taxation powers, Panchayati Raj Institutions have not utilised them fully. The Asoka Mehta Committee's findings reveal that these institutions have rarely utilised their taxation powers.

It observes:

- "In spite of all the exhortations on the need to raise their own resources by way of taxation, there is a general resistance by the Panchayati Raj Institutions to imposing taxes. This reluctance is visible not only in the case of Panchayats which are in face-to-face contact with the people but also in the case of the Zila Parishads even in such states as Maharashtra where they are performing a variety of developmental functions and need additional resources".

This unwillingness to mobilise the resources is due to the unpopularity of the measure and the representatives fear of their being unseated at the next election. There is no exaggeration that the minimum that an elective body can do to alienate the sympathies of its constituents and to ensure the defeat of its sitting members at the next polls is to give the people heavier doses of taxation.

Various committees which have examined, from time to time, the problem of local finance, have drawn pointed attention to this factor. Hence, the Asoka Mehta Committee recommended that some of the local taxes should be made compulsory. It observed, "The thesis 'no taxation, only representation' should be discouraged. Representation involves inescapable responsibility of raising resources for development and welfare work". Further, the borrowing facilities available to Panchayati Raj units are too restrictive. The Local Authorities Loans Act, 1914 under which these units can raise loans is not much suited to the needs of the modern times and requires a complete overhaul. It has been suggested that the scope of the purposes for which loans can be raised, the period and other conditions of repayment should be liberalised keeping in view the rural poverty. The establishment of a new financing body like a Panchayati Raj Finance Corporation in the states of Uttar Pradesh and Bihar to provide loans to Panchayati Raj Institutions to enable them to take up different types of remunerative enterprises has not been favoured by Asoka Mehta Committee.

The Committee was of the opinion that it is not likely to add to the total availability of the credit. What is required in this context is a greater rural orientation to all the financial institutions to Apart from this, the present system of grants-in-aid suffers from certain shortcomings. The grants are unrelated to the needs, these are irregular, uncertain and their release is sometimes based on political considerations. To fill up the gap between revenue and expenditure, the grants should be made available to these institutions on time and their release on political considerations should be avoided. Though there is a provision for government audit of Panchayati Raj Institutions, yet there are serious gaps in actual practice.

It has been noticed that the accounts, especially, of Village Panchayats, have remained unaudited for years at times. Panchayati Raj units have not cared to consider or remove the audit objections within the stipulated period. Hence, audit should be conducted regularly and the impression of its dispensibility should not be allowed to gain ground. The persons found guilty of misuse of funds should be given exemplary punishment and shown no leniency. In order to ensure that weaker sections of the society derive maximum benefits from the various plans, the Asoka Mehta Committee suggested that there should be an independent authority to carry out 'Social Audit' of the funds and programmes earmarked for the Scheduled Castes and Scheduled Tribes and to ensure that projects designed for them are implemented in a way that the desired impact is not diluted. Improper distribution of sources of income between the state and rural local bodies, limited financial autonomy, undeveloped trading enterprises, increased population pressure and functions etc., are some of the reasons for inadequate financial resources of Panchayati Raj Institutions. To improve the financial conditions of local bodies, creation of a separate tax-zone was strongly recommended by the Local Finance Enquiry Committee (1949-51) and the Taxation Enquiry Commission (1953-54). There is nothing new in this arrangement. It was practised during the period 1921-37 under the Government of India Act, 1919. The committees and commissions set up at the centre and the states have also suggested simplification of tax-imposing procedures, development of trading enterprises, appointment of State Finance Commission on the pattern of Central Finance Commission. Centralised purchasing, streamlining of financial management etc. are some of the remedial measures to augment finances of local bodies in India. If the suggestions described above are given a serious and fair trial, there is no reason why the shape of Panchayati Raj finances will not improve. These suggestions, when pursued, will go a long way in bridging the gap between needs and present supply of funds, putting Panchayati Raj finances on an even keel.

STRUCTURAL CHANGE

COLONIALISM

Colonialism is the establishment, maintenance, acquisition and expansion of colonies in one territory by people from another territory. It is a process whereby the metropole claims sovereignty over the colony and the social structure, government, and economics of the colony are changed by colonizers from the metropole. Colonialism is a set of unequal relationships between the metropole and the colony and between the colonists and the indigenous population.

The *colonial period* normally refers to the late 15th to the 20th century, when European states established colonies on other continents. During this time, the justifications for colonialism included various factors such as Christian missionary work, the profits to be made, the expansion of the power of the metropole and various religious and political beliefs. Colonialism and imperialism are ideologically linked with mercantilism.

DEFINITIONS

Collins English Dictionary defines colonialism as "the policy of acquiring and maintaining colonies, especially for exploitation." The *Merriam-Webster Dictionary* offers four definitions, including "something characteristic of a colony" and "control by one power over a dependent area or people."

The 2006 *Stanford Encyclopedia of Philosophy* "uses the term 'colonialism' to describe the process of European settlement and political control over the rest of the world, including Americas, Australia, and parts of Africa and Asia." It discusses the distinction between colonialism and imperialism and states that "[g]iven the difficulty of consistently distinguishing between the two terms, this entry will use colonialism as a broad concept that refers to the project of European political domination from the sixteenth to the twentieth centuries that ended with the national liberation movements of the 1960s."

In his preface to Jürgen Osterhammel's *Colonialism: A Theoretical Overview*, Roger Tignor says, "For Osterhammel, the essence of colonialism is the existence of colonies, which are by definition governed differently from other territories such as protectorates or informal spheres of influence." In the book, Osterhammel asks, "How can 'colonialism' be defined independently from 'colony?'"

He settles on a three-sentence definition:

- Colonialism is a relationship between an indigenous majority and a minority of foreign invaders. The fundamental decisions affecting the lives of the colonised people are made and implemented by the colonial rulers in pursuit of interests that are often defined in a distant metropolis. Rejecting cultural compromises with the colonised population, the colonisers are convinced of their own superiority and their ordained mandate to rule.

TYPES OF COLONIALISM

Historians often distinguish between two forms of colonialism, yet the two are not mutually exclusive:

1. Settler colonialism involves large scale emigration often motivated by religious, political, or economic reasons.
2. Exploitation colonialism involves fewer colonists where the focus is access to resources for export, typically to the metropole. This category includes trading posts as well as larger colonies where colonists would constitute much of the political and economic administration; but rely on indigenous resources for labour and material. When indigenous labour was unavailable, slaves were often imported prior to the end of the slave trade and widespread abolition.

Plantation colonies would be considered exploitation colonialism; but colonizing powers would utilize either type for different territories depending on various social and economic factors as well as climate and geographic conditions.

Colonialism often took place in pre-populated areas. This gave rise to culturally and ethnically mixed populations such as the mestizos of the Americas, as well as racially divided populations as found in French Algeria or Southern Rhodesia.

HISTORY

Activity that could be called colonialism has a long history. The Egyptians, Phoenicians, Greeks and Romans all built colonies in antiquity. The word "metropole" comes from the Greek *metropolis*—"mother city". The word "colony" comes from the Latin *colonia*—"a place for agriculture". Between the 11th and 18th centuries, the Vietnamese established military colonies south of their original territory and absorbed the territory, in a process known as nam ti□h.

Modern colonialism started with the Age of Discovery. Portugal and Spain discovered new lands across the oceans and built trading posts. For some people, it is this building of colonies across oceans that differentiates colonialism from other types of expansionism. These new lands were divided between the Portuguese Empire and Spanish Empire, first by the papal bull Inter caetera and then by the Treaty of Tordesillas and the Treaty of Zaragoza.

This period is also associated with the Commercial Revolution. The late Middle Ages saw reforms in accountancy and banking in Italy and the eastern

Mediterranean. These ideas were adopted and adapted in western Europe to the high risks and rewards associated with colonial ventures.

The 17th century saw the creation of the French colonial empire and the Dutch Empire, as well as the English colonial empire, which later became the British Empire. It also saw the establishment of some Swedish overseas colonies and a Danish colonial empire.

The spread of colonial empires was reduced in the late 18th and early 19th centuries by the American Revolutionary War and the Latin American wars of independence. However, many new colonies were established after this time, including the German colonial empire and Belgian colonial empire. In the late 19th century, many European powers were involved in the Scramble for Africa.

The Russian Empire, Ottoman Empire and Austrian Empire existed at the same time, but did not expand over oceans. Rather, these empires expanded through the more traditional route of conquest of neighbouring territories. There was, though, some Russian colonization of the Americas across the Bering Strait. The Empire of Japan modelled itself on European colonial empires. The United States of America gained overseas territories after the Spanish-American War for which the term "American Empire" was coined.

After the First World War, the victorious allies divided up the German colonial empire and much of the Ottoman Empire between themselves as League of Nations mandates. These territories were divided into three classes just as to how quickly it was deemed that they would be ready for independence. However, decolonization outside the Americas lagged until after the Second World War. In 1962 the United Nations set up a Special Committee on Decolonization, often called the Committee of 24, to encourage this process. Further, dozens of independence movements and global political solidarity projects such as the Non-Aligned Movement were instrumental in the decolonization efforts of former colonies.

Neocolonialism

The term neocolonialism has been used to refer to a variety of contexts since decolonization that took place after World War II. Generally it does not refer to a type of direct colonization, rather, colonialism by other means. Specifically, neocolonialism refers to the theory that former or existing economic relationships, such as the General Agreement on Tariffs and Trade and the Central American Free Trade Agreement, created by former colonial powers were or are used to maintain control of their former colonies and dependencies after the colonial independence movements of the post–World War II period.

COLONIALISM AND THE HISTORY OF THOUGHT

Colonialism and Geography

Settlers acted as the link between the natives and the imperial hegemony, bridging the geographical, ideological and commercial gap between the colonisers and colonised. Painter, J. and Jeffrey, A. affirm that certain advances aided the expansion of European states. With tools such as cartography, shipbuilding, navigation, mining and agricultural productivity colonisers had an upper hand. Their awareness of the Earth's surface and abundance of practical skills provided colonisers with a knowledge that, in turn, created power.

Painter and Jeffrey argue that geography as a discipline was not and is not an objective science, rather it is based on assumptions about the physical world. Whereas it may have given "The West" an advantage when it came to exploration, it also created zones of racial inferiority. Geographical beliefs such as environmental determinism, the view that some parts of the world are underdeveloped, legitimised colonialism and created notions of skewed evolution. These are now seen as elementary concepts. Political geographers maintain that colonial behaviour was reinforced by the physical mapping of the world, visually separating "them" and "us". Geographers are primarily focused on the spaces of colonialism and imperialism, more specifically, the material and symbolic appropriation of space enabling colonialism.

Colonialism and Imperialism

A colony is part of an empire and so colonialism is closely related to imperialism. Assumptions are that colonialism and imperialism are interchangeable, however Robert Young suggests that imperialism is the concept while colonialism is the practice. Colonialism is based on an imperial outlook, thereby creating a consequential relationship. Through an empire, colonialism is established and capitalism is expanded, on the other hand a capitalist economy naturally enforces an empire.

Marxist view of Colonialism

Marxism views colonialism as a form of capitalism, enforcing exploitation and social change. Marx thought that working within the global capitalist system, colonialism is closely associated with uneven development. It is an "instrument of wholesale destruction, dependency and systematic exploitation producing distorted economies, socio-psychological disorientation, massive poverty and neocolonial dependency." Colonies are constructed into modes of production. The search for raw materials and the current search for new investment opportunities is a result of inter-capitalist rivalry for capital accumulation.

Lenin regarded colonialism as the root cause of imperialism, as imperialism was distinguished by monopoly capitalism via colonialism and as Lyal S. Sunga explains: "Vladimir Lenin advocated forcefully the principle of self-determination of peoples in his "Theses on the Socialist Revolution and the Right of Nations to Self-Determination" as an integral plank in the programme of socialist internationalism" and he quotes Lenin who contended that "The right of nations to self-determination implies exclusively the right to independence in the political sense, the right to free political separation from the oppressor nation. Specifically, this demand for political democracy implies complete freedom to agitate for secession and for a referendum on secession by the seceding nation."

Liberalism, Capitalism and Colonialism

Classical liberals generally opposed colonialism and imperialism, including Adam Smith, Frederik Bastiat, Richard Cobden, John Bright, Henry Richard, Herbert Spencer, H. R. Fox Bourne, Edward Morel, Josephine Butler, W. J. Fox and William Ewart Gladstone.

Moreover, American revolution was the first anti-colonial rebellion, inspiring others. Adam Smith wrote in *Wealth of Nations* that Britain should liberate all of its colonies and also noted that it would be economically beneficial for British people in the average, although the merchants having mercantilist privileges would lose out.

Post-colonialism

Post-colonialism can refer to a set of theories in philosophy and literature that grapple with the legacy of colonial rule. In this sense, postcolonial literature may be considered a branch of postmodern literature concerned with the political and cultural independence of peoples formerly subjugated in colonial empires. Many practitioners take Edward Saïd's book *Orientalism* as the theory's founding work.

Saïd analysed the works of Balzac, Baudelaire and Lautréamont, exploring how they both absorbed and helped to shape a societal fantasy of European racial superiority. Writers of post-colonial fiction interact with the traditional colonial discourse, but modify or subvert it; for instance by retelling a familiar story from the perspective of an oppressed minor character in the story. Gayatri Chakravorty Spivak's *Can the Subaltern Speak?* gave its name to Subaltern Studies.

In *A Critique of Postcolonial Reason*, Spivak explored how major works of European metaphysics not only tend to exclude the subaltern from their discussions, but actively prevent non-Europeans from occupying positions as fully human subjects. Hegel's *Phenomenology of Spirit*, famous for its explicit ethnocentrism, considers Western civilization as the most accomplished of all, while Kant also allowed some traces of racialism to enter his work.

IMPACT OF COLONIALISM AND COLONIZATION

The impacts of colonization are immense and pervasive. Various effects, both immediate and protracted, include the spread of virulent diseases, the establishment of unequal social relations, exploitation, enslavement, medical advances, the creation of new institutions, and technological progress.

Impact on Health

Encounters between explorers and populations in the rest of the world often introduced new diseases, which sometimes caused local epidemics of extraordinary virulence. For example, smallpox, measles, malaria, yellow fever, and others were unknown in pre-Columbian America.

Disease killed the entire native population of the Canary Islands in the 16th century. Half the native population of Hispaniola in 1518 was killed by smallpox. Smallpox also ravaged Mexico in the 1520s, killing 150,000 in Tenochtitlan alone, including the emperor, and Peru in the 1530s, aiding the European conquerors. Measles killed a further two million Mexican natives in the 17th century. In 1618–1619, smallpox wiped out 90% of the Massachusetts Bay Native Americans. Smallpox epidemics in 1780–1782 and 1837–1838 brought devastation and drastic depopulation among the Plains Indians. Some believe that the death of up to 95% of the Native American population of the New World was caused by Old World diseases. Over the centuries, the Europeans had developed high degrees of immunity to these diseases, while the indigenous peoples had no time to build no such immunity.

Smallpox decimated the native population of Australia, killing around 50% of indigenous Australians in the early years of British colonization. It also killed many New Zealand Mâori. As late as 1848□49, as many as 40,000 out of 150,000 Hawaiians are estimated to have died of measles, whooping cough and influenza. Introduced diseases, notably smallpox, nearly wiped out the native population of Easter Island. In 1875, measles killed over 40,000 Fijians, approximately one-third of the population. The Ainu population decreased drastically in the 19th century, due in large part to infectious diseases brought by Japanese settlers pouring into Hokkaido.

Conversely, researchers concluded that syphilis was carried from the New World to Europe after Columbus's voyages. The findings suggested Europeans could have carried the nonvenereal tropical bacteria home, where the organisms may have mutated into a more deadly form in the different conditions of Europe. The disease was more frequently fatal than it is today; syphilis was a major killer in Europe during the Renaissance. The first cholera pandemic began in Bengal, then spread across India by 1820. Ten thousand British troops and countless Indians died during this pandemic. Between 1736 and 1834 only some 10% of East India Company's officers survived to take the final voyage home. Waldemar Haffkine, who mainly worked in India, who developed and used vaccines against cholera and bubonic plague in the 1890s, is considered the first microbiologist.

Countering Disease

As early as 1803, the Spanish Crown organised a mission to transport the smallpox vaccine to the Spanish colonies, and establish mass vaccination programmes there. By 1832, the federal government of the United States established a smallpox vaccination programme for Native Americans. Under the direction of Mountstuart Elphinstone a programme was launched to propagate smallpox vaccination in India. From the beginning of the 20th century onwards, the elimination or control of disease in tropical countries became a driving force for all colonial powers. The sleeping sickness epidemic in Africa was arrested due to mobile teams systematically screening millions of people at risk. In the 20th century, the world saw the biggest increase in its population in human history due to lessening of the mortality rate in many countries due to medical advances. The world population has grown from 1.6 billion in 1900 to an estimated 6.975 billion today.

Some believe that discussion of how diseases were spread has been scuttled by descendants of colonialists to conceal actual origins of how indigenous populations were purposefully infected with these new diseases. An argument here is that once European colonists discovered indigenous populations were not immune to certain diseases, they deliberately spread diseases to gain military advantages and subjugate local peoples. The most infamous case involves suggestions by Lord Jeffery Amherst, British commander in chief for America during the so-called French and Indian Wars between 1754 to 1763, although history is mute on whether his barbaric suggestions were carried out.

Many scholars have argued that evidence that supports this practice as having been executed on a larger scale across North America is weak. Yet, growing evidence is showing that other indigenous communities were purposefully infected, citing oral history from the descendants of said peoples. It has been regarded as one of the first instances of bio-terrorism or use of biological weapons in the history of warfare. There is, however, only one documented case of germ warfare, involving British commander Jeffrey Amherst. It is uncertain whether this documented British attempt successfully infected the Native Americans.

THEORETICAL FRAMEWORK FOR INDUSTRIALIZATION

Before analysing the Indian approach, we want to introduce the aims of industrialization, give a rough overview of the industrialization strategies for Less Developed Countries and identify indicators for the evaluation of the success of industrialization policies.

WHY INDUSTRIALIZATION?

What are the ultimate objectives of economic development? Different governments may have different objectives in mind. Generally, however, they will include a faster growth of national income, alleviation of poverty, and reduction of income inequalities. But how is industrialization expected to contribute to these goals? The experience of industrial economies shows a close association between development and industrial expansion. But industry is also thought to provide certain spillovers which would benefit other activities: enhancement of skills, training of managers, dispersion of technology, etc. Moreover, pessimism about the prospects of food and raw materials made the substitution of domestic for imported manufactured goods seem the most promising route to development for many countries.

Industrialization and Foreign trade

Economists and policymakers in the developing countries have long agreed on the role of government in providing infrastructure and maintaining stable macroeconomic policies. But they have disagreed on policies towards trade and industry. The form of government intervention in this area is the distinguishing feature of alternative development strategies.

A convenient and instructive way to approach the complex issues of appropriate trade policies for development is to set these specific policies in the context of a broader Less Developed Countries strategy of looking outward or inward. Outward-looking development policies encourage not only free trade but also the free movement of capital, workers, enterprises, the multinational enterprise, and an open system of communications. By contrast, inward-looking development policies stress the need for LDCs to evolve their own styles of development and to control their own destiny. Within these two broad philosophical approaches to development, a lively debate has been carried out between the free traders, who advocate outward-looking export promotion strategies of industrialization, and the protectionists, who are proponents of inward-looking import substitution strategies.

The advocates of import substitution– the protectionists – believe that LDCs should substitute domestic production of previously imported simple consumer goods and extend this later to a wider range of more sophisticated manufactured items – all behind the protection of high tariffs and quotas on imports. In the long run, IS advocates cite the benefits of greater domestic industrial diversification and the ultimate ability to export previously protected manufactured goods, as economies of scale, low labour costs, and the positive externalities of learning by doing cause domestic prices to become more competitive with world prices.

By contrast, advocates of export promotion of both primary and manufactured goods cite the efficiency and growth benefits of free trade and competition, the importance of substituting large world markets for narrow domestic markets, the distorting price and cost effects of protection, and the tremendous success of the East Asian export-oriented economies of South Korea, Singapore, and Hong Kong.

The balance of the debate has swung back and forth, with the protectionists predominating in the 1950s and 1960s, and the export promoters gaining the upper hand in the late 1970s and in the 1980s and 1990s, especially among Western and World Bank economists.

Indicators for Measuring Economic Development

Of course, any development policy has to be assessed by measuring the economic development it effects. India's first Prime Minister Jawaharlal Nehru declared on the eve of the departure of the British, on 14 August 1947, that India's task in the future included "the ending of poverty and ignorance and disease and inequality of opportunity".

These measures will be used to determine the success of the inward-looking policies he initiated, as well as to compare their success with the success of the reform policies. Therefore, growth of income per capita, alleviation of poverty and reduction of income inequalities are amongst the most important indicators.

To measure advances regarding inequality of opportunity and ignorance, several indicators pertaining to education and health will be used. These are two important public goods to which every individual is entitled; both for their intrinsic importance and for their enhancement of instrumental personal, social and process roles, and also empowerment and distributive roles.

HISTORY OF INDUSTRIALIZATION IN INDIA

Colonial Rule

Under colonial rule, India, as with most other developing countries, followed a non-industrial model. But many Indians believed that progress was retarded by this. It was believed that true economic progress lay in industrialization; Smith's and Ricardo's ideas of international specialization and mutually advantageous free trade were rejected, at least until India became an exporter of more sophisticated goods.

INDUSTRIALIZATION SINCE INDEPENDENCE

India's first Prime Minister, Jawaharlal Nehru, Premier from 1947 to 1964, saw industrialization as the key to alleviating poverty. Industrialization not only promised self-sufficiency for his nation that had just regained political sovereignty, but also offered external economies accruing from technical progress. Believing the potential of agriculture and exports to be limited, Indian governments taxed agriculture by skewing the terms of trade against it and emphasising import substitution, thus giving priority to heavy industry.

Nehru believed a powerful state with a centralised planned economy to be essential if the country was to industrialise rapidly. The Industries Act in 1951 laid the foundations for this administrative control on industrial capacity. But, over time, the licensing requirements became increasingly stringent and were accompanied by a gamut of procedures that required clearance by a number of disparate and uncoordinated ministries. In order to pursue IS, the Import Trade Control Order of 1955 subjected almost all imports to quantitative restrictions in the form of import licenses. These were supplemented by tariffs at rates that were among the highest in the developing world.

Indian state intervention in industrial development has been extensive. Unlike many East Asian countries, which used state intervention to build strong private sector industries, India opted for state control over key industries. At different times, nationalised industries included chemicals, electric power, steel, transportation, life insurance, portions of the coal and textile industries, and banking. To promote these industries the government not only levied high tariffs and imposed import restrictions, but also subsidised the nationalised firms, directed investment funds to them, and controlled both land use and many prices.

Under Prime Minister Indhira Gandhi, two major shifts took place in the role of the state. First, the neglect of agriculture was reversed through state activism in subsidising new seeds and fertilizers, agricultural credit, and rural electrification. The green revolution took off and by the mid-1970s India was self-sufficient in grain. The second shift was the further tightening of state control over every aspect of the economy. Banks were nationalised, trade was increasingly restricted, price controls were imposed on a wide range of products, and foreign investment was squeezed.

In 1973, dealings in foreign exchanges as well as foreign investment came to be regulated by the Foreign Exchange and Regulation Act. The act virtually shut out the inflow of new technology from abroad in the 1970s and 1980s, particularly when these involved large equity participation.

The Indian system of state planning went far beyond the usual inward-looking industrialization policies that most developing countries pursued after World War II. The government regulated the most basic business decisions for all firms above a certain size: borrowing, investment, capacity utilization, pricing and distribution.

The over-restrictive, and often self-defeating nature of the regulatory framework, began to become evident by the late 1960s and early 1970s. Comprehensive planning was increasingly criticised as planned targets were not met and many plans were not even implemented. The lack of success in some dimensions led to a new and more restrictive set of regulations. One example is the attempt to reserve sectors for small industries and to restrict the growth of large firms.

Beginning in the early 1980s, a mild trend towards deregulation started. Economic reforms were introduced, starting to liberalise trade, industrial and financial policies, while subsidies, tax concessions, and the depreciation of the currency improved export incentives. These measures helped GDP growth to accelerate to over 5% per year during the 1980s, compared to 3.5% during the 1970s, and reduced poverty more rapidly. However India's most fundamental structural problems were only partially addressed. Tariffs continued to be among the highest in the world, and quantitative restrictions remained pervasive.

Moreover, a significant government influence continued in the allocation of credit to firms and a discouragement of foreign investment. Relatively inefficient public enterprises, controlling nearly 20% of GDP, remained a drag on economic growth.

The government expanded antipoverty schemes, especially rural employment schemes, but only a small fraction of the rising subsidies actually reached the poor. Competition between political parties drove subsidies up at every election. The resulting fiscal deficits contributed to a rising current account deficit. India's foreign exchange reserves were virtually exhausted by mid-1991 when a new government headed by Narasimha Rao came to power.

In July 1991, India launched a second major economic reform programme. The government committed itself to promoting a competitive economy that would be open to trade and foreign investment. Measures were introduced to reduce the government's influence in corporate investment decisions. Much of the industrial-licensing system was dismantled, and areas once closed to the private sector were opened up. These included electricity generation, areas of the oil industry, heavy industry, air transport, roads and some telecommunications. Foreign investment was suddenly welcomed.

Greater global integration was encouraged with a significant reduction in the use of import licenses and tariffs an elimination of subsidies for exports, and the introduction of a foreign-exchange market. Since April 1992, there has been no need to obtain any license or permit to carry out import-export trade. As of April 1, 1993, trade is completely free, barring only a small list of imports and exports that are either regulated or banned. The WTO estimated an average import tariff of 71% in 1993 which has been reduced to 40% in 1995. With successive additional monetary reforms, the rupee, since 1995, can nearly be considered a fully convertible currency at market rates. India now has a much more open economy.

AGRO BASED ACTIVITIES FOR INCOME GENERATION

CROP PRODUCTION

There are several areas to improve the crop profitability and profitability. These include the introduction of improved varieties and new crops, soil and water conservation, wastelands development, organic farming, use of improved inputs and tools, post production processing and marketing of the produce. In many villages, farmers do not have threshing yards and appropriate tools to thresh, clean and dry the produce, before storage. As a result, farmers incur heavy losses due to damage, wastage and pilferage.

These problems can be solved by establishing post harvest facilities, such as creation of threshing yards and storage facilities, supply of threshers, cleaners, dryers and other tools particularly in those regions where farmers grow two crops and the rainfall distribution is bimodal.

Horticulture and Forestry

On marginal and wastelands, where crop production is uneconomical, afforestation can be a viable alternative. Afforestation can generate cash income by providing commodity outputs like fodder, fuel, timber, gum, rubber, wax, lac and raw material for paper, pulp and herbal medicines. Several fruit crops like ber, custard apple, cashew and mango have the potential to generate good income in dry areas where agricultural production is uncertain and uneconomical.

Programmes can be initiated to identify unproductive and marginal lands for dryland horticulture. Such plantations can improve the micro climate and boost the productivity of the adjoining farmlands.

The on going Social Forestry programmes to promote fodder and fuelwood production have not made any headway so far.

This could be due to lack of interest among the farmers to grow fodder and fuelwood species as these are presently collected from community wastelands free of cost.

Their response to develop community wastelands has been poor because of lack of foolproof systems to distribute benefits equally among the families in the community. As the present efforts to produce fodder and fuelwood are not showing expected response, focus can be shifted to produce other useful commodities such as fruits, nuts, bamboo and pole timber, which have a ready market. Some of the following activities can be introduced to sustain interest of the community and to adopt social forestry as an income generation programme, while ensuring environmental protection.

- Motivating women and youth to set up forestry and horticultural nurseries;
- Promotion of commercial tree plantations on marginal lands;
- Establishment of market outlets to provide minimum support price;
- Facilities to process wood and other non-wood forest produce in rural areas.

Kisan Nurseries

As non-availability of good quality seedlings is a constraint for promoting afforestation and horticulture, local nurseries can be established through young farmers. They can be trained in raising plants and grafting and budding techniques. They can be supported with the supply of good quality seeds, mother plants and finance during the initial stage.

Animal Husbandry

Scientific breeding and management of cattle, buffaloes, sheep, goats, poultry and pigs for milk, meat, eggs, wool and processing of these products have good potential for providing gainful self employment on a sustainable basis, particularly to empower the women. Animal Husbandry and agriculture are inter dependent and mixed farming facilitates effective cycling of nutrients, while providing stable income. Development of infrastructure for marketing the produce would further improve the profitability. Fishery development also has scope in limited areas, along the rivers, sea coast and reservoirs.

OFF FARM EMPLOYMENT OPPORTUNITIES

Unless the outside entrepreneurs set up industries, the scope for non-agrobased vocations is limited to rural areas. However, certain small scale units can be set up by individuals or groups, to operate tool production unit, agro service centres, food processing and packing, tailoring and garment manufacturing, handloom units, fibre extraction and rope making, handicrafts, *etc.* Service sectors can also provide good employment opportunities. Plumbing, masonry, carpentry, hiring of bicycles, auto service, electrical fitting, retail trading, carpentry, etc can also provide employment opportunities to a few youth in each village.

ACTIVITIES FOR BETTER QUALITY OF LIFE

Activities related to health, education and social development need smaller investment and time as compared to livelihood activities. Therefore, it should be possible to take advantage of the government schemes to provide the services needed for improving health, hygiene and educational facilities.

PROGRAMME IMPLEMENTATION

It is advisable to prepare a general plan of implementation and yearly plan of operation with quarterwise or monthwise break up of activities and budget. This would help to review the progress and monitor the programme. Logical Framework Analysis (LFA) is a good tool to develop an action plan before implementing the project. This helps in identifying the real problems, expected outputs, activities needed to be initiated to achieve the goals and the indicators of success at various stages.

The success of the rural development programme lies in developing local level organisations of the target groups to sustain the development, even after completion of the project. This can be done by formation of Self Help Groups (SHGs) and other village level organisations. While SHGs consist of 15 20 members, who can organise savings and initiate several income generation activities, a larger organisation will be useful for promoting community level welfare and service activities. This organisation should have a close link with the local Gram Panchayat, so that activities can be undertaken jointly and effectively. This would also ensure transparency in programme implementation.

It is however difficult to define a set procedure for such a linkage, as it depends on the attitude and ability of the Panchayat members towards the target groups. Gram Panchayats are also compelled to cooperate if the programme is implemented successfully and the self help groups gain strength.

Indicators of Development

With enhanced income, the rural families are likely to change their lifestyle. Some of the indicators of improvement in the quality of life are rise in food consumption, better clothing, renovated houses, building up of assets such as vehicles, ornaments, utensils, *etc.* Farmers may also invest in land development and irrigation facilities with the surplus money generated by them. Use of banking facilities is another indicator of progress.

Improvement in the educational status can be judged by the percentage of children attending school in a village, the number of newspapers in circulation and the importance given by the farmers in attending meetings of the Gram Sabha and local bodies, vocational training courses, *etc.* Indicators of improving health status in the villages are the quality of drinking water, the number of sick days per family every year, percentage of children covered under vaccinations, birth rate, infant mortality, nutritional status of women and children, *etc.* For evaluating the improvement in social development ('Aacharan') appropriate indicators are the priority on spending extra income and free time and attendance of family heads in social gatherings and political meetings. Consumption of alcohol, sources of recreation, number of gambling dens, incidences of crime etc in the village will also help in analysing the level of social development that has been taking place in the villages during the process of development. Reduction in the family size, school drop outs, women spending time in fetching water and fuelwood, improvement in housing, clean surroundings, are reliable indicators to measure the quality of life.

Continuation of the programme on a sustainable basis by the community even after termination of the project, without financial support from the donor agency, is another reliable indicator to measure the success of the development programme. The agencies engaged in rural development can easily use these indicators while monitoring the programme implementation and make necessary changes in the action plan to achieve the goals.

RURAL DEVELOPMENT FOR NATION BUILDING

Rural Development is not only needed for ensuring food security but also to boost the Gross National Product of the nation. Fortunately, India has plenty of natural resources, idle labour, necessary technology and good market both in India and abroad.

Presently, the people engaged in agriculture lack motivation and organisational strength at the grass root level. We need to act now, before it is too late.

ESSENTIAL ASPECTS OF RURAL DEVELOPMENT

The essential aspects of rural development are as follows:

- Agricultural development constitutes the crucial aspect of rural development. Agricultural development is possible through the use of better seeds, adequate fertilizers, manures, and pesticides, adequate supply of water and effective implementation of land reform measures.
- By effecting changes in the socio-economic institutions, rural development seeks to change the socio-economic structure of the rural community.
- The effectiveness of the rural development programmes necessitates political non-interference. The persons associated with these programmes should be given adequate freedom to carry out their plans and programmes with undivided attention.
- The success of the rural development programmes depends on the co-operative orientation and attitude among the ruralites. The functioning of the co-operative societies goes a long way in improving the conditions of the vulnerable sections of the rural set-up.
- Rural development programmes demand the active participation of the ruralites. While formulating these programmes the opinions, attitudes, drives and interests of the rural people should be taken into account. Further, dedicated and committed village leaders should come forward to guide the masses for bringing about rural development.

INTEGRATED RURAL DEVELOPMENT

It is claimed that the concept of Integrated Rural Development was originally propounded by the World Bank. In India the concept was put forward in the year 1976 at the All-India Science Congress by C. Subramanyam, the then Finance Minister of India.

He viewed integrated rural development as "systematic, scientific and integrated use of all our natural resources and as a part of this process enabling every person to engage himself in a productive and socially useful occupation and earn an income that would meet at least the basic needs."

He holds the view that the use of natural resources is possible only through the application of science and technology. Further, proper application of science and technology results in the fulfilment of basic social needs.

G. Parthasarathy refers to four 'routes' in the context of integrated rural development: (i) the institutional route of Gunnar Myrdal, (ii) the 'New Economics' route, (iii) the Neo-Marxian route and (iv) the Gandhian route.

V.K.R.V. Rao defines integrated rural development as "the optimum utilization of the natural and human resources of a given rural area for the enrichment of the quality of life of the population."

The concept of integrated rural development addresses itself to various rural problems like widespread poverty, unemployment, illiteracy, exploitation, inequitable distribution of land, poor health conditions *etc.* It signifies that various facets of rural development are integrally connected.

It is a holistic concept rather than a sequential one. K. Om Prakash and G. Satyanarayan rightly observe that integrated rural development embraces all the activities of enrichment and betterment of the overall quality of rural life through appropriate development of man power, resources, infrastructural facilities and provisions of minimum needs and livelihood. It has far-reaching socio-economic and political implications for the life of the ruralites.

INTEGRATED RURAL DEVELOPMENT APPROACH

The integrated development approach emphasis is the need of coordinating different agencies under a single management system of essential components (including education) required to get agricultural or rural development moving. The management system may be highly authoritarian credit may be designed to provide an important role for local people in planning, decision making and implementation of the programmers. The main emphasis is on rational development and coordination of all principal factors required for agricultural and rural development. The community development for agricultural India could not achieve the desired impact in increasing agricultural productions. As a solution to this situation the Intensive Agriculture District Programme (IADP) was launched in selected districts. The IADP used the integrated development approach in tackling the problem of rural development.

OBJECTIVES

In this Programme there was more emphasis on the package approach. In ten points included in the programme were:

- Adequate farm credit through strengthened cooperatives.
- Adequate supplies of fertilizers pesticides, improved seeds, implements and other essential production needs through strengthened service cooperatives.
- Price incentives to participating farmers through assured price agreements for rice, wheat and millet.
- Marketing arrangements and services to enable farmers to obtain a full market price for their marketed surplus.
- Intensive educational, technical and farm management assistance made available in every village.
- Participation of all interested farmers in farm planning for increased production.

- Village planning for increased production and village improvement programme by strengthening village organisations and leaderships.
- A public works programme using local labour and development works contributing directly to increased production.
- Analysis and evaluation of the programme from its inception and
- Coordination of all essential resources for maximum speed and effectiveness.

INTEGRATED WASTELANDS DEVELOPMENT PROJECT (IWDP) SCHEME

This scheme is under implementation since, 1989-90, and has come to this Department along with the National Wastelands Development Board. The development of non-forest wastelands is taken up under this Scheme. The scheme provides for the development of an entire micro watershed in an holistic manner rather than piecemeal treatment in sporadic patches.. The thrust of the scheme continues to be on development of wastelands.

Objectives

The basic objective of this scheme is an integrated wastelands development based on village/micro watershed plans. These plans are prepared after taking into consideration the land capability, site condition and local needs of the people.

The scheme also aims at rural employment besides enhancing the contents of people's participation in the wastelands development programmes at all stages, which is ensured by providing modalities for equitable and sustainable sharing of benefits and usufructs arising from such projects.

Activities

The major activities taken up under the scheme are:

- En-situ soil and moisture conservation measures like terracing, bunding, trenching, vegetative barriers and drainage line treatment.
- Planting and sowing of multi-purpose trees, shrubs, grasses, legumes and pasture land development.
- Encouraging natural regeneration.
- Promotion of agro-forestry and horticulture.
- Wood substitution and fuel wood conservation measures.
- Awareness raising, training and extension.
- Encouraging people's participation through community organisation and capacity building.
- Drainage Line treatment by vegetative and engineering structures
- Development of small water Harvesting Structures.

- Afforestation of degraded forest and non-forest wasteland.
- Development and conservation of common Property Resources.

COMMUNITY ORGANISATION

To restore the ecological balance in the degraded watersheds through sustained community action, mass mobilisation is needed. The programme can only succeed when the community is motivated enough to realize that the programme is not only for eco-restoration through watershed development but also to addresses their other pressing socio-economic needs.

The activities under this community organisation include organizing Self Help Groups and User Groups, Participatory Rural Appraisal (PRA) exercises, awareness camps, exposure visits and programmes on literacy, family welfare, social services, income generating activities *etc.* giving small contributions to SHGs or other village institutions like mahila mandals/ youth clubs/ anganwadis which are considered important for people participation. The idea is rapport building with the people at grass root level and PIA. The people must feel that the programme belongs to them and its success depends on them only.

Once the people realize that it is they who own the programme, the sustenance of the project evolves.

One of the notable features of this component is the flexibility available to the PIAs (Project Implementing Agencies). There is a provision for entry point activities for trust building exercise and speedy community organisation. Under this component they can even take up those works which are not directly related to conservation and wasteland development.

Certain works of great priority and importance to villagers such as repairing and construction of community and panchayat houses, sanitation improvement, provision of drinking water school building *etc.* can be taken up.

Effective community organisation is important to establish credibility of the Watershed Development Team and create a rapport with the village community who is ultimately going to own and implement the programme even after withdrawing the Government machinery.

COMPREHENSIVE INTEGRATED DEVELOPMENT IN RURAL INDIA

MAHILA MANDALS (WOMEN'S GROUPS)

Mahila Mandals, or women's group, provide a forum for women of a particular village to voice their personal challenges, be it at an individual, domestic or social level. The women, with village facilitators trained by CORD, work together to resolve their issues. By this process women are encouraged to continuously grow and take their personal transformation to heights of active community participation. Currently we have 555 Mahila mandals with approximately 21,943 women as members.

Some of the achievements resulting from Mahila Mandal activity over the past year include:

- International women's day was celebrated in the super focused Panchayat, and women from other Panchayat also participated at the local nodal Panchayats. A total of 1.363 members from 78 MM participated. For the first time ever, the programme was completely self funded by the women of the MMs themselves.
- International Women's day was celebrated at the CORD centre too with 128 participants to discuss their experiences and current challenges.
- International and National days were observed by MM (*e.g.* Swami Vivekananda Jayanti, Republic day, World Water Day, World Tuberculosis day, World Consumer rights day, World HIV/AIDs day etc.)
- There were 12 MM follow up sessions in the past year. On an average each Mahila Mandal is represented by 2-3 members. (MM follow up sessions are held on the first day of each month to review all MM activities).
- Resource persons were trained in the Super-Khas Panchayats-in the last quarter we trained 147 Balvihars, 166 Yuvati Samuh and 209 Single Women resource persons.
- Training on capacity building of women leaders of grade C & D (areas covered included, writing minutes; developing action plans; record keeping; training new leaders etc.)
- Closure of an illegal liquor shop
- Reporting of an alcoholic man to officials for beating his wife.
- Women tortured by their in-laws and sent to their parent's homes were brought back home.
- Forcing an alcoholic man to stop drinking (through a written statement).
- Forcing a woman to repay her loan received from the local bank.
- Providing an avenue of hope for women in desperate situations (*e.g.* widowed) through empowerment with the skills to earn a livelihood and so be independent.
- ₹One lakh was sanctioned by the Government for construction of local Mahila Bhawan (Lahuna).
- Funds were raised for the marriage of a poor girl, medical treatment of an old lady (₹5,000), and building a bowri in a village (₹.50,000)
- Kangra Eye Hospital organized an eye camp in Sartori Gram Panchayat to improve eye health for local villagers.
- Bakulja Panchayat in collaboration with the Agriculture Department conducted an agricultural camp.

- Bhuned Panchayat in collaboration with the Youth Mandal organized a programme to discuss issues including dowry and female feticide etc.
- Awareness programmes were organized by the police department of Indora block in collaboration with local Mahila Mandals to discuss issues of bootlegging, domestic violence, drugs and sexual assault and relevant preventative methods.
- Village clean up programmes were organized (Dheneta).
- Exclusive meetings were held with SUTRA at Passu and Gurkadi for the upcoming'Ekal Nari Shakti Sangathan' (organization working on the issues related to single women) March Past Programme for demands of single women, to be held on 1st-3rd April from Akri to Shimla. 408 women participated, of which 312 were from Mahila Mandals.
- Mr. Vishal Gupta and Mr. Vinod Pathania of MM programme attended a two day workshop on Empowerment of Women organized by SALTS (Social Action Litigation and Training Society) and ISI (Indian Social Institute) held in New Delhi on 25th-26th February.
- Mr. Vinod Gupta attended a DLCC meeting on the 28th of February in Dharamsala. The meeting promoted NABARD's programme launches.
- Mr. Sunil Mishra, Mr. Vinod Pathania, Mrs. Seema Thakur and Mrs. Indu Dhiman attended the 7 days National workshop held in October on Gender and Development at the Indian Social Institute, New Delhi.
- Mrs. Rajni Kayastha and Mr. Ajit Kumar attended a sensitization programme on Female Feoticide and Infanticide for the trainers of PRI's in September at NIPCCD, New Delhi.

YUVA MANDAL (YOUTH GROUPS)

Youth, being the future of tomorrow, need to have their energies and dynamism channelised in the most appropriate direction. Regular youth group meetings encourage building youth confidence, leadership skills, representation in local governance, natural resource management and even organizing social activities. Currently there are 220 Yuva mandals, involving 5,500 members. This year 186 resource persons were trained. Regular monthly follow ups at the centre continue with a variety of workshops, discussion groups, plays, and external speakers etc. Common activities that members of the Yuva mandal carry out include organizing awareness programmes for various topics, mentoring other youth and younger members of the village, construction activities (*e.g.* building roads, toilets etc.), national resource management activities (*e.g.* planting trees etc.), maintain community cleanliness, career building skills, and organizing sports tournaments. This list is continually increasing.

Some of the important achievements of youth mandal for the year:

- Encouraging increased participation in Up-gram sabhas through a special motivational programme held in three different blocks (Panchrukhi, Bhawarana and Nagrota).
- 350 youth held a rally in district Kangra to reduce pollution on World Environment Day.
- 66 youngsters trained in basic computer course through Chinmaya Yuva se Yuva programme.
- On 22nd April 2007, 86 youth participated in a workshop"Just Think" focused on discussing leadership and growth training
- On 11th May 2007, 105 youth participated in a workshop to increase awareness of Right to Information (RTI) and National Rural Employment Guarantee Scheme (NREGS).
- On 17th May 2007, a workshop"Achieve the Goal" was organized for 170 youth participants. Several differently-abled youth and the Canadian High Commissioner to India were in attendance.
- Celebrated Swami Vivekananda Jayanti as National Youth Day (January 12th). Plays, songs and speeches were performed to commemorate the contribution of Swami Vivekananda. The event received significant media coverage.
- An exposure trip was organized for the Yuva Mandal team to Ray Organisation (a youth organization created by the youth). The purpose of the trip was to see how a Yuva Mandal can create its own organization.

YUVATI SAMOOH (ADOLESCENT GIRLS GROUPS)

Yuvati Samooh is an integral part of our youth programme. Adolescent girls face many challenges as they mature into young women. To address these issues in an appropriate forum gives the girls both confidence and a valuable support system. Topics commonly addressed in such meetings include personal health and hygiene, sanitation, gender discrimination, dowry, leadership, women's contribution to society etc. Workshops are commonly held at CORD centre, combining awareness programmes with social activities. Each workshop averages an attendance of approximately 70-100 girls each. With increasing interest in such meetings we currently have 79 Yuvati groups with 1,157 members. Eventually the Yuvati Samuh groups merge with the mainstream Yuva Mandal groups.

Achievements for the year include:

- Celebration of International Women's Day with skits and cultural programmes.
- Village facilitator training was conducted, with an attendance of over 28 girls.

- Capacity building session was conducted on National Youth day in which 123 young girls participated.
- A cultural programme was conducted at the CORD center on National Youth Day, winners of which competed at a District level and won second prize.
- A workshop"Aaj ki Yuvati, Kal ki Nari" (Today's girls, tomorrow's women) was held in December 2007, with the purpose of empowering the future generation of women with the right vision of women's role in society. The programme was attended by 65 young girls.

BALVIHAR (6-14 YEARS CHILDREN'S GROUPS)

Moulding children from a young age to be moral and productive members of society can be achieved by imbibing in them good values and correct thinking. Besides empowering our Balvihars with moral and spiritual values, they are also sensitized to social issues from this early age through the Bala Sena wing. Bala Sena raises awareness on issues of plantation, sanitation, literacy etc. Furthermore, health awareness programmes are conducted throughout the year for both children and mothers (all topics ranging from HIV/AIDs to Alcohol Abuse are covered).

One specific programme undertaken this year, based on Natural Resource Management, was recycling days. On this day glass and plastic were specifically separated from other rubbish in almost 20 villages. Other activities included awareness programmes through plays performed for other villagers, construction of soakage and garbage pits, and training of resource persons. Due to the introduction of Anganwadis by the government, the playschool component of Balvihar has been withdrawn this year to prevent unnecessary overlap. Currently we have a total of 137 Balvihar groups, in both Khas and Super Khas panchayats, with 3,233 total members. These Balvihars are run by Mahila Mandal members voluntarily without any cost to the programme.

ADULT LITERACY

Literacy is one of the most fundamental tools of today's society. The unique'Roti and Sothi' method is used to teach the village folk who were not fortunate enough develop their literacy skills earlier. Village facilitators also adopt other unique methods to educate including teaching with leaves as well relating to interesting, relevant and understandable topics.

Some significant achievements this year include:

- Six differently-abled children from Sokni da Kot panchyat are educating people in their own village.
- A 71 year old woman from the Barballa village has completed the first book of the programme!

PANCHAYATI RAJ INSTITUTIONS (LOCAL SELF GOVERNANCE)

The PRI programme provides a universal platform for decentralized planning from the bottom up. We are working in over 225 Gram panchayats, with intense focus in 28 of them to ensure that Panchayati Raj Institutions function as instruments of local government. This forum is for the villagers, so it is essential for them to see this as an important aspect of development and use it to bring about change in their community. Therefore, community based organizations make efforts to sensitize local community members, particularly the youth, to increase their involvement. CORD is working in 225 Gram Panchayats.

This year CORD facilitated 133 Up-Gram Sabha meetings to strengthen Gram Sabha meetings. As a result, in this year CORD facilitated 191 Gram Sabhas, and 50% run successfully and completed their quorum. Major issues raised were inclusion of the poor people in the National Rural Employment Guarantee Scheme (NREGS) and Below Poverty Line (BPL); discussion on the Right to Information Act; devolution of powers and functions; micro-planning; and resource mobilization.

Women participation has been consistently around 44.5%. 40 people were trained as VVRPs in Panchayati Raj. Regular activities and follow ups conducted by PRI, include regular meetings with Panchayats on Panchayat Diwas (2nd day of each month), training of volunteers and resource people; networking and liaison.

Following initiatives of CORD during the year to strengthen PRIs:

- Training of Village Volunteer Resource Persons (VVRPs).
- Organizing Panchayat Diwas in the field and in the center on the 2nd of every month. Here panchayat representatives from different panchayats share their experiences and difficulties along with discussion of economic and social development schemes.
- Formation, nurturing, and awareness in the following CBOs: Mahila Mandals, SHGs, Yuvati Samuh, Yuva Mandals, and Balvihar.
- Eight training programmes have been organized for elected representatives held at the CORD center, and in the field.
- Meeting with satellite agents (far off block workers) on the 26th of each month to discuss activities done in the field.
- Mr. Narender Paul partook in a two day workshop on PRI- Indo-German bilateral capacity building of Panchayati Raj institutions in H.P. (Project Design workshop) held at New Shimla in November. He also attended the 2nd sustainability Summit Asia 2007 organized in New Delhi in December.
- In October, Mr. Vishal Gupta participated in a workshop on Village Resource Centres supported by ISRO (Bangalore) and Implementation

of NRHM in H.P. and the role of NGO's in National Rural Health Mission. Later in the same month, Mr. Vishal Gupta participated in the Indo-Norwegian Symposium on"Experience of local self-Government" at Vigyan Bhawan, New Delhi.

- Mr. Neeraj Gupta represented CORD in four days training in Dehradun organized by the Rural Litigation and Entitlement Kendra (RLEK) where various topics were covered such as the PRI system and its uses, communication, disaster management, networking and resource management.

ALCOHOL ABUSE AWARENESS (AAA) PROGRAMME

Excessive use of alcohol can have negative consequences on individual's health, personal relationships and the community. Awareness and education is an essential starting point to understanding alcohol addiction. In the previous year 900 people attended awareness programmes about the negative effects of alcohol and how to prevent alcohol addiction. Also, four Youth awareness programmes were facilitated in which over 500 people were in attendance. Further, a survey of alcohol consumption was conducted in four villages, in an attempt to understand better their needs and intervene accordingly. Treatment of people dependant on alcohol is two-fold.

The first step is awareness and counseling and the second step is the use of the Sinclair Method and medication. This year, we were fortunate to have Dr. Roy David Eskapa from London, to facilitate the progress of the Sinclair method in CORD. He predominantly used the medication Natrim (Naltrexone) as a withdrawal aid. In the past year we have provided counseling to 55 alcoholics and their families, of which 23 are currently on treatment, 22 have reduced their drinking, and 10 have stopped drinking altogether. One unique event included a trip to a country liquor manufacturer for education and research purposes.

The purpose of this trip to Parour village, where rice beer is manufactured was to gain insight into the process of production and attitude of producers. The particular type of rice beer produced at the Parour location is also used as a medicine to treat kidney stones and other kidney related ailments. It is cheap and has a wide appeal amongst the poor. However, like all alcohol, when abused it can lead to serious illness and addiction.

COMMUNITY BASED PRIMARY HEALTHCARE

Healthcare is addressed by looking at both treatment and prevention. CORD provides primary healthcare, through the outpatient's department as well as through awareness campaigns in the field. Ongoing training is given to the health guides, birth attendants and Balwadi workers.

Through this past year specific topics of health campaigns included:

- Diarrhea-understanding the preventable causes of diarrhoea and the usage of Oral Re-hydration Solution (ORS) for prevention of severe dehydration.
- Diabetes Mellitus-50 patients were given advice and medication by an endocrinologist from Delhi.
- Blood donation camp was set up in which 158 CORD volunteers donated blood.
- Plastic Surgery camp at local Medical College in Dharamsala.
- Pulse polio immunization programmes (both at centre as well as in the field).
- Health and relevant support services provided to bed-ridden patients.
- Other health awareness programmes covering HIV/AIDs, anaemia, pre and post natal care.
- Health checkups for children of 10 Balwadis.

In addition to health campaigns, the outpatient department is kept consistently busy with over 12,000 consultations through the year (including patients seen in our sub-centers). Patients whose care is beyond our scope are referred on to hospitals and other relevant facilities for further investigation. The typical presentations seen in OPD include respiratory disease, skin conditions, anemia, and worm infestations.

COMMUNITY BASED INTEGRATED SANITATION PROGRAMME

To promote better health and encouraging good sanitation habits essential. Through our sanitation and hygiene programme we have reached out to almost 15,438 people. Low cost toilets structures have been developed and promoted through practical demonstrations thereby discouraging open defaecation. Almost 689 basic toilets have been constructed through the year. In addition, we have facilitated the setup of 382 garbage pits, 394 soaking pits, 391 kitchen gardens, and held cleanliness drives in 633 villages. The Lions Club in Chicago in collaboration with Lions Club Dharamshala has supported toilet construction in 2 blocks of the project area. CORD's workers have raised approximately 50% of the cost of toilet by motivating individuals and rest is by Lions Club.

Other activities include:

- Awareness campaigns for local villages, schools, and factories.
- Proper segregation of solid waste (plastic, iron, glass etc.)
- Construction of garbage and soakage pits.
- Exposure trip to Kullu (an open defecation free village)
- Regular training of village facilitators is conducted.
- 57 segregation campaigns.
- Cleaned 134 natural water sources.

- Chlorinated 80 bowries.
- Conducted 40 sanitation programmes in schools and ran 68 awareness campaigns.
- 6 inaugurations programmes in different Panchayats with an average attendance of 80-100 people.

RESOURCE CENTE FOR SELF HELP GROUPS (SHGS)

Self Help Groups are a means for underprivileged people to learn micro-finance. Once they are established in those skills, they are able to borrow significant loans from the bank in order to earn a living and explore entrepreneurship options. Currently there are 1,473 SHGs, with over 20,000 members, with almost ₹18 crores in circulation (*i.e.* approximately US$ 4.5 million). The success of our SHGs enticed people from all over Himachal to understand micro-economics through SHGs. 25 people attending one such training included state government officials as well as 13 state level NGO representatives. Furthermore, regular trainings are conducted at the CORD centre for our own village facilitators. CORD continues to provide training to govt. departments in needs of training at the resource centre.

SOCIAL JUSTICE AND INFORMAL LEGAL CELL

Women's equality allows development of a society in all aspects including political, economic and social. Through monthly Mahila Mandal meetings, workers are able to reach the most victimized women and resolve their problems by networking with relevant agencies. Legal cases can be divided in two specific sections, individual cases and cases of public interest. The latter is generally a matter of providing awareness and legal literacy to members of the community. However, this year we specifically fought a case related to environment pollution by the municipal corporation, Dharamsala.

This case was ruled in favour of the public interest; a judgment was passed directly to the municipal corporation of Dharamsala to take the relevant measures to prevent garbage seepage into water resources as well operate the solid waste plants immediately. The majority of cases filed with CORD are those of individuals. The most common cases were in relation to matrimonial issues (*i.e.* domestic violence, divorce, demanding or giving dowry, ongoing maintenance). Thus far we have had 385 cases filed through CORD, of which 239 have been completely closed and 146 are continuing.

Attaining justice for the women is not our final destination; we ensure the woman is appropriately rehabilitated into her community with dignity and respect after the case is closed. We ensure that the community takes up the responsibility to accept that woman back into society and enable her independence. Keeping abreast of the changes and amendments to the law through attendance of trainings and workshops is an integral component.

In the last year, we have had workers attend the following:

- Women's Law training and workshop in Dharamsala.
- The regional workshop of Protection from Domestic Violence Act 2005 training in Chandigarh.
- Para-legal training for social activists.
- A workshop on"Human Rights Vis-à-vis margi-nalized communities in India with special focus on Uttarakhand"

We also conducted a legal literacy camp on 14th March 2008 in commemoration of International Women's Day. The purpose of the workshop was to increase women's awareness and knowledge of the legal system. It was facilitated by the Legal Service Authority, Dharamsala (Dist. Kangra). The members of Legal service authority, Honourable Judges, Advocates, CORD members and notable personalities from All India Radio were present. The Secretary of Legal Service Authority, Sri. Rattan Chand Thakur (Chief Judicial Magistrate) chaired the workshop.

COMMUNITY BASED REHABILITATION (CBR) FOR DIFFERENTLY-ABLED

The Community Based Rehabilitation programme continues to not just provide rehabilitation for the disabled but also provide the differently-abled with their constitutional rights. This is achieved by working in synergy with Chinmaya Umang. Chinmaya Umang is a forum for the differently-abled, their parents, friends and relatives to share their stories, voice their concerns and fight for their rights. To strengthen the Chinmaya Umang forum and their young leaders' capacities we increased their participation in the community groups, held regular meetings and training at the centre and build their confidence by involving them in decision-making and events organizing. Also their accessibility and participation in the community has been emphasized.

The aim of CBR to promote collective awareness and inclusion of differently-abled persons back into society is achieved through awareness camps, integration and networking with rehabilitation centers, welfare organizations, schools etc. Currently the programme works with 416 differently-able people in over 80 villages (in the field and in the centre), on various aspects of life depending on their needs and abilities. During the year, we have increased focus on Khas and Super-Khas Panchayats (Panchayats with special focus).

Some major activities during the year include:

- CORD worked with the National Disability Network to compel the Government of India to sanction the UN convention for the rights of the differently able and helped achieve its ratification by the Govt. of India with other NGO partners of NCPEDP. It is now mandatory for all types of government to implement the laws with accommodations for the differently-abled.

- CORD in collaboration with NCPEPD and supported by AIFU, organized a State level seminar on Inclusive Education; there were 66 participants (including disabled people).
- CBR team and Chinmaya Umang members participated in a seven day recreational camp organized by Indian Muscular Dystrophy association at Soghi. The emphasis was on schemes of cooperation for the differently-abled
- Mr. Mahendra, one of our differently-abled, participated in International Abilympics in Japan in knitting skill competition.
- Meetings were held with our district partners to strengthen the advocacy movement in Himachal. It resulted in the preparation of a district wide action plan to promote equal opportunity, and protection of rights of the differently ablcd.
- Mrs. Monika Kalia attended one day workshop at Shimla and Mr. Vijay Guleria attended a one day national seminar on the'Disability Rights Movement in India in Chandigarh. Both the programmes were organized by the Society for Disability and Rehabilitation Studies, New Delhi.
- Mr. Narender Paul and I represented CORD in the two days National Consultation on the UN Convention on Rights of Persons with Disabilities and one day National Partner's Meet organized by National Centre for Promotion of Employment for Disabled People from 27th-29th July 2007.
- Attended a national conference on 14th March -"Skills development of person's with disability in inclusive rural development" in Panchkula. The focus discussion of the seminar was opportunities available to the differently-abled in rural India, poverty alleviation schemes, and ensuring the schemes were inclusive of the differentlyabled.
- Regular attendance to statewide and national meetings on topics related to differently able people. Some included National Abilympics Association, training of trainees on topics of Disability Rights and Acts and the UN Convention, and meeting the director of social justice and empowerment (Shimla, HP) to standardize the Common Attitude Test (CAT) for diploma/certificate course for the differentlyabled.
- Attended Karuna Vihar and National Institute for Visually Handicapped (NIVH) in Dehardoon, Snehalaya in Gwalior.
- Participation in the regional consultation on PWD Act Amendment in Delhi.
- Participation in annual plastic surgery camp at the Dr. Rajendra Prasad Medical College in Dharmasala, where 20 patients underwent surgery.
- Escort individuals to the Polio surgery screening camp to help candidates for contracture release surgery to be chosen.

- Five day sign language training organized for CBR team and the hearing impaired.
- Six differently able girls recently completed a 6 month training programme on sewing and embroidery at I.T.I in Dari. They can now sustain their own livelihood this way.
- 15 awareness camps during the year, on average each camp has 30-35 participants.
- Inclusion of 11 differently able youth at the Yuva Mandal awareness rally on world Environment Day.
- On World Disability Day (December 3rd) a rally was organized by Chinmaya Umang in Dharamshala on December 1st, and a play"Wider access and quality education" was staged by its members
- Regular participation in the statewide Special Olympics. Two mentally challenged youths participated in national level basketball competition and six differently-abled attended the Winter Sports at the National level training camp at Narkanda for 1 week.
- State Level Ability Festival was organized at Dharmasala. Sports and cultural activities were conducted, and six differently able individuals from CORD participated.
- In October, a Festival of Differently-Abled (FODA) organized by Bishop Cotton School was held in Shimla (H.P). Sanjeev Gupta, ten disabled individuals and one resource person attended the cultural and sports event.
- Regular networking with government officers at district and block levels, welfare organizations, and schools etc.
- Three patients were taken to Walawalkar Hospital Chiploon, Maharashtra, for free hip replacement surgery.
- Regular meetings of Chinmaya Umang members are held on alternate months open to all members. On average 60-70 participants attend. Individuals can resolve any challenges they may be facing at these meetings. In the other months meetings are exclusively for Chinmaya Umang leaders to discuss the future directions.
- Public litigation appeal to Food and Supply Officer Kangra filed by seventeen members of Chinmaya Umang in March. Human Rights Law Network Advocate, Miss. Ruchi assisted them with the appeal which was to provide low cost cereals and oil in their respective villages through public food distribution system.
- Two of CBR's mentally challenged children, Kushal and Krishna, accompanied by Sanjeev Gupta, attended a basketball training camp held in Bareily (U.P) in September. Sanjeev also attended the valedictory function of special athletes going to Shanghai (China) in Shimla

- Sanjeev Kumar attended a 2 day meeting of NGOs in November. The discussion involved the conducting of common admission test for all the Diploma/Certificate level courses and charging fee at Directorate of Social Justice and Empowerment, Shimla.
- Mr. Narender Paul attended a 2 day workshop on disability surveying in Kullu by HPVHA, Shimla as well as a budget for children by the H.P Govt., analysed by HAQ, Delhi in November.
- Narender Paul and I represented CORD in the 5th National Disability Network's State Partners meet in New Delhi.

COMMUNITY BASED LIVELIHOOD (CBL) PROGRAMME

Community based livelihood explores avenues of income generation, through enhancing or upgrading people's skills and capacities. Agricultural farming is the main source of income for villagers of the Kangra District. CBL also provides other different avenues for income enhancement. Livelihood is divided into two broad categories, farmand allied sector and nonfarm and service sector.

NON FARM AND SERVICE SECTOR (NFSS)

Non-farm training delves into areas such as weaving, sewing, embroidery, knitting, soap making, Kangra painting, candle making, and food production. Training topics include quality and design improvement, demand based production, market orientation, exploring local resources etc. Once skills are established, entrepreneurship skills are taught to the women. Rural women have some level of difficulty approaching the competitive marketplace so CBL's first priority is local markets. Other skills include managerial and marketing skills and concepts of product quality, price, place, and packaging. Currently we have 366 training sub groups, of which 41 were created this past year. There are currently 2,355 total beneficiaries in focused areas in our 12 main activities (which has indirectly has benefited 4139). At year ending, the total number of fully trained resource persons for CBL-NFS is 76 people. Currently beneficiaries earning more than ₹ 500 per month are 3325 and those earning more than ₹1000 per month are 853. Exposure trips are also a relevant component to familiarize attendees to larger markets of finished goods, as well as to demonstrate how to acquire raw material in the wholesale market. This year a total of 53 such trips were organized. For example, one of the trips was organized to New Delhi for 3 villagers with Mr. Rajesh Kumar (of CORD), to purchase raw materials for candle making.

Some specific achievements of the CBL (NFSS) for the year 2007-08 include:

- We have trained a total of 628 people, through 75 trainings conducted at the CORD centre and 56 trainings conducted in the field
- A carpenters training programme was organized by Bosch in Chandigarh. 13 carpenters were trained on how to use power tools

as well as in areas of quality improvement, design development and market orientations

- During the Silver Jubilee celebrations of Hanuman Abhishekam, an informal training was given to many women on different products, colour combinations and designs. Various methods of packaging and price determination were also discussed. They then had the option to sell their products through their SHG shop, Guru Dhara Self Help Group, or independently.
- Kangra painting works done by talented hearing and speech impaired youth, was displayed at an exhibition held in Delhi (16th- 19th November) with the support of His Excellency Mr. David Malone, the Canadian High Commissioner to India. More than 120 guests from different embassies participated in the exhibition. SHG members of Kangra painting were able to sell their paintings and greeting cards for total ₹85180.
- Kangra painting and bamboo products were promoted at Kangra museum, Dharmasala on International Women's Day (8th March)
- Women entrepreneurs participated in the Mumbai SARAS Fair from 22nd December to 3rd January organized by NABARD
- CORD is acting as a Micro Enterprise Promotion Agency (MEPA) for Himachal Pradesh, currently covering 20 Gram Panchayats of Kangra and Nagrota blocks. MEPA is a livelihood programme introduced by NABARD as a pilot project in 9 states of India.
- We have established new networks with the Forest Department, Dharmasala for training and marketing of Bamboo products as well as with the Palampur University and Institute of Himalayan Bio-Resource Technology (I.H.B.T) for food products development.

FARM AND ALLIED SECTOR (F&AS)

Farm sector focuses on exploring and establishing multiple livelihoods based on agriculture and related fields. Activities include, production of off-seasonal vegetables and cash crops, poly houses construction, construction of vermi compost pits, pattal production (plates made out of leaves), livestock and animal husbandry, dairy farming, fishery, mushroom cultivation (Dhingri mushrooms), goat and sheep keeping, poultry, beekeeping, sericulture, turmeric cultivation, mushroom compost and farming, fruit production, horticulture, floriculture, sheep and goat rearing, sericulture, and bee-keeping.

Presently we have 7983 beneficiaries associated with our programme in which 855 are earning more than ₹3000; 583 earning more than ₹2000; 997 earning more than ₹1000; 1578 earning more than ₹500. One of our youth, Mr. Shammy, set an example by earning ₹5000 per month through vegetable cultivation.

Other major activities over the year include:

- Currently using 23 poly-houses in district Kangra by farmers with successful results
- Promoting use of low cost poly-houses through practical demonstrations
- Replication of the System of Rice Intensification (SRI) during Kharif season has been carried out by 115 farmers in 10 Panchayats.
- A one-day workshop was organized on SRI. Participated by CORD, 42 farmers of the Kangra district, 4 scientists from the Rice and Wheat Research Centre and a consultant from People's Science Institute (Dehradoon).
- A workshop on chemical free agriculture was conducted. Also, a field trip to Haripur Jevic Gram at Dehradoon was organized to learn practices of organic farming.
- Improved dairy farming, particularly with respect to raising awareness of food and fodder security, reproductive health and artificial insemination, nutrition, and disease control amongst cows.
- Selected farmers attended training on mushroom cultivation, conducted at Institute of Himalayan Bio-Resource Technology and Agriculture University, Palampur. The worskshop was conducted by the Indo-Dutch mushroom training centre
- Four camps on Dairy and Organic Farming were organized, with the agriculture department of Kangra

PARTICIPATORY NATURAL RESOURCE MANAGEMENT (PNRM)

CORD's integrated PNRM not only focuses on management and conservation of natural resources, but also on the building of community understanding to govern their own natural resources strategically.

Some of the achievements of 2007-08 are detailed below:

- Planted 6695 Mulberry species, 35568 of Napier grass, 3000 fruit and fodder trees
- 2267 trees were planted in many areas by the youth and mahila mandals
- Multiple projects in various sectors. For example, in Fatehpur, trenches were built to limit erosion and capture rainwater, thereby rejuvenating water resources.
- 20 exposure trips for 302 participants (including trips to Rajasthan and Uttaranchal)
- Six training programmes and one awareness programme was held.

Evaluation, training and capacity building of other satellite centres of CORD:

- Mohan Raj and Prabhkaran, two Chinmaya Yuva Veer from Tamilnadu (to be posted in CORD Siruvani and CORD Thamraipakkam respectively) and Shri Brahmananda Das, Subhash Gamango, Somanatha Sabar from Gajapati Orissa (where CORD envisages to setup a new centre), Sumit Sharma and Geeta Prasad Dhakal (two Chinmaya Yuva Veer from Sikkim), are attending six-week training programme from 20th March 2008 on comprehensive integrated rural development.

- I visited various CORD sites regularly throughout the year sometime alone and sometime with a team constituted of Mr. Narender Jamwal, Vijay Singh and Smt. Kaushalaya Devi from the resource centre as per need. The largest numbers of visits have been to CORD Deuladiha.
- I visited CORD-Vijay near Vijayawara Andhra Pradesh and Chinmaya Mission's orphanage near Thiruvanthpuram in Kerala for the first time while I was in the south visiting the CORD centers at Thamaraipakkam and Siruvani.

General highlights of networking, trainings and volunteers:

- CORD's 23 years work in comprehensive integrated rural development was acknowledged by the Government of India by bestowing the honour of'Padma Shree' award for our work in social sector to me on our Republic Day, the 26th January 2008. This moment became more memorable for CORD as on the day of declaration of this award many who have contributed to the work were present with the team. We were celebrating the Republic Day with Shri Joti Chakraburtty and Dr. Sneh Chakraburtty of Chinmaya Mission Halton Region, Dr. Odile Voinchet and the Multi-Purpose Health Workers who gather every year on this date to come back to their Alma Mater with their families. CORD started its work in health by training four batches of these 120 MPW (F) from 1985-1992.
- The first ever document of CORD at Sidhbari after 23 years entitled'Grace at work' written by Ms. Deepika Sondhi was released on 2nd March 2008 in Delhi by H.H Swami Tejomayananda, head of Chinmaya Mission Worldwide.
- I was honoured with Golden Jubilee Achievers award by my Alma Mater Maulana Azad Medical College, New Delhi at its Golden Jubilee celebration. Sh. M. Hamid Ansari, Vice- President of India was the chief guest on this occasion. The medical fraternity acknowledged our work and appreciated their colleague who brought a deeper meaning to holistic health by working in integrated rural development.
- Canadian High Commissioner His Excellency David Malone and Canadian Consulate General Ms. Helen Amundsun visited CORD to see its integrated development work on 17th May 2007.
- CIDA evaluated our programme in May 2007 when Ms. Louise

Mailloux visited CORD at Sidhbari. The evaluation concluded that"CORD Sidhbari's programme is relevant, cost-effective, designed appropriately, uses its resources appropriately, having partnership, local ownership, taking informed and timely action thereby meeting seven of CIDA's eight key success factors. However it raises its concern on one factor, sustainability, in terms of moving ahead in absence of diversified funding". She also made insightful recommendations to strengthen our 2nd tier of workers and our Result Based Management further.

- Mr. Narender Paul and I presented a paper in a two day Development Professional Meet 2007 at G.B Pant Institute for Social Sciences at Allahabad. The theme was'Managing Performance for Rural Development'. G.B Pant Institute honoured two developmental scientists in rural development. I was one of them.
- I was invited by National Bank for Agriculture and Rural Development (NABARD), Thiruvanthpuram, Kerala in March 2008 to address"State level seminar on women empowerment" as a chief guest speaker.
- Mr. Narender Paul attended training on basic and advanced data analysis using Statistical Package for Social Sciences (SPSS) organized by Sambodhi Research and Communications, New Delhi for four days in May.
- Mr. Narender Jamwal and I attended meeting on Natural Resources based Small Micro- Livelihood (SML) programme -Phase II with People Science Institute (PSI) Dehradoon. We have started implementing this programme in four villages with kind support from PSI and Sir Rattan Tata Trust, Mumbai.
- Mr. Narender Paul, Senior Programme Manager at CORD attended five days of training on proposal writing, project planning and resource mobilization at Sai Ropa, Kullu, organized by Grass-root Institute, Grass-root Trust India, New Delhi in May.

Volunteers and trainees:

- Our work has attracted volunteers not just from India but also from countries all around the world. Poonam and Pooja Merai, Bhavana ShivaKumar, Charlie Richter from USA and Suresh, Kanchan, Prem, Mohit Wadwani and Rishi Vadera, Seema, Bindiya, Bina Naran and Sikta Ghelani from UK, Ms. Yoshita Tewari (UK), Rajneel Kunaal Prasad and Pravesh Narayan (Australia), Priya Gopalan (Hong Kong), Nitish Shah (U.K), Dr. Mitul Kapadia (USA), Lavanya Venkateswarna, Paayal Kot and Abinav Koul (Canada), Dr. Odile Voinchet (France) Vandana Rai, (Singapore), Krupa Shah, (Australia), Neel Mansukhani, (USA), Sunil Kapur, (USA) and many others volunteered their services to our programme during this period.

- Three Chinmaya Yuva Veer, Rishi Seth, Vaishali Gandhi and Bhakta Prasad Dhakal are posted with CORD Sidhbari as volunteers by Swami Mitrananda to work in various programme of CORD.
- During this period, Ms. Maria Brun, Sheila Nezhad, Sarah Vig, Anil J. Mehta, Kajal Mehta, Kathryan Hansal, Pareena Lawarence, Kanika Metre and Professor Mary A. Buckley from USA came to study our development work.
- Five students of Master in Social Work (MSW) from Delhi School of Social Work and two students of MBA (Rural Development) programme from G.B. Pant Social Science Institute, Allahabad (U.P) studied our development work during their one month summer placement programme.
- A team of eight students with their Professor Ms. Suzane Feeny, Professor in International Development and her colleague Ms. Linda Golaszewski from University of Portland came to see and study our work in integrated development for a week in August-September 2007.
- Two MBA students Nikhat Pawane and Tarun Pal from S.P Jain Institute of Management and Research, Mumbai are doing their one month academic internship with CORD from 26th March-26th April 2008.

5

Trends in Rural Credit

The financial sector reforms since 1991 and the emphasis on implementation of prudential norms, *i.e.*, income recognition, asset classification, provisioning norms and Capital Risk Weighted Assets Ratio (CRAR), were instrumental in compelling the commercial banks to concentrate on financial efficiency and economic viability through rationalisation of their operating system, consolidation of their branch network, which resulted in relocation of many bank branches, concentrating on core strengths reducing surplus staff as also computerisation of operation.

Over time, the flow of credit to agriculture and rural sector has expanded impressively. The ground level credit flow had registered an increase (in real term with 1993-94 prices) from ₹ 13, 915 crore in 1991-92 to ₹ 49, 401 crore in 2003-04 and further to ₹ 92, 125 crore in 2005-06. The estimated annual compound growth in credit to the agriculture sector in real terms was 14.5 per cent (with 14.1 per cent growth in production credit and 14.9 per cent growth for investment credit during the above period).

While the annual growth rate in production and investment credit flow (in real term) during 1991-92 and 2003-04 were 11.5 per cent and 10.5 per cent respectively, their respective growth rates during 2003-04 and 2005-06 were 31.3 per cent and 45.1 per cent. However, the maximum growth in credit flow were registered during 2004-05 and 2005-06 when agricultural credit was doubled during two years instead of the targeted 3 years.

AGENCY-WISE CREDIT FLOW

The analysis of agency wise credit flow indicates that the cooperative banks were the major source of agriculture credit in 1991-92 constituting 53.7 per cent of the total ground level credit flow of ₹ 13,915 crore (in real terms with 1993-94 prices) followed by commercial banks at 41.2 per cent (₹ 5,731 crore) and regional rural banks at 5.1 per cent (₹ 712 crore). Though cooperative banks had dominated agriculture credit supply during the early reform period, commercial banks and RRBs recorded impressive growth rates. As a result, in 2005-06, the share of cooperative banks in the total institutional credit flow receded to 21.9 per cent and that of commercial banks advanced to 69.7 per cent.

Although the quantum of disbursement for cooperative banks increased, it could not keep pace with commercial banks in enhancing credit flow due to several reasons including its poor financial health, dual control, lack of internal controls and corporate governance norms and excessive dependence on other financial institutions. The reasons for the massive increase in the credit flow for commercial banks and regional rural banks could be attributed to the linkage of self-help groups (SHG) with banks since 1992, introduction of the scheme of Kisan Credit Cards (KCC) in 1998, formulation of the Special Agricultural Credit Plans (SACP) by the public sector banks since 2004-05, and monitoring under the scheme of doubling of credit in 2004-05.

Size-wise Credit Flow

Despite impressive growth in direct credit to farmers from the scheduled commercial banks between 1991-92 and 2003-04, contrary to expectation, credit disbursement to small and marginal farmers has not been encouraging. However for small farmers and other farmers respectively, the number of accounts increased from 44.4 lakh and 36.7 lakh in 1991-92 to 48 lakh and 43.8 lakh in 2003-04. The percentage of marginal farmers to total farmers came down from 42.8 in 1991-92 to 39.8 in 2003-04, while the same for other farmers increased from 25.9 to 28.7.

Further, the average annual growth rate in the number of accounts and the amount of credit outstanding during the period between 1991-92 and 2003-04 were 0.62 per cent and 6.2 per cent respectively. One important observation from the above findings is that the credit amount per account had increased without any increase in the number of accounts. Further, increase in credit flow favoured the richer farmers.

Region Wise Credit Flow

While analysing the pattern of credit flow, it is observed that the proportions of bank deposits and credit shares have moved in favour of the South, West and North regions. While the share of loans in the total disbursement of credit for agriculture and allied activities were the maximum for the South region (47.9 per cent in 1990-91 and 43.7 per cent in 2001-02), it was the minimum for North-east region (0.4 per cent in 1990-91 and 0.5 per cent in 2001-02).

The population per rural branch, which was estimated at 16,335 and 16,402 in the North-east and East regions in 1991, increased to 22,158 and 21,208 respectively in 2005. Further, when the number of savings accounts for every 100 persons in rural areas of the North-east region had shown a marginal rise from 16.1 in 1991 to 16.4 in 2005, during the same period, the number of savings accounts in Eastern region had declined from 17.7 to 16.9. Similarly, in the case of number of credit account for every 100 persons in rural areas, the number reduced from 4.4 and 7.2 in North-east and East regions in 1991 to 3.2 and 4.2 respectively, in 2005.

Advances to Priority Sector

Although with the rise in net bank credit, the credit flow for priority sector by the scheduled commercial banks had increased, in percentage term, it remained stagnant at around 36 per cent over the last 14 years. While the net bank credit of the scheduled commercial banks increased from ₹ 1,45,250 crore (in real terms at 1993-94 prices) in 1991 to ₹ 5,75,090 crore in 2005 at an annual compound growth rate of 10.3 per cent, the advances to priority sector increased from ₹ 53,125 crore to ₹ 2,05,000 crore at an annual compound growth rate of 10.1 per cent. As a result, the gap between these two has been widening.

Further, the zig-zag trend, *i.e.*, downward during 1991 and 1996 and upward during 1996 and 2005, of the priority sector lending as a percentage to the net bank credit of the banks during the period between 1991 and 2005 shows that no consistent effort has been made to step up advances in favour of the priority sectors. With the new norms for the priority sector announced by RBI in 2007, it is expected that commercial banks would be able to achieve the targets fixed.

Credit-Deposit Ratio

The credit-deposit ratio (CDR), which is an important indicator of deployment of the resources of bank, had been showing a downward zig-zag movement during the last 14 years. The deposits and credit of the scheduled commercial banks in rural areas, which were ₹ 36,961 crore and ₹ 22,168 crore (in real terms at 1993-94 prices) in 1991, increased to ₹ 1,09,005 crore and ₹ 56,254 crore respectively, in 2005. Thus, the credit-deposit ratios had declined from 60 per cent in 1991 to 51.6 per cent in 2005.

However, the credit-deposit ratios of the banks in urban areas had increased from 62.3 per cent in 1991 to 68 per cent in 2005. When the pattern of the credit-deposit ratios for rural and urban areas are observed, we find that the CDR of the banks operating in urban areas are positioned above the overall CDR and that of rural areas are positioned well below the overall CDR.

While the credit-deposit ratio of the rural branches of the scheduled commercial banks declined during the period between 1991 and 2004, that of urban offices had shown improvement with declining and increasing trend in some years during the same period. However, the credit-deposit ratio for rural and urban areas increased from 43.6 per cent and 60.4 per cent in 2004 to 51.6 per cent and 68 per cent respectively in 2005. During the period between 1991 and 2005, while the annual growth rates in the volume of deposits and credit for urban areas were 10.2 per cent and 10.9 per cent respectively, the same for rural areas were 8 per cent and 6.9 per cent respectively. Thus, while in urban areas, the growth rate of credit was higher than that of deposits, in rural areas, the growth rate in deposits was higher than that of credit.

Branch Expansion

The Indian banking system has acquired a wide outreach, judged in terms of expansion of branches and the growth of deposits and credit. The expansion of the branch network peaked in the phase of social banking during the 1970s and 1980s. Although the Narasimham Committee had recognised the need for continuing with the expansion of banking infrastructure in rural areas, in the process of executing financial reforms, the importance of rural financial infrastructure has got neglected and the number of branches of the scheduled commercial banks declined steadily in rural areas and increased in urban areas.

For instance, in 1991, there were 35,206 rural branches out of the total 60,220 branches of the scheduled commercial banks. But in 2006, while the total number of branches of the scheduled commercial banks was 69,471, the number of rural branches had reduced to 30,579. Thus, the financial system has become increasingly urban-centric. Urbanized staff members of commercial banks perceive rural postings as a punishment and serve out their mandatory rural postings, rather grudgingly. The Voluntary Retirement Scheme (VRS) in commercial banks has also ensured that rural branches remain under-manned. Rural postings are avoided because of poor Infrastructural facilities, lack of communication, poor transport facilities, lack of good educational opportunities and also due to reduction in perks and allowances.

The trend analysis presented above brings out the fact that financial inclusion by way of credit to rural sectors as also small and marginal farmers, is a distant dream and demands evolution of appropriate strategies. This aspect has drawn the attention of the Government, RBI and NABARD in recent years and a series of interventions have been initiated to enhance credit flow in favour of priority sectors and the disadvantaged sections of the society. Some of the initiatives have been enumerated in the next section.

RECENT INITIATIVES

In order to increase credit flow to the agriculture sector, the policy of doubling of agricultural credit in three years was introduced in 2004-05. In 2004, the Central Government constituted a Task Force to revive the rural cooperative credit institutions under the Chairmanship of Prof. A. Vaidyanathan. In order to expand the outreach of the banking services, banks made available basic banking 'no-frills' account with low or nil minimum balances as well as low or no charges in 2005. The regional rural banks were also specifically advised to allow limited overdraft facilities in 'no-frills' accounts without any collateral or linkage to any purpose. For opening account with banks, procedures have been simplified by introducing the concept of 'Know Your Customer (KYC)' drill. In January 2006, banks were permitted to utilise the services of Non-Governmental Organisations (NGOs), Self-Help Groups (SHGs) and other Civil Society Organisations (CVOs) as intermediaries in providing financial and banking services through the use of Business Facilitator (BF) and Business Correspondence (BC) models.

The BC model allows banks to do 'Cash in – Cash out' transactions at the location of the business correspondent and also permits branchless banking. With the objective of providing revolving credit to the rural people, banks in rural and semi-urban areas have been advised to provide a General purpose Credit Card (GCC) facility. For all borrowers having a principal amount of less than ₹ 25,000 and whose accounts have become Non Performing Asset (NPA), banks have been requested to offer a One Time Settlement (OTS) Scheme.

It is expected that such a provision will restore borrowing relationship of small borrowers with the formal system and thereby obviates the need to go back to the informal system. In June 2007, a multi-lingual web site in 13 Indian languages on all matters concerning banking was launched by RBI for credit counselling and financial education. In 2007-08, two Funds, *i.e.*, Financial Inclusion Fund (FIF) for promotional interventions and Financial Inclusion Technology Fund (FITF) for meeting cost of technology adoption are proposed to be established with the National Bank for Agriculture and Rural Development (NABARD).

NABARD

Complementing its core financing and developmental functions in tune with the emerging challenges, NABARD has been pioneering innovative rural interventions for ensuring sustainable development and prosperity. In its long journey for the development of farm and non-farm sectors through credit and other support services, initiatives such as Potential Linked Credit Plans (PLPs), District Development Offices, Participatory Watershed Development Programme, Non-Farm Sector promotional programmes, Self-Help Group – Bank Linkage programmes, Rural Infrastructure Development Fund (RIDF), Kisan Credit Card (KCC), Swarojgar Credit Card (SCC), Consultancy Services, Tribal Development programmes, Farmers' Clubs, etc have contributed immensely.

The initiatives of the Bank centre around (i) exploring innovative investment opportunities, (ii) investing partners for Financial/Technical assistance, (iii) creating infrastructure base, (iv) developing leadership, entrepreneurship and capacity building, (v) educating the rural masses, (vi) building sound network of rural financial institutions, (vii) continuous innovations in delivery procedures and systems, (viii) credit planning and (ix) support Research & Development activities in the areas of agriculture and rural development.

In order to augment the much needed institutional credit, NABARD included financing of housing in rural areas as an eligible activity for extension of refinance under investment credit to financial institutions since 1 April 2001 subject to a maximum of ₹ 5 lakh for a dwelling unit. Major initiatives of NABARD, which have had a direct impact on the rural credit delivery mechanism and touched and transformed the lives of millions of rural people, are as follows:

(a) *SHG-Bank Linkage Programme:* The SHG-Bank Linkage programme, which came as a corporate strategy in 1992, aims at improving access of the weaker and other sections of the society from formal financial institutions. It has been built around a simple but basic aspect of human nature – 'the feeling of self-worth'. The ability of people to pool their micro-savings, provide collective social collateral for banks to lend against and add to the SHGs' funds and the collective alteration of Funds to meet emergent credit needs of the SHG members, rates which reflect risks and management cost of Funds, are the unique feature of this movement which has enabled banks to assist in meeting the credit needs of very poor people without sacrificing their funds and has helpful rural women especially to empower themselves both economically and financially.

Over the last 15 years, the Micro-Finance initiative of NABARD has passed through various stages like Pilot testing (1992-95), mainstreaming (1996-98) and expansion (1998 onwards) and has assumed the shape of a micro finance movement in the country by linking around 30 lakh SHGs with the formal banking system by March 2007. Further, the programme has enabled an estimated 394 lakh poor households to gain access to Funds from the formal banking system. Studies conducted by various experts show that the programme has indeed helped in the social and economic empowerment of rural folk, especially women, causing significant up-scaling of social capital while at the same time delivering crucial financial services. Today, it has expanded to become the largest micro finance programme in the world in terms of its outreach and has extended banking services to people hitherto under-served by the banking system.

(b) *Joint Liability Groups (JLGs):* Absence of ability to provide adequate collateral security works as a major hurdle for landless/tenant farmers in securing loans. The inability of this section of farmers to provide collateral often excludes them from the purview of formal credit cover. Keeping this in view, a pilot project on financing Joint Liability Groups (JLG), was initiated for developing effective credit products for such clients, which reduce risk and transaction costs for the banks and also introduce a greater degree of flexibility for the credit user to determine their credit needs and priorities.

Joint Liability Groups (JLG), to be established under the pilot project, will be a group of 5-10 member clients who are together informally recognised by the bank as a group. The group members offer an undertaking to the bank that enables them to jointly receive such amounts as deemed eligible by the bank for pursuing any activity, individually or jointly, as found suitable by the group. The group serves as collective guarantor for loans extended to individual members by executing joint liability agreements, making them severally and jointly liable for repayment of loans to the group. Although the JLG credit model was pilot-tested for mid-segment farmers, the concept could very well be extended to tenant farmers/ oral lessees/ sharecroppers also.

With a view to promoting the scheme on a large scale, banks may be allowed to adopt "Agency Model" by involving civil society organisations, NGOs, Farmers' Clubs, Village Knowledge Centres, Panchayats, various User Groups such as Water Users' Associations, etc. Their services could also be made use of for performing various non-financial functions for the bank such as borrower identification, preliminary appraisal, promotion and nurturing of JLGs, etc.

(c) *Financing Rythu Mitra Groups:* An approach similar to TFGs or JLGs was also adopted in Andhra Pradesh, with the initiative of the State Government. The programme called Rythu Mitra Groups, which envisages bringing about holistic development in the lives of small/ marginal/land less farmers through collective action. RMGs are expected to serve as a conduit for technology transfer, facilitate access to market information and market, assist in carrying out activities like soil testing, training, health camps, assess input requirements, etc., for its members. NABARD provides resource and grant assistance for conducting training and capacity building initiatives to different stakeholders. During the year, 4437 RMGs were financed by 18 commercial banks, 9 RRBs and 9 DCCBs involving ground level credit flow of ₹ 28.11 crore. About 62,000 farmers have been assisted under the pilot project.

(d) *Kisan Credit Card Scheme:* During the year 1998-99, NABARD introduced the Kisan Credit Card (KCC) Scheme in conjunction with cooperative banks, commercial banks and regional rural banks to smoothen and strengthen the credit delivery system and more particularly, to make available timely and hassle-free crop loans to the farmers. As on 28 February 2007, 665.6 lakh KCCs had been issued by the banking system. Of the total 665.6 lakh cards, the cooperative banks accounted for the largest share of 49 per cent followed by commercial banks (38 per cent) and regional rural banks (12 per cent). Recognising it as an accepted mechanism for delivery of credit to farmers, the banking system has been routing crop loans through the Kisan Credit Cards.

To cover the KCC holders against accidental death/permanent disability and partial disability upto ₹ 50,000 and ₹ 25,000, respectively, an insurance scheme was formulated by the General Insurers' (Public Sector) Association of India (GIPSA) in close co-ordination with the NABARD. Banks have been advised to implement the scheme with effect from the Kharif 2001 season. All the KCC holders are required to be covered under the scheme by payment of a nominal premium amount. With a view to making KCC more user-friendly and comprehensive, NABARD has further enlarged the scope of the Scheme to cover long-term loans and consumption loans along with crop loans.

The joint studies conducted by NABARD and the financing banks on implementation of the KCC Scheme have confirmed that the Scheme was well received both by farmers and bankers and the flexibility in operations has resulted in improved loan recoveries. For many banks, some ground level constraints like adoption of selective approach in identifying beneficiaries, reluctance to extend KCC facility in mono-crop areas, levy of costly service charges and levy of stamp duty by some of the State Governments for issuing loans under KCCs, were observed.

(e) *Swarozgar Credit Card (SCC) Scheme:* The Swarozgar Credit Card scheme was introduced in 2003 for facilitating hassle free availability of credit for meeting investment and working capital requirements of small borrowers and rural micro-entrepreneurs. As on 31 March 2007, the banking system had issued 6.79 lakh cards involving credit limits of ₹ 2,700 crores.

(f) *Rural Infrastructure Development Fund:* With an objective of quicker completion of ongoing rural infrastructure projects, the Rural Infrastructure Development Fund (RIDF) was set up with NABARD during 1995-96 with an initial corpus of ₹ 2,000 crore. In the Union Budget for 2006-07, the XII tranche for RIDF was announced with an allocation of ₹ 10,000 crore raising the aggregate allocation to ₹ 60,000 crore. As on 31 March 2007, the cumulative number of projects sanctioned rose to 2,44,025 and the amount sanctioned increased to ₹ 61, 539.87 crore. Although initially it was meant mainly for incomplete projects in irrigation, rural roads and rural bridges, its scope has now been extended to cover major infrastructure projects in various sectors like irrigation, roads, bridges, power, market yards, go-downs, cold storages, information technology, primary education and health systems.

ISSUES AND CONCERNS

The Situation Assessment Survey (NSSO, 2003) indicated that out of the total 89.3 million farmer households in the country, 84 per cent (750 million) households were small and marginal farmers and more than half (51.4 per cent) of the total households were non-indebted. Further, out of the total 43.4 million indebted households, 20.3 million (46.8 per cent) households had availed financial services from informal sources.

The inference of these findings is that in spite of a large network of the institutional credit system, it has not been able to adequately penetrate the informal rural financial markets and the non-institutional sources continue to play a dominant role in purveying the credit needs of the people residing in rural areas. The results of the All-India Debt and Investment Survey (AIDIS, 2002) also indicate that the share of the non-institutional sources, in the total credit of the cultivator households, had increased from 30.6 per cent in 1991 to 38.9 per cent in 2002.

The ratio of rural lending to total lending has been steadily declining during the 1990s. In 1991, the total credit of the scheduled commercial banks, in nominal terms, had increased from ₹ 1,21,865 crore, to ₹ 15,13,842 crore in 2006. However, the share of rural areas in the total deposits and credit of the scheduled commercial banks, which were 15.5 per cent and 15 per cent respectively in 1991, decreased to 10.8 per cent and 8.3 per cent respectively in 2006, reflecting the inability of rural areas to absorb funds for developmental purposes.

While studying the flow of institutional credit to agriculture sector during the period between 1991-92 and 2005-06, an impressive growth in both production and investment credit has been observed. However, the pace of growth had definitely been accelerated during the operation of the scheme of doubling of credit. Production credit, which was 60.7 per cent of the total credit flow of ₹ 13,915 (real terms) in 1991-92, had declined to 58.5 per cent of the total credit flow of ₹ 92,125 crore (real term) in 2005-06. It is also a concern that although the cooperative banks are in close proximity with the rural people, the share of cooperative banks in the total credit flow for agriculture sector had declined from 53.7 per cent in 1991-92 to 21.9 per cent in 2005-06.

Further, the share of the regional rural banks in the total credit flow had increased from 5.1 per cent in 1991-92 to only 8.5 per cent in 2005-06, when with the existing branch network of over 14,494 branches, they could meet the credit needs of 25 per cent of the rural areas. During the period between 1991-

92 and 2003-04, while the number of accounts for marginal, small and other farmers had increased at annual rates of 0.03 per cent, 0.65 per cent and 1.48 per cent respectively, the credit flow to the respective categories of farmers had increased at 6.71 per cent, 6.73 per cent and 5.7 per cent.

Overall, during 1991-92 and 2003-04, while the annual increase in the number of accounts was 0.62 per cent, the increase in the amount of credit outstanding of farmers was 6.2 per cent. Thus, during the last 10 years, although there is no meaningful increase in the number of accounts in favour of farmers, there has been a meaningful increase in the volume of credit outstanding of the farmers. Further, during the period between 1991-92 and 2003-04, the percentage of the number of accounts with marginal farmers had been declining and that of other farmers had been increasing.

For instance, the share of marginal, small and other farmers in the total number of accounts, which were 42.8 per cent, 31.3 per cent and 25.9 per cent respectively in 1991-92, reduced to 39.8 per cent, 31.5 per cent and 28.7 per cent for the respective category of farmers in 2003-04. Thus, over time, while credit deepening has taken place, credit widening has not yet effectively addressed. Alternatively, it could be stated that farmers have become more prosperous, migrating to the better off categories.

Falling Advances to Priority Sector

Over years, priority sector lending as a proportion of net bank credit has been falling. For the public sector banks, priority sector lending as a percentage to net bank credit had decreased from 41.8 per cent in 1991 to 40.3 per cent in 2006. In the priority sector itself, the shares of agriculture and small-scale industries had decreased from 40.7 per cent and 39.1 per cent in 1991 to 37.7 per cent and 20.1 per cent respectively in 2006.

While in 1989, it had been stipulated that all banks need to provide 18 per cent of their net bank credit for the agriculture sector, by March 2006, only 10 public sector banks and one private sector bank had achieved it. Similarly, only 8 public sector banks and one private sector bank had met the sub-target of 10 per cent of the net bank credit for weaker sections.

REDUCTION IN RURAL BANK BRANCHES

In spite of the process of financial reforms in the country, the total number of bank branches of the scheduled commercial banks had increased from 60,220 branches in 1991 to 69,471 branches in 2006, at an annual rate of 0.96 per cent. While the number of bank offices in urban areas had increased from 25,014 branches in 1991 to 38,892 branches in 2006 at an annual rate of 2.99 per cent, the number of branches in rural areas had declined from 35,206 branches in 1991 to 30,579 branches in 2006 at annual rate of 0.93 per cent. The influence of the declining trend of the bank branches in rural areas had been felt in marginalisation of the disadvantaged sections from accessing institutional credit, especially in the underdeveloped regions of the country. This has to some extent been offset by the SHG-Bank linkage programme, which provided credit to very poor people, especially poor rural women.

Credit flow vs. Productivity

Although credit for the agriculture sector has shown an impressive growth over a period of time between 1991-92 and 2005-06, no significant change in the value of output has been observed during this period. The relationship between the value of input and the value of output over the last decade has remained more or less the same with the output being less than five times the value of input. It is relevant to note that even at the highest level of production, credit forms around 11 per cent (in real term in 1993-94 prices) of the total output value. Thus, expecting credit with so little a share in the output value to have any significant impact on the output or productivity values may not be in order.

Emerging Challenges

There has been a long history of concern regarding rural credit. The increase in share of institutional credit has been rather slow. The dependence of small and marginal farmers is still very high on non-institutional sources. Besides, the developed regions have greater access to credit as compared with less developed regions. Therefore, the key issue now is how to ensure that rural credit from institutional sources achieves wider coverage and expands financial inclusion. As the credit-off-take depends on the willingness and ability of the person to avail of loans (which is a function of perceived returns to investments) and the willingness of the banker to lend (which is contingent on bank's perception and assessment of lending risk), there is a need to address the problems from both the supply side as also the demand side.

While distance from the bank branch, branch timings, cumbersome documentation and procedures, unsuitable products, communication and staff attitudes are some important supply side constraints, lack of awareness, low income/assets and small-sized loan demands are some of the demand side constraints. Further, large number of villages (more than 6 lakh villages), lack of infrastructure, vast geographical spread, high transaction costs and poor loan recovery are some other problems faced by banks. In the absence of any alternative, the poor and other weaker sections of rural society depend on the unorganized financial system, which utilizes local knowledge, offers credit for a wide variety of purposes and operates quite flexibly, though at high costs and as an exploitative relationship.

One strategy that has achieved great popularity and wide acceptance is that of micro finance. The banks need to involve micro-finance agencies and other financial intermediaries, as business opportunities. They must understand, recognise and streamline different activities like retail activities, service sector initiatives, and construction and rural housing that take place in the rural economy, in addition to financing agriculture. However, this needs innovations in risk assessment, reduction in transaction costs, search for new credit channels and the use of cheaper information technology. Technology is another option.

It can be a vital component in integrating strategies for achieving inclusive growth. Its use can be critical in building up a reliable credit information system and database on customers, reducing transaction costs and facilitating better pricing of risk, improving the efficiency of the financial system, and thereby increasing the access of un-banked rural people in an efficient manner. It can reduce the transaction costs sharply and time taken by banks in processing applications, maintaining accounts and disbursing loans. It has the potential to address the issues of outreach and credit delivery in rural areas, in a cost effective manner. But how the IT platform will provide a variety of financial services to the rural clients at affordable costs and in time needs to be examined.

Access to information is the key to ensure wider participation of all in the process of development. The challenge lies in ensuring easy flow of public information to rural citizens. The growing innovations in the use of information communication technologies have opened up a new era of information dissemination. Credit counseling, awareness creation and financial education regarding the benefits of financial inclusion are important for effective expansion of financial services in rural areas. To do this, banks may utilise the services of non-governmental organisations, village youth clubs, village Panchayats, farmer clubs and self-help groups into confidence.

Banks need to develop an array of financial products and services that are adapted to the needs of the majority of rural people at affordable prices. Interest rate is an important component of cost to agricultural producers and will become more important as backward and forward linkages are strengthened. As per the current interest rate policy of RBI, the interest rate on loans for the agriculture sector by commercial banks is linked to the size of the loan. While commercial banks have reduced their interest rates on crop loans up to ₹ 50,000 to 7 per cent, RRBs and cooperative banks, for various reasons, have not been able to bring down their rates of interest on lending to any appreciable extent. To ensure competitiveness of Indian agriculture produce in the world market, various Committees have suggested several measures of reducing cost of funds, transaction costs and the risk costs. Risk management is another option.. While the farmers suffer from wide variety of risks like the climate risk, price risk, technology risk, etc., the bankers suffer from the problem of increasing non-performing assets and losses. These risks emanate from a host of factors including failure of investments, willful defaults, weather aberrations, improper appraisal of loans, diversion of funds, inadequate monitoring and follow up and inability to realize the securities available, are some of the cost drivers, which play a decisive role in determining the rates of interest charged by banks to ultimate borrowers in rural areas.

Therefore, if credit risk can be disaggregated into factors like failure of rainfall, price fluctuations, poor health and death of the borrower, these can be mitigated through non-credit financial products like insurance and derivatives. This could also facilitate the banks to provide credit at lower rates. On account of low levels of financial capacity as also awareness, risks affect lives and livelihood of the poor. Therefore, the risk management mechanisms should take into accounts the similarities and differences in the incidence of risks and seek to assist people to manage the consequences thereof. One possible risk management measure could be to enhance savings.

Creation of a large fund administered centrally or at each State levcl would be necessary to help peoplc affected by calamities and disasters. The manner of contribution, mode of assistance, etc., could be designed to provide quick response to calamity-affected regions. Price hedging mechanisms to safeguard farmers from price risks would be needed. The gradual introduction of forward markets and future trading in select crops/commodities should be extended to all major crops in a phased manner. An enforcement mechanism whereby the suppliers of technology are made accountable for failure of technology, etc., could mitigate technology risks faced by the farmers.

Further, the infrastructure support, policy framework and technology could play an effective role in mitigating risks in financing to the rural sector. There is also a need for providing immediate relief at the time of disaster or natural calamity, smoothening the liquidity flow to ensure that consumption requirements are not unduly affected besides compensating people for loss of income, assets and livelihood. The rural Micro Finance Institutions (MFIs), which has emerged as a powerful tool for fighting poverty, may be made a part of the financial system for effective delivery of rural financial services.

The banks need to gear up their rural branches for facilitating bank linkages of SHGs where the programme has not shown satisfactory progress. The Business Correspondence models (MFIs, NGOs, etc.), as recommended by the Internal Group on Micro finance (Khan Committee), may also be put in place, which will increase banking outreach.

COOPERATIVE CREDIT IN INDIA

Agriculture continues to be main stay of India's national economy . Its contribution to the India's Gross Domestic Product (GDP) is about 30per cent Almost 2/3rd of the population of India depends on this sector for the livelihood. The agricultural land is being taken away by all sectors.

Moreover, in the era of economic liberalization the agriculture is being increasingly recognised as commercial activity, and, therefore, the specific needs of the farmers for modern agricultural technology will, no doubt become complex. Over a period of years with the state support, the cooperatives have craved out a formidable niche for themselves in various fields of economy like rural credit and banking, fertilizers, sugar, dairy *etc.* There are at present 4.9 lakh Cooperative Societies engaged in diverse business activities with a membership of over 200 million. They have 100per cent villages and 67per cent of rural house holds.

The Cooperative Credit Institutions from the beginning of the 20th Century till 1950s in India have depended heavily for their credit needs on individual sources of finances such as moneylenders, traders, commission agents, landlords, relatives and friends. There sources by their very nature, were not capable of meeting the growing credit needs of the farmers. Moreover, the farmers were subjected to many unfair conditions including higher interest rates. Realizing these defects, both the Central and the State Governments in India took a number of policy decision and enacted necessary legislation to progressively institutionalize farm finance. Today, institutional credits accounts for a share of over 50per cent of total credit need compared to less than 10per cent in the fifties

The Flow of credit to the agriculture sector and the rural areas is met through institutional agencies like Commercial Banks, Regional Rural Banks and Cooperative Credit Institutions. The short term, medium term and long term needs of the farming and rural community are met by their credit institutions. The Cooperative Banks have played a dominant role in providing credit to the needy.

SHORT TERM AND MEDIUM TERM FINANCE

Strengthening financial resources base of the various cooperative credit institutions and enterprises is definitely a priority area for working out a competitive edge for cooperatives in the field of short term and medium term credit system. The cooperative banks like PACS at the fields of short term an medium term credit system. The cooperative banks like PACS at the primary level have to show a turnaround through implementation of Business Development Plans (BDP).

At the same time it is necessary to find out how far the implementation of BDPs have helped in shoring up the finances of the cooperative banking system through reduction of loan overdues? How far the PACs associated with losses have reappealed into profits in the wake of the implementation of various components of BDPs?

LONG -TERM FINANCE

In the field of long term finance the state ARDBs are providing long term investment finance to the farming community in the rural areas for financing minor irrigation, farm mechanization, land development projects, fisheries, poultry *etc.* The state ARDBs by and large are dependent on re-finance facilities extended by NABARD. The State ARDBs have to make serious efforts to increase their financial health through mobilization of deposits and in the process reduce their dependence on re-finance facilities of NABARD. In this context, they have to evolve attractive deposit schemes and at the same time, will have to evolve Deposit Insurance Schemes (DIS) to instill confidence among depositors.

APPLICATIONS OF PRUDENTIAL NORMS:

The RBI has directed the State Cooperative Banks to adopt prudential norms in terms of income recognition, assets classification, and provisioning for bad and doubtful debts. Prudential norms also includes capital adequacy norms and these norms have been fixed at 8per cent of the capital risk weighted assets. The Cooperative banking sector has been asked by RBI to adopt prudential norms by March 31st, 2000. Similarly, the Urban Cooperative Banks which constitute a self-reliant group of banks in urban area have been asked to adopt prudential norms.

Adoption of prudential norms by Cooperative Banking sector would imply considerable improvement in their financial health, reduction of loan overdues and greater mobilization of deposits in the coming years. The Non-performance Assets (NPAs) associated with cooperative banks have to be drastically reduced through appropriate measures. This process would help in the recycling of funds for lending to the farming community. Future lending should be based on careful analysis of loan application including risk assessment to be backed by ensuring utilisation of funds for the specified objectives.

GOVERNING CORPORATE IN COOPERATIVES

In the context of intensive competitive economic environment introduced in the wake of economic reforms, the Governing Corporate system in cooperatives is likely to undergo change in the coming decades of the 21st century. The national Cooperative policy which is under formulation in the Urban Ministry of Agriculture is likely to lay emphasis on gradual disengagement of Government from financing of various cooperative activities and cooperative enterprises. Keeping this scenario in view, the cooperative have to adopt stringent measures to improve their financial position through greater deposit mobilization and access to new ways of raising capital from capital market. In this context they also have to rely on cost reduction and cost effective technologies to control transaction costs as well as management costs. Cooperative Leaders have to work out on action plan for removing various restrictions which have been have been placed by the Government for the smooth functioning of cooperative enterprises. In this Action Plan, greater emphasis would have to be laid on members participation in decision making process and in arranging restructured Education and Training Programmes for the members and personnel engaged in cooperative development. Governance by the cooperative leaders would imply greater emphasis on promotion of information technology in various segments of cooperative movement.

COOPERATIVE MANAGEMENT

Access to latest information and policy decision having a bearing on the future of Cooperative movement will have to be constantly tied up with the information matrix availability to the cooperative management system. To safeguard their interests, the cooperative leaders will have to establish lobby with the help of opinion on leaders and members of parliament to safeguard the interest of cooperatives in the coming years.

For improving the efficiency parameters of cooperative management there is the need to remove false members, false leaders and false cooperative enterprises from the domain of cooperative Movement. Such a step is necessary to lift the cooperative movement out of the morass into which it has fallen in certain region of India.

The efficient management of cooperative would also imply the implementation of the policy relating to mergers and acquisitionary among cooperative enterprises. Attention should be given to information Technology at primary level to improve the Cooperative Management Information Systems. In the future years great stress would have to be laid on encouraging qualified dedicated members to fight the election for the top leaders of the Board of Management and Governing Council of Cooperative. This would help in improving the cooperative face the competitive economic environments with courage and determination.

REASONS FOR DETERIORATION IN THE COOPERATIVE BANKING SYSTEM

Short-term and Medium Credit Finance

- The base structure of agriculture credit -cooperative consisting of PACS at the ground level continues to be weak even after recognizing and revitalization schemes including BDP being implemented since, 1991. The impact of the implementation of BDP on the functioning of PACS needs consideration.
- The level of overdues in the Cooperative Banks continues to be an area of concern.
- The central government should extend adequate budgetary support to strength the capital base of the weak and non-viable cooperative banks in the near future.
- Various disciplines pertaining to credit limits for seasonal agricultural credit limits are imposed by NADARD. There conditions act as

constraints are full utilisation of credit limits sanctioned by NADARD. Relaxation of there constraint needs to be considered.

- The Cooperative Banks should take advantage of the deregulated interest rates on deposits and lendings. The State Government should not interfere in the fixation of the interest rates by the Cooperative Banks .
- The PACS should diversify their operations into non-credit activities like jewel loans, consumption loan *etc.* Keeping in the view requirements of the rural masses in their area of operation.

Long -Term Credit/ Finance

- The resource base of ARDBs needs to increased through mobilization of deposits and rural savings. This would require strengthening of owned funds by ARDBs. Also, further avenues for resource mobilization by ARDBs may have to be identified and discussed.
- Remedial measures for improving the recovery position may be considered and discussed.
- NABARD imposes rigid discipline on ARDBs while extending re-finance support. Their mobilization needs to be mobilized.
- Prudential norms have been made applicable to ARDBs with effect form accounting year 1997-98. The ARDBs should be try to classify their assets into specific categories like standard, sub-standard, doubtful and loss making assets. Thereafter adequate provisioning has to be made to take care of the risk elements involved in various types assets.
- Training of staff in non-farm finance and housing finance may be considered and discussed. The cooperative leaders and members need to be acquainted with the techniques such as project appraisal and project formulation. This would be in the interest of proper appraisal of loan applications by the ARDBs and would help in the reduction of loan overdues.

The State partnership, by way of government contribution to share capital, which was conceived as a measure for strengthening the cooperative credit institutions, has passed the way instead for an unnecessarily high level of state control, their increasing bureaucratization and politicization, culmination in virtually depriving the cooperatives of their inherent vitality and affecting their democratic and autonomous character.

In the milleu of liberalization and privatization, there is an urgent need to redefine the Government's role in developing and strengthening cooperative banks.

The various reforms initiated in different sectors, are yet to be introduced to the cooperatives.

MEASURES TAKEN TO FACE THE EMERGING CHALLENGES

Cooperatives are based on the principles of autonomy and independence and strive for becoming member owned and member controlled organisations. In putting this principles in practice, NCUI has been making concerted efforts to persuade the Government of India and the State Governments to remove the restrictive provision from the existing Cooperative laws and to modify them in tune with Model Cooperative Act enunciated in the Ch. Brahm Prakash Committee Report. There are reports that the central Cabinet has approved amendments in the Multi-State Cooperative Societies act 1984. However, these amendments are yet to be approved by the parliament. Similarly some State Governments like Andhra Pradesh have passed mutually Aided Cooperative Societies Act under which there is no interference from the government in the functioning of the cooperative societies. Other State governments like M.P., Rajasthan, Punjab are reported to have initiated steps to modify State Cooperative acts in tune with the provision of Model Cooperative Law.

With the approval of the Government of India and RBI, the Cooperative bank of India has been established to bridge the systemic gaps existing within the cooperative credit structure . However due to lack of an amendment in the Banking Regulation Act, it has not been possible so far to operationalise the functioning of the Cooperative Bank of India. Efforts are being made to persuade the Government of India and the Ministry of finance to issue a license to this bank so as to enable it to operationalise its functioning.

The government has extended a sizeable budgetary support to the public sector commercial banks for strengthening their capital base and for enabling them to implement prudential norms. Similar financial assistance to the weak and non-viable cooperative banks has not been extended by the government of India.The cooperative leaders feel that in the background of a level playing field approach, the Cooperatives should also be extended a reasonable level of budgetary support so as to enable them to clear their balance sheets. Such a process would help the weak cooperative banks to strengthen their financial resource base and would enable them to stand on their own feet to face the competitive challenges in the liberal market environment.

Emphasis is already being laid on building up strong human resource base in the cooperative sector. Efforts are being to lay greater emphasis to promote professionalisation in the management and training of the cooperative personnel so as to enable them to man the various post in the cooperative organisation. The training and the evaluation programmes are being restructured on scientific lines after capturing the core elements of the information technology and management information system. It is being recognised that only highly professionalized management cadre and trained cooperative personnel would be able to face the competitive challenges from the private sector. Keeping this aspect in view the various training programmes are being extended by VAMNICOM and other ICMS with a focus on professionalisation in management and efficiency of cooperative personnel.

HEALTH OF RURAL CREDIT COOPERATIVES

Despite the phenomenal outreach and volume of operations, the health of a very large proportion of these rural credit cooperatives has deteriorated significantly. The institutions are beset with problems like low resource base, high dependence on external sources of funding, excessive Governmental control, dual control, huge accumulated losses, imbalances, poor business diversification, low recovery, *etc.* Around half of the PACS, a fourth of the intermediate tier, *viz.*, the DCCBs, and under a sixth of the State-level apex institutions, *viz.*, the SCBs are loss-making. The accumulated losses of the system aggregate over ₹ 9,100 crore. Non-performing assets (NPA), as a percentage of loans outstanding at the level of SCBs and DCCBs, at the end of March 2006 were around 16per cent and 20per cent respectively. These institutions do not, therefore, inspire confidence among their existing and potential members, depositors, borrowers and lenders. Thus, there is a need to find ways for strengthening the cooperative movement and making it a well-managed and vibrant medium to serve the credit needs of rural India, especially the small and marginal farmers.

NEED FOR REVIVAL OF THE COOPERATIVE CREDIT INSTITUTIONS

Given the above indicators, there has been considerable debate on whether there is an imperative need for revival of these institutions. Herein, it may be pertinent to reiterate the following points:

In the first place, India is a country with a population of more than 100 crore, of which around 70 crore reside in a little over 6 lakh villages. As there are a little over one lakh PACS in the country, the first fact to be appreciated, therefore, is that every 6th village, on an average, has an existing cooperative credit outlet.

Secondly, although the rural credit system includes about 45,000 rural and semi urban branches of commercial banks and RRBs, if one would net out the cooperatives from the aggregate rural presence of all RFIs, the per outlet population coverage deteriorates from 1:4,393 to 1:14,893. The short point is that on grounds of outreach, cooperatives cannot be ignored.

Thirdly, the outreach is significant not merely in absolute numbers but also in terms of location of outlets. The number of PACS located in hilly terrains, deserts and other areas with poor access far exceed the number of rural branches of commercial banks and RRBs.

The same set of conclusions flow when the system is viewed in the context of its membership. Assuming an artificially low family size of 4, a back of envelope calculation shows that cooperative membership touches the lives of nearly 48 crore rural people which is more than half the aggregate rural population. As regards number of agricultural credit accounts, the credit cooperatives have 50per cent more accounts than scheduled commercial banks (including RRBs). Of these, 70per cent are estimated to be marginal and sub-marginal farmers. On the financial side, it is sometimes argued that in terms of deposits, rural and semi-urban branches of commercial banks have nearly six times more deposits than cooperatives. While this is true, it is also true that this is part of a historic policy infirmity which allowed cooperatives to be treated as "refinance windows" instead of incentivising them into becoming genuine thrift and credit institutions.

Coming to the assets side of the balance sheet we find that cooperatives have a 37per cent share in the aggregate crop loans provided by the RFIs. However, in many districts, particularly in remote, hilly and desert areas the share is upwards of 50per cent. 6.18 Notwithstanding a larger client base, the share of cooperatives in institutional credit is lower than that provided by the commercial banks. This is because the average loan size of cooperatives is smaller at ₹ 6,637 as compared to ₹ 31,585 of commercial banks which also confirms the claim that nearly 70per cent of the cooperative structure's clients are small and marginal farmers. A little known fact is that the system has nearly 64,000 godowns. Given an appropriate policy dispensation entailing private partnership, conditions can be created for holding of crops by farmers at the ground level in these godowns while allowing them to negotiate the godown receipts in the market. A specific plan to revitalize these godowns in cooperative sector be drawn to make them the nerve centres of rural economy on a 'kiosk' model providing storage and financial services.

COOPERATIVES AND THE REFORM PROCESS

In the backdrop of these credentials, a look has to be taken at the reform process and what it means to the cooperative credit institutions. The financial sector reforms have been components of the overall economic reforms undertaken in a phased manner from 1991-92 by GoI. These reforms also envisaged improving the efficiency and productivity of the rural credit delivery system which in turn would accelerate the requisite credit flow to the productive sectors of the economy.

The major objectives of these reforms in the cooperative sector were:

- To make the institutions competitive by removing external constraints having a bearing on their operations,
- To improve their financial health,
- To ensure transparency in their business operations,

- To improve their profitability, *and*
- Institutional building and strengthening.

According to the Task Force on Revival of Rural Cooperative Credit Institutions (Vaidyanathan Committee), the STCCS never realized the enormous potential opened up by its vast outreach owing mainly to a "deep impairment of governance". While they were originally visualized as member-driven, democratic, self-governing, self-reliant institutions, cooperatives have, over the years, constantly looked up to the State for several basic functions.

The Task Force has described in detail how the State Governments have become the dominant shareholders, managers, regulators, supervisors and auditors of the STCCS. The concept of mutuality (with savings and credit functions going together), that provided strength to cooperatives all over the world, has been missing in India. This "borrower-driven" system is beset with conflict of interest and has led to regulatory arbitrage, recurrent losses, deposit erosion, poor portfolio quality and a loss of competitive edge for the cooperatives. The Task Force Report also recognised that there is an impasse in the laws governing cooperative banking institutions in the country as cooperation is a State subject while banking activities are regulated by a Central Act. Further, the Task Force also took cognizance of the poor quality of internal control systems, house keeping and audit in addition to professionally not qualified human resources manning the CCS.

For the revival of the STCCS, the Vaidyanathan Committee Report has suggested an implementable Action Plan with substantial financial assistance for recapitalisation subject to introduction of strict legal and institutional reforms together with technical assistance for human resource development (HRD), establishment of a common accounting system and computerisation.

The implementation of the Revival Package would result in the emergence of strong and robust cooperatives with conducive legal and institutional environment for it to prosper. At the macro level, the Revival Package is expected to promote growth with social justice and greater financial inclusion. In this background, the following observations are noteworthy:

- With 127 million plus membership and 45 million plus borrowing membership, the STCCS already exceeds the combined client base of commercial banks and RRBs. With nearly 1.25 lakh outlets spread throughout the length and breadth of the country, the STCCS after implementation of the recommendations of the Vaidyanathan Committee would be adequately equipped and would be a highly appropriate mechanism to promote financial inclusion.
- Located in rural areas, governed by local community leadership and managed by the staff with roots in rural areas, the STCCS would be oriented for promoting financial inclusion more effectively.
- The CCS with large membership of small and marginal farmers would

have necessary ethos to promote and encourage financial inclusion of deprived sections of the rural economy.

- With limited overheads, the CCS outlets will be an appropriate medium for encouraging financial inclusion through "no frills" savings accounts *etc.*
- The rural populace will be more comfortable and will easily identify culturally with the STCCS.
- Payments under various social welfare schemes of Central and State Governments for instance old age pension, Employment Guarantee Scheme (EGS), scholarships for students, *etc.* could be made more transparent, safe and foolproof if routed through the STCCS and the recipients could receive the assistance at their doorsteps.
- As envisaged in the Vaidyanathan Committee Report, the membership of PACS should be open to all members of the village without any restrictions. For the purpose, the existing restrictions regarding land holding *etc.*, should be done away with. If need be, PACS could be rechristened as Primary All-purpose Credit Societies instead of Primary Agriculture Credit Societies.
- The STCCS would be an ideal instrument for promoting financial inclusion through SHGs. Many cooperatives could be transformed into SHPIs with proper sensitisation. Promotion of SHGs could, indeed, become a major component of the Business Development Plan of cooperative organisations of the STCCS.
- As the Vaidyanathan Committee is envisaging application of IT right from PACS to SCBs, the STCCS would be in a position to cope with the additional work load on account of promoting financial inclusion. This, in fact, would go a long way in improving the productivity of the credit cooperatives. With due internal controls and checks in place, PACS could ideally be developed as BCs of DCCBs as well as for commercial banks / RRBs wherever the reform process facilitates this.
- As financial inclusion also envisages delivery of financial services at an affordable cost, the STCCS being accessible at the door step of the financially excluded sections of the society will be in a better position to render these services more effectively.
- Located in the rural areas, the STCCS units will have better knowledge of their existing and potential clients and, as such, KYC will not be a major hindrance.

ROLE ENVISAGED FOR COOPERATIVES IN THE PLANNING PROCESS

The cooperative credit institutions are being called upon for a greater involvement in credit dispensation during successive Five Year Plans. The

Working Group on Agricultural Credit, set up by the Planning Commission, for the formulation of the X Five Year Plan, had made a projection of credit flow for agriculture at ₹ 736,000 crore at 4per cent growth rate in agriculture GDP. Of this, the cooperative credit structure alone was required to provide during the plan period ₹ 271,000 crore from ₹24,000 crore during the first year (2002-03) of the X Five Year Plan, on the assumption that it would maintain its share of at least 42per cent in the total credit purveyed. During the period 2003-04 to 2006-07, these institutions, put together, have purveyed credit to the tune of ₹ 136,229 crore for agriculture and allied activities.

IMPACT ENVISAGED POST IMPLEMENTATION OF THE RECOMMENDATIONS OF THE TASK FORCE

The Committee concurs with the Vaidyanathan Committee's view that cooperatives are heterogeneous and exhibit wide variations in terms of method of operations, quality of governance, working results, *etc.* The Committee also notes that in certain areas, cooperatives have done exceedingly well.

It is expected that with the implementation of the reform package as envisaged by the Vaidyanathan Committee (already 13 States have signed the MoU with GoI and NABARD, while another 5 States and 1 UT have indicated their "in principle" acceptance), the cooperatives will be able to emerge stronger.

Consequent on implementation of the Revival Package, there will be two sets of outcomes – one at the sector level and the other at the macro level. At the sector level the legal environment within which the sector functions will become more enabling and there will be institutional upgradation in terms of systems and procedures, HRD, technology, *etc.* This will improve the internal operational efficiency of the system leading to more robust fundamentals.

At the macro level, this process will complete the financial sector agenda in regard to capitalization of impaired entities. India embarked on its reforms in the financial sector in 1992 with the capitalization of commercial banks followed by that of RRBs. Capitalisation of the rural cooperative credit structure will bring this process to a logical completion.

The other area of impact would be on the national goal of growth with equity. As already indicated, nearly 70per cent of the membership of the rural credit cooperatives are small and marginal farmers. As cooperative institutions improve their health and methods of operation, the number of borrowing members as a percentage of total membership will increase, thus bringing larger number of small and marginal farmers within the cooperative fold. This will help in addressing the credit requirements of this segment of the rural population which is sometimes bypassed in the growth process. This is an important outcome in regard to financial inclusion.

EMERGING ROLE OF COOPERATIVES IN MICROFINANCE

The Andhra Pradesh Mutually Aided Cooperative Societies (APMACS) Act, 1995 has resulted in the creation of over 30,000 new Mutually Aided Cooperative Societies (MACS) in Andhra Pradesh. A vast majority of these are Village Organisations (VOs) of SHGs and about 800 are higher level federations of these VOs at the Mandal level (20-30 villages). All these have been formed as part of the Velugu Programme. However, about 600 MACS are independent of the Velugu Programme, and have been promoted by NGOs. These institutions are able to provide savings and credit services to their members and are fully autonomous.

The parallel Acts are also one way to federate SHGs and form community based MFIs. The founding NGO only plays a facilitating role and there are no external shareholders. Recommendations in regard to the cooperative credit institutions:

EARLY IMPLEMENTATION OF VAIDYANATHAN COMMITTEE REVIVAL PACKAGE

The Committee is in broad agreement with the recommendations of the Vaidyanathan Committee and suggests that all necessary steps should be taken for the early implementation of the STCCS revival package in all States. Consequent on the implementation of the Vaidyanathan Committee recommendations, the Committee hopes for the emergence of a more robust, well managed and self-reliant cooperative credit system with improved governance structures and technology applications.

COOPERATIVES IN SHG LINKAGE – NEED FOR ENABLING LEGISLATIONS

The Committee is of the view that cooperatives are a good forum for enabling financial inclusion through SHGs. This has been demonstrated in several districts such as Bidar in Karnataka, Chandrapur in Maharashtra and Mandsaur in Madhya Pradesh. The Committee notes that in certain States, legislation has been enacted, admitting SHGs as members of PACS and recommends the enactment of similar legislation in other States to enable the emergence of cooperatives as effective SHPIs.

The Committee also recommends that federations of SHGs may be registered in all the States under the Cooperative Societies Act or the parallel Self Reliant Cooperatives Act and availability of funds to these cooperatives for advancing loans may be considered by NABARD, based on objective rating criteria. NABARD may also set aside requisite funds for sensitising the cooperative movement in this regard.

USE OF PACS AND OTHER PRIMARY COOPERATIVES AS BUSINESS CORRESPONDENTS

There are a large number of PACS and primary cooperatives under the parallel Acts located in rural areas where there are no other financial services outlets. Many of these cooperatives are in districts where the DCCBs are defunct or moribund. Such PACS could provide valuable services to their members if they get access to a commercial bank. These PACS could originate credit proposals, disburse loans, collect repayments and even collect savings on behalf of the commercial bank. They could also act as payment channels. RBI has already listed Cooperatives as eligible institutions under the BF/BC Model.

In the circumstances, the Committee recommends that the Cooperatives may make use of this opportunity atleast in States which have accepted the Vaidyanathan Committee recommendations. NABARD may be asked to suggest appropriate guidelines for the purpose, subject to the approval of RBI.

COOPERATIVES ADOPTING GROUP APPROACH FOR FINANCING EXCLUDED GROUPS

Micro-enterprises, in order to be successful, require larger funding which NGOs cannot provide. It will, therefore, be necessary to develop / test a new form of community based organisation other than SHGs which may be more appropriate to support members who engage in micro-enterprises. Those members of SHG who opt to graduate to micro-enterprises could be formed into JLGs or some similar organisation.

Banks may be more inclined to lend to individuals in this group based on the performance of each member in the SHG as well as on the assumption that a JLG will provide some degree of mutual guarantee. There is evidence however, that the relations of mutual trust and support which is described as affinity in a SHG tend to be weaker in a JLG. Therefore, new forms of collateral or guarantee may have to be worked out. In this regard, NABARD has already circulated the guidelines which may be adopted by banks.

Further, the use of the BF model could be thought of to organize vulnerable segments of the population into JLGs. The pilot project presently under implementation by NABARD should be sufficiently broad based to cover the role of facilitators in formation and linkage of JLGs.

6

Development of Rural Economy

INTRODUCTION

The Indian economy has been passing through the trajectory of high growth for several years. The overall Gross Domestic Product (GDP) is estimated to grow at 8.4 per cent, with the agriculture and allied sector projected to bounce back with 3.9 per cent growth during 2005-06. The Government has also been consolidating its fiscal position, creating a conducive climate for investment activities. Investment demand in the economy is picking up, reflecting the growing dynamism in the industrial sector.

The exports have also assumed vibrancy. Thus, the Indian economy as a whole is poised for still higher growth in the coming years. The Rural Economy in India is wholly agriculture based and it is of tremendous importance because it has vital supply and demand links with the other Indian industries. Agriculture is the main stay of the Indian economy, as it constitutes the backbone of rural India which inhabitants more than 70 per cent of total Indian population.

The fertility of the soil has augmented the success of agriculture in India. Further, Rural Economy in India has been playing an important role towards the overall economic growth and social growth of India. India has been predominantly an agriculture-based country and it was the only source of livelihood in ancient time. During prehistoric time when there was no currency system the India economy system followed barter system for trading *i.e.* the excess of agricultural produce were exchanged against other items. The agriculture produce and system in India are varied and thus offers a wide agricultural product portfolio.

Today, the rural economy in India and its subsequent productivity growth is predicated to a large extent upon the development of its 700-million strong rural population. The agricultural economy of India is drafted according to the needs of rural India since majority of the population lives in about 600,000 small villages. In India, agriculture accounts for almost 19 per cent of Indian gross domestic products (GDP). The rural section of Indian population is primarily engaged with agriculture, directly or indirectly. The Ministry of Agriculture, the Ministry of Rural Infrastructure, and the Planning Commission of India are the main governing bodies that formulate and implements the policy related to rural economy in India and its subsequent development for the overall growth of the Indian economy.

The main agricultural products that controls the fate of the Rural Economy in India are as follows:-

- *Food Grains*: Rice, Wheat, Pulses, Cereals, Corn, Maize, Rice Bran Extractions, Sorghum, Soy meal, Suji, Parmal, Lentils, Jowar, Bajra, Chick pea
- *Fruits and Nuts*: Cashew Kernels, Cashew Nut, Cashews, Almonds, Roasted Dry Fruits, Peanuts, Groundnut, Walnut Kernels, Walnuts, Indian Peanuts, HPS Groundnuts
- *Fruits*: Bananas, Beans, Cherry, Cucumbers, Dried Fruits, Dried Truffles, Carrots, Lemon, Mandarins, Mango steens, Meslin, Shallots, Apples, Asparagus, Grapes, Oranges, Gherkins, Turnips, Oranges, Papaya, Pineapple
- *Vegetables*: Potatoes, Bitter gourd, Stripe Gourd, Pumpkin, cauliflower, Cabbage, Tomato, Onion, Green Pepper, Drum Sticks, Lady's finger, Banana, Papaya, Spinach, Cucumber, Mushroom, Mushroom Spawn, Radiata
- *Seeds, Buds, Plantation and Related Products*: Basil Seed, Cumin seeds, Dill Seed, Buds, Celery Seed, Hybrid Seeds, Sesame Seeds, Sesbania Seed, Sunflower Seeds, Mustard Seeds, Oil Seeds, Plant Products, Plantation, Plants, Psyllium Seed, Fennel Seed, Fenugreek Seed, Herb Seeds, Tamarind Seed, Vegetable Seeds
- *Spices*: Black Pepper, Chilli Powder, Chillies, Cinnamon, Cloves, Coriander Powder, Cumin, Curry Powders, Dry Ginger, Dry Red Chilly, Cardamom, Anise, Salt, Onion Powder, Pepper, Fenugreek, Clove, Ginger, Turmeric, Turmeric Powder
- *Tea and Coffee:* Black Tea, Coffee, Coffee Beans, Darjeeling Teas, Assam Teas, Instant Coffee, Leaf Coffee, Leaf Tea, Packaged Tea, Green Tea, CTC Teas
- *Tobacco and Tobacco Products*: Beedi, Betel nut Leaves, Betel nut, Bidi Leaves, Chewing Tobacco, Cigarettes, Arecanut, Jarda, Scented Tobacco, Smoking Tobbacco, Snuff, Opium, Pan, Chatni, Pan Masala, Gutkazarda, Zafrani Zarda
- Cotton, Rubber, Jute etc.

No. The uneven growth will never help India to grow faster or help achieving the projected results. I support the PURA model of President A P J Abdul Kalam which calls for rural development and uplift of BPL with a social cause. Finance is still the biggest problem for development of rural economy despite it being innovative. People in the rural areas have no money and often tend to go for high-cost borrowings. No venture capitalists or funders have ever come forward to help those community with social obligations in mind.

Who lends the money to those poor people without collateral securities despite having the entrepreneurial capabilities, innovativeness, creativeness and hard working abilities? It is a pity to say that in few districts where I visited, villagers happened to be bonded labourers to big money launderers due to high cost borrowings which has never been a easy task to repay. The development of the Indian Rural Economy can be credited to the liberal policy of the Ministry of Rural Development, Government of India and the Planning Commission of India.

India is still an agriculture-based country and the agrarian sector contributes substantially to the GDP of India.

Around seventy per cent of the Indian population still depends on agriculture and allied areas for livelihood.

- Glimpses of Rural Economy of India
- A target of ₹ 225,000 crores for farm credit has been set for the financial year 2007-2008.
- 50 lakh new farmers have been brought under the banking system.
- Agricultural Insurance to facilitate agricultural loans to the farmer.
- Allocation for the Rural Infrastructure Development Fund to be increased substantially.
- In the financial year 2006-07, 35 projects were successfully completed.
- Additional irrigation of 900,000 hectares has been targeted in the financial year 2007 - 2008.
- For better farm yields modern farming techniques has been set up.
- Direct disbursement of subsidy to rural Indian farmers has been arranged through a pilot programme.

ROLE OF REGIONAL RURAL BANKS

The importance of the rural banking in the economic development of a country cannot be overlooked. As Gandhiji said "Real India lies in villages," and village economy is the backbone of Indian economy. Without the upliftment of the rural economy as well as the rural people of our country, the objectives of economic planning cannot be achieved. In fact, the real growth of Indian economy lied in the emancipation of rural masses from acute poverty, unemployment, and socio-economic backwardness.

Keeping this end in view, various important plans and programmes of rural development have been conceived and implemented by the government of India since the commencement of first five-year plan from 1951-56. But an appraisal of the achievement of these programmes clearly reveals that much programmes failed to achieve the desired objectives due to the backward economic condition and lack of adequate finance to the poor people in the rural areas. Hence, bank and other financial institutions are of vital importance for development of rural economy of a country.

The present study is a modest attempt to make an appraisal of the credit needs of the rural people and the way Regional Rural Bank, *i.e.*, Arunachal Pradesh Rural Bank, has been extending its service to meet the same in the state of Arunachal Pradesh. It deals with the performance evaluation of Arunachal Pradesh. Rural Bank (APRB) for the economic development of the state. Further, an attempt has also been made to study the growth and performance of Scheduled Commercial Banks with special emphasis on Regional Rural Banks (RRBs) in Indian and North-East Region.

A NEW RURAL ECONOMY

It is very possible that villagers are investing a part of their small surpluses in non-farm enterprises. Are there some subterranean changes in rural India that get ignored in the wider debate on farmer distress? The provisional results of the economic census that was conducted in 2005 were released.

They suggest that there is a gradual increase in non-farm activity in our villages. Take two facts. First, the average annual increase in the number of rural enterprises since 1998 was 5.53 per cent. New urban enterprises cropped up at a slower pace of 3.71 per cent. Second, since 1998, average annual employment growth in rural India was 3.33 per cent, compared with 1.68 per cent in the cities.

What does this mean? It is very possible that villagers are investing a part of their small surpluses in non-farm enterprises. If this is indeed the case, then what we are seeing are the first signs of an overdue diversification of the rural economy. The new units are offering employment opportunities to young villagers. Farming still dominates, but watch this trend as well.

Through the past four years, India's Gross Domestic Product (GDP) has grown at a phenomenal rate of 8.6 per cent. The momentum has continued through the current fiscal as well. The challenge today, however, lies as much in sustaining this momentum as ensuring an inclusive pattern of growth. I expect two distinct thrust areas in the coming Budget: a focus on social and physical infrastructure, and initiatives to integrate the rural economy with the national economy.

Since shortage of skilled manpower constitutes a serious long-term challenge to the economy today, Indian industry would expect a concerted effort from the finance minister on the education and skill development platform. In line with the 11th Plan Approach paper, which prescribes allocation towards education be raised from the current 2.9 per cent to 6 per cent of GDP, I expect enhanced allocation towards creation of a robust education and skill development infrastructure in the country. We look forward to initiatives towards development of an institutional framework to devise and implement national, sectoral strategies to develop and improve the skills of Indian workforce. Such a move would help us graduate from a labour to a knowledge arbitrage economy. Given that over-stretched physical infrastructure is going to be a major concern area, Indian industry would expect significant initiatives in the area of resource mobilisation for infrastructure projects.

The country has by and large developed a consensus around accelerated inclusion of the rural economy in the wider growth process. We expect added thrust on two critical components of the rural economy: strengthening of irrigation infrastructure and a larger role for the private sector to improve agricultural productivity and rural income. The government needs to attract more private companies towards agricultural R&D through appropriate tax and financial incentives.

On the tax front, Indian industry would expect some reduction in overall tax burden and removal of tax-related anomalies to stimulate manufacturing. In the service sector, telecom would expect dilution in the overall incidence of various levies, which cumulatively stand at a staggering 30 per cent of operator revenues. Such an initiative would help operators penetrate further into the rural hinterland and enable telecom to play a key role in the integration of the rural to the national economy. On the whole, Corporate India expects a Budget that not only drives economic growth but ushers in the key instruments for equitable growth.

Higher Rural Allocation

Apart from providing loan waivers to more than four crore small and marginal farmers in the country, the Union Budget has essentially focused on revamping the rural agricultural Economy through various measures such as augmenting rural credit, increasing the resource base of banks that are into priority sector lending and increasing allocation to social sector schemes under the National Rural Employment Guarantee Act (NREGA) and Bharat Nirman. The agricultural credit of schedule banks, which is estimated to around ₹ 2.4 lakh crore during the current fiscal, would go up by ₹ 2.8 lakh crore during 2008-09, marking a significant 16.6 per cent hike.

The finance minister has also proposed allocation of ₹ 10,200 crore for increasing the resource base of financial institutions such as National Bank for Agriculture and Rural Development (Nabard), Small Industries Development Bank of India (Sidbi) and National Housing Bank (NHB) to meet the requirement of priority sector lending. "Financial inclusion can be carried forward by expanding the reach of these three banks," Union finance minister P Chidambaram said. A fund of ₹ 5,000 crore in Nabard would enhance its refinance operations to short-term cooperative credit institutions, he said. There are proposals for two funds of ₹ 2,000 crore each for risk capital financing and enhancing refinance capability to micro, small and medium enterprises. Besides, a fund of ₹ 1,200 crore in NHB would also be created to enhance its refinance operations in the rural housing sector.

The Gross Capital Formation in agriculture as a proportion of GDP in the agriculture sector has improved from 10.2 per cent during 2003-04 to 12.5 per cent during 2006-07. The government targets to raise it to 16 per cent during the eleventh plan for achieving a growth rate of 4 per cent in the agriculture sector. It implies that more investment in the agriculture sector is in the offing during the eleventh plan period. According to the Budget, more than ₹ 1,185 crore had been released to the four states following the recommendation of Vaidyanathan committee on reviving the short-term cooperative credit structure being implemented across 17 states.

There has been an agreement between the states and the Centre for implementation of the committee report on reviving the long-term cooperative credit structure. The Centre's share will be ₹ 2,642 crore or 86 per cent of the total burden. "All this thrust on the rural Economy would definitely ensure that farmers return to the farming," says Richard Mahapatra, coordinator, Centre for Science & Environment, a New Delhi based... NGO. He added that the agriculture sector is not only the biggest employer in the country, but also plays a crucial role in sustaining the rural Economy.

Besides, a higher allocation of ₹ 16,000 crore for NREGA—the Union government's flagship social programme—is expected to go a long way in reviving the agriculture sector as most of the recommended works relate to water conservation. "Some of the key initiatives such as expansion of NREGA scheme to 596 districts in the country will have a positively impact and create livelihood options for rural youth in horticulture, biofuels, etc," says Rana Kapoor, CEO, Yes Bank. The Budget also announced reduction on duty on vitamin premixes and mineral mixtures from 30 per cent to 20 per cent with the intention of reducing the production cost of cattle and poultry feeds. The duty on phosphoric acid has been reduced from 7.5 per cent to 5 per cent, while duty on bactofuges is reduced from 7.5 per cent to nil. This will boost the dairy industry.

Rural Economic Development

Nobel Prize winning economist Robert Lucas had remarked that once you start thinking about economic growth, it is hard to think of anything else. What are the causes of economic growth and how can the process be enabled is a question that has obsessively occupied some of the best minds in the world of economics and commerce.

The question takes on an unparalled urgency and importance when applied to the rural Indian economy because it presents an enormous challenge, and, consequently, presents an equally great opportunity for making a difference in the lives of hundreds of millions of people. India's economic development is predicated upon India's rural development because around 700 million Indians live in rural India. An astonishing one out of every ten living humans lives in rural India.

Rapid progress in GDP growth and globalization in the last decade has primarily impacted the urban economy. While software exports, business process outsourcing, etc, have helped urban economic growth, it has done relatively little for the rural economy. Without rural economic development, India has little chance of achieving growth rates required to become a developed nation. Furthermore, economic development is both a cause and a consequence of urbanization.

Clearly, in the Indian context, urbanization through further rural to urban migration is both unsustainable and socially disruptive. Therefore urbanization of the rural population will have to be achieved in the rural areas. Rural India is caught in what is called a development trap. Because of lack of economic opportunities, incomes are low. Therefore they are unable to pay for goods and services that would enable them to increase their incomes. This leads to low demand for goods and services. Consequently, firms don't find it profitable to do business in rural India. This leads to the inadequate provision of infrastructure, which in turn leads to lack of economic opportunities, and so on.

It is important to recognize that human capital is the scarce resource globally. Fortunately India is lavishly endowed with immense human capital. However, physical capital is in relatively short supply in India. The challenge therefore is to use the limited capital most efficiently to break out of the poverty trap by integrating the rural economy with the urban Indian economy and indeed the global economy.

Various models for rural economic growth have been proposed and implemented. Vinod Khosla and I have proposed a model which harnesses the power of the information and communications technology (ICT) revolution to accelerate rural economic growth. The model called Rural Infrastructure & Services Commons (RISC) has the potential for achieving the multi-faceted goals of sustainable development. It uses limited resources efficiently by focusing them in specific locations that are accessible to a sufficiently large rural population, such as that of 100 villages. RISC provides the benefits of urbanization by making available to rural populations the full set of services and amenities that are normally available in urban areas.

It brings the benefits of ICT and the increased access to global markets that globalization promises. The model recognizes that rural populations face a number of inter-related gaps, not just the celebrated digital divide. Bridging them simultaneously with a holistic solution is more likely to succeed than any partial intervention can. The model facilitates the coordination of the investment decisions of the private sector, the public sector, NGOs, and multilateral lending institutions. To achieve its goal, the model strikes a number of balances — between the local and the global, between planned infrastructure investment and market-driven service provision, between specialization and standardization. It does not require government subsidies for its continued operation, although the government does have a role in providing some critical functions such as risk alleviation, loan assistance, and enacting enabling legislation.

A typical RISC installation would provide services for about 100,000 rural people. These services, mostly but not all provided competitively by a large number of for-profit firms, will range from education, health, market making, financial intermediation, entertainment to government services, social services, etc.

Since all services themselves require the infrastructural services such as power, telecommunications, water, physical plant, etc., large specialized firms will provide the infrastructure. RISC obtains urbanization economies, which arise from the agglomeration of populations and infrastructure facilities. By installing RISCs to serve the rural populations of an entire state, economies of scale and scope are also obtained. Scale economies would be significant at each level of the model.

At the infrastructure level, there are transaction costs associated with the necessary coordination between the firms providing the core infrastructural services. At the services level, the cost of the services will be inversely proportional to the quantity demanded and supplied. A RISC provides a complete set of services and functions. Each service provider itself is a customer of other services co-located on the RISC. The banker uses the internet and postal services, and the internet service provider uses the banking and postal services, and so on.

They make each other mutually viable and even possible. All these economies essentially lower the cost of service provision and, in a competitive market, makes them more affordable. At a certain level of abstraction, the proximate causes of poverty can be seen as two gaps: the ideas gap and the objects gap. The objects gap is the lack of physical resources – too little land, too little capital stock, etc – that contribute to persistent poverty. The ideas gap is the lack of knowledge about how to make the best use of the resources available.

Fortunately, the cost of knowledge goods has dropped precipitously due to the revolution in information and communications technologies. Bridging the ideas gap is a much easier task than ever before. RISC uses ICT intensively towards that end. The transition from the concept to the actual implementation of the RISC model requires co-ordination of investment decision of the government and the large firms that provide the infrastructural elements. It is a non-trivial but surmountable challenge provided the political will and the vision exists among policy makers, private sector leaders, leading investors, and opinion makers.

RECONSTRUCTION OF THE RURAL ECONOMY

Skill and enterprise will take them part of the journey. But they cannot bring back the lost prosperity unless the entire economy of the province, now severely deficit in several directions, is placed on stable foundations. In any programme of reconstruction, means of irrigation take the first place. Four-fifths of the new allottees had holdings even in West Punjab in the lowest grade of ten standard acres and less.

At least a third of the evacuee land in East Punjab and Pepsu has gone to the small rural traders from the predominantly Muslim districts of West Punjab. Many of them may take to the land, but theirs will continue to be an impoverished economy, for the call on their traditional skills cannot but be meagre. In virtue of the land held by them they have obtained land now, and this will give each of them a home and a location, but not as a general rule an adequate living.

Individuals from this group of settlers need assistance and encouragement to leave their families at home and to venture out into other parts of the country, where their intelligence and resourcefulness will enable them to build a new composite way of life intertwined with their interests in their own province. In this way they can re-establish themselves. Tenants from West Punjab as well as those who cultivated for large Muslim holders in East Punjab present another important problem of reconstruction.

Altogether, reduced holdings and poorer lands, a fall in the number of actual workers on the soil, insufficient irrigation facilities, slender capital resources, and the rise of tenant interests, combine to produce a picture of increasing economic pressure, which the land may not long sustain. If the stresses are not to overwhelm the social economy itseif, the end of the resettlement operations should be followed by a period of bold administrative action, reform in the management of land, and investment of capital on a scale sufficient to produce results. The migration has brought to

East Punjab a peasantry uncommonly rich in experience and progressive in outlook, whose record of achievement over sixty years of colonization is second to none in the world. In this and in the spirit of enterprise, which raised the western districts of the Punjab to the highest level of rural prosperity ever, reached in the long history of India lies perhaps the best hope of the future.

The East Punjab Government propose to replace the present system of temporary allotments of evacuee lands by a new system of allotments which will take account of the holdings of evacuees in West Punjab. The new allotments will not confer rights of ownership or permanent occupancy, but the possession of allottees will be maintained. Claims of allottees will be dealt with in accordance with decisions reached eventually regarding the treatment of evacuee property. In the new scheme of allotments, land will be allotted only to those who, In West Punjab, were owners, occupancy tenants under the Punjab

Tenancy Act, and tenants under the Colonization of Government Lands Act and to certain other classes of grantees and holders of land in West Punjab to be of equivalent areas, while in the case of larger holders there will be graded specified by Government. It is proposed to give to small holders allotments cuts.

The definition of the " Small Holders " and the details of the graded cuts will be determined when detailed information regarding the available areas in East Punjab and the East Punjab States, the areas held by the popu-lation to be settled in East Punjab and the East Punjab States, and other relevant information becomes available. It is intended to complete the new system of allotments in East Punjab and the East Punjab States, not later than the 31st May, 1948. Governments are, however, anxious to introduce the new scheme as early as may be feasible and steps to this end will be taken at once.

Arrangements for collecting complete information regarding the land available for allotment in East Punjab and the East Punjab States and the land abandoned by individual evacuees will be taken in hand without delay and it is hoped also to make arranagements on a reciprocal basis to secure Information from records of rights in West Punjab. To ensure accurate information an Ordinance will shortly be promulgated prescribing punishment lor false information regarding claims to land and action by way of forfeiture and otherwise in respect of allotments taken on false information.

Claims to land will be invited on a form to be prescribed by Government. Until the new system of allotments can be introduced, the present system of allotments will continue and allotments made to the present holders will be maintained subject to a complete scrutiny of existing allotments, cancel-lation of unauthorised and excessive allotments, dispossession from illicit occupation and such other adjustments as may be necessary Including ad-justments in the unit of allotment decided upon by Government. Government desires that kharif crops including sugar-cane and cotton should be sown to the maximum extent.

Accordingly they wish to assure the present allottees that in the event of their being otherwise dispossessed before the kharif crops have been harvested. Government will make arrange-ments for compensation after proper verification, through sharing of the crop or in some other appropriate manner. 7th February, 1948.

LAND CLAIMS PROCEDURE

The purpose of this chapter is to outline in some detail the steps taken and the instructions laid down from time to time in working on land claim' applications submitted by about half a million individuals. This description is given for two reasons. For several years it will be necessary for revenue officials to refer to papers con-nected with the allotment of land to displaced persons and to check whether the entries were according to the instructions and also, in some particulars, what the precise object of the various entries was. Secondly, the circumstances under which work on land claims was done during 1948 and 1949 imposed certain difficulties.

Not all the difficul-ties could be anticipated and, as the work proceeded, new problems arose. The experience gained in dealing with large numbers of claims to property and the errors which came to light in the course of this work should be recorded, so that when similar work is under-taken in other fields, mistakes and omissions can be avoided. It is possible in retrospect to distinguish between features, which arose from the nature of the task handled, and those, which were due to local or particular factors.

Inviting Land Claims

In the press note, which was issued on the 7th February, 1948 with the concurrence of the East Punjab States and the Government of India, the East Punjab Government announced its intention to invite claims to land abandoned by displaced persons. The East Punjab Refugee (Registration of Land Claims) Ordinance, 1948 was thereupon promulgated and corresponding legislation was introduced by the States of Patiala, Kapurthala. Nabha, Jind and Faridkot. The ordi-nance provided definitions of expressions such as "claim", "land", "landholder", "refugee" and "registering officer". Claims were to be invited under the Ordinance from refugee landholders in respect of land situated in West Punjab, N.W.F.P., Sind, Baluchistan and States adjacent to these provinces, which had acceded to the Dominion of Pakistan, in other words, from displaced landholders from Western Pakistan.

The expression, "refugee" was defined in the Ordinance as:

> "A landholder in the territories now comprised in the Provinces of West Punjab, N.W.F.P., Sind or Baluchistan or in any State adjacent to any of the aforesaid Provinces and acceding to the Dominion of Pakistan, who has since the 1st day of March, 1947, abandoned or been made to abandon his land in the said territories on account of civil disturbances, or the fear of such disturbances, or the partition of the country."

This definition was amended by the legislature before passing the East Punjab Refugees (Registration of Land Claims) Act. 1948 to mean a—"landholder in the territories now comprised in the Province of West Punjab, or who or whose ancestor migrated as a colonist from the Punjab since 1901 to the Provinces of North-West Frontier Province, Sind or Baluchistan or to any State adja-cent to any of the aforesaid Provinces and acceding to the Dominion of Pakistan, and who has since the 1st day of March, 1947, abandoned or been made to abandon his land in the said territories on account of civil disturbances, or the fear of such disturbances, or the partition of the country."

On the 7th April, 1948 the relative responsibilities of the Central and the Provincial Governments for the rehabilitation of dis-placed persons were considered in the Joint rehabilitation Board, in which both Governments were represented.

The record of pro-ceedings sets out the discussion and the decision in respect of settle-ment on evacuee land:

> "After the East Punjab Government have made up their mind in regard to the refugees they are going to rehabilitate in the East Punjab and East Punjab States, the rehabilitation of the rest in the States of Bikaner, Bharatpur and Alwar will be the responsibility of the Centre. After some discussion, it was decided that the East Punjab Government will undertake the responsibility of rehabilitation in East Punjab and East Punjab States, of Sind. N.W.F.P., Bahawalpur and Baluchistan refugees who are of Punjabi extraction- Other refugees from Bahawalpur will be rehabilitated in Bikaner and else-where. Refugees from Sind, N.W.F.P. and Baluchistan who are not of Punjabi extraction will be rehabilitated outside East Punjab and East Punjab States, *e.g.*, Bharatpur, Alwar etc."

Penalties

No authentic records being available, it was felt that if severe penalties were provided, dishonesty in the submission of claims could be greatly reduced. The Ordinance provided rigorous imprisonment upto five years or fine upto ₹ 5000 or both as penalties for persons submitting false claims or a public servant abetting such an offence-In addition to these penalties, Deputy Commissioners were authorised to disqualify from allotment by an order passed in writing any person who has submitted a false claim and to cancel, either in whole or in part, any allotment which may have been made on the basis of a false claim. An appeal from such an order lies within thirty days to the Financial Commissioner whose decision is final and conclusive and cannot be called in question in any court.

The Claim Form

By rules made under the Ordinance, the East Punjab Govern-ment prescribed a form on which claims for land were to be submitted. The East Punjab Government's form was used also in the States. The form was sold at the price of one anna. It was printed in Urdu, Punjabi and English. It provided for an affidavit by the applicant, signature or thumb-impression by one witness and attestation by a competent authority. The rules under the Ordinance prescribed competent authorities for the purpose of attest-ing affidavits on the land claim application.

Lacuna In the Form

For every district in which land was abandoned by a dis-placed person, one claim form was to be filled. Details of holdings in different villages of the same district were to be entered on one form. Subsequently, in actual work, since the particulars of land held by a person had to be verified and completed village by village, supplemen-tary land claim forms were prepared in the Land Claims Office.

Copying of extracts from claims which were frequently incomplete or badly written on such an extensive scale led to mistakes in supplemen-tary forms. Again, when it became necessary to consolidate into a single account, land held by an individual in different villages in more than one district, it was a serious handicap to have begun with claim forms on a district basis. Experience showed that the right course would have been to have obtained a separate form for each single village in which an individual held land along with a covering form giving particulars of all villages together, whether situated in one district or in several. The form did not specially provide space and directions for entering an applicant's address. This omission was soon noticed and the necessary instructions were issued to registering officers. Direc-tions to applicants for intimating changes in their addresses should also have been given. A column in the form asked for particulars of village, tehsil and district of origin from applicant who was colonists from different districts. The word "colonist" was not defined.

Gradually, in the course of land claims work, the word has come ⁱo mean not one necessarily who goes out from a particular district and "colonizes" land, but one who belongs to a particular district, whether of East Punjab or of West Punjab, who held land in another district. Since the claims of colonies from West Punjab were to be consolidated with their West Punjab districts and the claims of colonists from East Pun-jab and the States were to be sorted out for settlement in their parent districts, the column came to assume increasing importance. Incomplete information in this column led later to many difficulties in con-solidating individual accounts.

Arrangements for Registration

The Registration of Land Claims Ordinance provided for "registering officers," a term which included revenue officers within their jurisdiction, a Land Claims Officer at the central office and spe-cially appointed officials known as Assistant Land Claims Officers. Claims applications were to be presented under the rules to registering officers either in person or through recognised agents or they were to be sent by registered post. In the case of minors, applications had to be submitted by their next friends or guardians. An application sub-mitted by post unaccompanied by an affidavit not attested by a compe-tent authority was not to be entertained.

Arrangements for registration were made at the offices of tehsils and sub-tehsils throughout East Punjab and East Punjab States. Each tehsil carried its own classification number. A receipt was given for every claim received.

Although the period 10th March, to the 31st March, 1948 was prescribed as the period for the registeration of land claims, the date was extended upto the 10th April, and even later small numbers of claims continued to arrive by post.

The work of registration was conducted satisfactorily. Nevertheless, it was felt that if more time had been given and claims had been written by trained hands there would have been a greater measure of accuracy.

Work in the Land Claims Office

The press note of the 7th February, 1948 had announced the intention of Government to complete the new system of allotment of land not later than the 31st May, 1948, but Government expressed its anxiety to introduce the new scheme as early as might be feasible and warning was given that the cultivation of the kharif crops including sugar-cane and cotton should not be allowed to suffer. Although not in theory, in actual practice this announcement reduced the period available for work in the central office to less than a month.

During the period available claims were tabulated at much pressure. Necessarily, the areas claimed to have been abandoned were included in the tabulation at their face value. The results of the tabulation left a general impression that there had been a certain degree of exaggera-tion in the claims and a number who did not hold land had claimed to be landholders. On the 14th May, 1948, Government felt bound to announce that without further steps for the verification of areas said to have been abandoned, the new scheme of land allotment announced in the press communique of the 7th February, 1948, would not be launched.

Verification of land Claims

At this stage there was no assurance that revenue records would be exchanged between the two Dominions. Correspondence on the subject had been inconclusive. There was a deep desire every-where to introduce a scheme of quasi-permanent allotment. It was decided to arrange for oral verification of claims. Verification took place at tehsils and sub-tehsils in East Punjab and East Punjab States between the 17th August, 1948, and the end of October, 1948. Centres were fixed at which the claims of individual villages of Western Pakis-tan were verified.

As a rule, a village was named against a particular centre if the largest number of claims of that village had been register-ed there. Brochures setting out the verification programmes in detail from the aspect of West Punjab districts as well as that of individual districts in East Punjab and East Punjab States were published. Addi-tional staff was recruited for the purpose and for the best part of two and a half months the energies of the revenue administration were employed on verification. For the first time an attempt was made to draw up lists of villages abandoned in Pakistan.

Without knowledge of hadbast numbers, following in many instances wrong names given by applicants, the lists contained errors, but these were gradually reduced. A form known as the parcha tasdiq was devised for recording the results of the verification. Verifying Officers were directed to read out to persons from any West Punjab village which was under verifi-cation the names of claimants as given in the claims and to ask lambardars and other persons present if they could give information concern-ing the area, the kind of soil or the nature of rights held by each individual in their village.

After clearing discrepancies as far as possible, Verifying Officers were to record in the parcha tasdiq their conclusions about the area, the kind of soil and the nature of rights possessed by each claimant.

In support of a claim, proof was to be considered in the following order of precedence:

(1) Entries in a jamabandi or other revenue record ; or
(2) Entries and references in any registered document;
(3) Entries or references in other documents of unquestionable genuineness;
and
(4) Oral evidence of reliable persons present at the verification.

Verifying Officers were also to record in the parcha tasdiq against each claimant whether he was personally present at the verification, whether he produced any documentary evidence, (if so. giving hrief description), and if a claimant was serving in the Defence Services, whether any relative had assisted in the verification of his claim. The assistance of non-officials was also sought in full measure. For displaced landholders residing outside East Punjab.

East Punjab States or Delhi, as well as for persons serving in the Defence Forces, personal attendance at verification was not suggested.

They were requested to give certain particulars and, among these, to answer the following questions:—

Do you want your allotment of land ?

(a) According to district, tehsil and residence of Pakistan ? or
(b) According to tehsil or district of origin ? or
(c) Along with landholders of one of the villages in which land was held. If so, name the village ? or
(d) According to the district and tehsil of present temporary allotment; or
(e) According to the village of present temporary allotment ? or
(f) In any other manner, which may be stated.

These questions were also included in the parcha tasdiq. The pre-ferences indicated by individuals were noted and considered later. But to an extraordinary degree applications giving new preferences or preferences stated with reference to particular villages poured in when the work of allotment was actually begun. Where the object of invit-ing claims is to distribute any form of property, it is necessary to evolve In advance a suitable procedure for indication of wishes and preferences, which should then be treated as firm without repeated opportunity or permission to change; or to evolve a procedure which makes individual preferences largely unnecessary. The parcha tasdiq record proved on the whole a useful source of information in later work.

Exchange of Revenue Records

On the 1st July, 1948 arrangements were made between the West Punjab and the East Punjab Governments for preparation of copies of revenue records with a view to mutual exchange. Public opinion in the province, while appreciating the importance of exchange of records, was in favour of making such arrangements as would facilitate progress towards quasi-permanent allotment without being wholly dependent upon records which might be received in exchange.

The exchange of copies of revenue records between the two Govern-ments began on the 22nd November, 1948 and about two-thirds of the records due were received by the end of January. 1949. Thereafter, copies of jamabandis continued to be received at intervals in smaller numbers.

Analysis and tabulation of claims on the basis of the original Claim applications and the parcha tasdiq began in the '/curth week of November. 1948. In the first instance, as jamabandis were being received in driblets and it was not certain when the exchange would be completed, the analysis and tabulation of claims was carried out on the basis of material already available without recourse to details of individual holdings as given in jamabandis. The circumstances in which the work was done dictated the procedure which was adopted. Under other circumstances, work on individual claims may have been deferred until all the jamabandis were available, or all the effort might have been given to the preparation of accounts from jamabandis, the claims being considered later.

It was felt, however, that from the pre-liminary work on claims and the parcha tasdiq, it was possible and necessary to obtain a picture of the problem of resettlement as a whole, so that the main lines of policy could be drawn up. The desire to com-plete the quasi-permanent allotment by the end of May, 1949 hastened work on whatever material was available. The procedure followed was, therefore, to draw material from the claims and the parcha tasdiq, check area totals for villages of each tehsil whose jamabandis had been received by about the middle of January, 1949, apply certain correction factors and arrive at approximate figures of area abandoned in each tehsil and district of West Punjab. Thus, there was a good deal of work connected with analysis and tabulation of claims which had to be done twice over, once before claims were verified against individual jambandi entries and, on the second occasion, after such verifications had taken place. Nevertheless the size of the problem and the policy issues on which decisions of Governments were called for became apparent six months earlier than they would have otherwise done. This led to clear and timely decisions which stood "' firm later in circumstances propitious to fundamental change.

THE PARCHA CLAIM

A form known as the parcha claim was devised in November, 1948 for extracting all information relevant to each individual's hold-ing and for working out various steps leading to the assessment and valuation of his total claim, and to the area due to him for allotment, and for recording the final orders of allotment. The parcha claim form is by far the most important document in the entire land resettlement operation and grasp of its details is essential. After its introduction most of the work centred upon its various columns. The parcha claim is divided into four parts. The first part, which may be described as preliminary, sets out general particulars such as the registration number of claim, name, father's name and caste, address, place of residence in Pakistan, details of origin and temporary allotment, wishes in the matter of allotment, details of co-sharers in the khewat, the nature of oral verification, if any, in the case of a landholder from outside West Punjab whether he is of Punjabi or of non-Punjabi extraction and finally, names of vil-lages in which the claimant held land.

The second part of the parcha claim comprises columns 1 to 12 and summarises the information given in' the original claim, in the parcha tasdiq and in other documents which may have been furnished by an individual with his claim. The second part thus ends with a find-ing concerning each person's area and rights upto the stage of oral verification. The third part of the parcha claim comprises columns 13 to 26. Columns 13 to 20 state the rights and details of area etc.

According to the jamabandi, if any received from the West Punjab Government. In columns 21 to 24 is entered the area abandoned by a person, as finally assessed on the basis of all the evidence available, against rights shown in columns 15 and 16. The extent of land, the classes of land and the rights abandoned by an individual being known, the next step is to value his claim. The value against each item in his claim is shown in column 25 of the third part of the parcha claim.

The fourth part of the parcha claim serves four purposes. It provides first a break-up of the claim of an individual according to different classes of land. For convenience of tabulation, seven cate-gories of land are adopted; namely, perennial nehri, other nehri, chahi and abi, barani, sailab, banjar jadid and qadim, and ghair mumkin.

Secondly, it has space for adding up the area abandoned by a person in different villages so as to give his total claim, there being a separate parcha claim in respect of each separate village in which land is held by an individual-

In the third place, the total claim being stated in terms of standard acres and units, space is provided for indicating the net allotment due to an individual after application of cut- Finally, the particulars of the village and tehsil in which land is allotted in East Punjab or in the Patiala and East Punjab States Union is shown in this part of the parcha claim.

The Parcha Claim Number

Reference has been made earlier to the registration number carried by each claim based on the centre at which the claim has been registered. For facility of work it became necessary to evolve a new notation. Every parcha claim carries its own index number. For instance a parcha claim numbered JG 1|88|55 would mean that the claimant concerned is listed as No. 55 in the claimants' list of village hadbast No. 88 of tehsil Jhang, or a parcha claim numbered ML 7|435| EB25 would mean that the claimant concerned is listed as No. 25 in the village list of Chak 435|EB of tehsil Vehari of Multan district.

The first part of the parcha claim number indicates the tehsil, the second part the serial number of the village and the third part the serial number of the claimant in the West Punjab village list of claim-ants. It is necessary to have ready reference lists which would give against individual registra-tion numbers of claims according to centres of registration, the rele-vant parcha claim numbers.

The preparation of this directory is sche-duled to be undertaken after allotments have been completed. With-out such a directory it is necessary to know the name of the village and the tehsil in which an individual's land is situated before his claim can be located and other particulars ascertained.

The First Part of the Parcha Claim

A number of items in the first part of the parcha claim explain themselves, but a few require elucidation. The blank spaces at the head of the first part are for purposes of categorisation. Thus, parcha claims of defence personnel carried the letter ' D ' and of ex-defence personnel, the letters 'ED' wherever information was avail-able. Similarly, colonists would be linked with their districts of origin by means of descriptions such as C|JL, C|SL, C\RP, and indicating colonists of Jullundur, Sialkot and Rawalpindi respectively.

Categories of Verification

The nature of the verification to which a claim has been subjected is indicated briefly against the eighth item in the first part of the parcha claim.

Seven categories of verification were drawn up:

(1) In the presence of a claimant along with documentary evidence;

(2) In the absence of a claimant, but with documentary evidence;

(3) In the absence of a claimant and without documentary evidence;
(4) In the presence of a claimant;
(5) Unverified;
(6) False claim;
(7) Disputed claim.

Against the ninth item in the first part of the parcha claim, entry has to be made as to whether a claimant who had abandoned land outside West Punjab was of Punjabi or of non-Punjabi extraction, for claims of persons of non-Punjabi extraction abandoning land in Western Pakistan outside West Punjab are not eligible for allotment of land in East Punjab and East Punjab States. During the oral verification, verifying officers were asked to take special care to ascertain particulars of origin given by displaced persons from Bahawalpur, N.W.F.P., Sind and Baluchistan. If a displaced person from these areas claimed to hold agricultural land or to be the owner of a house anywhere in the Punjab such proof or attestation as might be possible were to be secured before accepting the claim.

It was not sufficient for an individual to state, for instance, that some generations ago his ancestors had gone from the Punjab to settle in the province or territory from which he had now come. The East Punjab Displaced Persons (Registration of Land Claims) Act provided, as has been noticed earlier, for registration of claims only from those dis-placed persons from N.W.F.P., Sind. Baluchistan and Bahawalpur who and whose ancestors had migrated as colonists from the Punjab since 1901.

The land claim form, however, which was issued under the Ordinance which preceded the Act, stated that claims to land were to be presented by " refugee landholders from West Punjab and Bahawalpur and by colonists who migrated from united Punjab to N.W.F.P., Sind or Bahawalpur or to any State adjacent to the province and acceding to Pakistan "- On this account a considerable amount of sort-ing was necessary in the claims of displaced persons from those areas.

The staff of the Land Claims Office was instructed not to depart from the finding on this question during the oral verification unless there were specific orders to the contrary. For instance, a claimant who had given only a vague description of his origin in the united Punjab, sometimes not even having indicated the name of his village of origin, was not to be accepted as being a person of Punjabi extraction without the orders in writing of a gazetted officer. Against the tenth item of the first part were to be entered the names of villages other than the one to which the parcha claim related in which a claimant was known to have held land.

These entries, for reasons, which have been explained earlier, frequently remained in-complete and much labour had to be given at a later stage to linking up each individual's claims relating to different villages.

Classification of Rights

In the second and third parts of the parcha claim, the impor-tant questions to be determined were the extent of area the classes of soil, and the rights held by an individual claimant. Without records rights were difficult to assess, and even with records the problem was by no means easy. Not all rights could be regarded as eligible for allotment in East Punjab and East Punjab States. For the assistance of staff, rights other than rights in 'shamilat' were divided into seven main categories with certain sub-categories as follows:

Category No. 1:

(a) Full ownership free of mortgage;

(b) Full ownership with mortgage with possession in favour of a non-Muslim;

(c) Full ownership with mortgage with possession In favour of a Muslim;

Explanations:

(i) In each sub-category there may be an occupancy tenant who may either be a Muslim or a non-Muslim.

(ii) Land in which the same individual holds the rights of superior and inferior ownership is to be regarded as being under his full ownership.

(iii) Malik Qabza is taken as full owner.

Category No. 2:

(a) Inferior ownership under a non-Muslim superior owner;

(b) Inferior ownership under a Muslim superior owner.

Explanations:

(i) An inferior owner may have an occupancy tenant who may be a Muslim or a non-Muslim;

(ii) Rights of an occupancy tenant may be hem free of mortgage or may be mortgaged with possession in favour of a Muslim or in favour of a non-Muslim.

Category no. 3:

(a) Superior ownership with a non-Muslim as inferior owner;

(b) Superior ownership with a Muslim as inferior owner.

Category No. 4:

(a) Occupancy tenant under the Punjab Tenancy Act, 1887 with a non-Muslim as landlord;

(b) Occupancy tenant under the Punjab Tenancy Act, 1887 with a Muslim as a landlord.

Explanation:

Rights of an occupancy tenant may be held free of mortgage or under mortgage in favour of a non-Muslim or a Muslim.

Category No. 5:

(a) Grant or occupancy tenancy under the Punjab Colonization of Government Lands Act, 1912;

(b) Auction-purchase under the Punjab Colonization of Govern-ment Lands Act, 1912;
(c) Lease under the Punjab Colonization of Government Lands Act. 1912;
(d) Other rights under the Punjab Colonization of Government Lands Act, 1912;

Explanation

(1) In respect of land held as grantee or occupancy tenant or auction purchaser, details of installments paid to Gov-ernment or lease money paid and due were to be enter-ed in the parcha claim. In the case of leases, the period and other conditions were to be indicated.
(2) In (a) a grantee may be a non-occupancy tenant under the Punjab Colonization of Government Lands Act, 1912.

Category No. 6:

(a) Rights of mortgage with possession of land belonging to a non-Muslim;
(b) Rights of mortgage with possession of land belonging to a Muslim.

Explanation:

Rights of mortgage may pertain to land under full ownership or under inferior ownership or under occupancy rights.

Category No. 7:

(a) Rights of lease or mortgage for a limited period over land belonging to a non-Muslim;
(b) Rights of lease or mortgage for a limited period over land belonging to a Muslim.

The period of lease or mortgage with dates and particulars of the lands involved were to be indicated in the parcha claim.

Units of Area

In the second and third parts of the parcha claim area is to be shown in acres, kanal and marlas the karam being of 5 feet and six inches. Where different units of area are in vogue such as ghumaon 'higha and ghunta, these have to be converted, or where the karam is 'of a different size, the instructions given in nara 45 of the Punjab Land Records Manual have to be followed. Conversion is also necessary, for instance, when dealing with the Lower Chenab and Lower Jhelum Colonies where the 'killa is of 8 kanals and 18 marlas, while elsewhere it is equivalent to an acre. In certain parts of the Lahore District irrigated by the upper Bari Doab Canal, there are a variety of measures in use in different villages.

These have to be ascertained carefully before conversion calculations are carried out, In Sind, 5 ghuntas make one kanal and 40 ghuntas make one acre. These strategies and programmes constitute the "five year plan", for the purpose of simplicity the measures undertaken have been categorized in broad groups and then elaborated upon. In the end, an ideal model of rural development, which is in contrast to the current model, is proposed.

The rural economy, as much as urban economy, is an integrated part of the overall Indian economy. Any talk of overall development without rural development, particularly in a country where three-quarters of people below the poverty line reside in rural areas, is flawed. Poverty is indeed a global issue. Its eradication is considered integral to humanity's quest for sustainable development. Reduction of poverty in India, is, therefore, vital for the attainment of international goals. Poverty alleviation has been one of the guiding principles of the planning process in India. This can be substantiated by the fact that anti-poverty programmes have been internalized in the (particularly the ninth) five-year plan. This article sheds light on the various "strategies and programmes" that form the instruments of the plan.

URBANIZATION AND RURAL ECONOMY

One should avoid following the straight jacketed approach followed by our smartest of all political leaders to comment on such issues. A 'Neta' (Perhaps we need to change the meaning of this word in Hindi dictionaries now) vouching for rural votes will say 'No' and someone vouching for urban votes will say 'Yes'.

An interesting and intriguing incident has been the downfall of BJP government, a government riding high on 'India Shining' campaign. The downfall has been associated with observations that BJP was concentrated on Urban India only. The truth of the analysis is evident form the fact that the campaign was in worded in English was pointed towards BJP's urban India approach. Ahem!

The Congress therefore followed their slogan as 'Aam Aadmi ki sarkar', worded in Hindi and worded for rural people. They made their huge plans {I have deliberately used the word 'Plans'} to associate with the rural people. Such developments may lead to conclude "Yes - urbanization has hindered the growth of rural people". In fact, I have also been to an extent convinced with this philosophy though I have thought that why concentrate on one side, why cannot both sides develop simultaneously.

1. A study of consumption in last 26 years reveals that an increase in Urban Household consumption of ₹ 100 leads to an increase of ₹ 39 in the rural household income. The driver of such increase is non farm sector of rural economy such as manufacturing, construction and trade, hotels and restaurants.
2. During the last decade, the rural economy is estimated to have grown by 7.3 per cent as compared to 5.4 per cent of urban economy.
3. The rural economy is nearly as big as the urban. In 2000, the rural economy accounted for 49 per cent of the India's GDP.

4. Share of agriculture in Rural economy has dropped from 72 per cent in 1970s to 64 per cent in 1980s to 51 per cent in 2000
5. The rural-urban migration has fallen from 6.5 per cent in 1981 to 2.8 per cent in 2001.

The indications pointed by each point noted above leads to refute a number of myths such as rural people are suffering due to urbanisation; there is an India – C waiting to shine and many more - an encouraging realization!!!!

The major reason for this change, as noted by eminent researcher and economists is the growing and strengthening integration of the rural economy with the urban economy. Granted that logistics and supply chain for the route is no less than a shame for the progress we hope to achieve, yet the hope does exist. Perhaps an integration of the rural supply chains with the urban ones, steered by the boom in organised retail would provide the impetus to pass on the benefits lower down the pyramid. Just one problem though – Who will help Mayawati understand on the recent Reliance Fresh issues? Anyone ready to bell the cat?

Winds of Growth

There may finally be a silver lining to the gloomy economic picture prevailing in the country. Last week, there were economic forecasts from three important quarters that saw a better future for the country's economy in the current year. The Centre for Monitoring Indian Economy (CMIE) forecast a 6.3 per cent growth in real GDP in the current financial year against 5.2 per cent growth in GDP in the last fiscal.

Its forecast was quickly followed by estimates from the Reserve Bank of India (RBI) which saw the economy growing at over 6.5 per cent in FY2001-2002 and then the finance minister stated that he saw the economy turning around by the end of the calender year. In a nutshell, the picture for Indian economy appears to be brightening up as we go forward into the year.

However, the most remarkable feature of this improving economic outlook is that the growth is projected to come almost entirely from the agriculture sector. CMIE has forecast that growth in the agriculture production during the current year would be a whopping 9 per cent over the previous year. This would be almost the highest in the last seven years and comes after two consecutive years of shrinkage in agriculture sector.

Impact on Rural Economy

After having grown at over seven per cent annually during 1994 and 1997, India's GDP growth slowed down substantially because of the sharp fall in agricultural production and income. After an impressive 8.2 per cent rise in production in 1998-99, the pace of growth in the farm sector turned negative with output shrinking by 1.5 per cent in FY2000 and 4.5 per cent in FY2001.

This meant there was less disposable income generated in the rural areas and hence the demand pull from vast majority of population was absent. The last two years were marked by a drought in states like Gujarat, Maharashtra and Rajasthan which contribute significantly to domestic production and also account for substantial amount of consumer spending. With a pick up in income in these areas, the demand for goods and services is expected to pick up this year and that should contribute to the over all growth in economy.

Impact on Industry

Increased income in farm sector impacts the entire economy, however it has an almost immediate impact on some sectors like consumer durables and non-durables, tractors and motorcycles. There is also an increased demand for cement and steel from the resurgent housing sector. Heavy commercial vehicles too attract buying as transportation of goods picks up across the country and demand for services too is higher.

Therefore, the relationship between agricultural income and economic growth is almost direct. We expect FMCG companies, tractor manufacturers and motorcycle makers to feel an immediate pick up in demand once the kharif crop is harvested. This sentiment has already been reflected in the stock markets with the FMCG leader, Hindustan Lever attracting huge amount of buying by fund managers in expectation of a large top line growth this year.

We might also see a turnaround in the subdued sentiment in industries such as televisions, washing machines and refrigerators which have seen a fall in sales due to sluggish rural demand over the past two years. Higher demand for goods and services in rural areas necessitates increased movement of goods and hence a pick up in demand for commercial vehicles. This means increased demand in almost all sectors such as steel and engineering. Therefore, if the agriculture sector does grow at the projected 9 per cent this year, economy would receive a big boost by the end of the year.

Growth in Industry

The growth in industry suffers from poor demand in consumption as well as investments. Due to a decline in farm income over the past two years, demand from rural areas was poor and as result of this investment sentiment remains sluggish too. The situation can only reverse if consumption rises giving a boost to investment sentiment. However, as the impact of increased income in farm sector would be felt only from the end of the year, the growth in industrial production in expected to remain this year.

CMIE has projected that the growth in industrial production this year would be nearly 4.5 per cent, down from 5 per cent in the last financial year and the lowest level since 1998-99. The CMIE forecast notes that the index of industrial production (IIP) registered a growth of 5 per cent last year and 6.6 per cent in

1999-2000. While in April 2001 industrial production grew only 2.7 per cent and in May it was even lower at 1.9 per cent, the overall growth may be better as the impact of improved demand is felt later in the year. Morgan Stanley Dean Witter too has projected that the industrial activity will pick up in the second half of this calendar year and the IIP should be between 4 and 5 per cent for the year.

Gains from Rains

According to the CMIE study, the 2001 south west monsoon has been fairly widespread and intensive across most parts of the country. Between June 1 and June 27, 2001, as many as 29 out of the 35 meteorological sub-divisions in the country received excess to normal rains, covering almost 90 per cent of the gross cropped area. Out of this 75 per cent of the area received excess rains.

In comparison, in June 2000 only 72 per cent of the cropped area in 26 meteorological sub-divisions had received excess rains, the CMIE report states. Thus rains have not only been good they have also been evenly distributed leading to prospects of widespread growth. Rains have been particularly good for Eastern and Western UP, Haryana and Punjab, raising hopes of a huge demand rise in these states early net year. The only areas that have received deficient rainfall so far include Rayalseema in Andhra Pradesh, interiors of Karnataka and some parts of Tamil Nadu. Early and good rains have enthused farmers to go for kharif sowing operations ahead of the normal schedule. The CMIE report says that it expects kharif crop to be much better this year than the harvest of 2000.

Stocks to Watch

As we have stated earlier, the direct beneficiary of a surge in rural demand would be companies in the FMCG sector, like Hindustan Lever. HLL has seen a sluggish topline growth over the pat two years largely because of a slowdown in demand from rural areas. The company can be expected to capitalise heavily on a revival in farm income. The markets have already anticipated this and last week several prominent funds were buying into the counter. Infact, Hindustan Lever was one of the biggest gainers in the stock market index last week. Others that could gain too include Nirma, Colgate Palmolive, Britannia Industries and Tata Tea.

The other gainers could be tractor majors who have faced a sharp slump in demand over the past two years. The decline in farm income had forced a big slump in tractor sales. Tractors sales are almost first to be impacted by a change in farm income. We expect that tractor majors such as Punjab Tractors and Mahindra & Mahindra would be biggest beneficiaries of a look up in the prospects. Both the stocks, particularly, Mahindra & Mahindra, has taken a big hit in valuations due to the fall in sales. Both the companies are fundamentally sound and have very good management.

We could see a major re-rating of the industry in the coming months. Investors could watch out for these stocks. E also expect motorcycle sales to pick up and companies Hero Honda Motors could be the biggest gainers. While other two-wheeler makers should also see a pick up in demand, Hero Honda can outperform the market by a long margin. Other manufacturers of consumer durables like colour televisions, refrigerators and washing machines could also see a surge in demand driven by consumption in rural economy. Manufacturers such as Electrolux Kelvinator, Whirlpool and Voltas could see demand rising for their products. Electrolux and Whirlpool could be particularly fancied due to their large capacities and strong brand presnce.

A surge in rural economy would also mean more transportation needs, increased housing and larger demand for services. CMIE projects the growth in services at 7 per cent in the current year. We also expect commercial vehicle makers like Telco and Ashok Leyland to gain. Cement and steel could also see increased demand from a pick up in housing activity.

Overall, we may say that the worst may soon be over for the economy and things could begin to look much better from the second half of the year. Rural India is nothing but agriculture; and since agriculture has been growing at a mere 1.9 per cent since 1995-96, so is the rural economy. Therefore, per capita rural income has fallen in the recent past. "We have a dual economic structure in which a 1.9 per cent growth economy supports more than 60 per cent of the population, and a 7.3 per cent growth economy supports the remaining 40 per cent".

The rural-urban chasm is not only deep but also "has grown substantially over the past few years". For cell phones, other durables, consumer goods and services, penetrating the rural market will be limited by poverty and lack of growth, and that "companies might find themselves reaching saturation point much sooner than expected."

This gives a misleading picture of the economy, and would perhaps have been understandable if it had been a populist politician that had equated the rural economy with agriculture to say that two-third of India's population live on only 22 per cent of the country's income, while a third live in cities and lord over 78 per cent of the GDP.

Since April last year, we have constructed what is probably the most comprehensive picture of India's rural economy—a digitised database of economic, demographic, consumption data that has been extracted and harmonised across various sources, goes back over two decades, down to 530 districts. All the evidence that we have collected, processed and analysed tells us that rural is much more than agriculture. This is true not just for the present, but has been so for quite some time. In 1993-94, the Central Statistical

Organisation conducted its last rural-urban classification of India's net domestic product (NDP, which is GDP minus depreciation).

It showed that rural India accounted for 54 per cent of the country's NDP, while agriculture contributed to 31 per cent of India's GDP. So, even if one were to account for depreciation, the rural economy of 1993-94 was quite a bit more than just agriculture, forestry and fishing. The share of rural economy is more or less the same seven years later. Our analysis shows that in 2000-01, out of India's NDP of ₹ 1,062,400 crore (₹ 10,624 billion) at constant 1993-94 prices, the share of rural India was 52 per cent.

This is how rural NDP played out in 2000-01: agriculture accounted for 46 per cent; industry took up another 21 per cent; and services 33 per cent. Between 1993-94 and 2000-01, rural NDP at constant prices grew at an average of 6.2 per cent per year. Since agriculture grew at around 2 per cent during this period, clearly the rural economy has been much more than just agriculture. There is a lot of other evidence as well that demonstrates the growth of non-agricultural activities throughout rural India. According to the Annual Survey of Industries, even in 1993-94, rural India accounted for 29 per cent of the country's organised manufacturing units; 30 per cent of its employees; 32 per cent of its output; and 30 per cent of its net value added. In 2000-01, over a rising base, rural India could speak of 36 per cent of organised manufacturing establishments, 38 per cent of its employees, 43 per cent of output; and 41 per cent of net value added.

Consider also the Census of India. In 1991, 30.6 per cent of rural households had permanent (or "pucca") houses. By 2001, this had risen to 41 per cent, over a base that was growing at 1.7 per cent a year. Between 1991 and 2001, households using LPG for cooking rose from 1 per cent to almost 6 per cent, with Himachal Pradesh leading at 22 per cent. In 2001, almost a fifth of rural households owned TV sets, and the rural regions of 10 states were significantly above the national average.

Between 1991 and 2001, the percentage of rural households with electricity connections rose from 30 per cent to 43.5 per cent and 11 states ranked well over the national rural average. In 2001, over 30 per cent of rural households kept their funds in banks or postal savings accounts. All this doesn't square up with the age-old image of rural India — that of highly indebted, underfed peasants ploughing handkerchief-sized fields under the blazing heat of the mid-day sun. That may be still be partly true of agriculture; but not of the rural economy. We won't inundate you with more evidence. Instead, let's make three points.

One, there's more to rural than just agriculture; it has a thriving and growing manufacturing and services sector. Two, between 1993-94 and 2000-2001 per capita rural income grew at the same pace as urban income. The reason why total urban income was greater has much to do with higher population growth. Three, there is considerable pent-up demand for goods as well as services such as education, telecom, medical treatment and financial products.

Those in the top quartile of rural India have been discontinuously higher spenders than the average, spending at least ₹ 180,000 crore (₹ 1,800 billion) — NSS, 55th round — in 1999-2000, with expenditure patterns that are pretty similar to urban India. Consider this: services can't constitute 52 per cent of GDP on the rump of only the urban populace.

INTEGRATED RURAL DEVELOPMENT PROGRAMME

First introduced in 1978-79, IRBD has provided assistance to rural poor in the form of subsidy and bank credit for productive employment opportunities through successive plan periods. Subsequently, Training of Rural Youth for Self Employment (TRYSEM), Development of Women and Children in Rural Areas (DWCRA), Supply of Improved Tool Kits to Rural Artisans (SITRA) and Ganga Kalyan Yojana (GKY) were introduced as sub-programmes of IRDP to take care of the specific needs of the rural population.

WAGE EMPLOYMENT PROGRAMMES

Important components of the anti-poverty strategy, Wage Employment Programmes have sought to achieve multiple objectives. They not only provide employment opportunities during lean agricultural seasons but also in times of floods, droughts and other natural calamities. They create rural infrastructure which supports further economic activity.

These programmes also put an upward pressure on market wage rates by attracting people to public works programmes, thereby reducing labour supply and pushing up demand for labour. It encompasses National Rural Employment Programme (NREP) and Rural Landless Employment Guarantee Programme (RLEGP) which were initially part of the Sixth and Seventh five year Plans.

Employment Assurance Scheme (EAS)

EAS was launched in October 1993 covering 1,778 drought-prone, desert, tribal and hill area blocks. It was later extended to all the blocks in 1997-98. The EAS was designed to provide employment in the form of manual work in the lean agricultural season. The works taken up under the programme were expected to lead to the creation of durable economic and social infrastructure and address the felt-needs of the people.

Food for Work Programme

The Food for Work programme was started in 2000-01 as a component of the EAS in eight notified drought-affected states of Chattisgarh, Gujarat, Himachal Pradesh, Madhya Pradesh, Orissa, Rajasthan, Maharastra and Uttaranchal. The programme aims at food provision through wage employment.

Food grains are supplied to states free of cost. However, lifting of food grains for the scheme from Food Corporation of India (FCI) godowns has been slow.

Rural Housing

Initiated in 1985-86, the IAY is the core programme for providing free housing to families in rural areas, targets scheduled castes (SCs)/scheduled tribes (STs), households and freed bonded laborers. The rural housing programme has certainly enabled many BPL families to acquire pucca houses; the coverage of the beneficiaries is limited given the resource constraints.

The Samagra Awas Yojana (SAY) was taken up in 25 blocks to ensure convergence of housing, provision of safe drinking water, sanitation and common drainage facilities. The Housing and Urban Development Corporation (HUDCO) has extended its activities to the rural areas, providing loans at a concessional rate of interest to economically weaker sections and low-income group households for construction of houses.

Social Security Programmes

Democratic decentralization and centrally supported Social Assistance Programmes were two major initiatives of the government in the 1990s. The National Social Assistance Programme (NSAP), launched in August 1995 marks a significant step towards fulfillment of the Directive Principles of State Policy. The NSAP has three components: a) National Old Age Pension Scheme (NOAPS); b) National Family Benefit Scheme (NFBS); c) National Maternity Benefit Scheme (NMBS).

The NSAP is a centrally-sponsored programme that aims at ensuring a minimum national standard of social assistance over and above the assistance that states provide from their own resources. The NOAPS provides a monthly pension of ₹ 75 to destitute BPL persons above the age of 65. The NFBS is a scheme for BPL families who are given ₹ 10,000 in the event of the death of the breadwinner.

The NMBS provides ₹ 500 to support nutritional intake for pregnant women. In addition to NSAP, the Annapurna scheme was launched from I April 2000 to provide food security to senior citizens who were eligible for pension under NOAPS but could not receive it due to budget constraints.

Land Reforms

In an agro-based economy of, the structure of land ownership is central to the wellbeing of the people. The government has strived to change the ownership pattern of cultivable land, the abolition of intermediaries, the abolition of zamindari, ceiling laws, security of tenure to tenants, consolidation of land holdings and banning of tenancy are a few measures undertaken. Furthermore, a land record management system is a pre-condition for an effective land reform programme.

In 1987-88, a centrally-sponsored scheme for Strengthening of Revenue Administration and Updating of Land Records was introduced in Orissa and Bihar. Although these measures have been successful (to some extent) in curbing poverty, this model has a very basic flaw. Under this model resources are transferred from urban economy to rural economy just for short term political motives. This is affecting both areas, not letting rural economy develop on its own and hampering growth and investments in urban economy.

An ideal approach should include the government, panchayats and key village personals, NGOs and private companies. This will not only help reduce this imbalance but will have a multiplier effect on the overall economy. By aligning the goals of the two parts we can convert this seemingly zero sum game into a win-win situation. It would be a very long drawn and difficult battle with conventions but the reward is worth the effort.

7

Bank Performance

This study examines the relation between management ownership and firm performance for a sample of commercial bank holding companies. To measure bank performance, we use an economic measure: Stern Stewart and Co.'s *Economic Value Added* (EVA). Prior studies of firm ownership and performance have traditionally used accounting measures of corporate performance. Exceptions are Chen, Hexter, and Hu's and McConnell and Servaes, which use Tobin's *q* as a measure of performance, but which do not focus upon commercial banks. We find that, when an economic measure of performance is used, the relation between ownership and performance of commercial banks is not monotonic, but is significantly curvilinear.

This differs from the results of Pi and Timme. We also find that the question of whether or not the CEO also holds the title of chairman of the board has no impact on bank performance. We speculate that, in commercial banks, management entrenchment, as proposed in Morck, Shleifer and Vishny, may offset the effects predicted by the convergence-of-interest hypothesis of Jensen and Meckling. Jensen and Meckling's hypothesis suggests a uniformly positive relation between management ownership and the value of the firm. Jensen and Meckling propose that an inverse monotonic relation should exist between the ownermanager's control and agency costs, and that, as ownership increases, there is increased incentive for the ownermanager to maximize the value of the firm. Berle and Means show that as firm size increases, ownership becomes diffused, thus leading to conflicts of interest between owners and managers. Jensen and Meckling and Berle and Means assume that the owner-manager is a single owner who has reduced his or her equity position in the firm. We know that in most circumstances this is not the case with the modern public corporation and management.

Therefore, it is this relation, the one between management ownership and bank performance that is examined. Principal/agent conflicts arise due to the separation of the ownership and the control of the corporation. Berle and Means emphasize that when control is distinct from ownership, those in control may deploy assets in ways that benefit those in control rather than owners.

Jensen and Meckling demonstrate that when the owner-manager sells equity in the firm to outsiders, and if both parties are utility maximizers, the owner-manager's interest will diverge from the new principals. Jensen and Meckling refer to this failure to maximize the welfare of the principal as residual loss, and feel it is likely to be the most important cost due to the principal/agent conflict. Morck, Shleifer, and Vishny propose another model in which increased ownership by the management leads to entrenchment, where the manager will indulge in non-value-maximizing behaviour. However, management's self-indulgence is expected to be less than if he or she has control but no claim on the firm's cash flows. The entrenchment hypothesis predicts that the value of the firm will be less when management is free from checks on their control, and suggests that firm performance will decline as management ownership increases. Our findings of a significantly curvilinear relation between management ownership and firm value suggest that both the convergence-of-interest effect and the entrenchment effect are at work. Specifically, our results show that firm value increases, then declines, then increases with management ownership. The issue of management ownership and performance has been addressed extensively in the corporate literature, but has received little attention in the banking literature.

The corporate literature emphasizes the relation between management or insider ownership and the performance of the firm. These studies are important to this research because they indicate that a conflict exists as to whether control influences the performance of the firm. One study that does address control and bank performance is that of Pi and Timme. They investigate the principal/agent conflicts by examining variations in performance and the relations between performance, top management team and ownership structures, and the composition of the board of directors.

Their sample consists of large publicly traded US commercial banks. Their results suggest that top management team structure affects performance, and internal monitoring devices may not be an effective control. They find that when the CEO is also chairman of the board, principal/agent conflicts may be exacerbated because of the consolidation of the decision control processes. Their results indicate that when the CEO is also chairman, cost efficiency and return on assets are lower. Conversely, cost efficiency and return on assets are positively related to non-chairman-CEO ownership, and unrelated to institutional and large blockholders' ownership, and the proportion of inside directors. The next section explains the data and methodology. The third section presents the results, and the last section summarizes and concludes the study.

DATA AND METHODOLOGY

EVA

The sample consists of 100 bank holding companies obtained from the Stern Stewart and Co. 1997 database for year ending 1996. The EVA performance data were obtained from Stern Stewart and Co. The data required for calculating selected accounting measures were taken from COMPUSTAT, which was supplemented with information from the *Standard and Poor's Stock Guide*. EVA is defined as the current-period after-tax economic earnings net of the charge for the use of capital. The procedure for estimating EVA for each bank follows Uyemura, Kantor, and Pettit's methodology:

Equation:

EVA = NOPAT - Capital Charge

where NOPAT represents "net operating profits after-tax" and "Capital Charge" is the amount of capital multiplied by the cost of capital.

EVA differs form conventional earnings in two important ways. First, NOPAT reflects operational profits adjusted to minimize accounting conventions that misrepresent economic flows or that distort the proper matching of revenues and expenses. Second, EVA assumes that management must generate sufficient revenues to cover operating expenses, interest charges, and provide the return that shareholders require as compensation for assuming risks. Prior studies traditionally used *net income* (NI), *earnings per share* (EPS), *return on equity* (ROE), or *return on assets* (ROA); all are accounting measures of performance. None of these performance measures tells us how much management has increased shareholders wealth.

EVA can lead to management decisions that are different from those based on traditional measures. Traditional measures do not reflect risk and therefore promote behaviour that aims to maximize earnings or prevent the dilution of returns. Return or ratio measures do not accurately assess shareholder value creation; rather they only indicate average profitability. The advantage of EVA is that it is dollarbased and thus, EVA maximization correlates with wealth maximization. Uyemura, Kantor, and Pettit find that EVA has the strongest correlation with *market value added* (MVA).

To calculate EVA, we need NOPAT and the capital charge. NOPAT is the operational profits of the company restated in such a way that NI is adjusted to reflect the current economics of the business. Loan loss provisions, taxes, non-recurring events, and securities accounting are the four major adjustments that are the most common adjustments that are made when calculating EVA for banks. Capital is composed of shareholders' equity plus the following: loan loss reserves, other net deferred tax credits, non-recurring events, and unamortized securities gains or losses after taxes. This ensures that if an item is not considered a component of current operations that it will be capitalized and will be assessed a capital charge.

Ownership

Previous studies use Abrecht and Locker's *Corporate Data Exchange* (*CDE*). This data set contains principal stockholder ownership information of *Fortune*

500 companies for year-end 1980, and is updated through May 1981 for holders of 5 per cent or more. For this study, ownership data were obtained from proxy statements for the year-end 1996. One of the problems with using current ownership data is availability. The *CDE Fortune 500* directory was published only once in 1981. However, ownership data is available from other sources. Anderson and Lee examine ownership data provided by four databases and proxy statements. They suggest that data collected from proxy statements are superior to data from other sources but can be expensive to acquire and time consuming to extract.

METHODOLOGY

We sought to extract certain measures of performance, ownership and control, and to determine which of the ownership or control measures was statistically significant as a predictor of performance. Because EVA is a function of a bank's size, we standardized it using year-end capital. Therefore, for performance, we used standardized measures of EVA. For measures of ownership and control, we constructed the following variables: CHM is a dummy variable, which takes on a value of 1 if the CEO is also the Chairman of the Board, and takes on a value of 0 otherwise.

TEN is the natural log of CEO tenure, expressed in years. AGE is the log of the age of the CEO. INS-BD is the log of the ratio of inside directors to total board members. INSIDE is the log of the ratio of insider ownership to total ownership. Finally, MAN is the log of the ratio of management ownership to total ownership. In order to test for possible non-linearity in the relation between management ownership and performance, we also constructed squared and cubed values of MAN. After constructing these variables for ownership and control, we looked at the correlation matrix, presented. Because of the high degree of collinearity between variables, we concluded that only CHM and MAN were sufficiently uncorrelated with the other variables to be included in our model. We therefore dropped all other variables, other than CHM and MAN, and included the squared and cubed values of MAN in order to test for possible non-linearity.

FORM OF GOVERNMENT REGULATION

Bank regulations are a form of government regulation which subject banks to certain requirements, restrictions and guidelines. This regulatory structure creates transparency between banking institutions and the individuals and corporations with whom they conduct business, among other things. Given the interconnectedness of the banking industry and the reliance that the national economy hold on banks, it is important for regulatory agencies to maintain control over the standardized practices of these institutions. Supporters of such regulation often hinge their arguments on the "too big to fail" notion.

This holds that many financial institutions hold too much control over the economy to fail without enormous consequences. This is the premise for government bailouts, in which federal financial assistance is provided to banks or other financial institutions who appear to be on the brink of collapse. The belief is that without this aid, the crippled banks would not only become bankrupt, but would create rippling effects throughout the economy. Others advocate deregulation, or free banking, whereby banks are given extended liberties as to how they operate the institution.

OBJECTIVES OF BANK REGULATION

The objectives of bank regulation, and the emphasis, vary between jurisdictions. The most common objectives are:

- Prudential—to reduce the level of risk to which bank creditors are exposed
- Systemic risk reduction—to reduce the risk of disruption resulting from adverse trading conditions for banks causing multiple or major bank failures
- Avoid misuse of banks—to reduce the risk of banks being used for criminal purposes, *e.g.* laundering the proceeds of crime
- To protect banking confidentiality
- Credit allocation—to direct credit to favoured sectors

GENERAL PRINCIPLES OF BANK REGULATION

Banking regulations can vary widely across nations and jurisdictions. This section of the article describes general principles of bank regulation throughout the world.

Minimum requirements

Requirements are imposed on banks in order to promote the objectives of the regulator. Often, these requirements are closely tied to the level of risk exposure for a certain sector of the bank. The most important minimum requirement in banking regulation is maintaining minimum capital ratios.

Supervisory review

Banks are required to be issued with a bank license by the regulator in order to carry on business as a bank, and the regulator supervises licenced banks for compliance with the requirements and responds to breaches of the requirements through obtaining undertakings, giving directions, imposing penalties or revoking the bank's licence.

Market discipline

The regulator requires banks to publicly disclose financial and other information, and depositors and other creditors are able to use this information to assess the level of risk and to make investment decisions. As a result of this, the bank is subject to market discipline and the regulator can also use market pricing information as an indicator of the bank's financial health.

INSTRUMENTS AND REQUIREMENTS OF BANK REGULATION

CAPITAL REQUIREMENT

The capital requirement sets a framework on how banks must handle their capital in relation to their assets. Internationally, the Bank for International Settlements' Basel Committee on Banking Supervision influences each country's capital requirements. In 1988, the Committee decided to introduce a capital measurement system commonly referred to as the Basel Capital Accords. The latest capital adequacy framework is commonly known as Basel III. This updated framework is intended to be more risk sensitive than the original one, but is also a lot more complex.

Reserve requirement

The reserve requirement sets the minimum reserves each bank must hold to demand deposits and banknotes. This type of regulation has lost the role it once had, as the emphasis has moved towards capital adequacy, and in many countries there is no minimum reserve ratio. The purpose of minimum reserve ratios is liquidity rather than safety. An example of a country with a contemporary minimum reserve ratio is Hong Kong, where banks are required to maintain 25 per cent of their liabilities that are due on demand or within 1 month as qualifying liquefiable assets.

Reserve requirements have also been used in the past to control the stock of banknotes and/or bank deposits. Required reserves have at times been gold coin, central bank banknotes or deposits, and foreign currency.

Corporate governance

Corporate governance requirements are intended to encourage the bank to be well managed, and is an indirect way of achieving other objectives. As many banks are relatively large, with many divisions, it is important for management to maintain a close watch on all operations. Investors and clients will often hold higher management accountable for missteps, as these individuals are expected to be aware of all activities of the institution. Some of these requirements may include:

- To be a body corporate
- To be incorporated locally, and/or to be incorporated under as a particular type of body corporate, rather than being incorporated in a foreign jurisdiction.
- To have a minimum number of directors

- To have an organisational structure that includes various offices and officers, *e.g.* corporate secretary, treasurer/CFO, auditor, Asset Liability Management Committee, Privacy Officer etc. Also the officers for those offices may need to be approved persons, or from an approved class of persons.
- To have a constitution or articles of association that is approved, or contains or does not contain particular clauses, *e.g.* clauses that enable directors to act other than in the best interests of the company may not be allowed.

Financial reporting and disclosure requirements

Among the most important regulations that are placed on banking institutions is the requirement for disclosure of the bank's finances. Particularly for banks that trade on the public market, the *Securities and Exchange Commission* (SEC) requires management to prepare annual financial statements according to a financial reporting standard, have them audited, and to register or publish them.

Often, these banks are even required to prepare more frequent financial disclosures, such as Quarterly Disclosure Statements. The Sarbanes-Oxley Act of 2002 outlines in detail the exact structure of the reports that the SEC requires.

In addition to preparing these statements, the SEC also stipulates that directors of the bank must attest to the accuracy of such financial disclosures.

Thus, included in their annual reports must be a report of management on the company's internal control over financial reporting.

The internal control report must include: a statement of management's responsibility for establishing and maintaining adequate internal control over financial reporting for the company; management's assessment of the effectiveness of the company's internal control over financial reporting as of the end of the company's most recent fiscal year; a statement identifying the framework used by management to evaluate the effectiveness of the company's internal control over financial reporting; and a statement that the registered public accounting firm that audited the company's financial statements included in the annual report has issued an attestation report on management's assessment of the company's internal control over financial reporting.

Under the new rules, a company is required to file the registered public accounting firm's attestation report as part of the annual report. Furthermore, the SEC added a requirement that management evaluate any change in the company's internal control over financial reporting that occurred during a fiscal quarter that has materially affected, or is reasonably likely to materially affect, the company's internal control over financial reporting.

Credit rating requirement

Banks may be required to obtain and maintain a current credit rating from an approved credit rating agency, and to disclose it to investors and prospective investors. Also, banks may be required to maintain a minimum credit rating. These ratings are designed to provide colour for prospective clients or investors regarding the relative risk that one assumes when engaging in business with the bank. The ratings reflect the tendencies of the bank to take on high risk endeavors, in addition to the likelihood of succeeding in such deals or initiatives. The rating agencies that banks are most strictly governed by, referred to as the "Big Three" are the Fitch Group, Standard and Poor's and Moody's.

These agencies hold the most influence over how banks are viewed by those engaged in the public market. In recent years, following the Great Recession, many economists have argued that these agencies face a serious conflict of interest in their core business model. Clients pay these agencies to rate their company based on their relative riskiness in the market. The question then is, to whom is the agency providing its service: the company or the market?

Large exposures restrictions

Banks may be restricted from having imprudently large exposures to individual counterparties or groups of connected counterparties. This may be expressed as a proportion of the bank's assets or equity, and different limits may apply depending on the security held and/or the credit rating of the counterparty.

Restricting disproportionate exposure to high risk initiatives allows regulatory agencies to prevent financial institutions from placing investor capital at unnecessary risk.

Activity and affiliation restrictions

In 1933, during the first 100 days of President Franklin D. Roosevelt's New Deal, the Securities Act of 1933 and the *Glass-Steagall Act* (GSA) were enacted, setting up a pervasive regulatory scheme for the public offering of securities and generally prohibiting commercial banks from underwriting and dealing in those securities. GSA prohibited affiliations between banks and securities firms; further restrictions on bank affiliations with non- banking firms were enacted in *Bank Holding Company Act* of 1956 (BHCA) and its subsequent amendments, eliminating the possibility that companies owning banks would be permitted to take ownership or controlling interest in insurance companies, manufacturing companies, real estate companies, securities firms, or any other non-banking company. As a result, distinct regulatory systems developed in the United States for regulating banks, on the one hand, and securities firms on the other.

TOO BIG TO FAIL AND MORAL HAZARD

Among the reasons for maintaining close regulation of banking institutions is the aforementioned concern over the global repercussions that could result from a bank's failure; the idea that these bulge bracket banks are "too big to fail". The objective of federal agencies is to avoid situations in which the government must decide whether to support a struggling bank or to let it fail. The issue, as many argue, is that providing aid to crippled banks creates a situation of moral hazard. The general premise is that while the government may have prevented a financial catastrophe for the time being, they have reinforced confidence for high risk taking and provided an invisible safety net. This can lead to a vicious cycle, wherein banks take risks, fail, receive a bailout and then continue to take risks once again.

8

Role of Commercial Banking Industry

STRATEGIC IMPLICATIONS FROM A US PERSPECTIVE

The banking industry provides an interesting and important case study of how changes in technology and regulation influence competitive structure, business strategy and industrial evolution. Indeed a narrow focus on traditional bank products and performance measures conditioned on the rapid pace of technological change confronting the industry would lead one to conclude that banking is essentially a declining industry.

In fact, according to some observers the commercial bank-an institution that conducts the twin activities of accepting deposits payable on demand and originating loans-has outlived its usefulness. Such a focus, however, misses most of the true innovations that have taken place in the industry in recent years-most notably the move towards off-balance-sheet and information-based activities.

A broader perspective shows banks evolving in ways that are enabling them to provide the same basic functions as before, but in new, more efficient ways. In the past most banks thought of themselves as delivering a set of specific, largely unrelated products to different sets of customers. Today, as a result of technological change and competitive pressures, many banks are pursuing strategies that aim to strengthen their ability to perform various functions, including, for example, financial planning for retail clients and raising capital for middle-market companies, which tend to cut across old product lines.

As a result, and in contrast to most industrial firms, many banks are offering a more diversified range of products and services than ever before with the aim of exploiting potential synergies among those products. Much of this has been made possible by the recent advances in technology, typically associated with the so-called electronic banking revolution and spurred on by the rapid development and application of the Internet.

The economic rationale for banks' past existence relates directly to their two core activities-taking in deposits payable on demand and providing non-marketable loans. It seems clear that both activities essentially require the institution to come up with cash at short notice-that is, to provide liquidity. Economy of scale in the provision of liquidity thus explains why both activities are provided by the same entity.

Deregulation and technological innovations have served to increase competition in the financial services industry, which has forced commerical banks to concentrate on the essentials of liquidity provision. This is why the outward nature of bank activities has changed significantly for both retail and wholesale customers. For example banks around the globe often sell their loans instead of holding them on their balance sheets, offer consumers unsecured personal credit lines through credit cards and provide back-up lines for commercial paper instead of extending loans. Despite these different types of activity, it should be obvious to the astute observer that the underlying economic rationale for these activities-the provision of liquidity-has not changed.

Beneath the surface of the dramatic changes in financial products and services, the fundamental banking business of liquidity provision seems alive and well. Moreover, in the course of performing their traditional activities banks have acquired competencies that enable them to perform a variety of other financial and non-financial activities that deregulation and innovation have opened up to them.

RECENT TRENDS IN THE US BANKING INDUSTRY

Since the 1970s, what is commonly called the commercial banking industry in the US has evolved into two distinct and, for the most part, differently focused industries: the 'global banking industry' and the 'community', 'local' or regional banking industry.

As might be expected, banks operating in the global banking industry or market compete in national and international markets while community banks compete largely in local markets. This is at least partly because global banks have large corporate customers with special financing and information requirements compared with consumers and small businesses.

Thus US global banks face competition from different sources than those faced by community banks. For example global banks face competition from the commercial paper market, investment and merchant banks and major foreign banks, all of which compete in national or international markets.

Consequently the geographical market for many of these global bank customers and services is at least national in scope but is more often global. In contrast, the geographical market of the community banking industry is still largely local, approximated by metropolitan statistical areas (MSAs) or non-MSA counties. The preference of consumers and small businesses for local banks is presumably due to the lower information and transaction costs relative to their funds and may also reflect the information costs facing non-local financial firms. Whatever the reason, it is apparent that US bankers are keenly aware of this preference and treat community or regional banking as a very localised activity that often requires a local presence. For example the number of bank branches in the US increased by about 74 per cent between 1970 and 1990, even as the number of banks and banking organisations declined. For many years it has been apparent that community banks are significantly influenced by local market conditions that may influence only some, if any, of the activities of global banks. This has provided support for the view that local banking is a separate industry from the global banking industry. This view is also supported by studies of the cost structure of the US banking industry.

Many of these studies have found that global and community banks do indeed operate on different long-term average cost curves, that is, these banks operate in different industries. While firms in both of these industries operate as financial intermediaries, offer insured deposits and the other standard packages of services, local banks have traditionally served a distinctly separate class of customer and competed in fairly protected local markets. As a result it has been generally assumed that developments in the global banking industry will only marginally affect community or regional banks.

However, with the advent of dramatic technological change in the form of various electronic or Internet banking developments and the increase in the minimum efficient size of banks as a result of technological developments, local banks can no longer assume that their local markets will remain unattractive or inaccessible to global banks and their global networks.

Thus local and regional banks should be aware that their market share is at risk. This is easy to see given that the overlap between these two industries is limited in an important way that is indicative of the basic difference between the two industries. Specifically, while banking organis-ations that operate in the global banking industry can and do operate in the community or local banking industry, the reverse does not hold.

That is, community and local banks tend not to operate in the global banking industry. However, just as technological developments represent a threat to the long-term viability of community banks, when used appropriately they also present an opportunity for these banks to access the global banking market through the electronic networks offered by members of the global banking industry. Two interesting avenues for examining technological change and its influence on the banking industry are

- Regulation and the legal environment resulting from changes in banking technology, and
- Changes in the competitive environment facing financial institutions.

Regarding the regulation of Internet banking and related changes induced by technology, the current consensus among US banking scholars seems to be that market arrangements for electronic money and Internet banking should be allowed to evolve unencumbered by regulation and government intervention. This should remain the case as long as the safety, soundness and stability of the payments and financial system are not impaired by these developments. This essentially means that regulatory intervention in electronic money and internet banking will take place in a parallel fashion to the regulation that already exists for non-electronic non-Internet banking. That is, if the paper equivalent of an electronic transaction is regulated, then so should the electronic transaction. In this environment, regulatory attention is focused on evaluating the threat of those electronic transactions which have no paper equivalent to the safety and soundness of the payments and financial system.

Many concerns have also been expressed about the nature and structure of the US banking industry in the next 20 to 30 years; in particular, whether local and regional banks will be able to compete with the larger global banks and whether banking services will continue to be owned by traditional bankers or by software developers or telecommunications firms. As should be clear from this introduction, there is reason to believe that banking services will continue to be provided by banks (both global and regional), albeit in a much more competitive environment.

TECHNOLOGICAL CHANGE AND THE INDUSTRIAL ORGANISATION OF US BANKING MARKETS

The impact of technological change on the banking industry (both globally and locally), particularly the development of Internet banking, is best examined using the tools of modern industrial organisation theory. Though many banks might eventually offer combinations of electronic cash and electronic money, the decision to become a fully fledged provider of electronic or Internet banking services involves irreversible investment and output decisions.

This irreversibility, combined with uncertainty about customer demand for electronic banking services, implies that banks (and other firms for that matter) will typically face a precommitment decision when deciding whether to enter the Internet banking business and the scope of such involvement. This decision will uniquely influence the environment surrounding the emergence of an electronic or Internet banking technology.

Given these elements of irreversibility and demand uncertainty, if banks are profit-maximising firms we can expect incumbent or dominant banks (typically the large global banks in the US) to act strategically when deciding the scope of their involvement in Internet banking. Hence they can be expected to undertake entry-deterring investments to the extent that the marginal benefit of such investments (the profit that flows from reduced future competition) exceeds their current cost.

Investment in excess capacity is one such strategy. Whether or not investment in excess capacity constitutes a credible threat by dominant firms depends on what potential entrants think the post-entry regime will be, on whether or not there are economies of scale and scope in the provision of electronic and Internet banking services, and on the size of minimum output relative to the market.

Whether incumbents find investment in excess capacity profitable depends on their certainty that such investment will deter entry, and perhaps on the possibility of free-riding by other incumbent firms. Investment could also be used as a way of responding to entry rather than as a device for precluding entry.

If customers incur costs by switching from their current bank to a new provider of financial services, then incumbents or dominant firms may strategically expand output to attract customers and make entry more difficult. This involves some sacrifice of short-term profits and should be considered as a strategic investment in the customer base.

It is clearly costly for incumbent or dominant firms to carry excess capacity or to make other strategic investments to deter entry. If incumbents can raise the costs incurred by actual or potential rivals while suffering smaller cost increases themselves, they will generally find it profitable to do so.

The existence of significant demand uncertainty also implies that dominant firms find it worthwhile to engage in predatory or entry-limiting behaviour in order to create and maintain a reputation as a firm that will fight entry, or as a low-cost firm.

Although such a strategy may be unprofitable in the particular market in which it is carried out, it does discourage entry into other markets and thus may be optimal for dominant firms from an overall point of view.

Barring the success of the above strategies, cooperation may emerge as a key force behind the evolution of electronic and Internet banking. Such cooperative arrangement are commonly referred to as strategic alliances or joint ventures.

RECENT CHANGES CONSISTENT WITH THE PREDICTIONS OF MODERN INDUSTRIAL ORGANISATION THEORY

Two developments are responsible for the interest and growth in electronic and Internet banking around the globe. These developments are significant for both global banks and community and local banks in the US and elsewhere. First, computing costs have dropped steeply in recent years; second, electronic telecommunications innovations have simultaneously increased the capacity for communication usage in financial services and reduced the importance of geographically based financial services.

Historically, both global and local bankers viewed themselves as owning customers. They provided a range of services to customers, including current and savings accounts, credit cards and settlement and clearing procedures. Customers only had to choose a bank, deposit their money and withdraw it in whatever form they chose at some future date. In many countries, and especially the US, the types of service that banks and other financial firms could offer customers were restricted by law-for example, until recently US firms that issued securities were not allowed to accept deposits.

In addition there were statutory restrictions on the types of entity that could accept customer deposits. A prime example of this was the US Bank Holding Company Act, which prohibited companies from owning banks if the parent company was engaged in activities that were not closely related to banking.

The deregulation of banking and bank deposit activities has brought deposit rates to competitive levels in most banking markets. Indeed, with the depositor's cost of telephoning or e-mailing competitors falling to zero, banks have had to rethink their deposit and retail business. While synergies remain in liquidity provision, all banks enjoy this synergy, so the challenge is to build a competitive deposit business in ways that create rents for the bank.

In fact there are only a limited number of ways in which long-term profits can be made. The holy grail for all banks (both global and local) continues to be captive customers who are price-insensitive, that is, have inelastic demand curves. In the absence of this, banks must innovate continuously or find scale economies that enable them to become low-cost producers.

It helps, of course, if there is substantial first-mover advantage in a product so that the profits from innovation or scale can be reaped over a longer period. In the days when a customer had to be physically present to undertake most banking activities, proximity to a bank branch was important. A bank's customers were those who lived closest to the branch. Higher prices could be charged or lower interest rates paid to their customers because the customer's costs of switching to another bank were high. But today it is no longer clear which customers a bank should target. The geographical reach of any given bank has increased as a result of lower communication costs. At the same time the cost to the customer of switching banks has fallen.

Banks, both global and regional, have one big advantage when deciding who to target, how to bring them in and how to increase their switching costs: so-called customer inertia. Many customers have been slow to use the phone or other telecommunications media to reach other financial service providers-there seems to be considerable inertia and the learning curve is apparently steep. For example, while the number of ATMs in the US went up from 13 800 in 1979 to about 187 000 in 1998, the number of bank branches also went up over the same period. Many customers in the US still prefer to use bank branches for such activities as depositing cheques despite the fact that ATMs can do the job just as well as tellers in manned branches.

Local branches provide some human interaction, and hence are less technologically intimidating. Moreover bankers (at least in the US) have been seen as more trustworthy than other financial service providers, such as stockbrokers and insurance agents. Some bankers correctly view their branch network and current depositor base as an opportunity. Their idea is to use the branch as the gateway through which the depositor can access the entire financial system. They would like to convert the physical contact and trust they currently enjoy with depositors into high switching costs so that when depositors become more technically sophisticated, or when access costs diminish further, they are not tempted to switch banks.

There are a number of ways in which financial service companies can increase switching costs. Providing personal advisory services may be the costliest approach, but it also has the most potential to build personal bonds that are hard to break. Another approach is to offer a variety of services and to integrate them so that they appear seamless to the customer. For instance a bank that can offer to the customer mortgage, credit card and insurance services can link all these accounts to the deposit account, as well as to overdraft facilities and home equity loans. Within limits, authorised payments can be made automatically, if necessary by borrowing on behalf of the customer at the least-cost rate. The bank can also provide a consolidated statement to the customer at the end of every month. The advantage of being the sole access point is that the cost of switching to a different access point increases with the number of services provided (and if the customer uses software, with the degree of specialisation of the software needed to gain access).

Clearly this strategy is so designed that convenience is the most important feature, but this raises an interesting question: should the bank offer access to more than its own products and services? It should, and not simply because it will become more attractive as an access point if it is able to offer the best services. By offering other firms' services, it can also promise its customers that they will not be overcharged, ripped-off or gouged later if they lock themselves into the bank (economists call this technique a second sourcing). Moreover the bank that controls access is in a position to extract rents from the other service providers because it controls the prime asset: captive customers.

This approach has been successfully followed by the discount broker Charles Schwab, and by Intuit Home Banking. For example Schwab's mutual fund provides its customers with access to over 1100 mutual funds from over 100 fund families, consolidating all fund statements into one statement for the customer. The market power gained by Schwab through its customer control access is evident in Fidelity's decision to withdraw most of its popular funds from this scheme.

INNOVATION

Innovation is clearly one way in which a financial institution can differentiate itself from the pack. But most successful product innovations on the retail side are easily imitated (except those based on proprietary technology). One way to build sustained advantage is to use innovation to build a captive customer base. In a sense this is what Charles Schwab has done. It was one of the first brokers to allow customers to trade electronically. In the process it cross-sold a variety of products, including information services and mutual fund services that locked the electronic customer into a relationship with Schwab. At the same time these customers give Schwab the necessary scope to pursue further innovation.

Another kind of innovation is to identify activities with high transaction costs and to reduce those costs by internalising the transactions. To the extent that there are first-mover advantages to this approach, a bank can build a long-term franchise. For example Citibank recognised that there were still very high costs involved in making cross-border payments.

By setting up a global network of branches and developing tremendous expertise in foreign exchange transactions it succeeded in internalising cross-border payments. The savings in transactions costs coupled with the very high volume of transactions have made this a very profitable franchise. Moreover other banks are unlikely to challenge this franchise because of the high cost of setting up a competing network and the formidable position now occupied by Citibank.

TECHNOLOGY

It is clear that nothing beats being a low-cost financial services provider and that automation is a proven way to reduce costs. For example the real cost of an electronic deposit in the US fell from four times the cost of processing a cheque in 1979 to less than half the cost in 1998.

Since automation requires a substantial investment, large global banks have a competitive advantage. Indeed this may also explain the large-scale consolidation taking place in the US banking industry.

In recent years the percentage of assets in banks with over $100 billion more than doubled between 1979 and 1998 while the percentage of assets in small banks dropped by more than 50 per cent. Most economic analysts of the payments business suggest that it is a large-fixed-cost business. Thus the economics of the situation require the service provider to maximise its customer contacts in order to spread these fixed costs over a larger base.

Since variable costs are low, maximising the customer base maximises profits. Hence the private provider will be motivated to control a larger and larger share of the market. This could lead to increased market concentration and market (monopoly) power, with adverse consequences for small community and regional banks.

Given that there are large sunken costs in the business, standard economic theory implies that the incumbent provider will be able to sustain its monopoly position, that is, market forces will not keep the firm from exploiting its monopoly position. Being in a business that is subject to mild increasing returns to scale-that is, the larger the firm the cheaper its average cost of producing electronic financial services-dominant firms will naturally seek to become larger and will engage in entry-limiting and/or pricing behaviour to limit competition.

Again, this implies that small regional banks will find it difficult to compete. Finally, electronic payments systems are subject to significant network externalities, scope economies and economies of sequencing. A dominant firm with the industry standard software or hardware will have a definite competitive advantage over all new entrants, which must adopt this software or hardware in order to offer complete access.

The dominant firm is thus able to exploit scope economies and gain access to additional customers, again leading to increased market share and power. The business also has elements of economies of sequencing, which are present if an integrated technology is more productive than separate technologies.

ECONOMIES OF SCALE AND SCOPE

Scale and scope economies typically have important implications for the structure of an industry. If such economies are substantial, ceteris paribus an industry will tend to be relatively concentrated and entry will be difficult. There is a large body of literature on scale and scope economies in the commercial banking industry in most developed countries. Most of this literature focuses on data for banks with under $1 billion in total assets, which in essence are part of the community or regional banking industry.

The evidence suggests that scale economies (especially in US banking) are quite modest and are exhausted at low levels of output. This bodes well for the competitive viability of smaller regional and community banks. On the other hand, more recent studies of larger global-type banks show that significant scale economies are possible for these banks. This raises questions about the viability of local and regional banks throughout the developed world. What is one to make of these mixed findings?

Since the 1970s, with the onset of deregulation, increased expansion and new electronic technologies, questions have been raised about the competitive viability of small and regional banks. A fairly wide range of empirical evidence suggests that small banks are both viable and profitable. For example it has been argued that the scale economy research findings imply that smaller banks are able to compete on an equal footing with large global banks, or at least with respect to basic banking services.

Moreover, recent research on managerial inefficiency in US banking suggests that these types of inefficiencies dominate those identified with inefficient scale. If one believes these findings, small community and regional banks do indeed have a continuing role to play in the industry. Nonetheless there is reason to believe that small and regional banks will continue to be threatened by developments arising from technological change.

Studies of the impact of technological change in the US banking industry suggest that the minimum efficient size of banks (especially in the US) has increased as a result of technological change. This combined with the probable impact of electronic or Internet banking on the structure of the industry, strongly suggests that regional and small local banks will have a tougher time competing in the future.

AN INTERNET BANKING WORLD AND THE ROLE OF LOCAL BANKS

Even though fundamental competencies have not changed, in order to compete, global banks and community and regional banks can pursue different strategies in the world of Internet banking. Banking scholars have identified several strategies to deal with the technological revolution in the financial services industry. These strategies involve serving different customer segments in a variety of ways. Strategic decisions involve both operating decisions and product decisions and can be made locally on a decentralised basis or on a centralised basis.

Decentralised operating and product or service decision making has the advantage of keeping local bank decision makers in close proximity with the customer and local information. The disadvantage of this approach is that senior management may not have complete control over the operations side, while on the product or service side the bank may miss opportunities to exploit economies of scope and scale.

By default, this strategy is a natural one for small community and regional banks, given their size and/or lack of extensive branch networks. However some small banks have attempted to mitigate the disadvantages of the strategy by outsourcing back office operations and joining large electronic networks to enhance their customers' access. However, in attempting to circumvent the weaknesses of the decentralised strategy these banks may have to share a substantial proportion of the profits from their customer base with the access providers, and they also risk their customers being captured or stolen by the access providers.

Clearly the decentralisation strategy will pose significant risks and problems for small banks in the future as geographical location becomes less important in defining a bank's customer base. A strategy of decentralised operational decision making and centralised product and service decision making makes sense for banks that possess special localised knowledge about their markets, but recognise that retail customers (in all but the most remote and isolated markets) in an Internet banking world will have fairly low switching costs.

It will also be difficult for banks to make significant profits from traditional products that come to be offered on a commodity basis. Thus, it will become important for banks to offer customers a wide choice of a products and services (which emerge from a centralised product and services strategy) and to offer local or decentralised pricing differences and advice only for those products that are deemed to be of high value-added.

A strategy of centralised operational and product and service decision making recognises the growing standardisation of banking products generally, though not exclusively. Such a strategy also implies more uniformity in operations and products regardless of location, since location is less relevant in an increasingly electronic world.

Like the findings of studies on the cost effectiveness of banks using decentralised and centralised decision making more generally, it is likely that a totally centralised strategy will not be optimal for most banks. Such a strategy seems to work for the McDonald restaurant chain but it probably will not for most banks, given their special competency in local information gathering and processing.

Based on this discussion, it seems fairly obvious that a totally decentralised strategy, especially on the retail side, will become less and less profitable as we move into a more integrated electronic and Internet banking world. Customers will become more sophisticated, they will move up the learning curve, and the cost of electronic hardware and software will continue to decline, making this mode of transacting even more cost effective relative to paper and face-to-face contact. To be sure, no one knows exactly how long this will take, so the strategy may be profitable in the short run. A global strategy, on the other hand, is likely to be beyond the means of most small and medium-sized banks. For most banks, then, a strategy that exploits local market-information advantages and product synergies, scale economies and innovation seems most appropriate.

PERVASIVE COMPUTING: REALLY GETTING TO KNOW YOUR TOASTER

The avalanche of technologies developed in the last twenty years has conditioned consumers to expect a new wave of devices in ever-shortening cycles, yet the pervasiveness of technology is the least understood aspect, and its implications for a global society are only just beginning to come to light. Studying the application of bio-integration to the socio-economic fabric of human relationships and the interface to contemporary business has barely begun.

It is apparent that the consumer's love affair with electronic gadgetry is far from over; in fact, it could be argued that it is only just starting. The rate of technology adoption is increasing with each new generation of potential users. Although all members of society do not share this affection for technology, the pervasiveness of technology continues to impact each individual either by direct participation or as an indirect consequence. The pervasiveness of computing has many implications for financial services companies, and in some cases distracts from a clear value proposition.

Is new technology spawning a revolution in how we work and live or is our lifestyle driving the need for new technology? The architect/philosopher Richard Buckminster Fuller noted in 1980 that the time between the creation of a technology and its practical adoption by society varied by technical category and application. In his words:

My half-century experience also discovered the natural, unacceleratable lags existing between inventions and industrial uses in various technical categories, which occur as follows: in electronics – two years; aerodynamics – five years; automobiles – ten years; railroading – fifteen years; big-city buildings twenty-five years; single family dwellings – fifty years.

This commercialization time lag in technology represents the time span necessary to educate the population about the benefits of new technologies, convince society of the improvements that such new technologies bring and allow the business infrastructure to reach a point of production that will make it economically viable. Architects incorporate the practical advantages of new technology into structures that shape our behaviour, while architecture involves employing a more complex process of changing social taste. The matter of adoption of any sort of technology by individuals is an exercise in shaping the behaviour of consumers as new technological marvels emerge.

The same technological time lag can be equated to financial services products and the technologies found in the four bands in the technology spectrum (for example ATMs, credit cards, retina scanners, and the Internet) and should be a critical part of strategic technology planning. Individual technologies can be plotted along a maturity curve and compared to a similar curve indicating the level of social acceptance. The delta between the curves represents the opportunity to experiment and refine the application of the technology as well as a barometer to set the expectations of the firm on the return on investment.

Technologies mature at a predictable rate determined by the innovation of their components. However, social acceptance of technology occurs at a rate that varies from culture to culture or even within the socio-economic classes in one given culture.

For example, the use of mobile phones for banking is more popular in Scandinavia than high-tech Boston, Massachusetts. Furthermore, there is a synergistic relationship between technology, people, and how people work in the lifecycle of technology creation, adoption, impact and design. Fuller's observation on technological latency brings into question the accelerating rate at which society is adopting technology. Technological visions such as

Microsoft's Home of the Future and the Halifax's Future Retail Bank are early indications that the nature of work will radically change during the next twenty years.

It can be argued that not only will the nature of work change, but where one works will undergo a transformation. For example, retail banking will need to rethink how branches are designed in order to accommodate the shift from a transaction to an advisory business, which will indeed be different in each culture serviced. Organizations such as BWA\Chiat\Day, which have radically altered the way in which people think and work by inventing work spaces that stretch beyond the conventional designs of today's business, inadvertently provided financial services firms with a glimpse into the future of financial services.

Technological gadgetry – and the pervasiveness of computing – carries with it a familiar technology banner, resembling the messages from the early twentieth-century electric companies about removing the complexity of life and enabling users greater work efficiencies, that it will provide members of our modern society with additional leisure time. Alluring words, which should be remembered as you carry your laptop, mobile phone and personal digital assistant (PDA) on your next family vacation.

Stripping away the marketing hype, pervasive computing is capable of placing the user in the centre of the technological universe, allowing the individual to control the amount of intrusion permissible by other members in the connected society.

Technology is as pervasive as you will allow it to become. Business looks at pervasive computing as a new method of interacting with consumers, whereas consumers should view it as a way of employing technology to perform tasks on their behalf. The underlying dilemma that pervasive computing brings to the surface is the new balance that individuals must strike between work, leisure and social interactions. The product of this balance is a redefinition of when, where and how people work.

A strong argument can be made that the impact of technology will be the redefinition of the socio-economic contract with business and a reexamination of the nature of work. It is not incomprehensible that the result of society embracing pervasive computing is anytime, anywhere work. Technology is redefining where and how organizations work by removing the need to be in a specific geography, at a specific time. Many financial services firms, organized under traditional hierarchical command and control structures that were established because of the need to regulate the activities of subordinates, will find moving into a matrix structure difficult unless ample investment is made in training and education.

In today's world, manufacturing, consulting and research organizations are realizing that the ability to act unfettered by work hours, geography or corporate bureaucratic structure is not creating more leisure time for employees; in practice it is enabling a freeing up of work time, resulting in additional capacity. The proliferation of technology also creates opportunities to redefine the structure of organizations and establish new functional disciplines. A new skill that individuals will need to develop is striking a balance between these two diametrically opposed forces of work and leisure. As the lines between work and play become blurred, there may be opportunities for comingled activities to occur. For example, an employee working at home for some portion of the week can order supplies for the office and home at the same time on the same Internet site using two different payment technologies, as well as communicating with colleagues and customers on the telephone and Internet while performing many other traditional in-house tasks without commuting.

Described in a business context, pervasive technology operates within a framework which can be represented by a diagram comprising four levels of conductivity similar to concentric circles in which you are at the epicentre. Individuals can add 'layers' to their epicentre as they grow more accepting of technology and more adept at using its capabilities.

LEVEL ONE TECHNOLOGIES

The first level is composed of smart devices equipped with microprocessors, called appliances, which are attached to you and facilitate your lifestyle, including home devices, wearable computing and biometric feedback mechanisms. These devices are basically automated methods of recognizing a person based on a physiological or behavioural characteristic.

For financial services companies, these devices provide new avenues for secure transactions because of their ability to identify a single individual or entity. Level one technologies centre on the point of interaction or an interchange of value, either monetary, informational or data. Micropayments, billing data, usage information and other transactions can be used to develop a profile of customer behaviour in retail banking applications.

The same model can be applied to small businesses and other entities such as government departments, not to act as Big Brother, but to optimize operating expenses and plan future budgetary requirements.

LEVEL TWO TECHNOLOGIES

Level two technologies that represent you and perform duties on your behalf are commonly referred to as agents, including bio-enhancement, intelligent agents, robots and avatars. Intelligent agents are autonomous, adaptive computer programmes that operate within software environments such as operating systems and database networks. They assist users with routine computer tasks being tailored to accommodate individual user habits.

Avatars are three-dimensional representations of individuals in cyberspace that users may utilize to represent themselves in both form and task. At the moment, avatars are inanimate objects. However, in the near future they may be animated to further express the personality that end users wish to portray. These technologies give you the ability to represent yourself in the eEconomy, proposing the following question: When you select the physical appearance and personality of your avatar, will it reflect you or someone you would like to be?

Concerning the financial services community, level two technologies are a treasure-trove of opportunities in the development of intelligent agents that can seek out the highest yielding savings rate or the best mortgage terms to fit individual circumstances.

These agents could be employed to assess conditions on the stock market, interrogate individual securities, analyse currency rates and evaluate foreign market fluctuations. Intelligent agents will be crafted into a host of highly specialized functions that have yet to be imagined.

LEVEL THREE TECHNOLOGIES

Mechanisms on the third level are designed to keep you interfaced to the relentless stream of data generated by society by linking you to the information that is relevant to you. Technologies such as global positioning satellites (GPSs), bluetooth, wireless application protocol (WAP) and a host of new devices will act as data interchange brokers. Interface technologies are an integral part of the following example. With your smart card's stored value-chip in your mobile phone, you approach a cold beverage machine, make a selection and then transmit digital currency to it by pressing a key on the phone.

The machine accepts your token and dispenses the beverage, sends the token to the bank via its cellular modem and transmits the reduction in inventory to the beverage distributor.

In this scenario, cash has moved from your account to your card, from your card to the dispenser, and finally to the accounts receivable of the beverage company, eliminating the need for physical cash pick-up, armoured car services, lock box operations and a suite of support services.

Level three technologies present financial services firms with an opportunity to facilitate transactions across markets, suppliers, consumers, nations and all parts of the Internet. Put simply, these technologies are the tools of the twenty-first-century intermediary. The fees associated with these types of transaction will obviously be commoditized over time and command very thin margins, indicating that operational efficiency will be the key factor in sustaining long-term viability.

LEVEL FOUR TECHNOLOGIES

Finally, fourth level prescriptive technologies, called regulators, are designed to keep you within the designated limits of a process or a set of rules in society. They include radio-controlled ankle restraints, anti-theft devices for automobiles and the pet chip, an electronic dog tag that is inserted under the skin of your pet. These technologies can act both passively and actively.

The application of these technologies to financial services is in its infancy. One can imagine microsensors embedded throughout an automobile providing an insurance adjuster with the data to assess damage incurred during an accident.

DATA, INFORMATION AND EVERYDAY LIFE

Another aspect of pervasive computing is the challenge that it creates for data replication and information usability, including establishing corporate data-sharing policies to regulate the level and detail of information being passed to value chain partners.

One can speculate that if there is a direct relationship between data and value, the underlying value of information will be commoditized or worth less over time. Every piece of information has a half-life of usefulness to the individual or organization that assigns.

its original value. For example: for a stock trader, the value of up to the minute stock price information is extremely high; that same data on the following day is less valuable as a single piece of data, although it may still be valuable when plotted with similar pieces of data to form a chart or graph. Ultimately, to the stock trader, the individual stock quotation is almost valueless at some point in the future.

However, as that same element of data becomes less valuable to the trader, it increases in value to a stock analyst or fund manager. One can conclude that there is a direct relationship between information and its perceived value which is relative to who set the value on the information. This relationship between information and value is critically important to financial services organizations because of the nature of the data, received from third-party sources, passing through the business process within the firm to value chain partners.

Surprisingly, organizations are continually disappointed when they discover the often dysfunctional state of customer data that was in many cases a critical element in merger or acquisition negotiations. Often the value of the customer data is drastically reduced when the labour cost associated with bringing it up to date is applied.

Regardless of the data produced by these new technologies, it is difficult to predict how people during the next five years will use these technologies in everyday life. The more information that is collected about an individual, the greater the possibility that it can be mishandled and simply increase the cost of operations.

THE INTENT OF TECHNOLOGY

Often the purpose of a technology's initial design is derailed by the necessities of business or the way it is embraced by society. For example, the developers of television thought that its primary application was to give everyone the opportunity to receive a college education at home; however, today's television programming schedules are a long way from that ideal.

From the noble ideal of television's forefathers, its use was quickly transformed into an entertainment delivery device supported by product advertising, moving to its present state as a mechanism for selling products interrupted by entertainment programming. In order to draw a parallel between the pervasiveness of technology in everyday life, one can examine the pervasiveness of product advertising on television.

Television programming was merely supported by product commercials that provided the viewer with a view of life with the product in 10–30 seconds. Now, the products are simply integrated into the programming, noticeable as the actors or actresses in the programme strategically hold a beverage can so that the audience is able to read the label. Financial services organizations are presented with a wide range of opportunities to leverage these technologies into product offerings that supplement our everyday lives and streamline core banking services.

Pervasive technologies provide a financial services firm with the opportunity to rethink what they offer, how it is delivered and, more importantly, why a product or service offering is valuable to a customer. The long-term implications of these technologies are to change our view of technology as an asset and begin to manage it as a liability. This is not to say that technology should be treated as a liability; on the contrary, the management of technology should be as if its value declines over time.

So as to put this concept into perspective, the legacy of banking technology is rooted in the high capital equipment cost that was an investment with a useful lifespan, requiring maintenance and support personnel. Thus, the typical classification of technology as an asset depreciating over time while providing a mechanism for improved information flow. However, technology is advancing at an accelerated rate, making older technology not only less valuable, but commanding a higher cost to maintain.

Despite the rapid decay of technological value, technology is still regarded as an essential asset of the organization, one without which it cannot function. The idea of treating technology as a liability is not an oversimplification of the balance between technology investment and technology deployment; it is merely to say that the technology should be viewed and managed differently from the way in which it was managed in the past.

This can be seen in the following example: there is a fundamental difference between the strategy of an equity fund manager and a bond portfolio manager. Both specialists are managing assets with strategies that come from two very different philosophies on investing. Taking these conditions into account, the management of the technology liability will be different from core back office systems to end user or consumer devices. If one considers that consumer retail delivery devices, such as PDAs, PCs, WAP phones and many others, will continue to experience a high turnover due to the nature of the innovation of devices and the demand for new technologies by consumers, it can be concluded that the delivery of retail banking products using these technologies will have a half-life much shorter than a core processing system. Simply, the rate of the half-life of technology is proportional to the distance to the end user. Core systems are replaced at a rate of five to ten years and retail end user technologies range from six months to four years.

The key althought to consider when treating the management of technology as a liability is that each technology should be handled according to its application to the business process that it serves and linked to a realistic expectation of a phased retirement. Again, the closer a technology is to the consumer, the faster the rate of decay and the greater the tendency to overmanage the asset. For example, a consultant was engaged to review the operating cost of the technology group within a large bank, and found an ongoing cost of warehousing a stockpile of outdated PCs because they were a depreciated asset.

The cost of warehousing these non-functioning computers, coupled with the cost of the labour associated with inventorying and tracking these assets, was greater than the new replacement value. Put simply, for the amount of money being spent on storing these outdated PCs, they could be purchasing new ones, as indeed they were.

Pervasive computing amplifies the fact that technology is ever changing. A general rule can be applied to thinking about managing pervasive technologies: the closer the technology is to the end user, the more it will be subject to change. Therefore, the key to providing pervasive technology services is a robust architecture that anticipates a continuous change of delivery platforms. The by-product of combining pervasive computing with evolving Internet technologies is to rethink core banking operations and redesign how banks work.

THE DARK SIDE OF NEW TECHNOLOGY

It is not hard to imagine a darker side to pervasive technologies as the intrusion into everyday life moves from something controlled by a consumer to an action regulated by a governing authority. Combinations of technologies have been coupled together to allowing a pet owner to pinpoint a lost pet using GPS technology.

A pet owner can elect to have this technology implanted under the skin of a cat or dog (in the case of farmers, sheep, cattle, horses) to determine where an animal is located if it becomes separated from the owner. Several organizations have discussed making this technology available to parents, allowing a similar transponder to be implanted under a child's skin to eliminate the problem of missing or abducted children. It is not beyond the range of

Orwellian thinking to imagine the next evolution of this technology – a governing authority requires the insertion a GPS chip under the skin of citizens to monitor their actions and whereabouts. Regardless of the intent of these technologies, they will continue to raise questions about ethics, morality and social consciousness, creating new social responsibilities for business while redefining the relationship between technology and a diverse global population.

For financial services firms, another dark side looms in the distance. In a connected environment in which a customer's home provides massive amounts of usage data, for example lights, computer use, phone use and other data-supporting activities, the need to secure and encrypt this data arises because a criminal monitoring the data will know exactly when people are not home.

From a positive viewpoint, a variety of these GPS technologies could be employed in the physical world and cyberspace to track a variety of illegal activities, in order to reduce money laundering and drug trafficking, for example. As governments continue to develop new responsibilities for financial services providers to know the sources of depositors' funds, these technologies have an enormous potential to be used as a regulatory mechanism.

Regardless of the final evolution of the pervasiveness of technology, its potential over time to alter the social contract between employees and employer, taxpayers and governments, customer and financial services institutions is as predictable as the effect of radio, television and the PC.

The adoption of a technology will fundamentally interrupt the traditional relationships between parties and market forces, and, as has been proven, a planned design will not be able to reconfigure the way in which these relationships are maintained and executed. In conclusion, the implication to financial services is to develop a clear understanding of these trends, interpret how value can be added and create services that facilitate the transition.

9

Central Banking

Central Bank of India, a government-owned bank, is one of the oldest and largest commercial banks in India. It is based inMumbai which is the financial capital of india and capital city of state of Maharashtra. The bank has 4600 branches and 4 extension counters across 27 Indian states and three Union Territories. At present, Central Bank of India has overseas office at Nairobi, Hong Kong and a joint venture with Bank of India, Bank of Baroda, and the Zambian government. The Zambian government holds 40 per cent stake and each of the banks has 20 per cent. Recently it has also opened a representative office at Nairobi in Kenya.

Central bank of India is one of 18 Public Sector banks in India to get recapitalisation finance from the government over the next 24 months.

Central Bank of India has approached the Reserve Bank of India (RBI) for permission to open representative offices in five more locations - Singapore, Dubai, Doha and London. As on 31 March 2011, the bank's reserves and surplus stood at – 68688 million. Its total business at the end of the last fiscal amounted to – 2,22,124(approx) million.

THE MEANING OF CENTRAL BANK

Central bank is the supreme monetary institution, which is at the apex of the monetary and banking structure of a country. It is the leader of money market and as such controls, regulates and supervises the activities of commercial banks. It is the central monetary authority, which manages the currency and credit policy of the country and functions as a banker to the government as well as to the commercial banks. It is difficult to define central bank accurately.

However, different definitions have been given emphasizing one or more functions of the central bank. De Kock defined central as "a bank which constitutes the apex of the monetary and banking structure of the country."

According to Vera Smith, "the primary definition of central bank is a banking system in which a single bank has either a complete or a residuary monopoly of note issue."

According to the Bank for International Settlements, a central bank is defined as "the bank in any country to which has been entrusted the duty of regulating the volume of currency and credit in that country."

In the words of Kent, a Central bank is an "institution charged with the responsibility of managing the expansion and contraction of the volume of money in the interest of general public welfare."

FUNCTIONS OF THE CENTRAL BANK OF INDIA

Some of the most important functions of the central bank of India are as follows:

A central bank has been defined in terms of its functions. According to Vera Smith, "The primary definition of central banking is a banking system in which a single bank has either complete control or a residuary monopoly of note issue." W.A. Shaw defines a central bank as a bank which control credit.

To Hawtrey, a central bank is that which is the lender of the last resort. According to A.C.L. Day, a central bank is "to help control and stabilise the monetary and banking system."

According to Sayers, the central bank "is the organ of government that undertakes the major financial operations of the government and by its conduct of these operations and by other means, influences the behaviour of financial institutions so as to support the economic policy of the Government." Sayers refers only to the nature of the central bank as the government's bank. All these definitions are narrow because they refer only to one particular function of a central bank. On the other hand, Samuelson's definition is wide. According to him, a central bank "is a bank of bankers. Its duty is to control the monetary base.... and through control of this 'high-powered money' to control the community's supply of money." But the broadest definition has been given by De Kock.

In his words, a central bank is "a bank which constitutes the apex of the monetary and banking structure of its country and which performs as best as it can in the national economic interest, the following functions:

- The regulation of currency in accordance with the requirements of business and the general public for which purpose it is granted either the sole right of note issue or at least a partial monopoly thereof,
- The performance of general banking and agency for the state,
- The custody of the cash reserves of the commercial banks,
- The custody and management of the nation's reserves of international currency,
- The granting of accommodation in the form of re-discounts and collateral advances to commercial banks, bill brokers and dealers, or other financial institutions and the general acceptance of the responsibility of lender of the last resort,

- The settlement of clearance balances between the banks,
- The control of credit in accordance with the needs of business and with a view to carrying out the broad monetary policy adopted by the state." De Kock's definition is too long to be called a definition. For, a definition must be brief.

FUNCTIONS OF A CENTRAL BANK

A central bank performs the following functions, as given by De Kock and accepted by the majority of economists.

Regulator of Currency

The central bank is the bank of issue. It has the monopoly of note issue. Notes issued by it circulate as legal tender money. It has its issue department which issues notes and coins to commercial banks. Coins are manufactured in the government mint but they are put into circulation through the central bank.

Central banks have been following different methods of note issue in different countries. The central bank is required by law to keep a certain amount of gold and foreign securities against the issue of notes. In some countries, the amount of gold and foreign securities bears a fixed proportion, between 25 to 40 per cent of the total notes issued.

In other countries, a minimum fixed amount of gold and foreign currencies is required to be kept against note issue by the central bank. This system is operative in India whereby the Reserve Bank of India is required to keep ₹ 115 crores in gold and ₹ 85 crores in foreign securities. There is no limit to the issue of notes after keeping this minimum amount of ₹ 200 crores in gold and foreign securities. The monopoly of issuing notes vested in the central bank ensures uniformity in the notes issued which helps in facilitating exchange and trade within the country. It brings stability in the monetary system and creates confidence among the public. The central bank can restrict or expand the supply of cash according to the requirements of the economy. Thus it provides elasticity to the monetary system. By having a monopoly of note issue, the central bank also controls the banking system by being the ultimate source of cash. Last but not the least, by entrusting the monopoly of note issue to the central bank, the government is able to earn profits from printing notes whose cost is very low as compared with their face value.

Banker, Fiscal Agent and Adviser to the Government

Central banks everywhere act as bankers, fiscal agents and advisers to their respective governments. As banker to the government, the central bank keeps the deposits of the central and state governments and makes payments on behalf of governments. But it does not pay interest on governments deposits. It buys and sells foreign currencies on behalf of the government.

It keeps the stock of gold of the government. Thus it is the custodian of government money and wealth. As a fiscal agent, the central bank makes short-term loans to the government for a period not exceeding 90 days. It floats loans, pays interest on them, and finally repays them on behalf of the government. Thus it manages the entire public debt. The central bank also advises the government on such economic and money matters as controlling inflation or deflation, devaluation or revaluation of the currency, deficit financing, balance of payments, etc. As pointed out by De Kock, "Central banks everywhere operate as bankers to the state not only because it may be more convenient and economical to the state, but also because of the intimate connection between public finance and monetary affairs."

Custodian of Cash Reserves of Commercial Banks

Commercial banks are required by law to keep reserves equal to a certain percentage of both time and demand deposits liabilities with the central banks. It is on the basis of these reserves that the central bank transfers funds from one bank to another to facilitate the clearing of cheques.

Thus the central bank acts as the custodian of the cash reserves of commercial banks and helps in facilitating their transactions. There are many advantages of keeping the cash reserves of the commercial banks with the central bank, according to De Kock. In the first place, the centralisation of cash reserves in the central bank is a source of great strength to the banking system of a country. Secondly, centralised cash reserves can serve as the basis of a large and more elastic credit structure than if the same amount were scattered among the individual banks. Thirdly, centralised cash reserves can be utilised fully and most effectively during periods of seasonal strains and in financial crises or emergencies. Fourthly, by varying these cash reserves the central bank can control the credit creation by commercial banks. Lastly, the central bank can provide additional funds on a temporary and short term basis to commercial banks to overcome their financial difficulties.

Custody and Management of Foreign Exchange Reserves

The central bank keeps and manages the foreign exchange reserves of the country. It is an official reservoir of gold and foreign currencies. It sells gold at fixed prices to the monetary authorities of other countries. It also buys and sells foreign currencies at international prices. Further, it fixes the exchange rates of the domestic currency in terms of foreign currencies.

It holds these rates within narrow limits in keeping with its obligations as a member of the International Monetary Fund and tries to bring stability in foreign exchange rates. Further, it manages exchange control operations by supplying foreign currencies to importers and persons visiting foreign countries on business, studies, etc. in keeping with the rules laid down by the government.

Lender of the Last Resort

De Kock regards this function as a sine qua non of central banking. By granting accommodation in the form of re-discounts and collateral advances to commercial banks, bill brokers and dealers, or other financial institutions, the central bank acts as the lender of the last resort.

The central bank lends to such institutions in order to help them in times of stress so as to save the financial structure of the country from collapse. It acts as lender of the last resort through discount house on the basis of treasury bills, government securities and bonds at "the front door".

The other method is to give temporary accommodation to the commercial banks or discount houses directly through the "back door". The difference between the two methods is that lending at the front door is at the bank rate and in the second case at the market rate. Thus the central bank as lender of the last resort is a big source of cash and also influences prices and market rates.

Clearing House for Transfer and Settlement

As bankers' bank, the central bank acts as a clearing house for transfer and settlement of mutual claims of commercial banks. Since the central bank holds reserves of commercial banks, it transfers funds from one bank to other banks to facilitate clearing of cheques. This is done by making transfer entries in their accounts on the principle of book-keeping. To transfer and settle claims of one bank upon others, the central bank operates a separate department in big cities and trade centres. This department is known as the "clearing house" and it renders the service free to commercial banks.

When the central bank acts as a clearing agency, it is time-saving and convenient for the commercial banks to settle their claims at one place. It also economises the use of money. "It is not only a means of economising cash and capital but is also a means of testing at any time the degree of liquidity which the community is maintaining."

Controller of Credit

The most important function of the central bank is to control the credit creation power of commercial bank in order to control inflationary and deflationary pressures within this economy. For this purpose, it adopts quantitative methods and qualitative methods. Quantitative methods aim at controlling the cost and quantity of credit by adopting bank rate policy, open market operations, and by variations in reserve ratios of commercial banks.

Qualitative methods control the use and direction of credit. These involve selective credit controls and direct action. By adopting such methods, the central bank tries to influence and control credit creation by commercial banks in order to stabilise economic activity in the country.

Besides the above noted functions, the central banks in a number of developing countries have been entrusted with the responsibility of developing a strong banking system to meet the expanding requirements of agriculture, industry, trade and commerce.

Accordingly, the central banks possess some additional powers of supervision and control over the commercial banks. They are the issuing of licences; the regulation of branch expansion; to see that every bank maintains the minimum paid up capital and reserves as provided by law; inspecting or auditing the accounts of banks; to approve the appointment of chairmen and directors of such banks in accordance with the rules and qualifications; to control and recommend merger of weak banks in order to avoid their failures and to protect the interest of depositors; to recommend nationalisation of certain banks to the government in public interest; to publish periodical reports relating to different aspects of monetary and economic policies for the benefit of banks and the public; and to engage in research and train banking personnel etc..

IMPORTANT FUNCTIONS PERFORMED BY CENTRAL BANKS (6 FUNCTIONS)

Important functions performed by central banks are as follows: 1. Central Bank as a Bank of Note Issue 2. Central Bank as a Custodian of Foreign Exchange Reserves 3. Central Bank as Banker to Government 4. Central Bank as Banker to Commercial Banks 5. Central Bank as Controller of Credit 6. Central Bank as Promoter of Economic Development.

The powers and range of functions of central banks vary from country to country.

But there are certain functions which are commonly performed by the central banks:

- It issues the currency notes of the country.
- It is the custodian of the foreign exchange reserves of the country.
- It serves as banker to the government.
- It serves as banker to commercial banks.
- Being a monetary authority, it regulates the banks' credit creation activity and performs the function of a controller of credit.
- If promotes the economic development of the country.

CENTRAL BANK AS A BANK OF NOTE ISSUE

The central bank is legally empowered to issue currency notes – legal tender. Commercial banks cannot issue currency notes. The central bank's right to issue notes gives it the sole or partial monopoly of note issue, while in India, the Reserve Bank of India has a partial monopoly of note issue, for example, one rupee notes are issued by the Ministry of Finance, but the rest of the notes are issued by the Reserve Bank.

According to De Kock, following are the main reasons for the concentration of the right of note issue in the central bank:

- It leads to uniformity in note circulation and its better regulation.
- It gives distinctive prestige to the note issue.
- It enables the State to exercise supervision over the irregularities and malpractices committed by the central bank in the issue of notes.
- It gives the central bank some measure of control over undue credit expansion by the commercial banks, since expansion of credit obviously leads to an increased demand for note currency.

The central bank keeps three considerations in mind while issuing currency notes, namely, uniformity, elasticity and security. The right of note issue is regulated by law. According to law, every note issued must be matched with an asset of equal value (assets such as, government securities, gold and foreign currencies and securities). This is necessary to inspire public confidence in paper currency.

CENTRAL BANK AS A CUSTODIAN OF FOREIGN EXCHANGE RESERVES

The central bank holds all foreign exchange reserves – key currencies such as U.S. dollars, British pounds, and other prominent currencies, gold stock, gold bullion,' and other such reserves – in its custody. This right of the central bank enables it to exercise a reasonable control over foreign exchange, for example, to maintain the country's international liquidity position at a safe margin and to maintain the external value of the country's currency in terms of key foreign currencies.

CENTRAL BANK AS BANKER TO GOVERNMENT

As the government's banker, the central bank maintains the banking accounts of government departments, boards, and enterprises and performs the same functions as a commercial bank ordinarily performs for its customers.

It accepts deposits of commercial banks and undertakes the collection of cheques and drafts drawn on the bank; it supplies government with the cash required for payment of salaries and wages to their staff and other cash disbursements and transfer funds of the government from one account to another or from one place to another. Moreover, it also advances short-term loans to the government in anticipation of the collection of taxes and raises loans from the public. It also makes extraordinary advances during periods of depression, war, or other national emergencies. In addition, the central bank renders a very useful banking exchange required to meet the repayment of debts and service charges or for the purchase of goods and other disbursements abroad, and by buying any surplus foreign exchange which may accrue to the government from foreign loans or other sources.

The central bank also serves as an agent and adviser to the government. As agent of the government, it is entrusted with the task of managing the public debt and the issue of new loans and treasury bills on behalf of the government. It also underwrites unsold government securities. Moreover, the central bank is the fiscal agent to the government and receives taxes and other payments on government account. By acting as financial adviser to the government, the central bank discharges another important service: it advises the government on important matters of economic policy such as deficit financing, devaluation of currency, trade policy and foreign exchange policy.

The central bank also functions as a representative of the State in international financial matters. It is entrusted with the task of maintaining the nation's reserves of international currency.

CENTRAL BANK AS BANKER TO COMMERCIAL BANKS

Broadly speaking, the central bank functions as banker to commercial banks in three capacities:

- As custodian of cash reserves of commercial banks;
- As lender of last resort; and
- As clearing agent.

Thus, the central bank acts, as a conductor and leader of the banking system of the country. It acts as a friend, philosopher, and guide to commercial banks.

CUSTODIAN OF CASH RESERVES OF COMMERCIAL BANKS

Commercial banks find it convenient to keep their reserve requirements with the central bank because its notes command the greatest confidence and prestige and the government's banking transactions are conducted by this institution. Thus, in every country, commercial banks keep a certain percentage of their cash reserves with the central bank by custom or by law.

In fact, the establishment of central banks makes it possible for the banking system to secure the advantages of centralised cash reserves.

The significance of centralised cash reserves lies in the following facts:

- Centralisation of cash reserves in the central bank is a source of great strength to the banking system of the country as it inspires the confidence of the public in the commercial banks.
- Centralised cash reserves can form the basis of a much longer and more elastic credit structure than those scattered among numerous individual commercial banks.
- Centralised cash reserves enable the central bank to provide additional funds to those banks which are in temporary difficulties. In fact, the central bank can function as lender of the last resort on the basis of the centralised cash reserves with it.

- Centralisation of cash reserves is conducive to the growth of the economy and to the increased elasticity and liquidity of the banking system in particular and of the credit structure in general.
- Centralisation of cash reserves also enables the central bank to influence and control credit creation of commercial banks by increasing or decreasing the cash reserves of the latter, that is, through the technique of the variable reserve ratio.

Lender of the Last Resort

As lender of last resort, in periods of credit stringency, the central bank gives temporary financial accommodation to commercial banks by rediscounting their eligible bills. The central bank is the ultimate source of money in the modern credit system. The function of the lender of last resort implies that the central bank assumes the responsibility of meeting directly or indirectly all reasonable demands for accommodation from commercial banks. The central bank's function as lender of last resort has evolved out of its rediscounting function during emergency periods. The real significance of rediscount function, according to De Kock, lies in the fact that it increases the elasticity and liquidity of the entire credit structure. By providing a ready medium for the conversion in cash of certain assets of banks. It helps to maintain their liquidity. It also makes possible a considerable degree of economy in the use of cash reserves, since commercial banks can conduct a large volume of business with the same reserve and capital.

Clearing Agent

As the central bank becomes the custodian of cash reserves of commercial banks, it is but logical for it to act as a settlement bank or a clearing house for other banks. As all banks have their accounts with the central bank, the claims of banks against each other are settled by simple transfers from and to their accounts.

This method of settling accounts through the central bank, apart from being convenient, is economical as regards the use of cash. Since claims are adjusted through accounts, there is usually no need for cash. It also strengthens the banking system by reducing withdrawals of cash in times of crisis. Furthermore, it keeps the central bank informed about the state of liquidity of commercial banks in regard to their assets.

CENTRAL BANK AS CONTROLLER OF CREDIT

By far the most important of all functions of the central bank in modern times is that of controlling credit operations of commercial banks. Credit, the source of many blessings in a modern economy, also may become, unless we control it, a source of confusion and peril.

The social and economic consequences of changes in the purchasing power of money are serious and since credit plays a predominant part in the settlement of business transactions, it is essential that it should be subjected to control. Monetary policy is implemented by the central bank through the weapon of credit control.

CENTRAL BANK AS PROMOTER OF ECONOMIC DEVELOPMENT

The modern central bank accomplishes a number of development and promotional functions. Today, the central bank is regarded as an inevitable agency for promoting the economic growth of a country. It is an institution responsible for the maintenance of economic stability and for assisting the growth of the economy within the framework of the general economic policy of the State. Thus, the central bank has to take all such steps as are necessary, to meet the economic requirements of economic development of the country. It is responsible for the development of an adequate and sound banking system to cater to the needs not only of the trade and commerce but also of agriculture and industry. The central bank has to ensure, in the interest of economic progress, that the commercial banks operate on a reasonably sound and prudent basis.

Thus, the major task of the central bank lies in the development of highly organised money and capital markets that many help accelerate economic progress by assisting the huge investment activities in capital formation and other productive sectors. During the planning era, the central bank's role as adviser to government on economic matters in general, and on financial matters in particular, is of considerable importance. Thus, the central bank of a developing country has an important role to play in the process of development. In underdeveloped countries, the central bank has not only to provide adequate funds and to control inflation, through credit regulation, but it also has to undertake the responsibility of spreading banking facilities, providing credit at cheap rates to agriculture and industry, protecting the market for government securities and channeling credit into desirable avenues.

Moreover, in underdeveloped countries, there are institutional gaps in the money and capital markets which hinder economic growth. The banking system is not properly organised as a large section of the money market consists of unorganised, indigenous bankers. Thus, promotion of sound, organised, well-integrated institutions and agencies of money and capital market becomes an important function of a central bank in a developing economy. From deficiency of non-existence of institutions such as savings banks, agricultural credit agencies, insurance companies, and the like to collect and mobilise savings and make them available for productive investments is the main cause of the low rate of capital formation. Hence, the growth of such institutions in these countries is a precondition for capital formation which is a key to economic development. Evidently, therefore, the central bank of a developing country has a vital role to play in building such financial infrastructure for rapid economic development. As the Planning Commission of India puts it, central banking has to take "a direct and active role, first, in creating or helping to create the machinery needed for financing development activities all over the country and secondly, in ensuring that the finance available flows in the directions intended." The central bank also collects and disseminates economic statistics of a wider range. As such, the government of the country has to lean heavily upon the central bank for seeking economic and financial advice in the course of development planning.

In addition, the central bank may also undertake miscellaneous functions such as providing assistance to farmers through co-operative societies by subscribing to their share capital, promoting finance corporations with a view to providing loans to large-scale and small- scale industries, and publishing statistical reports on trends in the money and capital markets.

In short, a central bank is an institution which always works in the best economic interests of the nation as a whole.

In view of all these functions, as discussed above, it follows that a modern central bank is much more than a Bank of Issue.

Chart: Summarises the functions of a central bank.

Chart 1
Functions of Central Bank

MAIN POINTS ABOUTCOMMERCIAL BANKING

- Commercial banking (also known aswholesale banking) looks after the needs of businesses.
- Commercial banks offer many of the same services offered in retail banking, such as current (checking) accounts and other deposit or special interest accounts, with the facility to transfer money between accounts.
- They provide facilities to access money deposited, such as cheque books, debit cards and cashier services.
- They allow the payment of regular bills through standing orders or

direct debits. They also provide Internet banking so that companies can access up-to-date information about the state of their accounts.

- However, commercial banking divisions usually have specially trained people who understand the needs of businesses, so that they can offer the right financial advice to each company.
- Some commercial bankers will be specially trained to work with small businesses, whilst others are trained to work with large corporations because such companies can have very different needs.
- One of the most important functions of commercial banking is to provide a variety of debt finance (loans) to companies, to allow businesses to expand and become more profitable.
- Loan facilities include overdraft facilities and special accounts from which businesses can withdraw money as a loan, up to an agreed limit. The company will only be charged interest on the money that they actually withdraw, although most accounts do have an annual maintenance charge.
- The facilities can also include very large loans that can be paid back over anything from six months to 20 years. For larger loans the bank will want them secured against the company assets.
- Commercial bankers will help with payments to companies operating in other countries and will arrange special documents that authorise payments for goods (usually expensive goods) called 'letters of credit'.
- A commercial banker may offer to set up a lockbox service for a company. This is a special PO box where money owed to the company by its customers can be sent. The bank has access to this PO box and collects and processes the money for the company.
- As large companies have thousands of transactions passing through their accounts each day, commercial banking has to be able to offer the capacity to deal with such a huge volume.
- Commercial bankers often offer retail banking services as well - in fact most large high street banks offer both retail and commercial services.

FUNCTIONS OF THE RESERVE BANK OF INDIA

Major functions of the RBI are as follows:

ISSUE OF BANK NOTES

The Reserve Bank of India has the sole right to issue currency notes except one rupee notes which are issued by the Ministry of Finance. Currency notes issued by the Reserve Bank are declared unlimited legal tender throughout the country.

This concentration of notes issue function with the Reserve Bank has a number of advantages:

- It brings uniformity in notes issue;
- It makes possible effective state supervision;
- It is easier to control and regulate credit in accordance with the requirements in the economy; and
- It keeps faith of the public in the paper currency.

BANKER TO GOVERNMENT

As banker to the government the Reserve Bank manages the banking needs of the government. It has to-maintain and operate the government's deposit accounts. It collects receipts of funds and makes payments on behalf of the government. It represents the Government of India as the member of the IMF and the World Bank.

CUSTODIAN OF CASH RESERVES OF COMMERCIAL BANKS

The commercial banks hold deposits in the Reserve Bank and the latter has the custody of the cash reserves of the commercial banks.

CUSTODIAN OF COUNTRY'S FOREIGN CURRENCY RESERVES

The Reserve Bank has the custody of the country's reserves of international currency, and this enables the Reserve Bank to deal with crisis connected with adverse balance of payments position.

LENDER OF LAST RESORT

The commercial banks approach the Reserve Bank in times of emergency to tide over financial difficulties, and the Reserve bank comes to their rescue though it might charge a higher rate of interest.

CENTRAL CLEARANCE AND ACCOUNTS SETTLEMENT

Since commercial banks have their surplus cash reserves deposited in the Reserve Bank, it is easier to deal with each other and settle the claim of each on the other through book keeping entries in the books of the Reserve Bank. The clearing of accounts has now become an essential function of the Reserve Bank.

CONTROLLER OF CREDIT

Since credit money forms the most important part of supply of money, and since the supply of money has important implications for economic stability, the importance of control of credit becomes obvious. Credit is controlled by the Reserve Bank in accordance with the economic priorities of the government.

10

Development of Banking Operations

This Manual mainly deals with the Banking operations and is intended as a guide for staff functioning in Banking department and branches of the *Andhra Pradesh State Co-operative Bank* (APCOB). The operations of the Bank are fully computerized under a *Core Banking System* (CBS). As such, this Manual does not attempt to detail the accounting, calculation processes, vouchering etc., as would be relevant to the Manual environment. The procedures involved in handling the various types of accounts of customers are dealt with in this Manual for giving a better understanding and background reference to the front office functionaries in the Branches and Banking wing of the Bank. The current volume deals with the customer relationship aspects of Banking in the Bank and focuses on the handling of deposit accounts.

SALIENT FEATURES OF DEPOSIT SCHEMES

CURRENT ACCOUNT

Accounts under this type can be opened by Individuals, Sole Proprietary Concerns, Partnership Firms, Companies, Clubs, Associations, Trusts, Govt./ Local Bodies, Cooperative Societies etc. This Account is meant for Individuals/ Institutions having large number/ volume of transactions, mainly for meeting their day-to-day business and operational requirements for parking their operational fund balances. No interest is provided on the balances in Current Account as the Bank renders a considerable service in operation and maintenance of the Account.

These Accounts are operated only through the cheques provided by the Bank drawn either in individual or representative capacity, either singly or jointly. The Cheques, Bills, DDs etc of parties are collected through the Current Accounts and cash/clearing payments are made in respect of cheques issued by the Account holders.

Over Drafts, secured or otherwise, are provided as per the separate loan rules in this regard. For Accounts of individuals facility of withdrawal from ATM is also provided.

SAVINGS BANK ACCOUNT

The Savings Bank Accounts are meant for individuals operating singly or jointly with other individuals, Associations, Clubs etc. The Savings Bank accounts can be operated either with cheque book facility or without cheque book facility. Where cheque book facility is not provided or not opted for, remittances in cash and withdrawals through withdrawal slip are allowed. There is a limit on the number of transactions allowed in Savings Bank account and these accounts are not meant for business or trading activities etc. Interest at the rate as prescribed by RBI is paid on the monthly minimum balance maintained in the account between 10th and last day of the month.

The interest is computed for the full month on the above basis and credited once in 6 months to the account. Where cheque book facility is extended, the party can draw cheques on the account which can be collected by 3rd parties through the clearing office. Deposits in cash and cash withdrawals by way of cheque or through ATM is allowed. Cheques/ DDs etc., favouring the account holder are collected into the account. A special No Frills Savings Account called Abhyudaya S.B. A/c is made available by the Bank to facilitate financial inclusion of persons of lower economic standing, getting access to banking facilities. Under this, account can be opened with ₹ 25/-. There is no minimum balance stipulated. Ten withdrawals are allowed per quarter. Maximum balance at any point of time is stipulated at ₹ 25,000/-. There is no service charge or incidentals for these accounts and interest will be paid at the rate applicable for normal Savings Bank Accounts. No cheque book or ATM cards are issued for these accounts and collection of cheques and DDs are not undertaken through these accounts.

FIXED DEPOSITS

These are deposits of specified sum of money permitted to be made in multiples of ₹ 100/- for a specified period. For example, a Fixed Deposit of ₹ 5000/- for 12 months period. Fixed Deposits may be accepted for Days, Months, Years or their combination, as per request of customer. If the deposit is for a minimum period of 12 months, then interest may be paid monthly, quarterly, half-yearly or yearly. Minimum period of deposit is 7 days for ₹ 1.00 lakh or more and 15 days for deposits of below ₹ 1.00 lakh. Maximum period of deposit is 120 months or 10 years. These deposits are repayable to the customer on expiry of the period for which the deposit is made.

However, the account holders are permitted to make premature encashment of such deposits in case of exigency/ need – in such an event the principal amount is paid along with interest as applicable for the period for which the deposit was actually with the Bank, less penalty of 1 percentage points on the applicable rate of interest.

The interest is normally paid at quarterly rests for credit of the customer's Savings/ Current account as per standing instructions or allowed to be withdrawn in cash by the customer or paid to him by way of Bankers Cheque/ Pay Order and by way of D.D. for out-location customers.

The Bank will pay interest at monthly rests also if the customer so desires by duly discounting the interest for such monthly payment. Loans against the Fixed Deposit may be issued to the customers on surrender of duly discharged Fixed Deposit receipt with a letter of lien through a separate Depositor Loan A/c for which interest is charged at 2 per cent over the rate provided on the deposit. In the event of foreclosure of deposit, the depositor loan is also foreclosed with the rates of interest charged at 2 per cent over the rate allowed on the foreclosure of the deposit..

RECURRING DEPOSIT

Deposits under this category are in the nature of fixed amounts being paid in by the depositor every month subject to a minimum of ₹ 50/- and in multiples of ₹ 10/- thereafter for a specified period of years involving monthly payments ranging from 12 to 120 months. Under this deposit scheme, interest is cumulated at quarterly rests based on month-end balances in the account and pre-determined amount is fixed as payable at the end of the period of deposit.

The rules relating to foreclosure and grant of loan against this deposit are similar to that under Fixed Deposit except that in the event of foreclosure of a Recurring Deposit, interest is paid based on monthly balances without cumulation for the incomplete quarter. In computerized environment, the basic procedures of interest calculation etc., are inbuilt in the *Core Banking Solution* (CBS) and as such the users are fully guided by the system. However, the necessary verification and checking as required in respect of various operations are essential and need to be performed by the concerned functionaries.

CUSTOMER IDENTIFICATION AND INTRODUCTION: OPENING OF ACCOUNTS

Introduction of Customer Accounts

- It is important that every prospective customer who wants to open any type of deposit account in the branch must be properly introduced to the Bank by a respectable person known to the Bank or by an existing customer of the Bank with satisfactory conduct of transactions in deposit account. The introducer must normally call on the Bank and sign in the column specifically provided for the purpose in the account opening application form. Introduction is obtained primarily to get protection under Section 131 of the 'Negotiable Instruments Act' and all the members of the staff in the branch must be made aware of the importance of a proper introduction.
- The legal protection given to bankers in respect of cheques collected

"in good faith and without negligence" is available only if the account is opened with proper introduction.

- Once a party has been properly introduced to the Bank for opening an account that party need not bring fresh introduction at the time of opening another type of account
- However, if a party has Term Deposit with the Bank and such investment has been made without any introduction and he wants to open a Savings Bank or Current Account proper introduction is necessary to open such Savings Bank/ Current Account.
- The need for introduction in the case of limited companies is greater as they may form a convenient medium for questionable transactions.

Who can introduce a customer?

Introduction of a new customer by an existing Current/ Savings Bank Account Holder is considered to be the best form of introduction. However, a respectable person well known to the bank or a staff of the bank can also introduce a new customer.

Who cannot introduce a customer?

- A Term Deposit holder who has no Current/ Savings Bank Account cannot introduce another person to open a Current/ Savings Bank Account.
- A minor Account Holder cannot introduce.
- It is desirable that there should be a reasonable time gap of at least six months for a new Account Holder of the bank to introduce another new customer to the bank. This will enable the bank to assess whether the operations by the existing Account Holder are in order or not.

Method of obtaining introduction

- The bank must insist that the Introducer must come to the Bank in person and sign the document before the Officer. In case the Introducer does not come in person, then the introduction may be got confirmed by an official of the Bank by contacting the Introducer and recording the same in the opening form or by issue of letter.
- In the case of newly opened Branch it may be difficult to rigidly enforce this rule that new accounts must be opened only with proper introduction. Hence, accounts may be opened at new branches duly following the Know Your Customer Norms.

Verification of Introduction

- It is to be clearly understood that introduction is treated as a substantive step having real significance and not merely as a formality and any lapse in this regard will be viewed seriously. Hence, proper care is to be exercised in obtaining and verifying the introduction. Establishing the bonafides of a new customer is the main purpose of introduction and is to be handled accordingly.

- Even though the constituent is well introduced, it is still essential to enquire and record the name of his employer, changes in employment, if any, should also be noted in Ledger Account.
- Due customer identification under KYC norms is mandatory even for accounts being introduced by parties well known to the Bank.

OPENING OF ACCOUNTS

IMPORTANT

Accounts are opened by the Bank at its discretion and upon satisfaction of the Authorised official of the Bank as to the bonafides of the prospective customer and subject to the fulfillment of the various requirements stipulated in this regard including satisfaction as to veracity of introduction.

Salient features

- All new *Current Accounts* (C.A.), *Savings Bank Accounts* (S.B.), *Fixed Deposits* (FD), Term Deposits and Recurring Deposit Accounts (R.D.) shall be opened only with the authorisation of authorized officers in the branch.
- All applications for opening Current Accounts, Savings Bank Accounts, Term Deposits and R.D. Accounts etc. must be made in writing in the Bank's printed application forms only.
- The prospective customer should affix the signatures at all the relevant places on the forms prescribed in the presence of the Authorized official.
- In the Account Opening Form the residential address, office address and alternative addresses with phone numbers and e-mail id must be furnished.
- The customer also has to record nomination of the account at the relevant portion in the account opening application forms.
- The bank has to obtain *Permanent Account Numbe*r (PAN) of the customer while opening any type of accounts. In case, the PAN is not available, a declaration in Form No. 60/ 61 under Rule 114-B of I.T. Rules is to be obtained from the customer in duplicate.
- The particulars furnished by the prospective customer, after due verification and satisfaction must be entered in the relevant fields of the customer Id form and Account opening form in the system and duly authorized.

- The customer identification number and the Account No. which are automatically generated by the system for the Current Accounts, S.B. Accounts and R.D. Accounts, must be written in the Passbook, Specimen Signature Card, Account Opening Forms and also the Account Opening Register which is specially maintained for the purpose to record the details of the accounts opened.
- There is a provision in the system to generate, print out and send to the customers and also to the introducers, an acknowledgement or a letter of thanks for having opened/ having introduced the account, which must be sent.
- The requests of the customer for issue of cheque book, ATM card must be recorded in the relevant form and authorized. Whenever Cheque Books are issued, the details must be recorded in the system and duly authorized. The account number of the customer must be written/ stamped on each cheque leaf and on the cheque requisition slip in the cheque book.
- The cheque book issued to the customer must be acknowledged by the customer or his representative in the register of 'cheque books issued'. The cheque books should be issued in the serial number order and if for any reason the continuous serial number is skipped, such missing numbers should be recorded with the reasons and attested by the authorized officer.
- Requisite number of copies of photographs of the Account Holder, and all the Joint Account Holders in case of Joint Accounts have to be obtained while opening of accounts and affixed on appropriate forms, after due authentication of the authorized officer, as indicated for each type of account.

Photographs

- Branches should obtain recent passport size photographs of the customers at the time of opening of new accounts. The photographs submitted at the time of opening of account should be compared with the prospective customer/ account holder to satisfy about the resemblance and then only accepted. Recent passport size photographs of the prospective customer/ account holder/s are to be obtained and affixed at the appropriate places in the account opening forms, specimen card and pass book.
- In respect of Current and Savings Bank Accounts, one copy of the photograph each is to be affixed to the application form, the Passbook and the Specimen Signature Card.
- In respect of Term Deposits, the photograph of the customer has to be attached to the application form.

- In the case of joint accounts, *i.e.*, account being opened in the names of more than one person/ partnership accounts, separate set of photographs of all joint depositors/ partners have to be obtained.
- In the case of institutional customers, a set of photographs of all the officials authorized to open and operate the account must be obtained.
- Name of the account holder and the account number have to be written on the back of the photographs and the officer authorizing the opening of the account has to affix his signature on the reverse of the photographs with date before stapling the same to the application form.
- The officer authorizing the opening of Current and Savings Bank Accounts has to authenticate the same by affixing the round stamp of the branch and his signature with date at the bottom corner on the face of the second copy of photograph before affixing the same to the Pass Book.
- In the case of Savings Bank accounts opened by minors of age 12 years and above, photographs of the Account Holder has to be obtained.
- In the case of minor's account, operated by the Guardian, photograph of the Guardian is also to be obtained.
- In the case of *Hindu Undivided Family* (HUF) accounts, photographs of the "Karta" has to be obtained.
- In the case of Non-Resident Depositor, photographs of the depositor/ account holder has to be obtained.
- In respect of accounts opened by illiterate persons and blind persons three copies of recent passport size photographs have to be obtained. Further, passport size photograph of the depositor must be affixed on the specimen signature/thumb impression card, the pass book and the account opening form duly authenticated by the authorized officer. The signature of the Attesting Officer should be partly on the photos and partly on the account opening form/ specimen signature/ thumb impression card.
- A declaration shall be taken from the illiterate depositor on the account opening form to the effect that the contents of the account opening form as also the rules governing the deposit account have been explained to him, that he has fully understood the rules and that he had affixed his thumb impression after fully knowing the rules. This declaration should be authenticated by the depositor by affixing his thumb impression and it should be countersigned by a witness.
- In respect of accounts opened prior to 01.04.1994 photographs were not required to be obtained. However in all such accounts in which names have been either added or deleted after 1.4.1994, photographs

of all the Account Holders have to be obtained. However, it is advised to obtain photographs of all Account Holders who had opened accounts previously also, as and when they visit the branch for operation of their accounts.

- In the case where the same customer has more than one type of account separate photographs for each category of account need not be insisted. However, the account opening form to which the photo is tagged is to be mentioned in the application form of all other accounts.
- During the operations in the accounts whenever the passing officer or authorized official or the counter clerk notices a visible change in the resemblance of the photograph and the customer, particularly in the case of illiterate customers, a recent photograph should be obtained from the customer, duly attested and affixed at all appropriate places. This should be done at least once in every 3 years.

Eligibility to open accounts

The following persons/ institutions are eligible to open accounts with the Bank:

- Individuals in single name.
- Two or more persons in joint names in any of the following forms:
  a. Either or Survivor (E or S)
  b. Former or Survivor
  c. Jointly/ Jointly or Survivors (J or S)
  d. Any one or Survivor/ Survivors (A or S)
- In the names of Sole Proprietary Concerns, Companies, Associations, Partnership firms, Clubs, Religious and Charitable Institutions, Educational Institutions, Social Organizations, Co-operative Society etc.
- Minor above 14 years can open and operate Savings Bank account. However, Minor student of age 12 years and above can open Savings Bank account and operate by himself.
- Bank should not open more than one Savings Bank account for the same person in his individual name.
- At the time of opening joint accounts instructions regarding operations and survivorship should be obtained from all the account holders and properly recorded duly authenticated by an officer.

Prohibition against opening of Savings Bank accounts in the name of certain Bodies/ Organizations

- Savings Deposit account cannot be opened by banks in the name of:
  e. Government Departments
  f. Bodies depending upon budgetary allocations for performance of their functions.

g. Municipal Corporations or Municipal Committees
h. Panchayat Samitis
i. State Housing Boards
j. Water and Sewerage/ Drainage Boards
k. State Text Book Publishing Corporations
l. Societies
m. Metropolitan Development Authority
n. State/ District Level Housing Co-op. Societies etc.
o. Any trading business or professional concern whether such concern is a proprietary or a partnership firm or a company or in association
p. Political Party

- The above prohibition will not apply in the case of the following organizations/ agencies:

q. Primary Co-operative Credit Society which is being financed by the bank.
r. Small Farmer's Development Agency (SFDA)/ Fish Farmers Development Agencies (FFDAs).
s. Marginal Farmers' and Agricultural Labourers' Agencies (MFAL).
t. Drought Prone Areas Programme (DPAP).
u. District Development Authority (DDA).
v. District Rural Development Agency/ Society (DRDA/ DRDS).
w. Integrated Rural Development Programme (IRDP)/ Development of Women and Children in Rural Areas (DWCRA)/ Self-Help Groups (SHGs), registered or unregistered, which are engaged in promoting savings habit among their members/ Farmers Clubs – Vikas Volunteer Vahini (VVV), informal groups of rural farmers or entrepreneurs.
x. Integrated Tribal Development Agency (ITDA).
y. Agriculture Produce Market Committees.
z. Khadi and Village Industries Boards.

– Societies registered under the Societies Registration Act, 1860 or any other corresponding law in force in State or a Union Territory.
– Companies governed by the Companies Act, 1956 which have been licensed by the Central Government under Section 25 of the said Act, or under the corresponding provision in the Indian Companies Act, 1913 and permitted, not to add to their names the words 'Limited' or the words "Private Limited".
– Institutions other than those mentioned in clause (i) above and whose entire income is exempt from payment of income-tax under the Income Tax Act, 1961.

- Zilla Parishads/ Gram Panchayats only in respect of Jawahar Rojgar Yojana Funds.
- Nagar panchayats, Nagar Palikas and Municipal bodies in relation to funds given under Nehru Rozgar Yojana towards the components of:

i. subsidy and
ii. Training and Infrastructure of Scheme of Urban Micro Enterprise (SUME) and Scheme of Urban Wage Employment (SUWE) and interest earned on deposits under both the components of SUME and on deposits under SUWE subject, however, to the condition that no such account shall be opened with a bank other than public sector bank.

Operational Instructions

Operational instructions in the joint accounts have to be carefully followed. *They may be:*

- Joint Account without survivorship clause: This account is to be operated jointly by all the account holders. In the event of death of one of the account holders, operations in this account should be stopped and the balance in this account is payable to the survivors and the legal heirs of the deceased party.
- Joint or Survivor with Survivorship: This account is to be operated jointly by all the account holders. In the event of death of one of the account holders, the survivor/s can be allowed to continue to operate the account or the balance in the account can be paid to survivor/s.
- Either or Survivor: This account is opened in the names of two persons and this account can be operated by either of them. In the event of the death of one of them, the survivor can be allowed to operate this account or the balance in the account can be paid to the survivor.
- Anyone or Survivor: This account is opened by more than two persons and can be operated by any one of them. In the event of death of one of them, the right to operate the account rests with the survivors, but jointly. A fresh mandate has to be obtained from all the survivors, if the account is to be operated as E or S or otherwise. On the death of all except one of the account holders the balance in the account is payable to the lone survivor.
- Any variation in the instructions given by the joint account holder at the time of opening the account can be made only if it is authorised by all the account holders jointly.
- Original authority relating to the operations of joint accounts as well as the survivorship clause may be later on revoked by anyone of the joint account holder.

Conversion of Accounts – Single into Joint and Joint into Single

- To convert an existing single account into a joint or E or S account, a letter from the existing account holder attesting the specimen signature of the new person(s) has to be obtained and attached to the Account Opening Form. Specimen signatures of existing as well as the newly added person(s) have to be obtained in a fresh specimen signature card and maintained in the specimen signature card rack or in the specimen signatures loose leaf binder. All the changes have to be properly recorded duly authenticated by an authorized officer with dates of changes.
- In case the customer having a joint account with the Bank intends to convert the same into a single account, it is desirable to close such account by getting necessary instructions from the existing account holders and then open a new account in the name of the person in whose name the account is to be continued.

OPENING AND OPERATING OF ACCOUNTS UNDER DIFFERENT CATEGORIES

Minor:

- According to Indian Majority Act, a Minor is one who has not completed 18 years of age, but in the case of a Minor whose guardian is appointed by the Court, the minority status continues upto the age of 21 years.
- Any contract with a Minor is not a valid one. Hence no overdraft should be allowed to a minor. No collection of Cheques should be allowed in Accounts operated by Minor.
- An account may be opened in the name of a minor by the guardian and operated by the guardian. Proof of date of birth of the minor from appropriate authorities has to be obtained at the time of opening the account and should be retained in the records of the bank. Proof of date of birth by way of declaration by guardian is also valid for this purpose.
- The guardian must not be allowed to operate the minor's account once the minor attains majority status or in the event of the death of the minor. In the event of death of the minor, the guardian has to close the account.
- In the Account Opening Form as well as specimen signature card, the guardian must sign in representative capacity. For example, guardian should sign as "For and on behalf of minor................".
- Savings Bank account can be opened and operated by a minor student who is above the age of 12 years or a minor of the age of 14 and above.

- No cheque book is to be issued to minors who are operating their Savings Bank accounts by themselves.
- Accounts in the name of minor to be operated by the natural guardian or by the guardian or by the guardians appointed by the court or to be operated by the minor himself, must be opened in the ledger.
- Date of Birth of the minor must be noted and authenticated by an authorised officer of the Bank. On the date of minor attaining majority, the bank has to issue a notice in the prescribed format with regard to the eligibility of the minor to operate the account personally.
- On the date of minor attaining majority fresh Account Opening Form duly signed by the account holder in the status of a major with his fresh set of specimen signatures duly counter signed by the guardian should be obtained and retained in Bank records. Proper notings about the minor attaining majority status should be made and authenticated by an authorised officer of the Bank. From such date of minor attaining majority, the guardian should not be permitted to operate the account in the status of guardian.

Guardians:

- The natural guardian of a Hindu Minor in respect of Minor's property according to the Hindu Majority and Guardianship Act 1956 is:
  - in the case of a boy or unmarried girl the father and if the father is not alive, the mother;
  - in the case of illegitimate boy or illegitimate unmarried girl - the mother and if she is not alive the father;
  - in the case of a minor married girl - the husband. If both the father and mother are not alive, no one other than the person appointed by a competent court can act as a guardian of a minor.
- Under Mohammedan Law, the father is the guardian for the property of the minor but after the father's death, the following persons are entitled, in the order mentioned hereunder, to be the guardians of a minor:
  - The Executor appointed by the father's will;
  - Father's father;
  - The Executor appointed by the will of the father's father.
- If none of the above persons is alive only the person appointed by the competent court can act as the guardian of a minor.
- Under no circumstance mother can act as guardian of the minor under Mohammedan Law.
- In respect of Christians, either the Father or Mother is the natural guardian to the Minor.
- The RBI has advised that Banks could open Savings, R.D., and Term Deposit accounts in the names of minors with Mothers as Guardians.

Illiterate Persons:

- The rules relating to Savings Bank or other deposit account have to be clearly explained to an illiterate person intending to open such accounts in a language in which he understands. He should be advised that for withdrawing money from his account, he has to personally come to the bank with the Pass Book, every time.
- Cheque Book should not be issued to him under any circumstances.
- Left hand thumb impression of the constituent has to be obtained on the Account Opening Form and specimen signature card in the presence of the authorised bank officer and a person well known to the bank who will attest his thumb impression on the Account Opening Form.
- Three passport size photographs have to be obtained from the customer. One copy will have to be affixed on the Account Opening Form. At the lower portion of this photograph his *Left Thumb Impression* (LTI) has to be affixed in such a way as to half of the thumb impression is on the photograph and the other half on the Account Opening Form. The authorised officer of the bank will have to attest this thumb impression beneath that.
- Every time before passing the withdrawal, the Passing Officer should ask him whether he intends to withdraw the amount mentioned in the withdrawal slip. Only on getting his oral confirmation the withdrawal must be passed for payment.
- In the account, it must be clearly noted "after the name of the party" as "Illiterate person" and in the case of the customer operating his account with LTI that fact also must be recorded as thumb impression.
- An illiterate depositor if he intends to allow a literate person to operate his account, he has to submit on authorisation cum indemnity letter in the prescribed format.
- Current account should not be opened in the name of an illiterate person.
- In case the illiterate person wants to open an account jointly with a literate person such account must be opened with the condition that it can be operated only jointly by both. No illiterate persons account should be opened with operation facility of E or S or by "literate person only."
- No cheque book is to be issued even for such joint accounts.

Blind persons:

- There is no legal bar for a blind person to open a bank account.
- Due care must be exercised in opening accounts for blind persons as there may not be consistency in their signature. As they always depend on someone the chance for their being cheated is greater;

and it may not be always possible for blind person to come to the Bank in person and he may send a messenger for transaction whose reliability may be known to the bank.

- Three copies of recent passport size photographs of the blind person have to be obtained at the time of opening the account — one to be attached to Account Opening Form — second copy to the specimen signature card and the third copy to the Pass Book. The signature/ thumb impression of the blind person has to be attested by a person well known to the bank and countersigned by the authorised officer of the bank on the reverse of two photographs. The third photograph affixed to his Pass Book should not have his specimen signature.
- Signature of the blind person in the Account Opening Form and Specimen Signature Card are to be attested by a witness who must be a person well known to the bank or a longstanding customer of the bank.
- It must be boldly written as "BLIND" in red ink in the Account Opening Form, specimen signature card, noted in the system and the Pass Book.
- In the cases where the Branch Manager is satisfied, he may allow the blind persons to operate their accounts by themselves, or on merits of each case the Branch Manager may allow a next of kin of the blind customer to operate the account as representative after taking proper 'letter of authority' from the blind customer to that effect.
- Whenever inconsistency in the signature of the blind customer is noticed, his left hand thumb impression may be obtained by the Bank in addition to his signature.
- Entries and the balance must be made up to date at the time of each transaction by the blind customer and should also be read out to him when no other person is in hearing distance of the blind customer.
- No ATM Card will be issued to the Blind deposit Account holder.

Sole Proprietorship:

- The law does not distinguish between the Proprietor and the Proprietary Concern and therefore such accounts can be treated as individual accounts and he has to submit a declaration in the prescribed format.

Executors/ Administrators:

- An Executor is a person named in the will and derives title immediately after the date of death of Testator for the purpose of administration of the property of the deceased. He must obtain a Probate from a court of law before acting as an Executor.
- An Administrator is a person appointed by the Court to manage the property of the deceased who had died without leaving any will.

- Executors and Administrators cannot delegate power to third parties.
- Any power of attorney or authority given to third parties on the account of the estate should not be accepted unless they are cleared by *Head Office* (H.O.) after examination by the Legal Department/ Legal Advisor of the Bank.
- The opening of accounts for Executors/ Administrators has to be cleared by the Legal Advisor/ Legal Department of the Bank.
- Account Opening Form should be signed by all the Executors/ Administrators if there is more than one Executor/ Administrator - photographs of all Executors/ Administrators have to be obtained and retained on Bank records.
- Cheques drawn in favour of Executor/ Administrator should not be credited to the personal account of the Executor/ Administrator.
- Branch Officers must very carefully read the contents of the Will or Letter of Administration so that the operations in the account of Executor/ Administrator are allowed only as per the terms of the Will.
- The account should be opened in the name of the individual with the addition of the words "Executor" or "Administrator."

Hindu Undivided Family (HUF) Account:

- The Bank may open accounts in the names of joint Hindu families. The account should be opened in the name of 'Karta' or in the name of the family business. The bank has to obtain two copies of the photographs of the 'Karta', one to be affixed on the Account Opening Form and the other on the Specimen Signature Card.
- It must be written in bold letters in red ink as "HUF Account." in the Account Opening Form, Specimen Signature Card, Account in the system and Passbook. Further, the bank has to obtain the HUF declaration duly signed by the 'Karta' and the coparceners.

Power of Attorney:

- A person may authorise another person to open and operate a bank account on his behalf. This authority may be given by "Power of Attorney".
- The Power of Attorney may be 'special or general'. Special Power of Attorney authorises a person to act in a simple transaction. A General Power of Attorney authorises the person to have wide range of powers to carry out various transaction.
- The Power of Attorney must give specific authority to open and operate a bank account, to overdraw in Current Account, to borrow, to accept/ endorse bills of exchange, etc.
- Branch Officers must study the Power of Attorney very carefully and allow operations only as per the terms of Power of Attorney. If any

operation outside the terms of Power of Attorney is permitted in the account, such transaction will not bind the principal.

- The Power of Attorney can be revoked at any time by the grantor. It is also automatically revoked by the death, insanity or insolvency of the grantor and also by the death or insanity of Attorney. But in case, the Attorney becomes insolvent, he cannot receive payments on behalf of the principal but the authority given by the principal does not dissolve automatically. The principal, in such cases, has to give confirmation that the power holder will continue to exercise the powers conveyed in the Power of Attorney executed by him.
- Copy of the Power of Attorney should be carefully compared with the original by an Officer of the Bank who will attest the copy as "Compared with the Original".
- The branch must maintain the "Power of Attorney Register" bearing all relevant terms and conditions of the Power. It should be recorded and duly authenticated by an Officer. Main operational clauses should also be recorded in the system.

Partnership Accounts:

- It is desirable that the partnership firm is a registered one.
- Account should be opened in the name of the firm and not in the name of any partner.
- Account Opening Form should be signed by all the partners in their official capacity and also in personal capacity.
- While operating the partnership account the partners should sign for and on behalf of the firm and not as an individual.
- Partnership Deed should be very carefully examined and in case the branch offices have any doubt it is always desirable to refer such cases, before opening the account, to H.O. for examination and approval by Bank's Legal Department/ Legal Advisor.
- Once a partnership account is opened operations in such account should be strictly in conformity with the provisions of the deed. If there are any restrictive clauses in the Partnership Deed they must be clearly noted in Power of Attorney Register as well as system and strictly followed while allowing operations in the account.
- A Partnership letter should be obtained and signed by all the partners along with the Account Opening Form. This letter must be signed by all the partners in their individual capacity and not on behalf of the firm.
- Cheques payable to the firm should not be credited to the private account of any partners or any employee of the firm.
- In case any one partner in the firm advise the bank not to allow operations on the firm's account by the other partner(s), all operations

on the account must be stopped under intimation addressed as a joint letter to all partners as well as the firm. This letter must be sent to all the partners and the firm. In the event of death of any of the partner, the operation in the account is to be stopped and a fresh account is to be opened, provided the partnership deed permits the same.

Limited Company:

- While opening an account in the name of a limited company, the following documents are to be obtained along with the Account Opening Form. A separate file containing various documents as noted below should be maintained:
  - A certified true copy of the Certificate of Incorporation.
  - A copy of Memorandum and Articles of Association duly certified as true and up to date by a competent officer of the company for Bank's records. This document will contain a provision as to who is the competent officer of the company to certify the copy of the Memorandum and Articles of Association as "True and up to date." In case of any doubt these documents submitted to the Bank should be verified from the records of the Registrar of Companies.
  - Certified copy of the latest resolution of the General Body/ Board, etc., regarding opening of the account, with names and designation of persons authorised to operate the account.
  - In the case of Public Limited Company certified true copy of the "Certificate of Commencement of Business" duly verified with the original should be obtained.
  - An officer of the Bank who verified this certificate must authenticate on the copy submitted to the bank to the effect that "verified with the original". This is not required in the case of a Private Limited Company.
  - List of Directors/ Chairman and other office bearers of the institution with designation.
  - Before opening an account for such a company, the bank must satisfy itself that the said company is a well established one, or the directors of the company are well known to the Bank or properly introduced by a respectable person well known to the Bank.
  - Where an account for such a Company has been opened on the proper introduction of a well known person, the Bank must before accepting any cheque drawn in favour of the company for collection and issue of cheque book, make independent enquiry about the company and its Directors.

- Specimen signatures of authorised persons to operate the account duly countersigned by the Chairman of the meeting with the official seal of the company.
- Recent passport size photographs of the person(s) opening the account/ authorized persons to operate the account.

Trust Accounts:

- Before opening the account in the name of a Trust, a copy of Trust Deed must be obtained from the Trustee(s) concerned and carefully studied with particular reference to restrictive clauses regarding the amounts that can be withdrawn, provisions regarding the opening and operation of an account in the name of Trust, etc.
- A resolution adopted by the Trustees should be obtained with regard to operation of the Account.
- In case of a Public Trust, a copy of certificate issued by Charity Commissioner together with a copy of Trust Deed has to be obtained.
- Operational instructions and the name(s) of the Trustee(s), should be properly recorded and approved by an authorised officer.
- It should always be ensured that all payments in the Trust account are made only in accordance with the provisions of the Trust Deed.
- A Trustee can not delegate his powers.
- Trustees have no implied power to borrow unless such powers have been expressly provided in the Trust Deed.
- Cheques payable to the Trust should not be collected for credit of private accounts of Trustees.
- Bank has no right to set off against the Trust Fund for debts owed by Trustees in their individual capacity.

Others:

- Schools/ Colleges:
  - In the case of Schools/ Colleges, the Account Opening Form should be signed by the Correspondent/ Principal/ Headmaster.
  - A certified copy of the rules and regulations of the educational institution must be obtained and retained.
  - The operation of the account shall be strictly as per instructions of competent authority of the institution/ resolution.
  - In the case of Government aided School, the permission of Board of Secondary Education may be necessary for opening an account with the Bank.
- Insolvents:
  - No account should be opened in the name of an undischarged insolvent.
- Lunatics:
  - Though there is no legal bar to open an account in the name of a

lunatic it is desirable to refer such cases to Head Office (H.O.) for clearance by Legal Department/ Legal Advisor of the Bank.

- Liquidators:
  - Account in the name of a Liquidator has to be opened only with the prior approval of H.O.
- Staff Accounts:
  - It is desirable to restrict number of Savings Bank or Current Accounts to be maintained by each staff member.
  - In all the accounts of the staff member it must be prominently marked as "Staff Account".
  - While issuing cheque books to staff members it must be ensured that all the cheque leaves of the previous cheque books have been used.
  - If any cheque issued by the staff member on his account is returned unpaid for want of funds the facts must be informed to H.O. Administration/ Personnel Section for further action.
- Cooperative Societies:
  - For opening an account in the name of a Cooperative Society the provisions of the bye-laws of the society should be gone into and if the bye-laws provide for the same, account may be opened consistent with the provisions of the bye-laws.

Other Eligible Institutions:

- Various Govt. Departments/ Bodies which are dependant upon budgetary allocation of the Govt. for performing their functions are required to open Current Accounts as the banks cannot open Savings Bank Accounts in their names..
- However, certain institutions like the following few, are exempt from the above restrictions and the Bank can open Savings Bank Accounts for them.
  - District Rural Development Agency (DRDA)
  - Drought Prone Areas Programme (DPAP)
  - District Development Authority (DDA)
  - Integrated Rural Development Programme (IRDP)
  - Khadi and Village Industries Board (KVIB)
  - Integrated Tribal Development Agency (ITDA)
  - Agriculture Produce Market Committee (APMC)
  - Societies Registered under the Societies Registration Act 1860 or any other law in force in a State/ Union territory.
  - Institutions whose entire income is exempted from payment of Income Tax under IT Act 1961.
- Fiduciary Accounts:
  - There may be certain funds, mostly connected with recreation etc. and usually of temporary nature and are not Registered. For

example constituent may ask the Bank to open account styled as "Cyclone Fund", "Sports Fund" etc. Before opening such accounts the Manager must make full enquiry and satisfy himself about the genuineness of the parties concerned or if the proposal is from Government, a copy of relevant Government Order must be obtained and retained.

- No overdraft should be allowed in such accounts.

NOMINATION OF ACCOUNT HOLDER

SALIENT FEATURES

- Nomination facilities to bank's customer 's are provided in respect of DEPOSIT ACCOUNTS under the Banking Laws (Amendment) Act of 1983 and as per Cooperative Banks (Nomination) Rules, 1985 and they have come into force since 29.3.1985.
- Where the nomination has been made in the prescribed manner, the nominee shall on the death of the sole depositor or all depositors, as the case may be, becomes entitled to all the rights of the depositor(s).
- Nomination facility is available only in respect of deposits held in the depositor individual capacity and not in any representative capacity.
- This nomination facility is available only to individual customers.
- Nomination can be given only in favour of individual.
- Nomination facility is available for the following:
  - Deposits standing in their names in individual capacity,
  - Contents of Safe Deposit Lockers hired by them and
  - Items left by them in Safe Custody with the Bank.
- Branches should ensure that all customers are aware of this facility and give nominations at the time of opening the accounts.
- Branches should ensure that the existing Account Holders also give their nominations.
- If any customer does not wish to make nomination for any personal reasons, an endorsement may be made in the Nomination form attached to the Account Opening Form or in the Account Opening Form itself reading:
  "I/We.. do not require Nomination facility" under the signature(s) of the Account Holder(s).

Nomination for Deposit Accounts

Conditions/ formalities for accepting nominations in deposit accounts:

- Nominations should be obtained in the prescribed format.
- Branches shall accept nominations only in deposits held in the personal names of the constituents.

- Branches should not accept nominations in respect of deposits held in any representative capacity such as, director of a company, secretary in an association, partner of a firm, Karta of a Hindu undivided family etc.
- Branches should not accept nominations even in the accounts of proprietary concerns.
- Branches can accept nominations in the following types of accounts standing in the name(s) of individual depositor(s).
  - Savings Bank Accounts
  - Current Accounts
  - Term Deposit Accounts including Special Deposits and Recurring Deposit Accounts.
  - NRE and NRO accounts *i.e.* in respect of NRI accounts.
  - Accounts of Pensioners.
- In respect of Term Deposits, the nomination made during the currency of a deposit will continue to be valid after renewal of that deposit.
- Branches should note that only one individual in his personal capacity can be made as a nominee in respect of a particular deposit account.
- Acceptance of more than one nominee in any particular deposit account is prohibited.
- Where the depositor has more than one deposit account, branches should accept separate nominations in respect of each deposit account even though all the deposits stand in the name of the same depositor.
- Where the depositor wishes to nominate more than one person for a single deposit, branch may permit splitting of the deposit in proportion desired by the depositor, subject to the period and aggregate amount of the deposit not undergoing any change as a result of such splitting. Such a splitting will not amount to foreclosure and will not attract penalty.
- For each of the deposit Accounts, branch should obtain a separate nomination.

Nomination for Pension Accounts

- Nomination may be made by the pensioner in the account to which his pension amount is credited. Pension can also be credited to the Joint account of Central/ State Govt. Pensioner with his/ her spouse in whose favour an authorization for family pension exists in the Pension Payment Office.
- In case the pensioner has given nomination under "Arrears of Pension Rules, 1983" which will be applicable only for payment of pension arrears, it is in favour of Government for payment of arrears after

the death of the pensioner, whereas the nomination obtained for the bank account of the pensioner is to cover the credits already made into the account of the pensioner before the death of the pensioner.

- The Branches must persuade the pensioners to give separate nomination/s *i.e.* apart from the one given for arrears of pension.

Who Can Nominate

- Every depositor having a deposit in his individual name either singly or jointly with other individual(s) can give nomination for each one of the deposits standing in his name/ their names.
- Nominations in various deposit accounts may be accepted in the following names:
  - Accounts in the name of an individual: Nomination should be given by that individual Account Holder alone.
  - Accounts in the joint names of two or more individuals: Nomination should be made jointly by all the joint Account Holders in favour of one person only.
  - Accounts in the joint names of individuals with "E or S", "Any one or Survivor" or Former or Survivor" mandate: Nomination should be made jointly by all the joint Account Holders irrespective of the operational instructions.
  - Accounts of minors operated by guardian on behalf of the minor: Nomination should be made only by the guardian authorised to operate the account of the minor.
  - Accounts of minors operated by guardian held jointly with the guardian: Nomination should be made only by guardian both on behalf of the minor and the guardian himself.
  - Minor's Special Deposits Account *i.e.* Account operated by minor himself: No nomination should be accepted from the minor. Nomination can be accepted only from lawfully entitled/ empowered to act on behalf of the minor.
  - Accounts of Non Resident Indians: Nominations can be made by the Non- Resident Indians in their, Non- Resident (ordinary), Non-Resident (External) accounts in the same manner as in the paras (i) to (vi) above.

Who can be Nominated

- Branches shall ensure that only individual in their personal capacity is nominated in respect of deposit accounts. The Nominee may be:-
  - Any individual, who is a resident of India, in his personal capacity, named by the depositor.
  - A minor - represented by the guardian A non-resident Indian of Indian origin

 - A foreign national of Indian origin
 - A foreign national of non-Indian origin.
- A non-resident Indian can nominate a resident as Nominee and resident Indian can nominate a non-resident as a Nominee. However, remittance of funds from the account of a deceased depositor to the non-resident nominee will be subject to the 'Exchange Control Regulations', prevailing at the time of remittance.
- Where a nominee is a Minor, the sole depositor or all the depositors as the case may be, should appoint another individual not being a minor, to receive the amount of the deposit on behalf of the minor, during the latter's minority. Such individual need not necessarily be the natural guardian of the minor - nominee.

Procedures for Nomination

- Branches should provide the customers with prescribed 'Nomination Form'.
- Upon rcceipt of the duly filled nomination form from the depositor the branch should examine the same carefully to ensure that:
 - II columns are duly filled in and account number and name of the depositor and the name, address and date of birth of the nominee are clearly written.
 - It is signed by all the depositors.
 - Only one nominee is appointed on the nomination letter.
 - The eligibility criteria as prescribed in foregoing paras are satisfied.
- Then the officer should verify the signature of the depositor on the nomination letter and there after sign on the nomination form as well as the acknowledgement slip, attached to the nomination letter, under the round stamp of the branch.
- The acknowledgement slip should be dated and handed over to the depositor in token of having registered the nomination.
- Complete details must then be recorded in the "Nomination Register" maintained by the Branch.
- The Nomination letter must be retained with the relevant Account Opening Form.
- Branch need not obtain the signature of the nominee, while obtaining nominations.

Cancellation or Variation of Nomination

- A nomination once made can be changed or cancelled by the depositor any time during the Currency of the relative deposit.
- Instructions for 'Cancellation of Nomination' should be given in the

prescribed Form and change or 'Variation of Nomination' should be made using a separate format.

- In case the deposit is in joint names, branch should obtain the above forms duly signed by all the depositors irrespective of the operational instructions.
- In the case of joint accounts, on the death of one of the depositors, branch may allow cancellation and/ or variation of nomination during the Currency of the account. But it must be ensured that such cancellation/ variation is made jointly by all the depositors surviving at the time of cancellation or variation of the nomination.
- When a nominee is changed the branch should ensure that the new nominee satisfies the eligibility criteria provided in earlier paras.
- The authorized officer should verify the signatures of the depositor on the application with their specimen signatures available with the Bank for cancellation and variation.
- Upon ensuring that the application for cancellation and variation is in order the officer must sign on the nomination form as well as acknowledgement slip, attached to the form, under the branch round stamp and return this slip to the depositor.
- In case the application is for cancellation and the same is in order and accepted by the branch, the officer in charge must cancel the nomination letter given earlier by drawing a line across the face and writing there as "nomination cancelled vide application form dated............................" under his initials and date.
- Then the application for cancellation of the nomination should be attached to the relative Account Opening Form.
- In case the application is for variation of a nomination the officer in charge should proceed as "nomination changed vide application date............" under his initials and date.
- Then the application for variation of nomination should be attached to the Account Opening Form. Original nomination letter, which is cancelled, must also be retained with the relative Account Opening Form.
- The nomination made by the customer must be recorded in the appropriate para in the 'Nomination Screen' in the system.
- A nomination/ change of nomination/ cancellation of nomination will be deemed to be in force even when the relative Deposit is renewed, unless the nomination is changed, in which case, a fresh nomination is required.

Some clarifications

- Upon the death of the sole depositor in the case of deposit in the name of an individual or upon the death of one or all of the depositors in a deposit in the names of two or more individuals, the names of the deceased depositors in the deposit cannot be substituted by the name of the nominee. The name of the nominee cannot also be added to the name(s) of the surviving depositor(s). In other words under no circumstance a branch can permit the Nominee to become the depositor under the same account.

- The role of nominee is only to receive the proceeds of the deposit in the event of death of the depositor/ all depositors.
- Similarly no loan shall be granted to a nominee against the deposit standing in the name of the deceased depositor.
- But the claim should be settled first in favour of the nominee by following the procedures laid down for settlement of claims.
- By making payment of the deposit amount to the nominee, the bank gets a good and valid discharge. It is entirely the responsibility of the nominee to account the money with any legal heir(s) of the deceased and the bank is in no way concerned with it.

Nominations for Safe Deposit Lockers

- Branch may permit nominations only in respect of Safe Deposit Lockers hired by persons in their individual capacity and not in any representative capacity.
- Only individuals can be made nominees in respect of Safe Deposit Locker accounts.

Nomination for Articles held in Safe Custody

- Branch may accept nominations for items held in Safe Custody only if they are held in the personal name of a single individual and not in any representative capacity or as holder of an office or otherwise.
- Branches should not accept nomination in respect of persons jointly depositing articles for Safe Custody.
- Where a nominee is a minor, the person who makes the nomination may appoint another individual, not being a minor, to receive the items on behalf of the minor during the latter's minority.
- Branches should obtain a separate nomination in respect of each lodgment covered by a safe custody receipt. Such a nomination should be obtained on the prescribed form.
- Branches may permit cancellation/ variation or change of nomination at any time during the Currency of the safe custody agreement. Requests for these purposes should be made in the prescribed forms.
- The other formalities like issuing due acknowledgement, attaching the original nomination forms and subsequent applications, for change or variation or cancellation of nomination to the relative Account

Opening Form etc. to be followed as in the case of nomination for Deposit accounts.

- Similarly noting the details in Nominations Register, relative ledger folios/Registers, verification of specimen signatures, scrutiny of particulars filled in the application forms, preservation of records etc. are the same as those applicable for deposit accounts.

Nomination Register

- Particulars of nominations should be properly and fully recorded in the "Nominations Register". All the particulars in this Register should be checked by an officer with reference to the application form for nomination or cancellation of nomination or change of nomination and the entries must be authenticated by the officer.
- In addition, the following particulars should be recorded in the folio/ entered into the computer system with the approval of the checking officer.
  - Name of the Nominee
  - Serial number as per recording in 'Nominations Register'
  - Date of Registration of nomination in the 'Nominations Register' which should be the date on which the nomination is made by the Depositor/ Account Holder in writing.
- Renewal of deposits with nomination will not in any way affect the nomination. Whenever the deposits with nominations are renewed, the new deposit receipt number will have to be recorded in "Nominations Register".
- Customer can change the nomination at any time during the period when the account/ deposit remains with the Bank. Hence, changes are to be carefully recorded.

Death of a Customer

- An announcement of death of a customer of the Bank in a newspaper/ production of a death certificate or report from a reliable person, etc., is sufficient notice to the Bank to act upon.
- The fact should be recorded in the system with the date and source of information duly authenticated by an officer.
- On receipt of such notice or information of death or about insolvency or insanity of a customer, the Bank must ensure that no further payment out of this account is allowed or passed. Even the cheques dated prior to the date of death/ insolvency/ insanity when presented to the Bank after receipt of notice/ information of death/ insolvency/ insanity of the customer should not be honoured/ paid.

CURRENT ACCOUNT

Who Can Open

- A *Current Account* (C.A.) can be opened by:
  - Individual in his single name
  - Two or more individuals in their joint names with survivor clause like "E or S"/ "A or S:/ Jointly.
  - Sole proprietorship concerns.
  - Private/ Public Sector Companies.
  - Religious/ Educational/ Charitable Institutions.
  - Trusts/ Executors/ Administrators.
  - Clubs/ Associations.
  - Registered/ Unregistered Societies.
  - Government/ Semi government Departments/ Local Bodies.
  - Cooperative Societies.
  - Other Institutions on production of required and valid documents.

Who Cannot Open

- A Current Account cannot be opened by:
  - Minors. However accounts of minors to be operated by natural guardian may be opened.
  - Purdanashin women.
  - Illiterate persons.
  - Blind persons. In case a person after opening a Current Account after sometime becomes Blind must be advised to close the Current Account and to open a Savings Bank Account.

Procedure for Opening Accounts

- It must be ensured that:
  - All applications for opening Current Account must be in Bank's printed form only.
  - The account should be properly introduced.
  - All required documents applicable to that particular category should be submitted.
  - Photographs.
  - No account should be opened unless the same has been authorised by the Manager.
  - Introducer normally, must sign in the application form in the presence of the Manager.
  - Initial Deposit to open the account must be made in Cash. Opening of an account with the proceeds of a cheque/ DD should not be allowed.

- Normally cheques/ DDs dated prior to the date of opening the account even in favour of the account holder should not be collected unless the Manager is satisfied about their bonafide.

Opening the Account in the Ledger and other Operational Procedures

- In the Current Account Module:
  - The System Assigns the Account Number and the same is to be recorded in the application form.
  - Enter full name of the Account Holder with residential and Office/ business address with phone numbers. Name of the introducer and if he is also an Account Holder his Account Number must also be noted in the system.
  - Enter the type of account as "E or s"/ "A or S"/ "Joint Account"/ "Sole Proprietor"/ "Partnership" etc.
  - Enter operational instructions like "Singly by....." b/ Jointly by the Account Holders/ Secretary/ Treasurers etc.
  - In the case of Companies/ Government/ Quasi Government Departments etc. all the details of persons authorised to operate the account, period of office etc. is to be properly recorded as per relevant documents produced by the Account Holder.
  - Note down the details of cheque numbers issued as and when Cheque Books are issued to the customer in the system.
  - Write the Account Number in the Account Opening Form as well as specimen signature cards once the account is opened.
  - File the Account Opening Form in the respective file, *i.e.* "File of Current Account Opening Forms".
  - Add the Specimen Signatures Cards to "Specimen Signature Loose Leaf Ledger" retained under the custody of Passing Officer and scan the same for storing in the Computer System.

Posting in the Ledger

- It must be ensured that:
  - Date of operation is correctly entered.
  - In respect of credits to the account the mode of remittance like "By Cash"/ "By Clearing"/ "By OBC No. "/ "By transfer from...." etc must be entered.
  - The amount must be correctly entered.
  - "Debit" entries like payment of cheque out of this account must be correctly entered. If it is payment of a cheque drawn on that account the cheque number paid must be recorded. If the debit is owing to transfer of funds out of this account the reason for

such transfer like "As per standing instruction No......." etc. must be clearly recorded.

Posting of Cheques

- Before posting a cheque in the account, the following must be verified by the Assistant.
  - The cheque is from the drawer's current Cheque Book.
  - Date of the cheque - it must not be post dated or stale cheque - it must be either ante dated or current dated one.
  - Payee's name is filled up legibly.
  - Amount written in words and figures agree.
  - The cheque has been properly signed by the Account Holder/ Authorised Person.
  - In the case of business/ companies/ firms their rubber stamp is affixed and authorised officials have signed.
  - Whether the cheque is a bearer cheque or order cheque - whether the cheque relates to that account.
  - Whether there is sufficient balance available or overdraft arrangement is there to cover the presented cheque.
  - That all the alterations, if any, on the body of the cheque, have been duly authenticated by the drawer.
  - Ensure that the cheque presented for payment is not a "Stopped Cheque". There is no other restriction like notice/ information of death/ insolvency/ lunacy of the Account Holder or attachment order has been received from appropriate authority.
  - In the case of bearer cheque, the bearer is to be asked to sign on the reverse of the cheque and write his name and address.
  - Then issue a Token to the bearer, the token number must be recorded on the back of the cheque in one corner and draw a circle covering this token number.
  - Post the cheque in the respective Account and initial in the space provided in the cheque.
  - Then send the posted cheque to the Passing Officer.
- Passing of Cheques:
  - Before passing a cheque for cash payment the Passing Officer has to also verify and satisfy himself that:

i. the date of the cheque is valid one and that it is not a crossed cheque

ii. amount in words and figures agree

iii. the signature of the Account Holder agrees with the specimen signature on record with the Bank.

iv. the particular cheque has been entered in the correct account and the same has not been stopped by the account holder.

v. for order cheque the identification of payee is to be established to the satisfaction of the Bank.
   - Crossed cheques:

i. the cheques which bear the crossing must be presented through any other banker
ii. if the payee and the drawee has account with the same branch the drawee a/c can be debited and payee a/c credited with the proceeds of the cheque.
iii. if the crossing is "A/c Payee only", then the proceeds of the cheque has to be credited to the payee A/c only.
iv. if a crossed cheque has to be paid by cash, then the drawer has to cancel the crossing and write pay cash along with his signature.
   - And having been satisfied about the above the Passing Officer affixed "pay cash" stamp on the cheque with his full signature under that stamp and draws a line across the signature of the Account Holder in such way that the signature is cancelled.
   - Wherever financial/ passing power for different cadres of officers have been fixed by the Bank, all the vouchers/ instruments have to be passed only by the officer who is authorized/ empowered for the purpose.

Issue of Cheque Book

- Fresh Cheque Books must always be issued only on presentation of "Cheque Book requisition slip" attached to the previous Cheque Book, which bears the Account Number, seal of the Bank, name of the Account holder and the signature of Bank Officer duly signed by the Account Holder.
- In case the customer is unable to produce the "Cheque Book requisition slip" he must give acceptable/ valid reason in the letter in which he requests the Bank to issue him fresh Cheque Book. On receipt of the "Cheque Book requisition slip" the Assistant must verify whether all the cheque leaves of the previous Cheque Book have been used by him. He must record the position in that slip and hand over to the Officer for further action.
- On getting the authorisation of the Officer to issue fresh Cheque Book to the customer, the Assistant must pull out Cheque Book out of the stock with the Officer, which must be in serial order, and write on the outside wrapper of the Cheque Book - a) the Account Number, b) the name of the Account holder. Then write the Account Number on cheque leaves and also in the Cheque Book requisition slip attached to the Cheque Book with the Manager signature.
- The Assistant must write the name of the Account Holder also in this slip, record the Cheque Book issue particulars in "Cheque Book

Issued Register" and release the Cheque Book to him after obtaining his signature in this Register.

Cheque Returned Book:

- Whenever the Assistant finds before posting a cheque in the relative Current Account that there is no sufficient balance in the account to meet the cheque, he must record all relevant details in the "Cheque Returned Book" and circulate this book to local "Clearing Section" and "Bills Section" of the Bank/ Branch.
- These sections will record details of cheques lodged by the Account Holder pending realisation. If there is no cheque pending realisation for credit of the said account they must record "NIL" in the relevant columns of the "Cheque Returned Book."
- The Manager on receipt of this book will pass orders therein either to return or to pass.
- The Assistant on receiving back this register will act as per the orders of the Manger therein.

Cheque Returned Outward Register

- The Assistant will record all the required particulars in this Register whenever a cheque has been ordered to be returned unpaid by the Manager.
- He will also prepare the "Cheque Return Memo" by writing/ marking the relevant objection/ reason for which the said cheque is returned unpaid.
- Passing Officer will sign both the register and the cheque return memo.
- This cheque along with the return memo will be sent to designated clearing section/ HO of the Bank for being returned to collecting Bank through Clearing House.

Stop Payment

- Whenever stop payment instructions are received from customer it has to be verified whether the cheque for which stop payment is issued is already passed or not by perusing the account. If the cheque is unpaid as of the time of receipt of the stop payment instructions, it would be accepted by the Manager/ Officer and the fact has been recorded by him on the letter of instruction. Then all relevant particulars must be entered into the system by the Assistant under "Stop Payment" option and get duly approved by the Manager/ Officer.

Pass Books/ Statement of Accounts

- On the outside wrapper and also in the inside first age full particulars like i) Account Number, ii) Name of the Account Holder, iii) Full Postal address as given, must be written.

- In the inside first page date of issue of Pass Book must be written and the Branch seal must be affixed in the space provided for the officer to sign. The Officer will initial on this seal with date.
- This Pass Book must be issued after obtaining the signature of the customer in the register Last few pages of "Cheque Book Issued Register" may be used for this purpose.
- A list of such abbreviations may be supplied to the customer for his reference. Few examples are:
  - *Ch:* Cheque
  - *Clg.:* Clearing
  - *TT:* Telegraphic Transfer
  - *MT:* Mail Transfer
  - *DD:* Demand Draft
  - *Int.:* Interest
  - *Com.:* Commission
  - *Dr.:* Debit
  - *Cr.:* Credit
  - *OBC:* Outward Bills for Collection
  - *C/o:* Carried over
  - *B/F:* Brought Forward
  - *CB:* Correct Balance etc.
- Depending upon the number of operations in the account the periodicity of issue of statement of account may be decided.

Withdrawals/ Payments/ Remittances

- All withdrawals by the Current Account Holder must be through cheques only.
- All payments to the third parties must be made by the Account Holder only through cheques.
- Bank can effect payment to the debit of the account if the Account Holder has given written instruction or a regular standing instruction for the purpose.
- Remittances for credit of the Current Account either by the Account Holder or third parties must be made only through the Bank's printed challans.
- All transfer/ clearing credits will be made by the Bank through internal transfer vouchers.

Other types of Current Account

- Partnership Firms:

- Partnership Firms must use only the Bank's printed application form specified by the Bank for "Partnership account". No partner has power to do the following:

i. Open a bank account on behalf of the firm in his own name.
ii. Withdraw a legal suit filed by the firm.
iii. Admit any liability in a suit or proceed against the firm.
iv. Acquire or transfer immovable property on behalf of the firm.

- Any of the partners has powers to countermand the payment of a cheque drawn by another partner.
- For opening a Current Account for a partnership firm the following documents must be obtained:

i. Current Account opening form signed by all the partners.
ii. Specimen signature cards signed by all the partners.
iii. Partnership letter signed by all the partners in their personal capacity and not under the seal of the firm.
iv. Original Partnership Deed with a certified copy.
v. Complete instructions regarding the person(s) authorised to operate the account with specimen signatures of the authorised persons with their designation or capacity in which they will operate the account.
vi. Certificate of Registration, in case of a registered partnership firm.

• Hindu Undivided Family (HUF), Joint Stock Companies, Clubs, Associations etc. Trusts, Executors/ Administrators, Government Departments etc.
  - These types of Account Holders must submit application forms as pr Bank's format together with all required documents.
  - In the case of HUF accounts the Current Account opening form and the joint Hindu Family Letter both have to be signed by all the adult members of the joint family.
  - Where the joint family consists of male minors, the Karta should sign the Account Opening Form on behalf of the male minors apart from signing in the capacity as Karta.
  - Under Hindu Law a woman cannot become a coparcener of the HUF.
  - Only the Karta has the eligibility in law to enter into contracts for a HUF and hence the name of the Karta who is authorised to operate the HUF account should be noted in the Ledger.
  - In the case of Joint Stock Company, in addition to getting the Account Opening Application Form and Specimen Signature Card as per Bank's format the following documents should also be collected. Certificate of Incorporation, Certificate of

Commencement of Business, Copy of Memorandum and Articles of Association, Certified copy of Board Resolution authorising the opening and operation of Bank Account signed by the Chairman of the meeting of the Board of Directors and a mandate giving specific instructions concerning the way in which operations on the Bank accounts are to be made.

- In the case of unregistered bodies like Clubs/ Association/ Committee a resolution passed in the appropriate forum as per their Bye-laws regarding opening a Bank account and persons with their designation authorised to operate such Bank account should be obtained.
- In all cases of registered/ unregistered bodies like Clubs/ Association etc. copy of their Bye-laws/ Rules should be obtained. This will help to cross verify whether the account has been opened and the persons authorised to operate the account are as per their Rules/ Bye-laws provisions.
- In the case of Trusts, a copy of Trust Deed should be obtained and compared with the original and authenticated by the concerned Officer. A Trust Letter and resolution signed by all the Trustees should also be obtained.
- The Account Opening Form should be signed by all the Trustees and the account must be opened in the name of the Trust.
- In case there is no Trust Deed and still the Branch receives a request to open an account in the name of a Trust, such cases must be referred to Legal Department of the HO for guidance.
- Before opening accounts for Executors/ Administrators, 'Original will' and probate of the will, if any,/ Letter oaf administration should be called for verification. A certified copy of the same must be retained in Bank's files.
- Such accounts are to be opened in the name of individuals. But after the name of the individual "Executor" "Administrator" must be added in the Account. In the same way it must be entered in the system/ Pass Book/ statement/ cheque books etc.
- In the case of Government Departments, copy of Government Order (G.O.) or Notification authorising the officers to open a Bank account should be obtained.
- In all the cases cheque books must be issued only after obtaining all the necessary documents.

• Temporary Overdraft (TOD):
  - Wherever there are specific provisions in the Current Account Rules/ permission in writing through policy circular or office order has been given by the HO, Temporary Overdrafts can be given

to good and trustworthy customers against their written request.

- Only the Manager/ Officer empowered should sanction TODs. Granting of TOD is at the sole discretion and risk and responsibility of sanctioning Officer/ Manager.
- A written request for TOD from the Account Holder should be obtained.
- Demand Promissory Note should be furnished by the Account Holder.
- An application requesting to admit him as 'B' Class member should be obtained from the Account Holder.

SAVINGS BANK ACCOUNTS

- Who can open Savings Bank Accounts (S.B.A/c):
  - Savings Bank Accounts may be opened in the name of:

  i. Individuals singly or jointly with other individuals with survivor clause like "E or S"/ "A or s".

  ii. minors or on behalf of minors, by their guardian.

  iii. associations, clubs or similar other non-trading institutions provided their by-law/rules are found acceptable and strictly adhered to. They must also be eligible as per the guidelines of RBI.
- Procedures:
  - The procedure for opening the Savings Bank Account:

  i. Opening of a Savings Bank Account must be authorized by the Manager.

  ii. For opening a Savings Bank Account the relevant printed application form of the Bank must only be used.

  iii. The Account Opening Forms as well as Specimen Signatures Card must be signed by the customer in the presence the Manager.

  iv. All the accounts should be properly introduced by the existing Account Holders or persons known to the Bank. The Introducer must also sign before the Manager or the introduction got confirmed and duly recorded. If the Introducer is also on Account Holder his Account Number must also be noted in the Account Opening Form.

  v. It must be ensued that the customer furnishes fully/ complete details like his name, residential and office/ business and full postal address with phone numbers in the application form.

  vi. In case he wishes to have nomination facility the same must be indicated in the Account Opening Form itself.

  vii. Two recent passport size photographs must be obtained from all

viii. Savings Bank Account Holders. One photograph must be affixed to the Account Opening Form and another photograph to the Pass Book/ Specimen Signature Card, as may be applicable.

ix. Initial deposit to open a Savings Bank Account must be received in cash, remitted through Savings Bank Remittance Challan/ Pay in Slip, duly signed by the depositor.

- Other Documents required:
  - The other documents required for opening a Savings Bank Account in the case of Associations/ Clubs etc. in addition to the Account Opening Form and Specimen Signature Cards shall be:

  i. Certified copy of Rules/ Bye-laws/ Memorandum and Articles of Association of the Institution.

  ii. Original certificate of incorporation/ Registration issued by appropriate authority along with a certified copy. The original will have to be returned to the customer after verification with the certified copies.

  iii. Original certificate issued by the Registrar regarding commencement of Business along with a certified copy. The original will have to be returned after verification.

  iv. Certified copy of the General Body/ Board/ Committee regarding opening of a Bank account, names and designation of persons authorised to operate the account and Regulation and conduct of account.

  v. Specimen Signatures of authorised persons duly attested by the Chief Executive of the Institution or the Chairman of the meeting wherein the relevant resolution was passed.

  vi. List of Directors with their designation.

  vii. Any other document specifically required by the Bank.

- Minimum Balance:
  - The minimum balance as prescribed/ fixed by the Bank form time to time must always be maintained by the customer. Whenever the balance in any account falls below the prescribed minimum balance such customer must be advised to regularize the account.
  - If any account holder continuously maintains less than the prescribed minimum balance in his account the Bank may exercise its right to close such an account and penalty charges as applicable has to be charged.
- Method of Opening Savings Bank Account and Maintenance of books:
  - On getting the Account Opening Form duly authorised by the Manager, customer identification must be entered in the Customer ID Form and the initial deposit in cash to open the account, the new account will be opened in the Savings Bank

Module by entering the name, nominee details, full postal residential/ business address, phone numbers if any, operational instructions wherever applicable. The Account Number allotted by the system must be written prominently.

  - In case the account holder is a Minor/ Blind Person/ Illiterate person or if it is with "E or S"/ "A or S"/ Joint operation clause the same must be entered into system and the Pass Book prominently in Red ink.
  - Pass Book must be issued with the Account Number, name of the Account Holder, Postal address on the wrapper page and first inner page. The initial deposit made to open the account must be recorded with date duly attested by the Supervising Officer.
  - As and when Cheque Books are issued to the Savings Bank Account Holder, the cheque numbers must be recorded in the respective account and authenticated.
  - While posting proper recording under "particulars" column must be made.
- Withdrawals:
  - Every Bank prescribes a minimum number of withdrawals, say about 150 withdrawals per Half Year and the rule prescribed must be followed.
  - For withdrawing amounts, from Savings Bank Account either cheques or Bank's withdrawal forms alone must be used. The blank withdrawal forms must be always kept under the custody of the Assistant and should not be placed on the open counter.
  - However, the Savings Bank Account withdrawal form cannot be issued in favour of third parties. It must only be used for withdrawing cash by the Account Holder.
  - Withdrawal form must be accompanied by the Pass Book. This will help the Assistant to properly identify/recognize the bearer/ presenter.
- Posting in the Ledger:
  - The account number on the Savings Bank Account withdrawal form must be checked with the number on the Pass Book and the amount is posted in the correct account.
  - A token is issued after marking the number of the Token on the back of the withdrawal form/ cheque in one corner and by drawing a circle around that token number.
  - Before posting a withdrawal form/ cheque in the system, the Assistant must verify the Date, amount in words and figures, Account number, drawer's signature, name of the payee and only when he is satisfied that the withdrawal form/ cheque qualifies

in all respects, he must post the same in the system.

- The Assistant must initial at the appropriate place in the withdrawal form/ cheque after posting the withdrawal in the system.
- The Pass Book must be updated immediately and the same along with the withdrawal form/ cheque must he handed over to the Passing Officer.
- There must be adequate balance to honour the withdrawal. When there is no sufficient balance in the account to honour the withdrawal/ cheque presented to the Bank, the assistant must record the position and details in the Cheque Returned Book and send it to the Manager/ Passing Officer for authorisation to return the same unpaid.
- On such confirmation/ authorisation the Savings Bank Account withdrawal form/ cheque must be returned together with "Cheque return memo" to the presenter or collecting bank as the case may be.
- No overdraft is allowed on Savings Bank Account.

• Passing of Cheques:
  - Before passing a cheque for cash payment the Passing Officer has to also verify and satisfy himself that:
  i. the date of the cheque is valid one and that it is not a crossed cheque
  ii. amount in words and figures agree.
  iii. the signature of the Account Holder agrees with the specimen signature on record with the Bank.
  iv. the particular cheque has been entered in the correct account and the same has not been stopped by the account holder.
  v. for order cheque the identification of payee is to be established to the satisfaction of the Bank.
  - Crossed cheques:
  i. the cheques which bear the crossing must be presented through any other banker
  ii. if the payee and the drawee has account with the same branch the drawee a/c can be debited and payee a/c credited with the proceeds of the cheque.
  iii. if the crossing is "A/c Payee only", then the proceeds of the cheque has to be credited to the payee A/c only.
  iv. if a crossed cheque has to be paid by cash, then the drawer has to cancel the crossing and write pay cash along with his signature.
  v. And having been satisfied about the above the Passing Officer affixed "pay cash" stamp on the cheque with his full signature

under that stamp and draws a line across the signature of the Account Holder in such way that the signature is cancelled.

vi. Wherever financial/ passing power for different cadres of officers have been fixed by the Bank, all the vouchers/ instruments have to be passed only by the officer who is authorized/ empowered for the purpose.

- Pass Books:
  - For all Savings Bank Accounts Pass Books have to be prepared at the time of opening the account and must be issued to the customer after getting his acknowledgement.
  - Customers must be advised to present the Pass Books at frequent intervals so that entries in the pass Book will be mostly upto date.
  - The pass book must be correctly placed in the PB Printer for getting the entries printed.
  - While all the pages in a Pass Book are exhausted with entries, a continuation Pass Book must be issued. It must be prominently marked on such Pass Book as "Continuation Pass Book".
  - On a written request by the customer, duplicate Pass Book will have to be issued only when authorised by the Manager and after levying the prescribed charges. on such Pass Book it must be prominently marked as "DUPLICATE PASS BOOK".
  - Pass Books received over the counter which may have to be retained for a day or two for updating the entries must be kept under lock and key.
- Interest on Savings Bank Accounts:
  - Rate of interest payable for Savings Bank Accounts will be as decided by the Bank Management from time to time and as per the RBI guidelines.
  - Interest will be calculated on the basis of monthly products. The lowest balance in a Savings Bank Account between 10th and last day of each month will have to be taken as product for the month. Interest will have to be calculated on the TOTAL PRODUCTS of six months.
  - Periodicity of payment of interest on Savings Bank Accounts is once in every six months. Interest on Savings Bank Accounts is paid at the end of February and August. Interest amount will be credited to customers accounts on or before 10th March and Sept. each year.
  - No interest will be paid if he interest earned by any Savings Bank Account in a half year is less then ₹ 1/-.
  - Interest payable in deposit accounts will be rounded off to the nearest rupee.

- Non-Eligibility for Interest:
  - As per the instructions of RBI certain institutions are not eligible for interest on Savings Bank Account balances. Therefore Savings Bank Accounts should not be opened in the names of such institutions.
- Preferential Rate of Interest:
  - 1 per cent preferential rate of interest over the standard rate is allowed.

  i. On deposits held individually or jointly with dependents in the case of employees of the bank/ retired employees/ widows of employees/ widows of retired employees etc..

  ii. On deposits of an Association or a Fund all the members of which are the members of Bank Staff.

  iii. A declaration has to be obtained from the person/ association eligible for the preferential rate.

  iv. Before extending preferential rate of interest to eligible retired employees/ widows of retired employees/ widows of employees etc. documentary evidence of service/ retirement/ identity of the widow should be scrutinized and kept attached to Account Opening Form.
- Transfer of Accounts:
  - At the written request of the customer his Savings Bank Account can be transferred from one branch to another branch of the bank free of any charges.

  i. While transferring a Savings Bank Account the monthly products qualifying for interest must be clearly indicated in the transfer credit advice so that transferee branch could record the same.

  ii. The Account Holder must surrender all unused cheque leaves to the old branch. The new branch must ensure by perusing the account through the system that all unused cheque leaves have been surrendered by the Account Holder before issuing a new Cheque Book.

  iii. The receiving branch must re-open the account with the first entry as "Deposited by transfer of account from........Branch" with the same customer ID.

  iv. The Account opening form and specimen signature card must be transferred to the branch where the account is sought to be transferred to, by retaining xerox copy in the branch.
- Inoperative Accounts:
  - All Savings Bank Accounts, on which there have been no operations for a period of one year, must be changed to 'Dormant Account".

  - Such accounts remaining without any operation for a continuous period of three years must be transferred to "Inoperative Status" which must be kept under the custody of the Officer.
  - In case an Account Holder subsequently wants to withdraw the entire amount of balance in the account and if he is properly identified, the same may be permitted.
  - In case the Account Holder wants to withdraw only a part amount and retain the balance amount in the account and would like to revive the operations in the account, first the account must be transferred from inoperative status to operative status and allow the operations.
- Conversion of Accounts:
  - Conversion of individual account into joint account is permitted.
  - For all such accounts Fresh Account Opening forms duly signed by all the proposed Joint Account Holders must be obtained along with a letter of request for such conversion into Joint Account from the existing single Account Holder.
  - Recent passport size photographs of all Account Holders must be obtained.
  - In the system the names of the Joint Account Holders must be added. Operational instructions like "E or S"/ "A or S"/Jointly must also be entered.
- Staff Accounts:
  - It is desirable to restrict the number of Savings Bank Accounts that may be opened and maintained by each staff member of the bank in his individual name or in joint names with family member(s). Such accounts must be conducted strictly in accordance with the Rules.
  - The Branch Officers must ensure that all cheques drawn by the staff members on their accounts when presented in clearing, are personally scrutinized by the Officer particularly with reference to the balance available in the account..
  - Third Party cheques/DDs should not be permitted to be collected in Staff Account.
  - If the account is operated with disproportionately huge amounts the Manager must watch such accounts.
  - In all the Savings Bank Accounts Staff members, it must be prominently marked as "Staff Account".
- Balancing of Accounts:
  - For periodical balancing of savings Bank accounts, all OK statements have to be generated to check for differences if any.
- Interest on Inoperative Accounts:

- In order to have a correct position of Pand L accounts of the Branch, it is desirable that even for all interest bearing S.B. Accounts in "Inoperative Status" the interest is calculated as in the case of operative accounts.
- When an account holder requests the Bank to issue a certificate of interest paid during the year the same must be issued.

- Closing of Account.
  - Savings Bank Account may be closed at the request of the Account Holder in writing. In case of Joint Accounts, all account holders will have to sign the request letter for closure of the account.
  - Together with such request letter the account holder must surrender all the unused cheque leaves and also the Pass Book.
  - After closing the account the Pass Book, if required by the customer, may be returned after making the entries upto date and marking "Account Closed" after the last entry and also in all pages in the Pass Book.
  - For payment of the balance in the account, a cheque/withdrawal form must be obtained from the Account Holder, at the time of closing the account.
  - In the "Accounts Opened and Closed Register" it must be noted against the serial number of the closed Savings Bank Accounts as 'CLOSED' with date of closing and the account number may be rounded off. Similar noting must be done in the computer system also.
  - The relevant account opening form as well as the specimen signature card of the closed account must be removed from the files/records and two parallel lines must be drawn across them within which a note as 'CLOSED ON.......' to be made with the signature of the Officer and kept separately.
- ABHYUDAYA Savings Bank Account: This is a No Frills variant of the normal Savings Bank Account. This type of account is introduced to facilitate financial inclusion of persons of modest financial standing. The following are the salient features:
  - Allowed to be opened on single individual name.
  - No minimum balance is insisted upon and no service charges or penalties are levied. Maximum balance is ₹ 25,000/-.
  - Account can be opened with a minimum of ₹ 2-.
  - Number of withdrawals allowed are 10 per quarter. Pass Book is provided.
  - No Cheque Books or ATM Cards are issued. Cheques are also not collected in this account. Operation upon account is only by way of cash remittance and cash withdrawals.
  - Nomination facility is available.

MAINTENANCE OF ACCOUNTS AND OPERATIONAL PROCEDURES

- Salient Features:
  - Only bank's printed application form must be used for opening of an account and the person who intends to open the account must fill all the details and sign before the Branch Manager.
  - Introducer must preferably sign before the Manger of the Bank or the introduction should be got confirmed and recorded as seen with the signature of the Officer/ Manager.
  - In the Account Opening form both residential and office address with phone numbers will have to be furnished along with the photographs.
  - In case the customer would like to have the Nomination facility the same must be recorded in the Account Opening Form.
  - Whenever an account is closed it must be prominently marked in Red ink as account closed with the date of closing in the Account Opening Form and also in the computer system and ledger printouts.
  - Specimen signature cards must be kept locked and under the custody of an officer of the Bank and specimen signature has to be scanned for storing in the computer system.
  - All inoperative accounts must be marked as inoperative in the computer system.
  - All Current/Savings and Recurring Deposit account will be assigned serial number by the system. Once the account number is allotted the same should be recorded in the Account Opening Form.
  - While opening the account, the following details should be properly recorded in the computer system without fail.

i. Name of the Account holder

ii. Full postal address of both residence and office.

iii. Residence and Office phone numbers

iv. Date of opening the account, cheque numbers and date of issue

v. Operations instruction, if any,

vi. Whether "E or S" or "Joint Account" must be recorded properly.

vii. Introducer's name and his account number.

viii. In the case of minor – Date of Birth and guardian details

ix. In the case of Blind or Illiterate person it must be prominently written on the ledger sheet as "Blind", "Illiterate" and a photograph of the person must be attached to ledger sheet scanned and stored in computer system.

x. Nomination details

xi. address for correspondence
xii. PAN Number.

- Separate Index Register in alphabetical order of the customers for Current, Savings and Recurring Deposit account should be maintained.
- Minimum requisite amount for opening the new account has to be paid in cash.
- Pass Book should bear the photograph of the customer.
- A separate Index Register for Term Deposit holders and Safe Deposit Locker holders should be maintained.

• Return of Cheques:

- All the cheques returned un paid by the Bank must be recorded in "Cheque Returned Book" initially. After getting the orders of the Manager to return the said cheque proper entry must be made in "Cheque Returned Book" wherein the reason/objection for return of the cheque should be recorded.
- Issue of advice for cheque deposited by customers for collection or clearing and also for cash remittances through 'pay-in-slips', counter foil duly stamped and signed by an officer of the Bank must be given to the customer.
- For Credits and Debits made to customer's account ie., for transfer type of transactions resulting in such debits/credits in the customer's account, copy of advice must be sent to the customer.

• Cash Payment of cheques:

- Before entering cash payment cheques in the system, Ledger Assistant has to ensure that:

i. it is bearer cheque and relates to the account
ii. it is dated current date or previous dates and not stale or outdated or non-existent date
iii. signed by the Account Holder properly, in the case of illiterates the LTI has to be attested affixed.
iv. amount in figure and words agree,
v. there are sufficient funds in the account to honour the cheque
vi. the particular cheque has not been stopped by the Account Holder
vii. the balance in the account has not been attached/ frozen by any appropriate authority.
viii. no notice of death/insanity/insolvency of the Account Holder has been received.
ix. tokens are to be issued and the number of which must be marked on the back of the cheque for all cash payment cheques, and
x. the Assistant has to initial at appropriate place on the cheque for having entered the cheque in the system.

xi. cheque should contain the name of the payee

xii. any alterations in the cheque has to be authenticated by the drawer with his full signature.

xiii. All particulars in the cheque has to be written in ink or typewritten.

xiv. At the time of payment also the signature of the bearer has to be verified by the paying cashier.

- Passing of Cheques:
  - Before passing a cheque for cash payment the Passing Officer has to also verify and satisfy himself that:

i. the date of the cheque is valid one and that it is not a crossed cheque

ii. amount in words and figures agree.

iii. the signature of the Account Holder agrees with the specimen signature on record with the Bank.

iv. the particular cheque has been entered in the correct account and the same has not been stopped by the account holder.

v. for order cheque the identification of payee is to be established to the satisfaction of the Bank.

- Crossed cheques:

i. the cheques which bear the crossing must be presented through any other banker

ii. if the payee and the drawee has account with the same branch the drawee a/c can be debited and payee a/c credited with the proceeds of the cheque.

iii. if the crossing is "A/c Payee only", then the proceeds of the cheque has to be credited to the payee A/c only.

iv. if a crossed cheque has to be paid by cash, then the drawer has to cancel the crossing and write pay cash along with his signature.

- And having been satisfied about the above the Passing Officer affixed "pay cash" stamp on the cheque with his full signature under that stamp and draws a line across the signature of the Account Holder in such way that the signature is cancelled.
- Wherever financial/ passing power for different cadres of officers have been fixed by the Bank, all the vouchers/ instruments have to be passed only by the officer who is authorized/ empowered for the purpose.
- Payment of cash:

i. Before making payment the Cash Assistant has to ensure that:

1. the cheque is properly dated bears the signature of the drawer, posted by the Ledger Assistant and passed by the Passing Officer.
2. the receiver of the cash payment surrenders the correct token as indicated on the back of the cheque.

3. as an additional step to ensure that payment is made only to the correct receiver the Cash Assistant may politely ask the receiver to sign again on the reverse and also to state the amount to be received by him,
4. on all payment vouchers/cheques on their backside the Cash Assistant must note the denominations in which he had made the payment and also affix "Cash Paid" stamp with date and enter the denominations in the computer system.
5. In the case of *Any Branch Banking* (ABB) transaction, the Account holder only has to receive cash and no bearer can be allowed payment.
   - Stop Payment:
   i. the drawer of the cheque can give stop payment instructions for stopping the payment of a particular instrument.
   ii. the drawer has to give the correct cheque No. in the requisition along with his signature as per Bank's record.
   iii. the Manager has to immediately satisfy himself whether the instrument is already paid or not. If it is unpaid the details have to be immediately entered into the computer system for ensuring non- payment of the cheque.
   iv. the bank cannot honour the cheque after getting the clear stop payment instructions from the customer.
   - Revoking of stop payment:
   i. the drawer of the cheque can give the revokal instructions asking the bank to honour the cheque when presented.
   ii. this revokal requisition can be given by the drawer by giving the correct cheque number along with his/her signature as given in the Bank's record.
   iii. when the stop payment is revoked the Bank can honour the cheque on presentation.
   iv. In the case of joint account, all the authorised signatories have to sign for giving the revokal.
   - Remittance in A/C:
   i. Cash/cheque – Either the customer or his representative can remit cash/cheque.

1. Cash:
   a. the cashier after satisfying himself can accept the cash and give the counterfoil of the pay-in-slip to the person remitting the cash.
   b. the Staff Assistant on the Counter should enter the amount to the account to which it relates.
   c. the Manager after satisfying himself would authorise the credit into the account.
   d. remittance of ₹ 50,000/- and above in cash is to be accompanied after verifying the PAN No. and noting the same in the voucher.

2. Cheque:
   a. the Staff Assistant on the counter after ensuring that the A/c number, date, amount in words and figures, payee name is correct would give the acknowledgement of the cheque on the counterfoil of the pay in slip.
   b. the cheque has to be sent either in local clearance or outward bills cheque for collection A/c depending on the place of the payable branch and on realization the proceeds of the cheque has to be credited to the customer's A/c.
   c. if the cheque has "A/c payee" crossing, then the proceeds on realization has to be credited to the A/c of the payee only.
   d. Third party cheques should generally be not credited to the customer's account to prevent any wrongful conversion.
   – Security Measures:
   i. Issue of cheque books:
1. Cheque books for newly opened account must be issued only after getting written request from the customer. In the case of new Savings Bank accounts the Cheque book(s) may be issued after assessing the need of the customer.
2. All cheque Books must be issued only after being authorized by the Manager.
3. in the case of existing accounts, fresh cheque books must be issued only against the presentation of the "Cheque Book requisition slip" taken out from the previous cheque book.
4. As a measure of precaution and as far as possible fresh cheque book must be issued only after the previous cheque book is exhausted.
5. while issuing a cheque book it must be ensured that all the cheque leaves bear the name of the branch as well as the Account number. Whenever Cheque books are issued the details of cheque leaves should be noted in the system.
6. the cheques issued has to be entered in cheque issue register and the customer has to sign on the register in the column provided for having taken the cheque if the cheque book sent by post, the same has to be noted.
7. cheque issued has to be entered in the computer system and authorized by the Manager.

   ii. Issue of Loose Cheque Leaf:
1. Loose cheque leaf must be issued only to Account Holder.
2. Loose cheque Leaf must be issued only against specific written request by the customer with valid reason that satisfies the Manager. Only against the authorization of the Manager, a loose cheque leaf should be issued.

3. This loose cheque leaf must also be issued only after entering the details in "Loose Cheque Leaf Issue Register" and after getting the signature of the customer as acknowledgement.
4. The number of the loose cheque leaf issued to the customer should be recorded in the system.
5. for issuing loose cheque leaf a fresh cheque book must be used, on which "To be issued as Loose Leaf" must be marked in Red ink and retained under the custody of the Manager.
6. unused cheque leaves surrendered by a customer whose account has been closed should not be used for issuing loose cheque leaves.
7. The following details must also be recorded on the face of the loose cheque leaf issued to the customer.
   a. Loose Leaf issued to Shri................A/c No.
   b. "Pay Self Only"
   c. Valid for ....(the date of issue of this loose cheque to be noted here.
8. The loose cheque leaf must be used on the same day of issue and it must be used only for withdrawing cash.
   - Transfer of Accounts:
   i. Transferring Branch:

1. At the written request of the customer his account may be closed and transferred to another branch of the bank.
2. In the case of joint account the request for transfer must be signed by all the joint holders.
3. Unused Cheque Books/cheque leaves must be surrendered by the customer at the time of closing the account for transfer to another branch.
4. Before closing and transferring an account all the cheques issued on this account by the customer must have been presented for payment.
5. In the transfer credit advice all relevant particulars like name of the Account Holder, new address etc., are to be furnished. Together with this credit advice he Account Opening Form, Specimen signature card, Pass book duly stamped as "Transferred" with upto date entries must be forwarded to the Transferee Branch.
6. If any outstation cheque is pending collection for this account the fact of transferring this account to another branch must be noted in "Bills Lodged Register so that on realization the proceeds may be remitted to the Transferee branch.
7. All standing instructions for transferring/remitting out of this account must be closed under intimation to customer.
8. Make a noting in the accounts opened and closed Register against this account as "Transferred to .... Branch" with date.

– Transferee branch:

i. When an advice regarding transfer of an account from another branch is received, the receiving branch must open a new account in the branch in the name of the customer.

ii. It must be recorded in the system account that "The account transferred from .... Branch".

iii. New Pass Book must be issued with the opening balance being the amount received from another branch as per transfer credit advice.

iv. New cheque book must be issued against written request of the customer.

v. New Pass Book together with old Pass Book received from another branch must be issued to the customer after obtaining his acknowledgement.

vi. Proper entry must be made with the new account number against which it must be noted as "Account transferred from ....Branch" in the "Accounts Opened and Closed Register".

– Stocks of Cheque Books/DD Books/Pay Orders and Stationery items:

i. The Branch must maintain separate stock registers for (i) Cheque Books/ DD Books and Pay order Books, (ii) Term Deposit receipt Books, (iii) Stationery items and (iv) Furniture and Fitting items.

ii. As and when fresh stock of Cheque Books/DD Books and Pay Orders are received by the branch they must be added to the respective group like 100 leaves/50 leaves/20 leaves/10 leaves cheque Books, DD Books of AIMAS (MICR and NON-MICR), DD Books of State Drafts Scheme etc. In addition to recording number of books received it must also be recorded in this stock register the serial numbers/DDs/Pos received by the branch.

iii. Cheque Books/DD Books/Payorder books have to be withdrawn from the stocks, for being issued to customers, only in the serial order and should not be pulled out at random. All withdrawals must be recorded in the stock register.

iv. All the Cheque Books/DD/PO books and even the serial numbered Term Deposit receipt books must always be kept under lock and key.

v. These all are called Security Instruments and therefore the stock must be physically verified at the end of each month and reported to the HO quarterly in the prescribed format.

– Inoperative Accounts:

i. Under Sec.26 of BR Act a return must be filed to RBI furnishing the details of Current/Savings Bank Accounts which remain dormant, ie., inoperative for a continuous period of 10 years and above.

ii. In view of the same, the Bank has to maintain "Inoperative Accounts status" in respect of those Current and Savings Bank Accounts which remain inoperative for 10 years and above.

iii. With a view to exercising proper control over the accounts and to avoid any manipulation by the Bank's staff members or others, it is desirable to shift those Current and Savings Bank Accounts which remain inoperative for a continuous period of 3 years and above to a separate inoperative status which may be styled as "Inoperative Accounts – 3 years and above Accounts". The regular inoperative ledger will be styled as "Inoperative Accounts 10 years and above Accounts".

iv. However the accounts operations of which have been stopped by court orders or attachment orders by appropriate authorities or when the account shows debit balance should not be transferred to "Inoperative Accounts".

v. Any credit/remittance is received for an inoperative account the fact must be brought to the notice of the Manager who will examine the position and decide about the status of account from 'inoperative' to 'operative' after proper proof to the satisfaction of the bank.

vi. Interest at applicable rate must be credited for every half year and every year for all interest bearing inoperative accounts.

vii. No transactions by the concerned Account Holder be permitted in an "Inoperative Account" other than close the account or to transfer it to "Operative Accounts".

viii. All debits to "Inoperative Accounts" must be passed by the Branch Manager.

ix. When any remittance is received for credit to "Inoperative Accounts" the same should be brought to the notice of the Branch Manager/Checking Officer, immediately.

x. In case the customer desires to revive his 'Inoperative Account' he must be asked to give a request letter explaining the reasons for the account remaining dormant and why he wants to revive the operations in the said account.

xi. When the Branch Manager is satisfied with the explanation of the customer, he may authorize transfer of such account from 'Inoperative Accounts status' to 'Operative Accounts status'.

xii. New cheque books should be issued to the inoperative Account Holder on revival under the authority of the Branch Manager only after ensuring that the Account Holder is properly identified.

– Exceptional cases:

i. The following categories of accounts, even if they remain 'dormant' need not be transferred to "Inoperative Accounts status".

1. Where operations in the account have been stopped under Garnishee order or any Court Order.
2. Where the nature of account itself permits only periodical and not regular operation.
3. Where the account is under lien or charge for advances allowed to the same customer in another account.
4. Where the account is showing DEBIT BALANCE.

– Procedure for submission of Records to Statutory orities:

i. Whenever orders are received in writing from the Court/IT Authorities/Police Department in criminal cases calling for certain records, the Bank has to necessarily produce such records.

ii. In all such cases when the originals are removed from the Vouchers for submission, Xerox copies of the Vouchers have to be inserted in the respective position in the Voucher bundle duly attested by the Manager/Officer of the Bank duly stating the purpose of such removal.

iii. Notice received from the above said authorities will have to be retained in a separate file under the custody of the Manger. Acknowledgements received from them relating to the records furnished by the Bank have also to be retained same file.

iv. Originals as and when returned to the bank must be again inserted in the same place in the voucher bundle and the xerox copies have to be removed and filed in the respective file duly noting that originals are received and placed in voucher bundle.

– Attachment Orders:

i. Garnishee Order is an attachment order issued by a Court under order 21, Rule 46 of Civil procedure code. It is an order of the Court obtained by the judgement creditor attaching the funds belonging to a judgement debtor with the Bank. Here the Bank is the Garnishee.

ii. Time and date of receipt of Garnishee order must be recorded in the Ledger Account with the attestation of the Manager.

iii. If no specific amount is mentioned in the Garnishee order the order simply attaches all the sums due and accruing to that customer as on the date of receipt of Garnishee order by the Bank.

iv. The Court may issue such Garnishee order in two parts. First order called as "Order NISI" will be seeking the explanation of the Bank why the balances in the accounts of the 'judgement debtor' with the bank should not be attached and utilized towards settlement of dues to the 'judgement creditor'. On receipt of such order the Bank must immediately stop payments out of such accounts and also inform the customer about this court order and the fact that the Bank could not allow any payment/withdrawal from the account till the Court issues revised orders. On receipt of the second order of the Court which is called "order absolute" the Bank will have to remit the attached funds to the Court out of the account of the 'judgement debtor' with the Bank.

v. With a view to ensuring that no payment by oversight is made out of such account it is always desirable to transfer the attached amount to suspense account.

vi. If the amount available in the attached account is less than the amount indicated in Court order the amount so available must be transferred to suspense account and if no specific amount has been mentioned in the court order the entire balance available in the account must be transferred to suspense account.

vii. A Garnishee order in the name of an individual will not attach the account operated by the said customer as a Trustee/Executor/Administrator.

viii. In the case of a joint account, Garnishee order specifying only one of the joint Account Holders does not bind other joint holders and the Court must be approached for withdrawal of such order. However if the order specifies all the joint Account Holders, such order will attach not only the balance in the joint account but also the balances in the individual accounts of the joint Account Holders.

– Weeding out Unremunerative/Undesirable Accounts:

i. Unremunerative Accounts are the accounts in which balances quite often fall below the minimum balance prescribed and/or the accounts which have been opened and maintained with very meagre balance just to avail other facilities like purchase of DDs etc.

ii. Undesirable Accounts are the accounts wherein cheques are often drawn for amounts in excess of balance available and without any arrangement, which results in return of many cheques.

iii. It is desirable that bank sends notices to such customers maintaining unremunerative/undesirable accounts informing them the intention of the bank to close such accounts and a reminder after a month. Give them two months time and then close such accounts and remit the balance amount due to the customer by a Payorder/DD.

iv. In respect of Undesirable Accounts the officers must keep constant vigil to ensure that no cheque is inadvertently passed when there is no sufficient funds in the account.

v. When the bank sends notice to the customer maintaining such unremunerative/ undesirable accounts, the bank should not issue fresh cheque Books to such customers.

vi. At the time of closing such accounts, the Bank must take all steps to collect unused cheque leaves/books from such customer.

– Other Attachment Orders:

i. Other attachment orders are normally issued by competent authorities like Income Tax/Commercial Tax officers/PF/ Employees State Insurance authorities. On receipt of such attachment orders, the fact should be noted in Ledger with date and time of receipt of such order duly attested by the Manager.

ii. Account Holder must be informed through Registered post about receipt of such attachment order and that the attached amount has been set aside by the bank and the same could be released to the Account Holder only if he is able to get orders from the authorities concerned withdrawing the attachment order and produce to the bank within reasonable time.

iii. If the attached amount is lying in a Current/Savings Bank Account the amount must be transferred to suspense account. If the attached amount is in Term Deposit it must be prominently noted in Red ink, "Under Attachment by IT/Commercial Tax Authorities" duly attested by the Manager. No foreclosure of such attached Term Deposit should be allowed, similarly, no loan against such attached term deposit should be sanctioned.

iv. Bank should also acknowledge receipt of such attachment order and also seek time to comply with their notice as the matter has been referred to Bank's Head Office for guidance.

v. The Branch must refer such cases to Head Office Legal Department for guidance.

–. STANDING INSTRUCTIONS:

i. The customer of the Bank can instruct the Bank in insisting along with his signature to carry out certain functions at fixed periodicity like:

1. Transferring amount from SB A/c to RD A/c
2. Transferring interest on Term Deposit to SB A/c or any other A/c
3. Transferring amount from SB A/c to certain loan account etc.
4. Payment of Insurance Premium etc.

ii. These instructions have to be entered into the computer system.

iii. At the beginning of the day, the Manager/Assistant has to verify whether such instructions are recorded for being executed and invoke the relevant option in computer system.

iv. The customer can stop the instructions given by him in writing along with his signature.

CASH AND IT'S CUSTODY

General

- The Cash and Small Coin Balances must be kept in the Strong Room in the joint custody of the Head Cashier/ Cashier and an authorised Supervising Official, who will be the Manager to perform this duty.
- Managers should see that no member of staff other than the Cashier/ Teller receives money over the counter from depositors. Notices to this effect should be prominently displayed in English and also the regional language in two places, one near the cash department and the other near the entrance.

Strong Room/ Safe

The Strong Room or Safe must be under the double lock of the Cashier and the Supervising Official in charge of cash. Both officials must be present when the Strong Room/ Safe is opened and as far as possible, all receptacles in the Strong Room which are used for storing Cash and Small Coin balances must also be under the double lock of the Cashier and the Supervising Official, with the exception of the receptacle used for the Cashier's hand balance which should be under his single lock. It must be ensured that the locking mechanism of all receptacles is effective and that the doors of all cupboards etc. are securely fastened before being locked.

Cash Balance of the Bank

- The bulk of the Cash Balance should always be in the Strong Room/ Safe under joint custody, while the remainder which will be kept as low as conveniently possible, will be left with the Head Cashier/ Cashier during the day for the day's transactions. Only cash sufficient for the day's requirements will be withdrawn in the morning from joint custody.
- The amounts of all notes and coins withdrawn from, or deposited in, the joint custody portion of the bank's Cash Balance will be entered immediately in the Reserve Cash Register under the initials of the joint custodians. The Reserve Cash Register must always remain in the Strong Room.
- The particulars of the Bank's Cash Balance at the close of business each day will be recorded in the Cash Balance Book, which will be

checked and signed by the Head Cashier/ Cashier and the Supervising Official after the latter has compared all the items of cash balance taking into account the cashier's hand balance, reserve cash and coins balance. The Manager will also sign the Cash Balance Book after agreeing the combined total of the 'Joint Custody' balance and the Head Cashier's/ Cashier's Hand Balance with the Closing Balance of his Cash Scroll.

Checking of Cash Balance

- Before taking notes and coin into the 'Joint Custody' balance, the Supervising Official will check their correctness in the following manner:
  - He will personally count ALL notes of denominations above ₹.10/ - and will verify a portion of all other notes on the 'clip system'. Under this system a few notes in each book of notes are clipped together at the top. The remainder is counted by an employee other than the one responsible for its correctness in the presence of the Supervising Official who verifies the total by counting the clipped notes. Notes of the same denomination are banded together into books of one hundred pieces each, every ten such books being tied up into a bundle of one thousand pieces. As counting machines are supplied to branches, the supervising officer/ Manager will check all the note bundles using the note counting machine personally.
  - The Supervising Official will have all bags of coins weighed in his presence and a few number of bags emptied to verify that the contents are genuine coins.
  - He will take and count a few pieces and leave the remainder to be counted in his presence same as in the case of 'Clip System' for notes. He will also verify the relative denomination slips in the bags at the same time.
  - Occasionally this will also be done in the case of small and uncurrent coins.
  - The Supervising Official will verify at the close of the working day that the 'Joint Custody Balance' corresponds exactly with the entries in the Cash Balance Book.
  - He will also invariably check the entire Head Cashier's/ Cashier's hand balance of loose notes and also check the loose packets in Hand Balance and initial against the items checked in the Cash Balance Book.
  - After the closing cash is checked by the Supervising Official, he must also ensure that the notes and coins held in the Head

Cashier's/ Cashier's Hand Balance are kept in the Cash Box and locked in his presence.

- He should also accompany the Cashier to the Safe Room when the Cash Box is kept under joint custody.
- Before the safe is closed, the Supervising Official, Head Cashier and the Cashier should check the bundles kept in the vault and verify the same with the Reserve Cash Register.
- At least once a week on different days, the officer holding charge of cash will check the whole of the bank Cash Balance by test check of different denominations and Register evidence of such check in the Cash Balance Book under his signature and date.

Shortage or Excess in cash

- Accounting for shortage or excess in cash has to be carried out as follows:
  - Any shortage in the Cash Balance should be recovered the same day from the Head Cashier/ Cashier, who will in turn recover it from the concerned employee of the Cash Department.
  - Failing recovery on the same day, the amount of shortage should be debited to the Suspense Account taking the signatures of the members responsible for the shortage on the reverse of the voucher under report to the Head Office and adjusted on recovery from the concerned members.
  - Head Cashier/Cashier is responsible for any shortage either in Hand or Vault Balance. In case of any shortage in any book of notes, the Cashiers who have signed the Denomination Slips, will be responsible for the shortage.
  - Any excess in the Cash Balance must be credited to Sundry Creditors Account on the same day itself.
  - Items which have been lying unclaimed for more than six months will be transferred to Head Office.

Insurance

Insuring the cash in transit/ safe shall be carried out as follows:

- All cash remittances in transit are covered under the Blanket Insurance Policy obtained by the Bank.
- It must be ensured that the maximum limit laid down therein for any one carriage is not exceeded under any circumstances.
- Cash in safe and on the counter should be kept within insured limit as directed by Head Office from time to time,
- Care should be taken particularly in the case of cash on the counter to ensure any excess over the insured limit amount is placed immediately inside the safe under joint custody and the Head Office intimated to lift the surplus cash.

Custody of Keys

- Particulars of all important keys, including those of the Head Cashier/ Cashier, must be entered in the Key Register. The Register should show what originals and duplicates exist and where they are to be found and must be initialed by every incoming Manager.
- The main keys of the branch may on no account leave the possession of the officials to whose charge they have been entrusted except as specified by the bank or in the case of incapacitation for duty when they will be taken over by another Bank official deputed by their Central Office/ Regional Office. The grave consequences that may result from any slackness in the observance of this instruction should be strongly impressed on officials, particularly those responsible for the safe custody of cash, gold ornaments, securities and other valuables.
- When the keys of the Strong Room or cash safe are kept in the personal safe of the Manager, the key of the safe in which they are lodged must not leave his custody. The officials holding custody of the safe/ strong room should not move freely to places other than the place of work or their residence while in personal possession of the keys.
- Subordinate employees or other unauthorized persons must never be allowed to handle the keys of the Strong Room and safes for any purpose whatsoever.
- The above instructions apply with equal force to the Head Cashier/ Cashiers in joint charge of cash and valuables.
- In case of safes previously handled by unauthorized officials, the Manager must arrange with Head office for the levers of the locks thereof to be changed.
- Great care must be taken with all locks and keys. Any important key showing signs of serious wear should be informed to the Head Office and handed over in sealed packet, in order that a new lock may be ordered and the duplicate can be issued for use in the meanwhile.
- No important key pertaining to cash counters, safes, lockers, strong rooms, almirahs, main entrance may be made and no repairs to such locks be got carried out without the prior permission of Head Office.
- All repairs, if permitted, must be carried out under the personal supervision of the Manager and the Head Cashier/ Cashier if he has joint control over the Strong Room door or safe under repair.

Duplicate Keys

The Banks must follow the instructions as mentioned below with regard to the Duplicate Keys:

- The officials holding the keys of the Strong Room/ safe room and safes/ cupboards containing cash, gold ornaments under pledge to the Bank and other securities, will pack their duplicate keys individually in a strong cloth lined envelope which will be sealed by them with seals. Before they are packed the keys must be greased and labelled.

- The sealed packets must be placed in a strong wooden or tin box locked or otherwise secured and wrapped in water-proof cloth.
- It must then be sealed in the presence of the officials concerned and the sealed box will be labelled with the name of the branch and should bear a docket reading as under:
  - This packet contains duplicate keys of .... Branch of the .... Bank and is deliverable against the joint signature of the Manager and Cashier of the branch for the time being".
- It should be signed by the Manager/ Cashier or the Supervising Official whose keys are deposited therein. These instructions should also be conveyed to the branch of the Bank holding the box in safe custody by means of a letter signed by all the officials holding the keys.
- The keys relating to the Head Office branch will be lodged in State Bank of India, Local Head Office.
- In all cases, the relative safe deposit receipt will be entered in the Branch documents Register and kept in the personal custody of the Manager in a safe or cabinet. Under no circumstances should the receipt be kept in any other safe, the duplicate key of which is held in safe custody with another branch or bank, as in the event of the loss of the original key or keys, the duplicates may not be available without the production of the safe custody receipt.
- Duplicate keys must be withdrawn from safe deposit and the keys rotated once every year.

Security measures

The security measures as advised by the Head Office in respect of security guards deployed and use of alarm system etc. should be scrupulously followed.

CLEARING

General

- The Head Office clearing section acts as "Service Branch" and functions as a Clearing Centre for all the instruments such as Drafts, Cheques etc. received from its Head Office customers and those of its branches.
- These instruments will have to be presented for collection through the "Clearing House".

Clearing House

- Bank Of India is conducting clearing in Hyderabad.
- The Clearing House will function during the stipulated hours which will be communicated to all Member Banks. The Member Banks will have to strictly adhere to these Clearing House hours.
- Delayed Participation in the Clearing House Operations will result in Non- Acceptance of the cheques presented by that Bank by all other Member Banks which in turn will cause serious damages to that Bank.
- The Clearing Operations may take place 2/3 times in a day in the following order:
  - MICR inward Clearing – received by 9.00 AM
  - High Value Clearing -11.30 AM
  - Returns Clearing – 1 PM
  - ECS - 9.30 AM
- On Saturdays high value clearing is not held.
  - *Note*: Timings are subject to change as may be notified by the Clearing House.

Operations in the MICR Clearing at Branch

- At the Branch when the cheques are received for collection form the customer, the payees name on the instrument and on the pay-in-slip has to be verified which is to be one and the same, unless otherwise the instruments are not crossed and are endorsed by the payee in some other person's favour.
- The amount on the instrument and that on the pay-in-slip should be one and the same.
- After ensuring that the instrument is drawn on local bank it should be sent for collection in the immediate next clearing as far as possible.
- While booking the instruments for presentation in outward clearing, the information should be completely filled in, including the Bank and Branch Code. *e.g.* Andhra Bank, Somajiguda – 011 047.
- After tallying with the total presentation and affixing the clearing stamp, crossing stamp etc., the bundle of instruments have to be sent to the Head Office, Clearing Dept. strictly by the stipulated time advised by the Head Office.

Operations in the MICR Clearing at Head Office

- The Head Office has a time schedule depending upon the Clearing House hours to collect the cheques from all the Branches to be presented in that day's clearing.
- The instruments received from Branches are encoded in the machine

after taking the information of that branch by means of floppy from the CBS and uploading into the MICR encoding batch..

- After consolidation of all the instruments and bundling bank-wise, the instruments are taken to the clearing house for presentation to various banks.

Pre-requisite for sending cheque in clearing

- APCOB Clearing Stamp:
  - All the instruments presented through the Clearing House should bear the 'Clearing' Stamp with Bank and Branch abbreviation with specific code number and the date of presenting in Clearing House.
  - Normally in Non-MICR Centers this 'Clearing' Stamp of the Bank will be affixed on the face of the Instruments.
- APCOB Crossing Stamp with MICR code.
- Verify name of payee on cheque and on pay-in-slip which should be one and the same in all respects and in the status also.
- Verify the amount on the cheque and that on pay-in-slip which should be one and the same.
- Cheques with a/c payee crossing must be collected to the Payee a/c. only.
- The branches will have to send the unpaid Return Cheques_ through the branch courier to reach the Head branch before stipulated time *i.e.* 12.30 PM.

Inward Clearing Cheques

- The Head Office will arrange to collect the inward clearing instruments from the Clearing House by 8.30 AM and by 9.30 AM send to respective Branch through courier.
- On getting the inward clearing instruments, the staff of the clearing section, Head Office, will have to verify the number of cheques as per the claim slip received from Clearing House. Then record the number of instruments and the total value against the respective branches in the inward clearing Register and debit the respective Branch for the total value of the presentation on the Branch. It will then send the claim slip to the Branch along with the relative instruments.
- With the Claim slip the clearing cheques will be sent to the respective branches which will be delivered to the branches between 9.30 am and 10.00 am through the bank's courier.
- While verifying the inward clearing instruments with the Claim Slip received from the clearing section, Head Office. if there is any difference in the amounts claimed, the same will be notified to the Head Office clearing section.

- In respect of Missing Instruments, the Head Office clearing section will advise the presenting bank in FORM – A under a copy to the Clearing House by the Head Office clearing section.
- In respect of Unclaimed amounts *i.e.* the cheque will be there in the bunch of inward clearing cheques but the amount relating to the particular cheque may not find place in the claim list, then the fact will be reported to Clearing House in FORM – B by the Head Office clearing section.
- Under the latest system, the Clearing House is imaging all the clearing instruments processed through the computers and if any bank represents about a missing cheque giving all the relevant details as per Inward Clearing Cheques – Claim statement, then the clearing cell will provide a copy of the instruments for verification and action.

Outward Clearing Cheques – Encoding

- All the outward clearing instruments received from the branches with a covering schedule called Local Clearing Cheques List, the clearing section staff will first count the number of instruments attached to such a list and verify whether the same agrees/ tallies with the number of cheques recorded therein.
- Then the cheques will be Encoded. Under the process of Encoding only the amount for which the said cheque is drawn will be printed in the white Band at the bottom of the cheque.
- For each branch a "Batch Ticket" will be prepared which will relate to presenting branch code number, number of instruments and total value of cheques presented in outward clearing.
- For the bank as a whole a "Block Ticker" will be printed which will contain bank code number, service branch code number, number of Batch tickets and total value of outward clearing cheques lodged.

High Value Clearing

- All instruments of value Rupees 1 lakh and above shall be separately presented in High value clearing. This will have to be done after loading all relevant details about the cheques presented in a floppy. This floppy together with a printout will be presented in High value clearing cell.
- High value returns will be known by stipulated time ie. 4.00 PM. Since the high value cheques are received by the service branch/HO only before 11.00 AM to be presented in the high value clearing on the same day.

Electronic Clearing System (ECS)

- Some companies for payment of periodical interest on the deposit of customers and also for payment of annual dividends, other payments/

refunds etc., and companies like BSNL for collecting telephone charges obtain a Mandate from the customers for directly crediting/ debiting the amounts to the their accounts.

- In respect of ECS, the details relating to our Bank are downloaded and will be uploaded into the Central Data Base by the clearing section and the passing officials of Head Office main Branch and branches must also verify correct account number and authorize the transactions.
- On the same day the respective branch will have to debit/ credit the customers account. If there is no adequate balance in any of the customer 's account to meet such debit under ECS, the same will have to be treated as regular return using objection memo. Similarly in the case where the branch is not able to properly identify the customer's account for crediting the amount then such amount must also be returned to the Clearing House following the procedure of returning the instrument by generating the "System generated cheque return memo".
- In respect of cheques returned unpaid: The cheques returned unpaid by the branches have to be presented in Clearing House in return clearing by 2.30 PM in the Clearing House.

Clearing House Account Reconciliation

- Sometimes, on account of handling huge volume of cheques in Outward as well as Inward clearing operations, banks do commit mistakes while recording the cheque amounts either in the Clearing Schedules or while booking Clearing. Such differences are noticed only after the Clearing House hours when the bank's Day Book does not balance.
- When such a discrepancy/ difference is noticed, first it is to be got confirmed by the other bank involved in that particular transaction. Then Pay Orders to or from that bank is to be issued/ collected and the amount adjusted to the Clearing House account to make good the difference.
- All such amounts either payable or receivable owing to clearing differences must be recorded in a Register called "Clearing House Reconciliation Register":

Balancing of Clearing House Account

- The clearing section at Head Office and the Branches are to daily verify and satisfy that the amount in the Clearing House Account in the GL corresponds only to the total value/ amount of the cheques presented in clearing and pending realization. This has to be ensured before end of each day's transactions.

- Similarly, the cheques returned account is also be balanced on a daily basis and the amount should only reflect the amount of cheque standing as returned in clearing. This has to be realized by funding from clearing house after realization on day to day basis.

TERM DEPOSITS – GENERAL

What is Term Deposit

A deposit received by the bank for a fixed/ specific period which is normally withdrawn only after the expiry of the deposit period is called TERM DEPOSIT.

Types of Term Deposit

- Fixed Deposit (F.D.).
- Reinvestment Deposit/ Cumulative Time Deposit
- Recurring Deposit.
- Special Deposits.

Period of Deposits

- As per RBI directive the minimum period and maximum period of accepting Term Deposits have to be fixed by the Bank from time to time.
- Now the minimum period of F.D. is 7 days and the maximum period for which a Term Deposit can be accepted is 120 months.

Rate of Interest

- The rates of interest payable for Term Deposits are governed by the directives of the RBI and as decided by the Bank from time to time.
- The minimum period to qualify for getting interest on Term Deposit will be as per the directive of the RBI.
- Interest can be paid monthly or Quarterly at the option of the depositor. However the interest paid monthly will be at discounted factor. So that the total interest paid for a period of 3 months on monthly basis will not exceed the actual amount of interest to be paid on that Term Deposit for a Quarter.
- Special/ additional rate of interest is paid to some special class/es of depositors as approved by the bank from time to time based on declaration and/or proof of a/c or other conditions as the case may be.

Who can invest in Term Deposits?

All persons who are eligible to open a Current or Savings Bank Account with the Bank are eligible to invest in Term Deposits, subject to the same conditions like proper introduction, photographs, Pan no., proof of addresses etc.

Procedure for Investment/ Opening the Account

- The depositor has to fill up Bank's Account Opening Form prescribed for Term Deposits.
- Bank Officer will have to ensure that the Account Opening Form filled up by the depositor has all the required information such as:
  - Full Name,
  - Full Postal Address with phone numbers,
  - Amount proposed to be invested,
  - Whether he prefers interest to be paid monthly/ quarterly,
  - Photographs of all depositors are enclosed, and
  - Proper introduction has been given.
  - Pan No.
  - Mode of payment of periodical interest.
- Bank Officer will have to fill up the correct rate of interest in the space provided for the same in the account opening form.
- This account opening form must be authenticated by authorised Officer.
- Once the above formalities are over the pay-in-slip relating to Term Deposit investment must be prepared by the Assistant attached to term Deposits Section and handed over to the Depositor/ Investor for remittance of cash at the Cash Counter.
- The Cashier receives the cash along with the 'Remittance Voucher' and affixes the 'Cash Received' stamp and other information and passes on the said voucher to the 'Scrolling Officer' for his signature before the necessary Term Deposit receipt is issued.

The Assistant has to prepare the Term deposit receipt after the funding is received and the authorized officer approves the same.

Investment by Cheque

- Investment in Term Deposit can also be made by the depositor through a cheque with some other bank.
- In all such cases the Term Deposit Receipts must be issued only after the proceeds of the cheque deposited by the investor have been realised. The Term Deposit will be made effective from the date of deposit of the Cheque if the deposit is for a term of six months and above.
- If the cheque lodged by the depositor is an outstation cheque the commission for collection of such cheque may be waived, if permitted to that effect; otherwise the commission will have to be separately collected from the depositor/ or reduced from the gross amount and term deposit account should be credited with net amount.
- A customer of the bank may also invest in Term Deposit through an authorisation cum request letter to the Manager to debit his Current

or Savings Bank Account with the proposed amount and to invest the same in Term Deposit. In his letter he must give clear instructions regarding the name of the person favouring whom the Term Deposit Receipt will have to be issued, type of account like E or S/ A or S/ F or S/ Jointly, periodicity and mode of payment of interest on Term Deposit and period of investment.

- In the above case the signature of the investor on the request letter must be compared with his Specimen Signature available with the bank and the passing officer must record in the request letter as "Signature Verified" and affix his initials.
- For such investment through an authorisation cum request letter, the Bank Staff will have to prepare necessary Account Opening Form as per the instructions in the request letter of the investor. However the signature of the investor will have to be obtained on the Account Opening Form at a later date when the investor comes to the Bank.

Maturity Notice

- The Bank will have to send a Due Date/ Maturity intimation to all the Term Deposit investors based on maturity Register Due Date Register at least 15 days prior to the actual due date and the letter can be generated in the system.
- In case the depositor has given specific instruction to the Bank not to send such intimation, the Bank should not send maturity intimation to such investors.

Repayment of Term Deposit

- Repayment of a Term Deposit on or after the due date can be made by cash or by crediting party's Current or Savings Bank Account with the Bank or by a PO/ DD as per the specific instructions of the depositor.
- In all such cases the Term Deposit Receipt will have to be duly discharged by the depositors on the reverse of the Term Deposit Receipt at the space provided for the same. However if the repayment is to be made by cash, discharge should be obtained from the depositor on revenue stamp of requisite value.
- If the proceeds are to be paid by a DD/ PO or to be credited to party's account, mere discharge is sufficient *i.e.* without revenue stamp.
- As per the provisions of Income Tax Act [Amended Sec. 269 (T) of IT Act] repayment of proceeds of Term Deposit cannot be made in cash for deposits of ₹.20,000/- and above.
- If the amount of principal + interest of a Term Deposit of ₹.20,000/-

and above payment should be made by way of crossed PO/ DD or to be credited to party's account with the Bank.

- In the case of a Term Deposit issued in favour of two or more persons, with E or S clause, no payment can be made at maturity to one of the parties, and the discharge of all parties on the reverse of the Term Deposit Receipt must be insisted. Since the Bank can pay cash only to one person all the other joint depositors should give a letter to the Bank authorizing one among the joint depositors to receive the payment of the proceeds of the Term Deposit.

Renewal of Term Deposits

- Term Deposits can be renewed from the date of maturity even after the date of its maturity by providing interest rate ruling on the date of maturity, without giving effect to subsequent revisions in the interest rate.
- In the case of overdue deposits where the overdue period does not exceed 14 days the rate of interest payable on the deposit amount so renewed shall be the appropriate rate of interest for the period of renewal as prevailing on the date of maturity.
- In the case of overdue deposits, where the overdue period exceeds 14 days the rate of interest payable on the deposit amount so renewed shall be the appropriate rate of interest for the period of renewal as prevailing on the date of maturity or at the time of renewal whichever is less.
- Additional amount should not be accepted along with the overdue deposit, if the renewal is to be made after the date of maturity.
- Interest for the overdue period can be allowed if the deposit or part there of is renewed from the date of maturity and not from the date of presentation.
- A portion of overdue deposit, if so required by the depositor, can be renewed for a further period from the date of maturity Interest in such case can be allowed only on the renewed portion of the deposit.
- In case of deposit standing in the individual name if deceased, if such deposit is not renewed on maturity interest for the overdue period can be paid from date of maturity till date of payment to legal heirs/ representatives at the rate ruling on the date of maturity.

Addition/ Alteration/ Substitution of name[s]

- Addition of names may be permitted with the written consent of the existing depositors.
- Name can be deleted or substituted with the written consent of all existing depositor provided the name of at least one of the original depositors is retained.

- At the time of addition/ alteration/ substitution of names, the amount, period, due date, rate of interest etc. should not be changed.
- Name of a staff member of the bank should not be subsequently added to get the benefit of preferential rate of interest.

Preferential Rate of Interest

- 1 per cent preferential rate of interest over the standard rate is allowed.
  - On deposits held individually or jointly with dependents in the case of employees of the bank/ retired employees/ widows of employees/ widows of retired employees etc..
  - On deposits of an Association or a Fund all the members of which are the members of Bank Staff.
- A declaration has to be obtained from the person/ association eligible for the preferential rate.
- Before extending preferential rate of interest to eligible retired employees/ widows of retired employees/ widows of employees etc. documentary evidence of service/ retirement/ identity of the widow should be scrutinized and kept attached to Account Opening Form.

Issue of Duplicate Receipt

- In case of loss of Term Deposit Receipt the Bank may issue Duplicate Deposit Receipt provided.
  - The depositor/ all the depositors in the case of joint deposit makes a written intimation to the Bank about the loss of Term Deposit Receipt and request to issue a Duplicate Deposit Receipt, and
  - Furnishing of an Indemnity Bond by all the depositors to the account.

Procedure

- On getting the intimation from the depositor about the loss of Term Deposit Receipt.
  - First make note of the same in the special instructions in the system.
  - Ensure that there is no lien on the deposit or that the deposit receipt is not already lodged with the Bank as security for loan.
  - Then issue a Duplicate Deposit Receipt after the same is authorised by the manager.
  - The Duplicate Receipt must contain the same details as in the original *i.e.* the date, amount, name of investors, rate of interest, period of deposit, due date, etc. There should be no change in any of the above.

- On the face of the Deposit Receipt it must be boldly written in red ink as Duplicate Receipt.
- The serial number of the Duplicate Receipt must also be noted in the special instructions.
- For the Duplicate Receipt issued No Separate account should be opened.
- In case the original receipt is produced, after issue of Duplicate Receipt, no payment should be made against the original receipt. The party with a covering letter must surrender such original receipt to the Bank which will cancel the same and retain on Bank's records.
- After the Duplicate Receipt has been issued to the party payment should be made only against the Duplicate Receipt.

Term Deposit Receipts: Non – Negotiable

- Term Deposit Receipt is NOT TRANSFERABLE and are not negotiable.

Nomination

- Facility of nomination is available for Term Deposits and it should be in favour of individual only.
- Nomination/ Variation or Cancellation of Nomination can be made at any time during the period the deposit held with the Bank and it must be made prior to Due date.

FIXED DEPOSITS

What is Fixed Deposit

A deposit invested for a fixed time/ specific period, repayable on maturity/ due date with agreed rate of interest, payable as simple interest, either monthly or quarterly is known as Fixed Deposit.

Opening

The prospective depositor must make an application in the prescribed application form of the Bank, providing all relevant information and the specimen signatures.

Issue of Deposit Receipts

- Separate pre-printed receipt for FD should be used.
- The Fixed Deposit Receipts is to be issued only in the order of serial numbers either from the stock of 'Loose Leaves' or from the booklets or running stationery.

- On getting the 'Remittance Voucher' duly stamped "Cash Received" and signed by the Cashier, and after verifying the system as to the funding of the account the Assistant in Term Deposit Section will write the Deposit Receipt, with particulars such as Name[s] of the Depositor[s], Date of investment, Period of investment, amount involved, Rate of Interest, Due Date, Specific instructions of the depositor like "E or S" or "A or S" etc.
- It must be ensured that all the Deposit Receipts bear the branch name.
- If the Receipt Books have counterfoils then all the particulars as in the Receipt must be filled up in the counterfoil also.
- Two authorised officers will have to sign the Receipts and the counterfoils.
- The Deposit Receipt is to be issued to the Depositor against his acknowledgement on the reverse of the relative counterfoil. If the Receipts do not have counterfoils then acknowledgement must be obtained in a separate Register called as "Term Deposit Receipts Issue Register".
- The printed serial number of the Deposit Receipt Number must be noted in the system, Account Opening Form and also in the Remittance Voucher.

Due Date

Due date provided by the system must be checked before the receipt prepared.

Payment of periodical interest

- Instructions regarding periodicity of payment of interest *i.e.* monthly/ quarterly must be noted in the system as well as in 'Standing Instruction Sheet' along with the reference account ID.
- Entries in the Standing Instruction must be authenticated by an Officer.

Interest Payment

- Interest at agreed simple rate of interest will have to be paid monthly/ quarterly as specified by the Depositor and noted down in the 'Schedule for Payment of Interest'.
- Must be paid by running the Standing instructions in the system.
- Interest on monthly basis will have to be paid on a discounted basis as RBI permits payment of interest only on quarterly basis so that such monthly interest paid on a FD for a continuous period of three months shall be equal to the interest calculated for the same FD on a quarterly basis.

Interest Provisions

- At the time of half year and Annual Closing of Accounts *i.e.* as on 30 September/ 31st March ever year the actual accrued interest on each FD upto 30th September/ 31st March on the basis of number of days will be applied in the system.
- The account level interest payables on all the deposits accounts must tally with the respective General Ledger Heads.

Renewal of Fixed Deposits

- On the Due date:
  - The deposit receipt must be surrendered by the depositor duly discharged. with a request on the same receipt to renew for further period.
  - However fresh Account Opening Form should be obtained.
  - If the party desires to renew only the principal amount then credit the interest against to his Current or Savings Bank Account or pay in cash as desired by the depositor.
  - For the principal amount prepare credit voucher and follow the procedure as in the case of opening a new FD account.
- After the due date:
  - In case of overdue deposits where the overdue period does not exceed 14 days
  - In the case of overdue deposits, where the overdue period exceeds 14 days the rate of interest payable on the deposit amount so renewed shall be the appropriate rate of interest for the period of renewal as prevailing on the date of maturity or at the time of renewal whichever is less.
  - Other procedures will be as detailed under paragraphs relating to Renewal of Term Deposits.

Foreclosure

- In case a FD is foreclosed before the minimum qualifying period for earning interest then no interest is to be paid.
- First calculate the actual number of days or period for which the FD was with the Bank.
- Then find out the rate of interest applicable for that period as on the date of investment of amount in FD.
- Deduct 1 per cent from that rate for calculation of interest and calculate interest on the FD for the period for which it has remained with the Bank.
- In case the FD submitted for foreclosure is under monthly interest payment schedule and if the total amount of monthly interest so far

paid on the said FD exceeds the eligible interest at the time of foreclosure, then such excess amount paid will have to be recovered out of principal amount of FD and only the Balance will have to be paid to depositor.

- Vouchers for interest payment and for repayment of FD will have to be prepared as explained in earlier paragraphs.
- The interest calculated by the system in some cases must be randomly verified.

Procedure

Whenever such Premature Extension is entertained by the Bank the under mentioned procedures will have to be followed.

- Get the Deposit receipt duly discharged by all the Depositors.
- Get a letter signed by all the depositors requesting the bank to extend the period of investment from this date for a further period in order to get benefit of enhanced interest rate.
- While passing the above entries the interest for the period from the date of original investment till this date at the applicable rate as explained in previous paragraphs should be paid/ credited to party's the account.
- A new FD Receipt must be issued to be effective from that date for the renewed period.
- Cancel the old FDR in the FD Ledger by recording as " Premature Extension with effect from...................".
- In the Due Date/ Maturity Register score off the old FDR as premature Extension.

Penal Interest for Foreclosure

- Whenever the amount invested in Fixed Deposit with the Bank is withdrawn by the depositor at any point of time before the due date, the Penal interest at applicable rate will have to be applied.
- Only in cases where the deposit is renewed before original due date the Penal provision will not be applied as there is no withdrawal of the amount by the depositor.

Closure of Account

At the time of foreclosure, renewal on due date, renewal after due date, premature renewal the "TD closure" activity in the system has to be utlised including "Auto renewal" option must be used appropriately in the system.

Loans against FD

- Loans may be sanctioned against the security of the Fixed Deposit of the Bank.

  - Margin: The Margin will be fixed by the bank from time to time or as per the directives of the RBI. Presently, the margin is 15 per cent.
  - Interest on Loan: The rate of interest on such loans will be as fixed by the Bank from time to time or as per the Directives of RBI. Presently, the Rate is 2 per cent points extra over the rate offered on the deposit.
- Interest on loans will be charged at quarterly rests. While paying the monthly/ quarterly interest on FD, the interest due on the loan against such FD must be first recovered/ adjusted and only the balance amount of interest to be credited to party's Current or Savings Bank Account as the case may be.
- Normally the above procedure will have to be followed, however certain customer may insist that the periodical payment of interest on his FD may be continued and he will separately remit the interest due on loan against his FD. It is advised to politely turn down such requests explaining that in case of any delay or default by the customer in remitting the interest due on the Loan Account on due date that amount will attract penal interest at the same rate at which interest is charged for the loan amount.
- The lien on the Fixed Deposit towards the loan should be entered and got authorised.
- On maturity, the loan with interest should be recovered from the proceeds of the fixed deposit.

Foreclosure of FD under loan cover

In case the depositor wants to foreclose his FD against which he had availed a loan:

- First arrive at the eligible rate of interest for the FD applying foreclosure norms.
- Then charge interest for the loan at 2 per cent above the eligible interest as arrived above, if the loan account is still alive on the date of foreclosure of the said FD.
- Recover/ Adjust the entire dues under the loan account *i.e.* the principal and interest due up-to-date, out of the proceeds of the FD.
- Finally, pay the balance amount of the proceeds of the FD to the depositor.

TAX DEDUCTION AT SOURCE (TDS)

Tax is to be deducted at source on the interest paid or accrued on a term deposit if it exceeds ₹.10,000/- in a Financial year or as may be revised by the Govt. of India from time to time for depositor other than DCCBs, who are our voting members and as such entitled to non-deduction of tax at source. This is statutory deduction which is to be deducted and remitted to the Government before 7th of succeeding month. This is statutory deduction which has to be explained to the depositor at the time of making deposit and if customer computes his taxable income and seeks exemption from deduction of tax at source by the bank, the customer has to submit a declaration in duplicate, in form 15 H or 15 G as per the existing rules which is to be submitted to the Income Tax department by 7th of the succeeding month. At the time of opening of the term deposit a/c and also at the beginning of the each financial year, such declaration has to be taken from the customer and the status in the system has to be changed appropriately for deduction of tax at source or otherwise. For the Term Deposit accounts, for which the customers have furnished the 15 H/ 15 G form, which will exempt such accounts from deduction of Tax at Source, the Branch Managers and Managers are hereby advised to cause immediate modification in the accounts concerned immediately from the:

"TDS – YES" to "TDS-NO"

This modification has to be done before applying interest provision for the half-year and year ending, otherwise the tax is deducted by the system "as per default setting". If it is noticed that the tax is deducted for any account such deduction should be reversed immediately on 30th September/ 31st March, as the case may be and also TDS Yes/ No to be modified suitably.

Exemption to TDS provisions

The following depositors are exempted from the scope of TDS provisions and hence, no income tax should be deducted from the interest being paid/ credited to them:

- The Government, or
- The Reserve Bank of India, or
- A Corporation established by or under a Central Act which is, under any law for the time being in force, exempt from income tax on its income, or
- A Mutual Fund specified under Clause (23 D) of Section 10 of Income Tax Act, 1961
- Banking Companies including Cooperative Banks and Land Mortgage Banks
- Any Central or State Financial Corporation
- Life Insurance Corporation of India
- Unit Trust of India
- Any Company or Co-operative Society carrying on the business of insurance
- Persons or Organizations notified by the Central Government in the Official Gazette for this purpose.

LOCAL CHEQUES, DEMAND DRAFTS AND OUTSTATION CHEQUES – PURCHASE/ INSTANT CREDIT

General

- This facility can be extended to select customers only who are maintaining good operative account with good standing.
- The customer to whom this facility is extended should be in a position to make good the amount in short notice in case the purchased instrument is returned unpaid by the Drawer bank.
- This is a facility provided to the customers who desire to encash the local Demand Drafts/ cheques drawn in their favour immediately without waiting till the proceeds of said instruments could be realized by the bank in the normal course.
- Since no other collateral security is available and this facility is a clean accommodation. This facility is sparingly used.
- Personal cheques of individuals shall not be discounted under any circumstances where the value exceeds ₹ 2.00 lakhs without specific instructions from Head Office.
- The purchase of the Negotiable instrument is restricted to DDs issued by reputed Banks, Interest Dividend warrants issued by reputed Companies, cheques issued by State/ Central Govt., LIC, UTI, PF, Universities, PPO, AGs Office, PAO, APSEB and Public Sector Undertakings.

Safe guards to be observed

The bank will have to establish the following in order to get a good title as "Holder for value".

- The bank should not have notice of any previous dishonour of the Cheque or any defect in the title of the customer.
- It should not have given value for the Cheque in good faith.
- It should not have paid the value under suspicion of forgery of the Cheque.
- The Cheque should not have been crossed "Not Negotiable".
- The cheques should be drawn in favour of the customer who wants the same to be purchased.
- The cheques should be crossed by the constituent before tendering to the Branch.
- The cheques must be drawn on well-known and sound banks.
- If the purchased/discounted cheque is returned unpaid for want of funds or due to stoppage of payment by the drawer the customer for whom the said cheque has been purchased should not be extended the same facility again.

- Cheque should prima facie be in order in all respects *viz.* date, amount in words and figures, alteration if any duly authenticated by the drawer etc.
- Post-dated or Outstation cheques should not be discounted.

Books

The Branch should maintain 'Bills Purchased Register' for the instruments purchased.

Procedure

- The Bank should collect a request letter from the customer for purchasing the cheque/ DD drawn in his favour which he lodges for realization and credit to his account with the branch.
- The Branch Manager should Authorize the same.
- Prepare necessary vouchers for purchasing the said cheques.
- Pass the necessary "purchase" entries and send the cheque to HO/ next immediate Clearing House for collection of proceeds.
- Make necessary adjustment entries upon realization of the cheque amount.
- The applicable cheque discounting charges and the service tax thereon has to be collected from the customer at the time of purchase of the instrument. However, if the proceeds of the discounted cheque is intended for being invested in Term Deposit, no discounting charges need to be levied
- Proper follow up has to be ensured so that the fate of the cheque discounted is known within the stipulated time.
- The bank has fixed ceilings in amount of the DD/ Cheque permitted for discounting by the branches based on their deposit position subject to a maximum of ₹ 2.00 lakhs per instrument per day. The same may be followed apart from the other precautions stipulated in this regard.

DEMAND DRAFTS AND PAY ORDERS

General

- The Demand Draft are the instruments issued/sold to the customers by a bank on request. A Demand draft is an order to pay money, drawn by one office of a Bank upon another office of the same Bank for a specified sum of money payable to order on demand and the 'Pay Order' is like a Banker's Cheque payable locally.
- Sale of Drafts constitutes an important function of the Bank.
- Despite the growth of new modes of transfer of funds like "Electronic funds Transfer" etc., the sale of Demand Drafts in banks has not reduced in volume.

Custody

- The stock of Demand Draft books and Pay order Books supplied by HO must be first recorded in the Branch "Stock Stationery Register" and then kept under lock and key under the effective custody of the Officer.
- While receiving the stock if any irregularity in the numbers or number of books etc., is noticed the same should be immediately informed to HO in writing with particulars.
- Even the Draft book and Pay order book, which are currently in use must be kept safely locked overnight.
- Each evening *i.e.* after close of business for the day the number of DDs/Pos issued on that day should be verified with the "DD Issued Register" and " Payorder Issued Register" to ensure that the balance of DD leaves and PO leaves are intact in the books.
- Each morning before starting the sale of DDs and POs the Officer must check the commencing numbers of DD and PO with reference to the last leaf issued the previous day.

All India Mutual Arrangement Scheme (AIMAS) and State Drafts Scheme (SDS)

- The SCBs and DCCBs are operating this DD business through AIMAS & SDS.
- Non-members of AiMAs have their own arrangements with select centres in India on which place their customers and other local population want DDs.
- For issue of DDs/honouring of DDs/maintenance of relevant Books, Accounting procedure etc. AIMAS Manual may be referred to.
- Similarly for issue of DDs/Honouring DDs/ reconciliation of accounts/ remittance of funds etc. under State Drafts Scheme all the terms and conditions and instructions issued from time to time may be followed.

Sale (issue) of DDs and Pos

- The purchaser of DD or PO will have to fill up the relevant application form in whih he has to furnish his name and full address in addition to other particulars:- place on which the DD is required, amount for which the DD is required and in favour of whom.
- Commission as per the rates fixed by the Bank from time to time and service tax will have to be collected along with the DD amount.
- Cashier who received the remittance for DD should check up whether the correct commission and Service Tax is provided in the DD application form.
- Customer may, instead of remitting the DD amount, enclose a cheque

on his account with the Branch to the DD application form. In such case it has to be verified whether the amount of the cheque is inclusive of DD issue Commission and Service Tax also. In case this amount has not been included in the cheque Amount, then a separate letter from the customer authorizing the bank to debit the charges to his account, must be obtained.

Procedure

- Before preparing a draft the concerned staff member should ensure that the amount for the DD along with commission and service tax is received and the relative voucher is passed by authorized officer.
- All other procedures for issuing a swell as honouring DDs have been explained in detail in AIMAS Manual.
- If any concession is allowed by the Bank on the commission, only then the commission need not be collected.

Unclaimed DDs

- A Bank draft is valid for a period of six months from the date of issue after which it becomes stale.
- Amounts of DDs which are unclaimed and outstanding for more than six months in the books of the Branch should be transferred to HO for credit of "HO Account Unclaimed DDs" furnishing in the advice full particulars such as the date of draft, numbers of DDs, Payee's name, amount of DDs etc.

Payment of unclaimed DDs

- Branches may receive for payment either the original DD orduplicates, whose amounts are not outstanding in their books, but transferred to HO, as unclaimed DDs. Before paying such Drafts, the Officer in charge should ensure:
  - That the draft is duly revalidated by the issuing branch.
  - That the relative advice from the issuing branch for the issue of duplicate draft for its revalidation has been received.
- While paying such DDs whose credits have been transferred to HO, the drawee branch should:
  - *Debit:* "HO Account Unclaimed DDs"
  - *Credit:* "DDs Payable Account" and then
  - *Debit:* "DDs payable account" &
  - *Credit:* "Payee's account".

Cancellation of DDs

The purchaser of the Demand Draft can request the Bank in writing along with his signature as in the DD application form for cancellation of a particular instrument. In such case he must enclose the said DD to his request letter. The Bank can cancel such DDs after establishing the identity of the purchaser to the satisfaction of the Bank and charging the fee prescribed for the same. Stop payment instructions are not accepted from the purchaser for the DDs already issued.

Safeguards to be followed while issuing DDs/Bankers Cheques

- While indicating the amount in figures and words on the instrument, there should not be any scope for unauthorized insertions *i.e.* no gaps should be left between the last words or figures as also between the last figure and the notation; similarly there should be no gap between the amount in words and the word 'only'.
- There should not be any alterations as far as possible and every alteration has to be attested in full by each of the drawing signatories.
- There should not be any discrepancy or ambiguity in the amount in figures and words.
- Appropriate crossing has to be made on the instrument.
- DD's for an amount of ₹ 50,000/- and above per day to single party have to be issued only through debit from the account and not by accepting cash.
- Cellophane tape should be pasted on the amount in figures and words, as well as on the name of the payee.
- A rubber stamp should be affixed on the face of the instrument with "Not over ₹___________" in both figures and words.
- While preparing the instrument, it should be ensured that there is a reverse carbon on the back of the instrument so that the impression falls on the reverse side of the instrument.
- Fortnightly reconciliation of the accounts with APCOB Head Office on which the cheques or Demand Drafts are issued shall be made regularly.
- Appropriate punching shall also be made in case of Demand Drafts.
- Full address and identity of the applicant of the Demand Draft shall be ensured while issuing DDs.
- Specimen signatures of the authorized officials up-to-date should be on record with APCOB. Further, the Joint authorized signatories should be invariably mention each of their allotted code on the cheque/ DD after signature.

Arrangement with notified Bank

The Bank has entered into an agreement with ICICI Bank for issue of Cheque on outstation centers payable at par. The safeguards to be followed are the same as enumerated for DDs. The specific instructions issued based on the guidelines of the Bank with which arrangements are made are also to be scrupulously followed.

Procedure for issue of duplicate Draft

- Letter from the purchaser of the DD be obtained containing the details like DD number, date, amount, favouring, drawn on which Bank and Branch, a request for issuance of a duplicate demand draft in lieu of DD reportedly lost, address of the applicant etc., and it is to be ensured that the signatures on the letter and application at the time of purchase of DD are one and the same.
- The drawee bank's branch has to be addressed to (a) confirm whether the subject DD is paid at their end (b) if not paid, to note caution of reporting that the original DD is lost in their records, and (c) to obtain confirmation in writing from the drawee bank that the subject DD is not honoured at their level and noted the relative caution.
- On getting written confirmation only from the drawee branch, the Branch/ Bank has to obtain an indemnity bond on the non-judicial stamp paper duly executed by the purchaser of the original DD.
- The secured correspondence in the matter *i.e.* letter from the purchaser, copy of letter written by the Branch to the drawee bank, letter received from the drawee bank, original indemnity bond are to be tagged together and kept in separate file and this file should form part of charge list upon transfer of Branch Managers.
- On completion of all the above formalities, a duplicate DD can be issued duly collecting the charges for issue of duplicate DD. On the duplicate DD it is to be mentioned that "Duplicate DD issued in lieu of original DD No. ________ dated _______".

SAFE DEPOSIT LOCKERS

General

- Safe Deposit Locker facility is one of the ancillary services offered by the Banks.
- The relationship between the Bank and Locker hiring customer is basically that of the BAILOR & the BAILEE and incidentally it is also that of a "LESSOR" & "LESSEE".
- The Bank is not required to know what is kept inside a Locker but is charged with the responsibility to exercise reasonable precautions against the loss of the contents of a Locker. That is why Safe Deposit Locker facility is provided only in those branches where a "Safe Vault" or a strong room is available to ensure safety and security to the Lockers.

Renting the Lockers

- Lockers should be rented or hired to Savings and Current Account holders only who are properly introduced to the branch.
- Lockers can be rented to:
  - Individuals - singly or jointly including NRIs, illiterate customers & staff members.
  - Trusts
  - HUF concerns
  - Societies/ Clubs/ Associations
  - Proprietary/ partnership concerns
  - Limited companies
  - Government Departments/ Courts
- However, Lockers should not be rented to MINORS.
- The usual precautions/ formalities observed in the opening of Deposit Accounts for the categories/ types of constituents should be strictly observed in hiring out Lockers.
- In the case of individuals having the Locker in the joint names like "E or S"/ "A or S", any one of them can have access to the Locker.
- In the case of Partnership Firm, Trusts, HUF, Clubs, Societies, Association etc. their Bye laws/ rules/ Memorandum and Articles of Association/ Certificate of Incorporation/ Board Resolution, as the case may be, should in clear terms, specify the person/ persons who are authorised to operate the Lockers.
- Normally in the case of Societies/ Clubs/ Associations etc. the Locker must be operated jointly by two authorised officials. In the case of partnership firm, it should be operated by at least two partners jointly.

Illiterates and Lockers

- Renting of Lockers to illiterate customers involves potential risk and hence should be strictly in exceptional cases only and where the Branch Manager is satisfied about the genuineness of the need and bonafides of the customer.
- The following procedure should be adopted when a Safe Locker is rented to an illiterate customer.
  - The hirer should be properly introduced to the Bank/ Branch.
  - His/her left-hand thumb impression should be affixed on the Bank documents in the presence of the Manager.
  - The Manager should at least get the *Left Hand Thumb Impression* (LTI) of the hirer both in the Locker Agreement/ Memorandum of Hiring as well as Specimen Signature Card.
  - It should be recorded in the "Locker Agreement Form", by the Manager that all the terms and conditions have been read to the hirer in a manner in which he could understand.

- A copy of recent passport size photograph of the hirer, duly authenticated by the Manager, should be attached to the Locker Agreement form and to the Specimen Signature Card.
- Whenever he operates the Locker his LTI should be obtained on "Locker Access Register".

Staff Members and Lockers

- A declaration should be obtained from the staff member who want to hire a Locker from the branch that he is not maintaining another Locker in any other branch of the bank either in his name or jointly with another family member availing "Staff concessional rent" facility "Staff concession rent" should be restricted to one Locker only.
- No member of the staff shall be permitted to hire a Locker jointly with a constituent of the bank or any other third party.

Terms for Hiring Lockers

- Lockers are given on hire for a period of one year.
- The desiring customer should submit an application, in Bank's form, furnishing complete particulars like:
  - Name and full address of the applicant with phone number.
  - Occupation and Business address.
  - Whether to be operated singly or as "E or S" or "A or S" or jointly should be clearly mentioned.
- The names and specimen signatures of other Joint Holders should be furnished.
- Specimen Signature Cards and "Stamped Locker Agreement Form"/ "Memorandum of Hiring" should be kept under lock and key under the custody of the Officer-in-Charge of Lockers.
- Each Locker hirer will have to sign the stamped "Locker Agreement Form" and "Memorandum of Hiring" wherein the terms and conditions under which the Locker is rented to him are detailed.
- The key of the Locker should be tested *i.e.* to check whether it opens and locks the assigned Locker smoothly, before handing over to the hirer.
- When the Locker Units are installed by the supplier the keys of the individual Locker units and the Master key will be handed over to the Branch Manager by the company.
- The Manager should first, prior to renting out the Lockers to customers, check whether all the keys open and lock the respective Locker smoothly. Then each key must be kept in a small cover and sealed noting on it the Locker number and key number.
- These sealed covers should be kept in a box arranged in the order of

Locker number and this box should be kept in a vacant Locker or inside cash safe.

- As and when a Locker is rented out then the sealed packet relating to that Locker should be taken out and the seal removed in the presence of the hirer and the key has to be tested to check whether it opens and locks the particular Locker. While doing so the officer should explain to the hirer how the Locker could be opened only with both the keys and how it could not be opened by solely by the Locker key or by the Master key.
- When a locker is allotted to more than one person, clear instructions regarding operation and surrender of the locker must be taken at the very beginning to avoid future complications. It should be ascertained whether the locker will be operated by anyone or more or all persons and whether, in the event of death of one of the parties, access may be given to the survivors without reference to the legal heirs of the deceased, and such instructions should be got signed by all the persons. Also special instructions should be recorded on the specimen signature cards.

Addition and Deletion of Names

- Additions of new names to the hired Locker can be made only when all existing hirers agree in writing to such proposal.
- However one or more names from a Joint Locker Account should not be deleted.
- If such deletion is insisted by the hirers, then they have to be advised to surrender the existing Locker and a fresh Locker should be allotted to them following all the regular formalities.
- Nomination facility is also available.

Locker Rent

- Rent for each type of Locker will vary. These rent rates will be fixed and revised from time to time by the HO.
- To ensure that Locker rents for all Lockers are collected without delay or default, it is desirable to fix a date to collect the annual rent in advance for the whole year.
- It may be the first week of April every year. In which case the Branch should send "Rent due notices" and collect the rent, either by debit to the customer's ccounts or by Cheque or cash. Proper follow up action should be taken to collect the annual rent before 7th April every year.
- If the rent is paid after 7th April penalty at the rates fixed by the Bank should also be collected.

- It is desirable to advise the customer, at the time of hiring the Locker, to place a specific amount in FD the annual interest of which will be equivalent to the yearly rent payable by the hirer. Such FD must be made for 2/3 years with an irrevocable letter to transfer the interest accrued towards Locker rent every year and to renew the deposit periodically as long as the Locker facility is required.
- If the Locker customer already has FD with the Branch the same could be earmarked by the customer in writing as above.

Locker left open by the Hirer

- At times the hirer may go out of Vault/ Locker Room with out properly locking his Locker. Even though the Bank has no knowledge of and takes no cognizance of the contents of the Lockers, following precautionary measures may be adopted to safe guard the contents in the interest of the hirer.
- The Bank officer should immediately contact the hirer and request him to come to the bank/ branch immediately with the Locker key. While calling him, no indication should be given to him about his unlocked Locker. Only when he comes to the branch he must be informed of the position and asked to check the contents of his Locker. A declaration should be obtained from him to the effect that the contents of the Locker are verified and found correct.
- In case the hirer who has left his Locker unlocked and has also taken the Locker key with him, is not immediately available then the contents may be listed in the presence of the Manager, another officer, cashier and 2/3 customers and the articles should be kept in a vacant Locker or in the safe in sealed cover/ bag. When the hirer subsequently comes to the Bank, he must be asked to check the contents in the sealed cover/ bag and certify in writing that the contents are intact.
- In case the Locker key has been left behind by the hirer in the Locker itself which he has not properly locked, then after following the above procedure the contents may be kept in the same Locker and may be locked with the help of the key left behind by the hirer. The Locker key must then be left under the joint custody of the Manager and Accountant or Manager and Cashier. The key should not be left with the officer in charge of Locker who is holding the Master key. When the hirer subsequently comes to the Bank he should be asked to check the contents of his Locker and certify in writing that the contents are intact.
- In addition to the above precautions, at the end of each working day, before closing the vault doors, the officer in charge of Lockers

(CUSTODIAN) should first check that no one is still inside the Locker room (vault) and then should check with reference to the "Locker Access Register" all the Lockers which were operated during that day to ensure that they have been properly locked by the hirers and no article/ valuables are left behind by the Locker hirers in the strong/ Locker room.

Shifting of Locker Units

- At the time of shifting the Branch/ the Locker units from one premises to another, a notice to the hirers of all the Lockers to temporarily vacate their Lockers, should be sent under "Registered Post with Acknowledgement due", at least 30 days in advance prior to the proposed date of shifting the Locker units.
- In the case of Joint Hirers such notice should be sent to all of them individually.
- All undelivered/ returned covers should be kept unopened and preserved till such time the hirer visits the new premises to operate his Locker.
- In case few hirers fail to turn up within the prescribed time, the Locker units with the contents should be shifted with utmost care and in the presence of the CUSTODIAN or a responsible bank staff.

Surrendering of Locker

- When a Locker is surrendered by the hirer, the Locker key should be collected from him. He has to sign in appropriate place in "Memorandum of Hiring"/ "Locker Agreement Forms." Locker Rent should be collected, if not already collected, till date of surrender of Locker.
- No refund of rent should be made for the unexpired period of the contract.
- If the Locker is in joint names, then all the hirers should sign the Locker Agreement Form and also the letter informing the bank about their surrendering the Locker.
- The lock of the surrendered Locker must be inter-changed with that of a vacant Locker. In case no vacant Locker is available in the branch then a spare lock should be procured from the company which supplied the Locker units and the same should be fitted in the surrendered Locker retaining the lock of that Locker as a spare one.
- Only after changing the lock of the surrendered Locker the same could be hired out to another customer.

Dealing with cases of missing person

- While Section.107 of the Indian Evidence Act, 1872 deals with presumption of continuance of life, section.108 deals with presumption of death. As per secion.108 of the Indian Evidence Act, when the question is whether a man is alive or dead and it is proved that he/she has not been heard of for seven years by those who would naturally have heard of him/her if he/she were alive, the burden of proving the existence of the person will be shifted to the person who affirms it.

- Again as per the provisions of Section.108 of the Indian Evidence Act, presumption of death can be raised only after a lapse of seven years from the date of his/her being reported missing. As such, the nominee of a missing depositor has to raise an express presumption of death of the subscriber under Section.107 & 108 of the Indian Evidence Act before a competent Court. If the court presumes that the person is dead, then, the nominee will be entitled for settlement of outstanding amount or the safe custody article of the missing subscriber.

Death of a Locker Hirer

- On the death of one of the two Joint Hirers, in an "E or S" account, the survivor alone is entitled to have access to the Locker.
- In the case of sole hirer, the legal heir(s) of the deceased should be advised to submit a "CLAIM" and unless and until the claim is sanctioned by the HO, the contents of that Locker should not be parted with. *i.e.* till the claim is settled no one should have access to the Locker of the deceased.
- However access may be allowed to known heirs of the deceased or persons authorised by the Court for making an inventory of the contents in the presence of their solicitors or lawyers.

Nomination

- Branch may permit nominations only in respect of the Safe Deposit Lockers hired by persons in their individual capacity and not in any other representative capacity. Only individual could be the nominee.
- In the case of Joint Hirers, branch may accept more than one nominee. However at any time the total number of nominees must not exceed the total number of Joint Hirers.
- Separate nomination should be obtained in respect of each Locker account. However at any time the total number of nominees should not exceed the total number of Joint Hirers.

Prohibitory Orders

- Access should not be allowed to the hirer of a Locker on which a valid prohibitory order from a competent authority or a Court appointing a Receiver in respect of the Locker is received.

- In the event of the competent authority bringing an order for making an inventory of the content of the Locker and accompanied by the hirer, the access of the Locker should be allowed. However, the hirer should be made to sign the Locker Access Register as usual.

Breaking open of Locker

- Breaking open of a Locker is an extreme step. It should not be resorted to without exhausting all available remedies. Prior permission should be obtained from HO for breaking open a Locker.
- All rents to the Lockers are strictly payable for one year in advance. On failure to pay the rents in advance or to deliver possession of the Locker with key, the Branch will be at liberty to break open the Locker.
- For breaking open the Locker following procedure should be followed:
  - Notice demanding the rent should be sent to the hirer calling upon him to pay up the rent immediately.
  - If the rent is still unpaid, at least Three Reminders should be sent at an interval of 10 days, under certificate of posting.
  - Even after the reminders the hirer does not pay up the rent, then issue a final letter giving notice that the Bank would break open the Locker. This letter should be sent by Register Post with Acknowledgement due.
  - If there is no response for the Register letter the Branch should depute a responsible staff member to ascertain the following information of the hirer.

  i. latest address of the hirer,

  ii. whether the hirer is available at this address, and

  iii. if not, what do the enquiries at the address reveal. d. If all the above efforts to collect the Locker rent fail then the Bank may wait for a further period of 3 months.
- After expiry of this 3 months period, another registered letter may be issued informing him that the Locker hired by him will be broken open, without further intimation to him, if the rent is not paid within 10 days from the date of notice.
- If the rent is not paid within the notice period, then the Bank will have to break open the Locker.
- The Locker should be broken open in the presence of:
  - Manager of the Branch.
  - A Senior Officer from HO/ Legal Counsel
  - At least two respectable customers.
- The contents, if any, found in the Locker should be placed inside a vacant Locker or Iron Safe with double lock which should be under

the joint custody of the Manager and another Officer/ Cashier of the Branch.

- The fact should be recorded in a separate Register called "Register of Lockers Broken Open" which will be authenticated by both the custodians.
- After breaking open the Locker due notice are to be sent to the concerned hirer in the following manner, a specimen of such notices as follows is given in the Annexures.
  - Locker found empty
  - Locker found with articles
  - After auction of contents
- A report/ inventory should be prepared and signed by all the persons in whose presence the Locker was broken open.

Report of Locker Broken Open

The specimen of the "Report of the Locker broken open" is as follows:

Locker number..............relating to hirer Shri/Smt..............................was broken open this............... day of............. 20, in the presence of Manager... Bank Ltd............................. Branch, Shri......................... Senior Officer from H.O. and Shri...................................... and Shri................................. Customer of the Bank. There were no contents/ an inventory of contents/ An inventory of contents found in the Locker is given below:

a. (Signature of the Branch Manager)
b. (Signature of HO Officer)
c. Witness (i)
   Witness (ii)

This report should be prepared in Duplicate, a copy of which should be sent to HO and the second copy should be kept in the Branch inside the safe under double lock. The report should be copied in "Register of Lockers Broken Open."

Care of Locker Keys

On no account, should the Manager or Officer in charge of Lockers receive the key of a rented Locker from the customer/ hirer, even for a temporary period.

11

Capital Control and Banking Policy

CAPITAL CONTROL

In economics, capital control is the monetary policy device that a country's government (*i.e.*, sovereign power) uses to regulate the flows into and out of a country's capital account, *i.e.*, the flows of investment-oriented money into and out of a country or currency. The decade since the Asian Currency Crisis in 1997-1998 has rekindled debate over the wisdom of developing markets having capital controls. As globalisation advanced with the formalisation of the World Trade Organisation and Uruguay Round of General Agreement on Tariffs and Trade (GATT), developing countries were urged by the International Monetary Fund and others to liberalise their capital controlled environments.

As it became clear that countries doing this, including Malaysia, Thailand and Mexico, essentially ceded control of their economies to external forces, namely international capital movements, hot money and capital flight; and countries that did not, like China and India, retained control and were not nearly as vulnerable to the volatility of international capital movement, some argued that capital controls were advisable for smaller economies to use, and to transition away from them only over long, general evolutionary timelines. Malaysia is an example of a country that switched regimes, from open in the late 1990s, to closed.

Economists supporting capital controls in certain cases were not only from the left, but also liberal economists like Jagdish Bhagwati and news publications like The Economist.

Banking Policy and Trends Policy Measures

The major policy measures taken in the current financial year as part of the annual monetary and credit policy statement, including its mid-term review. These include freedom for banks to lend at interest rates below their respective PLRs to exporters and other creditworthy borrowers (including public enterprises), permission to formulate fixed deposit plans offering higher and fixed interest rates to senior citizens, flexibility in the composition of working capital as between cash credit and loan components, reduction in exposure limits for borrowers, revised guidelines for exposure of banks to capital market, and guidelines for investment in non-SLR securities through the private placement route. The initiatives specially aimed at strengthening the operational efficiency of banks relate to the Voluntary Retirement Plan, the Banking Service Recruitment Boards, Credit Information Bureau, and enlargement of the reach and scope of the electronic funds transfer facility.

Voluntary Retirement Plan (VRS)

VRS was implemented by 26 out of 27 public sector banks in 2000-2001. Indian Banks Association (IBA), the total staff strength in public sector banks at the end of March 2000 was 8, 63,188 out of whom 1, 26,714 or 14.7 per cent applied for VRS. About 80 per cent of the number of applications were accepted, and the staff relieved under VRS until December 31, 2001 were 1, 01,300. This constituted 11.7 per cent of the total staff strength at the end of March 2000. Banks were advised by the Reserve Bank to treat the ex-gratia payment as deferred revenue expenditure (DRE), which would not be reduced from Tier I capital. The position will be regularised by the end of the accounting year in which the DRE gets totally wiped out. The maximum period of deferment has been fixed at five years, including the year of acceptance of VRS applications by the banks.

Banking Service Recruitment Boards

In pursuance of the announcement made by the Finance Minister in his Budget speech, the Banking Service Recruitment Boards (BSRBs) have been abolished. Accordingly, banks have been advised to frame their own recruitment strategies, with the approval of the respective Boards, to meet future requirements. While framing such strategies, banks are required to ensure, *inter alia*, that the recruitment policy is transparent and fair, with due representations of the members of SC/ST and minority communities in selection committees. Banks have also been advised to ensure that reservations in posts and related concessions/relaxations in fees and marks, as laid down by the Government of India, are strictly followed.

Electronic Funds Transfer (EFT)

EFT facilitates transfer of funds electronically within and across cities and between branches of a bank and across banks. EFT is operated by RBI, and is available for funds transferred across 13 major cities in the country as on January 11, 2002. With effect from October 1, 2001, large value transactions upto ₹. 2 crore have been permitted under EFT. Transfer of funds on a "same-day" basis was implemented effective from January 2, 2002 at the four metro centres with three settlements per day.

SMALL AND MEDIUM ENTERPRISES (SMES)

Problems Facing the SSI Sector

The SSI sector confronts several problems despite its strategic importance in any industrialisation strategy and its immense potential for employment generation. The problem which continues to be a big hurdle for the development of the sector is lack of access to timely and adequate credit. The Abid Hussain Committee on SSIs (1997) examined the problems of the SSI sector and recommended a package of policies to restructure the industry in the context of current global economic changes.

The Expert Committee was of the view that the existing institutional structure for delivering credit to SSEs needs a thorough overhaul. It endorsed the recommendations of the Nayak Committee and urged the RBI to implement the same. The Committee recommended restructuring of financial support through SFCs and SIDCs, tapping of other sources of funding for SSEs, extending credit rating servcies to small units, and addressing the credit needs of tiny units to ensure that they are not bypased by the commercial banking system. The overall credit availability for SSIs during 1991-1996 amounts to only 13 per cent of the value of production. The Nayak Committee had recommended a desirable norm of 20 per cent of the value of production to be made available by way of working capital through term-lending institutions and commercial banks A norm of 75 per cent was set for fixed capital assets whereas actual availability is only 55 per cent. Lack of finance has been one of the major causes of sickness in the SSI sector, blocking access to technological modernisation and other growth possibilities. There is an urgent need to enlarge flow of credit to the SSI sector from institutional sources. The creation of a facilitating environment for SSIs will centre on access to credit. The Ninth Five Year Plan estimates additional working capital funds at ₹. 1420 to 1460 billion for the small sector. Lowering interest-rates, specifying a time-frame to clear loan applications and adherence to norms set down by the Nayak Committee are some of the minimum measures that need to be taken. Legislative measures have a role to play with regard to funding and financing of small scale units. There are measures which can basically ensure that impediments to credit availability are removed. These measures include:

- Right to reasonable credit from commercial banks as per RBI guidelines framed after consultation with representative Board
- Protection against non-normative demands for security
- Appeal and enforcement by Ombudsman/Board
- Access to public funds by way of debentures, deposits, securities
- Government guarantee for loans from banks

The measures to support Marketing and Competitiveness are as follows:

- State to exempt from contract security

- Prompt return of contract securities in case of others
- Prompt payment measures
- Protection against undue bundling of contracts by the state
- Protection against restrictive and monopolistic trade practices
- Ombudsman/arbitral services for enforcement

IMPACT OF WTO

The emerging challenges to the small-scale sector are to come from the impact of the Agreements under WTO to which India is a signatory along with 134 member countries. The setting up of the WTO in 1995 has altered the framework of international trade towards non-distortive, market-oriented policies. This is in keeping with the policy shift that occurred worldwide since the early 1980s in favour of free market forces and a tilt away from State regulation/intervention in economic activity. This is expected to lead to an expansion in the volume of international trade and changes in the pattern of commodity flows. The main outcomes of WTO-stipulated requirements will be brought about through reduction in export subsidies, greater market access, removal of non-tariff barriers and reduction in tariffs. There will also be tighter patent laws through regulation of intellectual property rights under the TRIPS Agreement which lays down what is to be patented (both products and processes), for what duration (20 years instead of the present 7 years under India's 1970 Patent Law), and on what terms. The responses by trading countries and the reframing of domestic economic policies which will result from the impact of WTO and the repercussions on the global economy of all these changes are highly uncertain as they involve several unforeseeable factors. However, there are certain indications of the shape of future trade patterns. Increased market access to imports (of around 3 per cent of domestic production to be raised to 5 per cent) will mean opening up the domestic market to large flows of imports. The removal of quantitative restrictions (QRs) on imports has been speeded up to 2001. At present 714 items are in the restricted category but imports of these items will soon be freed from all restrictions as announced in the recent EXIM policy. Increased market access under WTO requirements will also mean that our industries can compete for export markets in both developed and developing countries. But the expected surge in our exports can come about only if the SSI sector is restructured to meet the demands of global competitiveness which is the key to the future of small industries in the present context.

REFORMATION OF BANKING SYSTEM

SITUATION APPRAISAL

Monetary policy of the Belarusian authorities is distinguished by its unique character among the post-socialist countries of Central and Eastern Europe.

Using, in contravention of the current legislation, "a printing press" as a source of covering low-effective public expenditure and levying thus enormous inflation tax on the population, the Government and the National Bank have achieved dubious economic growth and retained unproductive employment. As a result the country's economy has turned up in the financial and technological deadlock.

The following can be furnished to dramatise this thesis. Within the last six years net domestic ruble credit of the National Bank increased about 120 times, ruble money mass - approximately 210 times, official exchange rate of the Belarusian ruble decreased 111 times while consumer prices went up 161 times. These figures are undoubtedly indicative of the fact that "soft" monetary policy advocated by the present-day economic ideologists as presuming point-like public support to some branches at the expense of credit emission by the principle "emission to finance production of the goods does not lead to inflation" has appeared invalid.

Unique character of the monetary policy in Belarus is stipulated by the following causes. First, this is incredible economic incompetence of the Belarusian ruling elite as well as its total dependence upon the Head of the State. For some years the Government and the National Bank took and implemented decisions in the monetary sphere that were far away not only from the generally accepted practice in the civilised countries but also common sense. That concerns first of all the policy of covering public expenditure by credit emission of the National Bank, actual refusal of positive real interest rate, and attempts of administrative regulation of inflation and exchange rate.

Instead of real evaluation of financial possibilities of the country and use of budget resources, the authorities engaged in developing numerous programmmes without effective facilities of implementation. Second, this is deep-rooted disrespect of own country that turned into chronic inferiority complex not allowing the majority of political elite representatives to get rid of the "provisional men" feeling. Out of ten years of its existence the Belarusian monetary system had perspectives of independent development for about one and a half years (end of 1994 - beginning of 1996). All other years passed under the sign of either a portion of the Russian money system (91-93) or pending fast "unification" (ruble zone of "new type", attempts to eliminate the Belarusian ruble in April of 1994, preparation and signing of the agreement on union state in 1996, etc.).

As a consequence long-term goals and benchmarks were absent in the monetary policy, facilities of its implementation were weak, qualified specialists left for commercial structures, relations with the international financial organisations were actually broken. Third, this is absence of the market reforms in the real sector of economy that would have forced the political power to pursue general economic and monetary policy facilitating the development of private business.

Specifics of slow reformation of the real sector shown by the absence of systematic approaches and integrity in the introduced economic transformations have resulted in the fact that private sector has not received adequate development, and consequently middle class capable of sounding its economic interests has not been formed.

Shadow and semi-criminal business took the advantages of the effected economic policy. Economy of the country turned up eventually dependent on economic position of the public sector enterprises. In this situation all attempts, initiated by the specialists, to suggest and accomplish market plans of the monetary sphere were doomed to fail. Fourth, this is typical of the former USSR republics and extremely die-hard relapse of socialist attitude to legality when the laws are applied commensurate with their usefulness for a particular office holder.

In case of the monetary system this principle can be emphasised by the following example. The Law on The National Bank in effect from 1991 to 2000 stipulated that the latter could grant credits to the Government "for a term, as a rule, up to 6 months". Nevertheless, accretion of long-term credit amounts made up 122.6 billion rubles in 2000 alone (credits to cover budget deficit would be referred afterwards to the increase of domestic national debt). The Law on Banks explicitly barred the Government to interfere into activity of the banks. But that did not inhibit the Government to force the banks to provide credits to the Agro-Industrial Complex.

Such a queer way to interpret the laws has led to the fact that the enterprises and banks acted, as far as they could, in the same manner and avoided transparency of their operations at the money market. As a result steady and negative attitude was formed to the policy of the monetary authorities, and this is inadmissible in the pursuit of stabilisation of the national monetary unit. Fifth, this is voluntarism in the formation of priority tasks of the economic policy and their misbalance. The State lived beyond its income. Target parameters of volume indices (volume of housing construction, volumes of industrial output by the branches, etc.) passed over to the line ministries and departments were established arbitrary without taking available financial recourses of the State into account. Economic policy turned into a hostage of the populist political goals such as attainment of the GDP physical volume of 1990 in 2000.

Economic policy aimed at the growth of production at any expense by monetary expansion has brought about higher rates of inflation. Since 1997 the parameters of credit emission by the National Bank and growth of money mass in national currency invariably exceeded the target figures approved every year in the Major Directions of the Monetary Policy.

The situation was aggravated by directive maintenance of the Belarusian ruble exchange rate at the overestimated level with introduction of mandatory surrender of the foreign currency receipts. That resulted in the appearance of multiple exchange rates and shadow foreign exchange market, more numerous barter deals, foreign currency deficit to pay for critical import, and a number of other adverse consequences. For instance, share of housing construction in the total amount of credit emission of the National Bank made up 59 per cent in 1999 and 38 per cent in 2000 whereas this share is to total 90 per cent as indicated in the forecast of the social and economic development for 2001.

The housing construction credits were extended at a reduced interest rate of 5 per cent per year (while average monthly inflation, for example, in 1999 was as high as 11 per cent) and for long terms (up to 40 years). A narrow circle of people who got the opportunity to build dwellings under such conditions, was indirectly subsidised at the expense of other people who carried the burden of inflation tax. Weak and shadowed to a large extent economy could not generate a strong and civilised banking system.

The state of the Belarusian banking system within last five years can be characterised in the most general way by the following features. First, this is its chronic financial weakness.

Assets of the Belarusian banks do not demonstrate noticeable tendencies to increase, and are in the state of deep stagnation. During the five-year period they decreased in currency calculation by 6 per cent. The residue of credits on 01.01.2001 amounted to about 95 per cent as compared with analogous index on 01.01.1996. Percent of doubtful loans was on steady uprise - 17.9 per cent of the balance of credit arrears on 01.01.2001 in comparison with 13.2 per cent five years earlier.

Second, this is differentiation of the commercial banks by major indices. A privileged position and demonstrate unconditional support of the public sector of economy. Their share of resources amounts to 80-90 per cent by main articles of the aggregated balance of assets and liabilities of the banking system. The share of Joint Stock Saving Bank "Belarusbank" exceeds in some cases the official index of monopolisation - over 35 per cent.

From the economic point of view this means that the most effective private business is limited in credit support by the banking system while the authorised banks being actually public, cannot expect significant preferences from external financial markets. As a result the banks and real sector are not able to feed each other, and are doomed to financial weakness.

Third, this is formality in observing the regulations of safe banking activity. The National Bank performed insurance of the deposits of the population only in the authorised banks. Up to 2000 the regulations of obligatory reserve formation were always lowered in practice - amount of reserves made up frequently only 5-6 per cent with the official reserve norm of 16-18 per cent. Fourth, this is insufficient transparency of the banks. Over last nine years no trustworthy bank was set up in the country, and the information on financial position of the banks is accidental and published as a rule in non-public editions with small circulation. Therefore confidence of the enterprises and population to the banking system that is needed to accumulate free financial resources under the conditions of reliability and return is at the extremely low level in the present situation. It is no wonder that economic agents prefer to use any opportunity to export capital out of the country.

The problems of the Belarusian banking system together with the current monetary policy make any perspectives of its development indefinite. As a consequence that leads to financial isolation of a rather numerous group of the banks within the small and poor state and inevitable liquidation of the majority of them. The Belarusian authorities will have to face a new problem in 2001 - inconsistency between the declared rigid monetary policy and financial requirements of the unreformed real sector.

Some indications were felt in 2000 when the National Bank merely tried to limit the rate of credit emission. With the statistical GDP growth of 5.8 per cent the investments dropped by 3.4 per cent, income on the sale of products - by 14.9 per cent, profitability reduced by 2.3 per cent, specific weight of loss-making enterprises increased by 6.4 percent points to 23.5 per cent of all enterprises. More rigid monetary policy will bring about bankruptcy of many enterprises and associated banks. That occurred at the stage of financial stabilisation in practically all post-soviet republics.

General Conditions

Main directions and measures of the monetary policy for a middle-term period were suggested proceeding from the following circumstances:

- Beginning from February 2000 the Government and the National Bank pursue more weighted and considered monetary policy that includes limitation of credit emission by the National Bank to cover budget deficit, transfer to positive real interest rates, cancellation of the majority of currency market limits, and abolition of multiple currency exchange rates.
- Signature of the agreement with the Russian Federation on the transfer to common money unit in 2005 and monitoring programme with the IMF for a period of April-September 2001 (provided the agreement has been realised) forces the President Administration and the Government to take a number of certain measures towards reformation of the real sector of economy (liberalisation of pricing, privatisation of public sector, bankruptcy of loss-making enterprises, lift of the barriers for the development of small and medium business).

Nevertheless, despite definite successes in the monetary sphere achieved in 2000, growth rates of prices are still at the inadmissibly high level.

The first objective source of inflation in the Belarusian economy has not been removed - high level of money mass growth. Failure to pay and deficiency of working capital of the enterprises in the real sector of economy caused by low economic efficiency generate constant demand for financial resources. In order to avoid bankruptcies of the loss-making enterprises and reduction of employment the Government, in the absence of other sources (foreign credits and private investments), meets the requirements predominantly at the expense of emission crediting. The National Bank has to carry on emission financing of current cash gaps and deficit of the republican budget on the whole. Besides, methods of extra-economic character are used to force the commercial banks to continue crediting of the public programmmes in the field of the Agro-Industrial Complex at their own resources.

The current macroeconomic policy must be based on the following principles:

- Systematic approach - mutual consistency of the measures and parameters of monetary, fiscal, foreign economic, structural, and institutional policy. The policy of financial stabilisation should be accompanied with active privatisation, and should produce conditions for restructuring of the real sector of economy, for creation of stimulating institutional environment to develop private business and attract foreign investments;
- Balanced targets of macroeconomic policy - radical inventory and review of the volume targets in the public programmmes (housing construction, Agro-Industrial Complex, etc.) in order to make them consistent with the financial possibilities of the State.

TASKS OF THE MONETARY POLICY

Principle objective of the monetary policy is to form confidence on the part of business and households in the national money unit in the near future.

To attain this objective the following tasks have to be solved:

- To reduce the rate of inflation to 25 per cent in the first year, 15 per cent in the second, 5-10 per cent in the third, and keep it afterwards at a level not exceeding 5 per cent per year;
- To maintain positive real interest rate of all financial instruments denominated in the national currency. Attractive deposit policy will make it possible to increase specific weight of time ruble deposits in the money mass, which are the main source of credit resources for the needs of the real sector of economy. Owing to higher confidence in the national currency dollar-filling of the economy will be reduced, structures of the broad money mass will be improved by higher specific weight of the national currency in its total volume, monetisation coefficient will be increased;
- To introduce the regime of floating exchange rate and secure convertibility of the Belarusian ruble in current operations. Activities

of the National Bank should be limited by ironing out local, market fluctuations of the exchange rate and speculative misbalances in the currency demand and supply. Expediency of this exchange rate regime is determined by the fact that it corresponds to a great extent to the interests of small countries with transitional economy having export-oriented structure since the level of business activity and load of the available producing capacities directly depend on the demand for domestic products in the world market. This regime will make it possible to ensure competitiveness of the domestic goods due to the tendency of real exchange rate to reach an effective level. Taking moderate inflation within the period of stabilisation into account (unlike the regimes with fixed exchange rate) burdensome currency interventions may be avoided.

- To set up a regulative base for the system of non-public financial institutions capable of servicing internal and external payment transactions as well as insuring safety of the money accumulations of the enterprises and savings of the households;
- To bring expenditure and revenue of the republican budget into balance.

Directions of Implementation

- Consecutive reduction of the accretion of net crediting of the budget deficit by the National Bank and its complete discontinuation by the third year of reforms. Positive effect consists in eliminating the major inner source of inflation and lowering the national currency exchange rate. Besides, the Government will be called "to live within its means".
- Reduction of the growth rate of net internal ruble credit of the National Bank to average 2-3 per cent per month at the beginning of reforms and afterwards to 15-20 per cent per year. That will generate rigid budgetary restrictions for all economic entities.
- Regulation of the growth rate of aggregate internal credit (ruble and foreign currency) in order to support the medium-term economic programme of the Government in proportion to expected growth of GDP.
- Securance of steady annual growth of net foreign assets of the National Bank to reach complete coverage of the national currency money base at the current exchange rate. In the given case the requirement for annual growth of foreign currency reserves has primarily psychological character that increases confidence in the current monetary policy.
- Preparation of the conditions (accumulation of net foreign assets and

permanent control over the growth of ruble money mass) to tie up the Belarusian ruble to Euro with subsequent integration of the country into European Economic Community. The Authorities will have to demonstrate adherence of the country to the European vector of development and to accept economic rules of the civilised market behaviour.

- Limitation of the growth rate of broad ruble money mass to average 2-3 per cent per month in the first year of reforms and subsequently to 3.5-5 per cent per year. As the rate of inflation goes down preconditions will appear to increase the coefficient of monetisation of GDP.
- Successive reduction of the norm of obligatory reserves to 5-10 per cent with total abolition of all privileges to the commercial banks. That will allow, first, to decrease the cost of ruble and foreign currency credits for the real sector of economy, and, second, provide the banks with the possibility to maintain sufficiently attractive interest rate on time deposits.
- Elimination of all restrictions in the domestic currency market to reach internal convertibility of the national money unit with subsequent transfer of the Belarusian ruble to convertibility on current operations.
- Regulative promotion of settlements in the Belarusian ruble within CIS and close neighbours - Poland, Baltic countries, Russia - to free the resources of convertible currencies for investment projects.
- Maintenance of the refinancing and interest rates in the money market at the level exceeding current level of inflation to stimulate saving and to promote investment process.

The measures must be executed in package. They will make it possible to augment confidence in the national money unit, to gradually edge out dollar as means of saving and circulation, to considerably increase foreign currency reserves of the National Bank. Furthermore, the suggested monetary policy is a prerequisite of integration of Belarus into the European Community.

THE BANKING SYSTEM REFORM

Principle purpose of reformation and restructuring of the banking system is to form a community of credit and financial institutions that are able to accumulate free internal and external financial resources with their profitable disposition, and to render all banking services to domestic and foreign customers. Main problems of the Belarusian banking system consist in its general financial weakness (as against 01.04.2001 it had assets totaling only 2 billion dollars out of which own resources were less than 17 per cent, 44 per cent - resources of the customers, and 10 per cent - those of the National Bank).

About half of all assets of the banking system are disposed as credits to the legal entities, majority of which are low-efficient and loss-making enterprises of the public sector. Total amount of doubtful, overdue and prolonged credits make up 19.2 per cent out of the loans provided.

About 8.7 per cent of the assets are disposed in the low-profit public securities. Deductions to obligatory reserves make up 4.7 per cent. The banking system of Belarus does not practically possess financial instruments that are able to ensure accumulation of money resources in real calculation. Concentration of approximately 78 per cent of all assets in six authorised semi-public banks that have to service public programmmes associated with crediting of the low-efficient Agro-Industrial Complex and housing construction, produces a rather negative effect on the financial position of the banking system. The privileges on obligatory reserves and interest rates granted in return, do not permit to effectively regulate the money market by the market instruments and bring about certain distortions in its work.

Financial rehabilitation of the banking system must include two directions:

- Arrears of the real sector enterprises to the banks should be restructured;
- Recapitalisation of the banks should be performed through attraction of additional financial resources to the banking system.

Restructuring of doubtful to redeem arrears of the enterprises to the banks can be implemented by two means: by conciliation procedures and by compulsory measures. In case the enterprise refuses to strike a conciliation agreement, the bank will have a right to initiate the procedure of bankruptcy irrespective of the form of property of the given enterprise in accordance with the current legislation (the Law on bankruptcy).

Recapitalisation of the banks during the period of common recovery of the economy may include the following measures:

- For the purpose of operational safety of the attracted resources extraordinary provisional measures are to be taken in all commercial banks to restore general liquidity of the banking system.
- Aggregate own capital of the Belarusian banks is to be significantly enlarged within first two years after beginning of the radical reforms.
- Spectrum of crediting and financial institutions is to be widened by setting up specialised non-banking institutions (investment, mortgage, leasing companies, societies of mutual crediting, etc.) assuming that some banks that do not have possibilities to enlarge their own capital, will be transformed into such institutions.
- A group of leading Belarusian banks is to be encouraged to get acknowledgement at the international financial markets including corresponding credit rating.
- International rules of accounting are to be used by the Belarusian

banks. Main statistics on the commercial banks are to be passed over to independent analytical centers for systematic processing and publication of domestic bank rating.

- Transactions in the active accounts of the banks that fail to form reserves on doubtful credits are to be restricted (as against 01.04.2001 a sum of doubtful credits amounting to 153 billion rubles was covered by reserves only by 84 per cent without prolonged and overdue credits, if such credits are taken into consideration - 57 per cent).
- All banks with overdue arrears on extended credits in excess of 5 per cent out of all granted credits, are to work out a plan of own rehabilitation including a schedule of expected conciliation agreements with the borrowers and initiation of the procedure of bankruptcy.

The banks should be encouraged to develop a set of measures aimed at own financial rehabilitation:

- To adopt within 2-3 years a practice of preservation of the general licenses only for the banks having international rating;
- To work out a facility of coercive sale of the controlling block of stock of those banks that regularly fail to observe prudential norms and jeopardise the safety of the entire banking system. This right should be entrusted a banking supervision department or bank restructuring agency;
- To establish ultimate specific weight of the enterprise shares in the bank assets so that to encourage the banks to restore liquidity as fast as possible.

The Government and the National Bank should undertake in short order the following actions:

- Legal and actual restoration of sovereignty of the National Bank from the executive power as essential necessity of developing a modern banking system responsible before creditors and depositors.
- Withdraw the resources of the State and the National Bank from the equity capital of the commercial banks, primarily from Belarusbank and Belagroprombank, with their subsequent sale at free auctions. This is required, first, to make the conditions equal for all banks, and, second, to exclude possibility of non-market pressure of the Authorities and the National Bank on the money market through independent of them banks.
- Restoration of the specialised Saving Bank servicing exclusively the households and working in the money market. That will allow to raise the safety of household savings and to strengthen the market of long-term money resources.
- Reorganisation of Belagroprombank by means of its division into six (by number of regions) local land banks with transfer of the controlling

block of shares to local authorities. That will allow development of regional financial markets around local land banks in the future.

- Creation of the third level of crediting and financial institutions - specialised non-bank crediting and financial institutions with limited license commissions and without the right to maintain settlement accounts of the legal entities and physical persons (investment, trust, mortgage and other companies, societies of mutual crediting, credit unions, etc.). As a result additional resources will be attracted to the money market including the ones from the "gray" economy. Specialisation and better-quality crediting and financial services will be ensured, too.
- Setting of a special non-public fund as stock company to insure deposits of the households and time deposits of the legal entities. The fund will be replenished by proportional unrequited contributions of the banks and non-bank crediting and financial institutions. That will increase confidence in the banks and thus enlarge their resource base.
- Restriction of operations in the active accounts of the banks that fail to form reserves for doubtful credits.
- Development of a facility of accelerated lawsuits against enterprises-borrowers who are not able to redeem extended bank credits, their bankruptcy and property transfer for provisional management by recommendation of the bank-creditors.
- Development and adoption of a facility of coercive sale of the controlling block of stock of those banks that regularly fail to observe prudential norms and jeopardise the safety of the entire banking system. That will allow speeding up the procedure of owner change in the inefficient banks without their bankruptcy and public commotion, to attract more professional management, and to reduce a share of problem banks in the banking system.
- Creation of the Union of commercial banks is to be initiated. The Union will assume jointly and severally responsibility for the financial position of the member-banks, up to setting up a special non-public company insuring deposit risks of the depositors and creditors of the "union banks" on one side, and providing recommendations to the agency supervising the banks on coercive sale of the controlling block of shares of the banks suffering financial problems, on the other side. That should prevent unexpected bank bankruptcies.
- The service in charge of surveillance over the commercial banks should be removed from the National Bank. An independent agency is to be set up on its base. That will allow to split the functions of licensing, regulation and supervision of the banking system, and to increase its transparency.

- Calculation of all prudential regulations proceeding from own capital of the banks and not from their equity capital. That will allow to abandon artificial attraction of new shareholders and to enlarge capitalisation of already issued shares and their market value.
- Branches of reliable foreign banks are to be attracted to the country; their participation in the capital of already operating Belarusian banks will be encouraged, for example, through issue of American and European depositary receipts. That will allow to attract additional resources to the banking system and to intensify competition between commercial banks.
- Transfer to the international standards of financial reporting of the Belarusian banks for the purpose of their prompt adaptation to the world financial markets and procuration of appropriate bank ratings.
- Development of necessary actions aimed at getting credit rating for Belarus and appropriate bank rating for the commercial banks. The banks that do not possess commonly accepted international rating, will have limited foreign currency licenses. Furthermore, the banks that do not possess internal national rating, will have limited domestic license to service the households.
- Review of all current banking legislation of the country in the following directions:
  - Distinct differentiation of powers between monetary entities;
  - Competition between monetary entities;
  - Supremacy of law in regulation of monetary relations;
  - Consideration of disputable issues by courts;
  - Material, administrative and other responsibility of any entity, including state authorities, for the damage inflicted by wrongful actions;
  - Transparency in relations between entities;
  - Provision of information to the public on the National Bank policy and position of the monetary institutions.

The measures suggested are aimed at financial strengthening of the Belarusian banking system, making it dynamic, transparent, including entry to the world financial markets as a full member. Unlike the block of monetary policy, their implementation does not require comprehensive approaches and may be executed any time as economic and political conditions get ready.

PERFECTION OF BANKING LEGISLATION

APPRAISAL OF THE SITUATION

Analysis of the monetary policy pursued in 1995-2000 has displayed that within the frames of the present institutional arrangement of the monetary sphere no regulating efforts on the part of the monetary authorities are able to radically improve its position, and relative stabilisation of the money market is of short-term character. The legislation administering banking activities in Belarus proceeded from market principles on some positions.

In the second half of the 90-ies when backtrack from the economic reforms began, bank regulating acts appeared unprotected from the edicts and decrees, equated to laws, of the President. Legal field of activity of the National Bank and commercial crediting and financial institutions was considerably deformed. Suffice to note, that by the Presidential Decree of March 21, 1998 the National Bank, contrary to the Constitution, was subordinated in operative terms to the Government and remained in this position till June of 2000.

The only way out is to develop and to introduce promptly the legislative base needed to implement market reforms in the monetary and banking system, and coordinated with the legislation in the real sector of economy. Adopted in the fall of 2000 a variant of the Banking Code of the Republic of Belarus does not meet the given requirements since it has retained to a great extent the drawbacks of the preceding legislation and in some positions deterioration has taken place.

Major Directions Banking Legislation Perfection

- Market principles applied in the majority of dynamically developing countries will be laid down in the basis of legislation regulating the banking activity.
- Transition to the monetary system of open type and market-based determination of the national currency official exchange rate should be sounded by legislation.
- Introduce historic name of the national currency - taler. That will emphasise final selection of the country development as a sovereign state.
- To establish the object of money regulation - amount and structure of money base, and total money mass in circulation as well.
- To determine main instruments and methods of money regulation, principles of arranging money turnover, and order of cash money circulation.
- To set a rigid ban on using monetary emission to finance budget deficit and any public or other projects as well as banks for a period of over one year.
- To introduce limitations for participation of the emission bank in economic activity including participation in the capital of commercial banks.
- To secure exclusive responsibility of the National Bank for the development and execution of the monetary policy in the Republic of Belarus.

- Maximum transparency and openness of the National Bank should be established by legislation.
- The norms connected with central bank status should be significantly changed.

The most important legislative provision ensuring independence of the National Bank should be its accountability before the Parliament. Principle objectives and tasks of the National Bank are suggested to be defined in a legislative way: maintenance of price stability, securance of steady purchasing power of the national currency and its exchange rate with foreign currencies.

Independence of the National Bank of the executive power should be based on three chief principles: institutional, financial, and personal. Institutional independence means that no agency of state power and management as well as the highest state officials cannot give instructions to the National Bank in terms of its activity. Financial independence presumes own budget of the National Bank. That includes also establishment of the level and forms of labour compensation of its employees.

Personal independence of the National Bank management is arranged by strictly regulated order of appointment and dismission of its highest officials by the Parliament. The provision that stipulates the status of the Chairman of the Board of Directors of the National Bank as member of the Government should be cancelled. By virtue of the suggested autonomy of the National Bank the norms should be provided for regulation of interrelations between different levels of its management - Board and Council of Directors, by removing them from the internal statute of the central bank.

The law should legally arrange relations of the central bank with the government (prohibition of direct centralised crediting of budget deficit, commitments to secure liquidity of public short-term liabilities), mutual responsibility for pursued common monetary policy, and division of surveillance functions over crediting and financial institutions. An important part of the law is legal arrangement of the limits of licensing and surveillance powers of the National Bank, rules of their application, as well as the order of presentation of surveillance information on the activity of the banks and non-bank crediting and financial institutions to other agencies of state management and mass media. A new approach is needed to perform surveillance of the commercial banks and non-bank crediting and financial institutions.

State registration, licensing and cancellation of licenses of the commercial banks, establishment of main norms associated with regulation of the money market in the country should be left with the National Bank. Surveillance of the banks and non-bank institutions should be passed over to a special committee on surveillance of the activity of the crediting and financial institutions, rights and obligations of which will be defined in a special law. Licensing and regulation of the activity of the non-bank crediting and financial institutions should be entrusted with the Ministry of Finance.

Furthermore, all prudential supervision (control of liquidity, solvency, large risks, etc.) of the activity of all crediting and financial institutions will be given to a special supervising committee. Practice of the recent years has shown inefficiency of concentration of all functions in the National Bank. To temporary suspension of any license issued by the National Bank or Ministry of Finance. The supreme governing body of the committee is to be set up on a parity basis out of the representatives of the National Bank, Ministry of Finance, and members of the committee itself.

The following provisions should be specified in the law on the non-bank crediting and financial institutions:

- Non-bank institutions must not perform exclusively banking functions - attraction of deposits, extension of credits on their own behalf, and account keeping;
- Non-bank institutions must not have correspondent accounts in the single payment system;
- Specialisation of the non-bank institutions should be maintained by issuing a limited number of licenses (not more than three);
- Relatively low start-up equity capital;
- Licensing of the non-bank crediting and financial institutions by the Ministry of Finance that suggests participation of the latter in pursuing of the financial policy coordinated with the National Bank.

New Banking Code will be structurally composed of a package of independent laws - on monetary system, on central bank, on banking universal and specialised crediting and financial institutions, on active, passive and intermediary banking operations, on non-bank crediting and financial institutions, on banking trust, on foreign currency operations and foreign exchange control, on mutual crediting of small business entities, on surveillance of the activity of the crediting and financial institutions (banking supervision) and some other legislative acts. Each of them regulates in a legislative manner a separate sphere of monetary activities and defines responsibilities of separate legal entities and corresponding public authorities. Advantages of the suggested structure consist in the following: some component parts of the general code may be adopted and refined not as a whole but successively as corresponding economic conditions change, and as public authorities are ready to guarantee their observation and economic entities - their implementation.

REFORM IN INDIAN BANKING

Measured by share of deposits, 83 percent of the banking business in India is in the hands of state or nationalised banks, which are banks that are owned by the government, in some, increasingly less clear-cut way. Moreover, even the non-nationalised banks are subject to extensive regulations on who they can lend to, in addition to the more standard prudential regulations.

Government control over banks has always had its fans, ranging from Lenin to Gerschenkron. While there are those who have emphasised the political importance of public control over banking, most arguments for nationalising banks are based on the premise that profit maximizing lenders do not necessarily deliver credit where the social returns are the highest. The Indian government, when nationalising all the larger Indian banks in 1969, argued that banking was "inspired by a larger social purpose" and must "sub serve national priorities and objectives such as rapid growth in agriculture, small industry and exports."

There is now a body of direct and indirect evidence showing that credit markets in developing countries often fail to deliver credit where its social product might be the highest, and both agriculture and small industry are often mentioned as sectors that do not get their fair share of credit.

If nationalisation succeeds in pushing credit into these sectors, as the Indian government claimed it would, it could indeed raise both equity and efficiency. The cross-country evidence on the impact of bank nationalisation is not very encouraging. For example, La Porta et al. find in a cross-country setting that government ownership of banks is negatively correlated with both financial development and economic growth.

They interpret this as support for their view, which holds that the potential benefits of public ownership of banks, and public control over banks more generally, are swamped by the costs that come from the agency problems it creates: cronyism, leading to the deliberate misallocation of capital, bureaucratic lethargy, leading to less deliberate, but perhaps equally costly errors in the allocation of capital, as well as inefficiency in the process of mobilising savings and transforming them into credit. Unfortunately the interpretation of this type of cross-country analysis is never easy, and never more so than the case of something like bank nationalisation, which typically occurs as part of a package of other policies. For example, Bertrand et al. study a 1985 banking deregulation in France, which gave banks much greater freedom to compete for clients.

They find that deregulated banks respond more to profitability when making lending decisions. After the reform, firms that suffer a negative shock are much more likely to undertake restructuring measures, and there is more entry and exit in bank-dependent industries. Micro studies of the effect of bank nationalisation are rare: an important exception is Mian who examines the privatisation of a large public bank in Pakistan in 1991.

He finds that the privatised bank does a better job both at choosing profitable clients and monitoring existing clients, than the commercial banks that remained public. Micro data from a nationalised bank to evaluate the effectiveness of the Indian banking system in delivering credit.

The Indian financial system is characterised by under-lending in the sense that there are many firms that could earn large profits if they were given access to credit at the current market prices. The work with the aim of using that evidence and evidence from other research by ourselves and others, to come to an assessment of the appropriate role of the Indian government vis a vis the banking sector. We first provide a very brief history of banking in India.

We begin by presenting evidence that there is substantial under-lending in India. To understand what role public ownership of banks may play in underlending, we identify differences between public and private banks in the sectoral allocation of credit between public and private banks. In particular, we focus on the question of whether being nationalised has made these banks more responsive to what the Indian government wants them to do. We report results, based on work by Cole showing that on many of the declared objectives of "social banking," the private banks were no less responsive than the comparable nationalised banks, with the exception of agricultural lending.

Finally, the last sub-section compares the performance of public and private banks as financial intermediaries and concludes that the public banks have been less aggressive than private banks both in lending, in attracting deposits and in setting up branches, at least since 1990. We find that official lending policy is very rigid. Moreover, loan officers do not appear to use what little flexibility they have. We argue that the evidence suggests that bankers in the public sector have a preference for what we may call passive lending.

To understand why this is the case, we examine the incentives and constraints faced by public loan officers. We focus on whether vigilance activity impedes lending, and whether public sector banks prefer to lend to the government, rather than private firms. The penultimate part compares the performance of public and private banking in two other areas. First, we examine how nationalisation of banks has affected the availability of bank branches in rural areas, and find that, if anything, nationalisation appears to have inhibited the growth of rural branches. Second, we try to say something about the sensitive issue of NPAs and bailouts.

While the dataset we have now is rather sparse, it appears that the bailouts of the public banks have proved more expensive for the government, but once we control for differences in size between the public and private banks, it is less clear-cut. We conclude in a short discussion of the implications of these results for the future of banking reform.

BACKGROUND

India has a long history of both public and private banking. Modern banking in India began in the 18th century, with the founding of the English Agency House in Calcutta and Bombay. In the first half of the 19th century, three Presidency banks were founded. After the 1860 introduction of limited liability, private banks began to appear, and foreign banks entered the market.

The beginning of the 20th century saw the introduction of joint stock banks.

In 1935, the presidency banks were merged together to form the Imperial Bank of India, which was subsequently renamed the State Bank of India. Also that year, India's central bank, the Reserve Bank of India (RBI), began operation. Following independence, the RBI was given broad regulatory authority over commercial banks in India. In 1959, the State Bank of India acquired the state-owned banks of eight former princely states. Thus, by July 1969, approximately 31 percent of scheduled bank branches throughout India were government controlled, as part of the State Bank of India. The post-war development strategy was in many ways a socialist one, and the Indian government felt that banks in private hands did not lend enough to those who needed it most.

In July 1969, the government nationalised all banks whose nationwide deposits were greater than ₹.500 million, resulting in the nationalisation of 54 percent more of the branches in India, and bringing the total number of branches under government control to 84 percent. Prakesh Tandon, a former chairman of the Punjab National Bank (nationalised in 1969) describes the rationale for nationalisation as follows: Many bank failures and crises over two centuries, and the damage they did under 'laissez faire' conditions; the needs of planned growth and equitable distribution of credit, which in privately owned banks was concentrated mainly on the controlling industrial houses and influential borrowers; the needs of growing small scale industry and farming regarding finance, equipment and inputs; from all these there emerged an inexorable demand for banking legislation, some government control and a central banking authority, adding up, in the final analysis, to social control and nationalisation.

After nationalisation, the breadth and scope of the Indian banking sector expanded at a rate perhaps unmatched by any other country. Indian banking has been remarkably successful at achieving mass participation. Between the time of the 1969 nationalisations and the present, over 58,000 bank branches were opened in India; these new branches, as of March 2003, had mobilised over 9 trillion Rupees in deposits, which represent the overwhelming majority of deposits in Indian banks. This rapid expansion is attributable to a policy which required banks to open four branches in unbanked locations for every branch opened in banked locations. Between 1969 and 1980, the number of private branches grew more quickly than public banks, and on April 1, 1980, they accounted for approximately 17.5 percent of bank branches in India.

In April of 1980, the government undertook a second round of nationalisation, placing under government control the six private banks whose nationwide deposits were above ₹. 2 billion, or a further 8 percent of bank branches, leaving approximately 10 percent of bank branches in private hands. The share of private bank branches stayed fairly constant between 1980 to 2000. Nationalised banks remained corporate entities, retaining most of their staff, with the exception of the board of directors, who were replaced by appointees of the central government. The political appointments included representatives from the government, industry, agriculture, as well as the public. (Equity holders in the national bank were reimbursed at approximately par). Since 1980, has been no further nationalisation, and indeed the trend appears to be reversing itself, as nationalised banks are issuing shares to the public, in what amounts to a step towards privatisation. The considerable accomplishments of the Indian banking sector notwithstanding, advocates for privatisation argue that privatisation will lead to several substantial improvements.

Recently, the Indian banking sector has witnessed the introduction of several "new private banks," either newly founded, or created by previously extant financial institutions. The new private banks have grown quickly in the past few years, and one has grown to be the second largest bank in India. India has also seen the entry of over two dozen foreign banks since the commencement of financial reforms. While we believe both of these types of banks deserve study, our focus here is on the older private sector, and nationalised banks, since they represent the overwhelming majority of banking activity in India.

The Indian banking sector has historically suffered from high intermediation costs, due in no small part to the staffing at public sector banks: as of March 2002, there were 1.17 crores of deposits per employee in nationalised banks, compared to 2.05 crores per employee in private sector banks. As with other government-run enterprises, corruption is a problem for public sector banks: in 1999, there were 1,916 cases which attracted attention from the Central Vigilance Commission.

While not all of these represent crimes, the investigations themselves may have a harmful effect, if bank officers fear that approving any risky loan will inevitably lead to scrutiny. Advocates for privatisation also criticise public sector banking as unresponsive to credit needs. We use recent evidence on banking in India to shed light on the relative costs and benefits of nationalised banks. Throughout this exercise, it is important to bear in mind that the Indian banking sector is going through something like a transformation. Thus, it is potentially a dangerous time to evaluate its performance using historical data. Nevertheless, data from the past is all we have, and we believe things are not changing so quickly that the lessons learned are not useful.

Under-lending therefore is a characteristic of the entire financial system: the firm has not been able to raise enough capital from the market as a whole. In other words, while as suggested, focus on the clients of a public sector bank, if these firms are getting too little credit from that bank, they should in theory have the option of going elsewhere for more credit. If they do not or cannot exercise this option, the market cannot be doing what, in its idealised form, we would have expected it to do. However, we know that the Indian financial system does not function as the ideal credit market might. Most small or medium firms have a relationship with one bank, which they have built up over some time–

they cannot expect to walk into another bank and get as much credit as they want. For that reason, their ability to finance investments they need to make does depend on the willingness of that one bank to finance them. In this sense the results we report might very well reflect the specificities of the public sector banks, or even the one bank that was kind enough to share its data with us, though given that it is seen as one of the best public sector banks, it seems unlikely that we would find much better results in other banks in its category. On the other hand we do not have comparable data from any private bank and therefore cannot tell whether under-lending is as much of a problem for private banks. As suggested, however, later report some results on the relative performance of public and private banks in terms of overall credit delivery. Our identification of credit constrained firms is based on the following simple observation: if a firm that is not credit constrained is offered some extra credit at a rate below what it is paying on the market, then the best way to make use of the new loan must be to pay down the firm's current market borrowing, rather than to invest more.

This is because, by the definition of not being credit constrained, any additional investment will drive the marginal product of capital below what the firm is paying on its market borrowing. It follows that a firm that is not facing any credit constraint will expand its investment in response to additional subsidised credit becoming available, only if it has no more market borrowing. By contrast, a firm that is credit constrained will always expand its investment to some extent.

A corollary to this prediction is that for unconstrained firms, growth in revenue should be slower than the growth in subsidised credit. This is a direct consequence of the fact that firms are substituting subsidised credit for market borrowing. Therefore, if we do not see a gap in these growth rates, the firm must be credit constrained. Of course, revenue could increase slower than credit even for non-constrained firms, if the technology has declining marginal return to capital. These predictions are more robust than the traditional way of measuring credit constraints as the excess sensitivity of investment to cash flow.

Our approach inscribes itself in a literature that tries to identify specific shocks to wealth in order to identify credit constraints. In Banerjee and Duflo we test these predictions by taking advantage of a recent change in the so-called "priority sector" rules in India: all banks in India are required to lend at least 40 percent of their net credit to the priority sector, which includes small scale industry (SSI), at an interest rate that is required to be no more than 4 percentage points their prime lending rate. If banks do not satisfy the priority sector target, they are required to lend money to specific government agencies at low rates of interest. In January, 1998, the limit on total investment in plants and machinery for a firm to be eligible for inclusion in the small scale industry category was raised from ₹. 6.5 million to ₹. 30 million. Our empirical strategy focuses on the firms that became newly eligible for credit in this period, and uses firms that were always eligible for priority sector credit as a control. The results from our analysis are reported brie fly in the next sub-section.

The Evidence for Under-lending

Data: The data we use were obtained from one of the better-performing Indian public sector banks. We use data from the loan folders maintained by the bank on profit, sales, credit lines and utilisation, and interest rates.

The loan folders also report all numbers that the banker was required to calculate (*e.g.*, his projection of the bank's future turnover, his calculation of the bank's credit needs, etc.) in order to determine the amount to be lent.

We have data on 253 firms (including 93 newly eligible firms). The data is available for the entire 1997 to 1999 period for 175 of these firms.

Specification: Through much of this section we will estimate an equation of the form

$$y_{it} - y_{it} - = \alpha_y BIG + \beta_y POST_t + \gamma_y BIG_i * POST_t + \in_{yit}, \qquad (1)$$

with y taking the role of the various outcomes of interest (credit, revenue, profits, etc.) and the dummy POST representing the post January 1998 period. We are in effect comparing how the outcomes change for the big firms after 1998, with how they change for the small firms.

We are in effect comparing how the outcomes change for the big firms after 1998, with how they change for the small firms.

Since y is always a growth rate, this is, in effect, a triple difference–we can allow small firms and big firms to have different rates of growth, and the rate of growth to differ from year to year, but we assume that there would have been no differential changes in the rate of growth of small and large firms in 1998, absent the change in the priority sector regulation.

Using, respectively, the log of the credit limit and the log of next year's sales (or profit) in place of y in equation 1, we obtain the first stage and the reduced form of a regression of sales on credit, using the interaction BIG * POST as an instrument for credit. As suggested, present the corresponding instrumental variable regressions.

Results: The change in the regulation certainly had an impact on who got priority sector credit. The credit limit granted to firms below ₹. 6.5 million in plant and machinery (henceforth, small firms) grew by 11.1 percent during 1997, while that granted to firms between ₹.6.5 million and ₹. 30 million (henceforth, big firms), grew by 5.4 percent. In 1998, after the change in rules, small firms had 7.6 percent growth while the big firms had 11.3 percent growth. In 1999, both big and small firms had about the same growth, suggesting they had reached the new status quo. This is confirmed when we estimate equation 1 using bank credit as the outcome. The coefficient of the interaction term BIG * POST is

0.95, with a standard error of 0.033. Column (1) estimates the probability that a firm's credit limit was changed: the coefficient on BIG * POST is close to zero and insignificant, suggesting that the reform did not affect which firm's limits was changed. This corresponds to the general observations that whether or not a firm's file is brought out for a change in limit has nothing to do with the needs of the firm, but respond to internal dynamics of the bank. As suggested, make use of this fact to partition the sample into two groups on the basis of whether there was a change in the credit limit or not: the sample where there was no change in limit can be used as a "placebo" group, where we can test our identification assumption.

Finally, column (3) gives the estimated impact of the reform on loan size for firms whose limit was changed: the coefficient of the interaction BIG * POST is 0.27, with a standard error of 0.10. This increase in credit was not accompanied by a change in the rate of interest. It did not lead to reduction in the rate of utilisation of the limits by the big firms (column (5)): the ratio of total turnover (the sum of all debts incurred during the year) to credit limit is not associated with the interaction BIG * POST. The additional credit limit thus resulted in an increase in bank credit utilisation by the firms.

The coefficient of the interaction BIG * POST in the sales equation, in the sample where the limit was increased, is 0.19, with a standard error of 0.11. By contrast, in the sample where there was no increase in limit, the interaction BIG * POST is close to zero (0.007) and insignificant, which suggests that the sales result is not driven by a failure of the identification assumption. The coefficient of the interaction BIG * POST is 0.27 in the credit regression, and 0.19 in the sales regression: thus, sales increased almost as fast as loans in response to the reform. This is an indication that there was little or no substitution of bank credit for non-bank credit as a result of the reform, and that firms are credit constrained. Additional evidence is provided in column (2).

We restrict the sample to firms which have a positive amount of borrowing from the market both before and after the reform, and thus have not completely substituted bank borrowing for market borrowing. In this sample as well, we obtain a positive and significant effect of the interaction BIG * POST, indicating that these firms must be credit constrained. In column (3), we present the effect of the reform on profit. Because our dependent variable is the logarithm of profit, we can only estimate the impact on firms whose profits were positive. The effect is even bigger than that of sales: 0.54, with a standard error of 0.28.

Here again, we see no effect of the interaction BIG * POST in the sample without a change in limit, which lends support to our identification assumption. The large effect on profit is not sufficient to establish the presence of credit constraints: even unconstrained firms should see profits increase when they gain access to subsidised credit, because they would substitute cheaper capital for more expensive capital. However, if firms were not expanding, we should not expect to see sales (column (1)) or costs (not reported) expand as well.

Note that the coefficient is a lower bound of the effect of working capital on sales, because the reform should have led to some substitution of bank credit for market credit. The IV coefficient is 0.75, with a standard error of 0.37. The effect of working capital on sales is very close to 1, a result which would imply that there cannot be equilibrium without credit constraint. The IV estimate of the impact of bank credit on profit is 1.79, though again the sample is limited to firms with positive profits. This is substantially greater than, which suggests that the technology has a strong fixed cost component. However, these coefficients also allow us to estimate the effect of credit expansion on profits. We can use this estimate to get a sense of the average increase in profit caused by every rupee in loan.

The average loan is ₹ 8, 6800. Therefore, and increase of ₹. 1,000 in the loan corresponds to a 1.15 per cent increase in loans. Taking 1.79 as the estimate of the effect of the log increase in loan on log increase in profit, an increase of ₹. 1,000 in lending causes a 2 per cent increase in profit. At the mean profit (which is ₹. 36,700, this would correspond to an increase in profit of ₹. 756. A last piece of important evidence is whether big firms become more likely to default than small firms after the reform: the increase in profits (and sales) may otherwise reflect more risky strategies pursued by the large firms. In order to answer this question, we collected additional data on the firms based in the Mumbai region (138 firms, a bit over half the sample). In particular, we collected data on whether any of these firm's loan had become non-performing assets (NPA) in 1999, 2000 or 2001, or were NPA before 1999.

The number of NPAs is disturbingly large (consistent with the high rate of NPAs in Indian banks), but large and small firms are equally likely to have a non-performing loan: 7.7 per cent of the big firms and 7.29 per cent of the small firms (who were not already NPA), default on their loan in 2000 or 2001. Among the firms in Mumbai, 2.5 per cent of the large firms, and 5.96 per cent of the small firms had defaulted between 1996 and 1998. The fraction of firms that had defaulted thus increased a little bit more for large firms, but the difference is small, and not significant. The increase in credit did not cause an unusually large number of big firms to default. Default rate, and the higher cost of lending to the firms in the priority sector, is not sufficient to narrow significantly the gap between our estimate of the rate of returns to capital and the interest rate. Using these estimates and our previous estimates of the cost of lending to small firms, we compute that the interest rate banks should charge to these firms is close to 22 per cent (rather than the 16 per cent they are charging on average). This means that the gap between the social marginal product of capital is at least 66 per cent. These results provide clear evidence of very substantial under-lending: some firms clearly can absorb much more capital at high rates of return. Moreover the firms in our sample are by Indian standards quite substantial: these are not the very small firms at the margins of the economy, where, even if the marginal product is high, the scope for expansion may be quite limited. These data do not tell us anything directly about the efficiency of allocation of capital across firms.

However, the IV estimate of the effect of loans on profit is strongly positive, while the OLS estimate is not different from zero. In other words, firms that have higher growth in loans do not generate faster growth in profits, suggesting that normally banks do not target loans enhancements to the most profitable firms. This is consistent with evidence reported in Dasgupta15, that the interest rate paid by firms and by implication the marginal product of capital varies enormously within the same sub-economy. It is also consistent with the more direct evidence in Banerjee and Munshi showing that there is very substantial variation in the productivity of capital in the knitted garment industry in Tirupur.

Furthermore, while we have no direct data on this point, banker's lore suggests that the firms that have relatively easy access to credit tend to be the bigger and longer established firms. The underprovision of credit to small-scale industry was one of the key reasons cited for nationalisation in 1969: thus, it might in fact be the case that while the public sector banks provide relatively little credit to SSI firms, private banks are even worse.

Bank Ownership and Sectoral Allocation of Credit

An important rationale for the Indian bank nationalisations was to direct credit towards sectors the government thought were underserved, including small scale industry, as well as agriculture and backward areas.

Ownership was not the only means of directing credit: the Reserve Bank of India issued guidelines in 1974, indicating that both public and private sector banks must provide at least one-third of their aggregate advances to the priority sector by March 1979. In 1980, it was announced that this quota would be increased to 40 percent by March 1985. Sub-targets were also specified for lending to agriculture and weaker sectors within the priority sector. Since public and private banks faced the same regulation, in this part we focus on how ownership affected credit allocation. The comparison of nationalised and private banks is never easy: banks that fail are often merged with healthy nationalised banks, which makes the comparison of nationalised banks and non-nationalised banks close to meaningless.

The Indian nationalisation experience of 1980 represents a unique chance to learn about the relationship between bank ownership and bank lending behaviour. The 1980 nationalisation took place according to a strict policy rule: all private banks whose deposits were a certain cutoff were nationalised. After 1980, the nationalised banks remained corporate entities, retaining most of their staff, though the board of directors was replaced by nominees of the Government of India. Both the banks that got nationalised under this rule and the banks that missed being nationalised, continued to operate in the same environment, and face the same regulations and therefore ought to be directly comparable.

Even this comparison between banks just nationalised and just not nationalised may be invalid, because policy rule means that banks nationalised in 1980 are larger than the banks that remained private. If size influences bank behaviour, it would be incorrect to attribute all differences between nationalised and private sector banks to nationalisation. In this part, based on Cole, we adopt an approach in the spirit of regression discontinuity design, and compare banks that were just above the 1980 cutoff to those that were just below the 1980 cutoff, while controlling for bank size in 1980. The idea behind this comparison is that the relationship between size and behaviour should not change dramatically around the cutoff, unless nationalisation itself causes changes in bank behaviour.

This will allow for credible causal inference on the role of bank ownership on bank behaviour. In order to get a sense of the magnitude of lending differences among bank types, we first divide the banks into five groups, based on their size in 1980: State Bank of India and its affiliates, large nationalised banks (nationalised in 1969), "marginal" nationalised banks (nationalised in 1980), "marginal" private banks (relatively large, but just too small to be nationalised in 1980), and small private banks. Because the geographic districts in which banks are located vary (soil quality, rural population, etc.), and face different economic shocks, we focus here on comparing differential bank behaviour within each district. Our outcomes of interest include average loan size, residual interest rate, 20 and share of bank lending to the following areas: agriculture, rural credit, small scale industry, government credit, and "trade, transport and finance."

To estimate bank-group effects, we regress credit outcome variables for each bank group g in district d on D district dummy variables, and $BG_1 ..., BG_G$ bank group dummy variables. Specifically, we estimate:

$$y_{b,d,t} = \sum_{i=1}^{G} \gamma_i BG_i + \sum_{i=1}^{G} \delta_i \, District_i + \varepsilon_{b,d,t} \qquad (2)$$

The estimated bank group effects, $\hat{\gamma}_1 ..., \hat{\gamma}_G$ give the average share each bank gives to each sector, after controlling for differences across districts. For example, the estimated $\hat{\gamma}$ for the average loan size from banks in the State Bank of India group is ₹ 56,190. Compared to the average loan size of the State Bank of India, nationalised banks gave slightly smaller loans (an average of 6,430 ₹ lower), while marginal nationalised banks gave slightly larger loans (the average was 8,350 ₹ greater), marginal private banks gave much larger loans (35,310 ₹ more), and small private banks gave loans much larger on average (58,500 ₹ more). These results appear to confirm conventional wisdom that nationalised and public banks give smaller loans than private banks. The most informative comparison is between what we called the "marginal" nationalised and the "marginal" private bank, which were similar in size, but the former were nationalised while the latter weren't. Many of the differences between the marginal nationalised and the marginal private banks are large: the marginal private banks gave 5 percentage points less credit to agriculture than the marginal nationalised banks: given that the all-India share of credit to agriculture is 11 percent, this difference is substantial.

The results also suggest that nationalisation led to more credit to small scale industry (an increase of 2 percentage points relative to the private banks; India-wide small scale industry receives 9 per cent of total credit), four percentage points more credit to rural areas (compared to a national average of 12 per cent), and slightly more to government enterprises. These increases come at the expense of credit trade, transport, and finance (nationalised banks gave 6 per cent points less, compared to the national average share of 21 per cent).

The rural and government lending differences are significant at the 5 percent level, while all others are significant at the one percent level. While this is suggestive that private and public banks behave differently, the values in the table vary not only between marginal private and marginal nationalised banks, but across other bank groups as well. Thus, from this data alone, we cannot rule out the possibility that the difference in lending behaviour is attributable to bank size, rather than ownership.

To obtain an accurate measure of the impact of nationalisation, we examine lending behaviour at the individual bank level, adopting a full-fledged regression-discontinuity approach. We first estimate bank effects analogous to the group effects estimated in equation (2), by replacing the Bank Group dummy indicators with individual bank dummy indicators, to obtain coefficients $\hat{\beta}_1 \ldots \hat{\beta}_B$.

These coefficients tell us to what extent bank *b* behaves differently from other banks, after controlling for the characteristics of the districts in which each bank operates. We then regress the individual indicators $\hat{\beta}_b$ b on log deposits of the bank in 1980 ($size_b$), an indicator variable (Nat_b),which takes the value of one when the size was larger than the cutoff and the bank therefore nationalised, and an interaction term.

Banks are ordered by the size of their deposits in 1980, so that banks below the cutoff of 14.5 are private, while banks above were nationalised in 1980. Contrary to the results obtained by simple comparison of means, there does not appear to be any significant difference in lending to small-scale industry between public and private banks that are of similar size. That is, we cannot reject the hypothesis that nationalisation had no effect on credit to small-scale industry. On the other hand, nationalization appears to have had the effect of lowering the amount of credit banks provide to trade, transport, and finance. Nationalisation appears to have had a large effect on credit to agriculture.

There is a relationship between size in 1980 and lending to agriculture in 1992: larger banks lend more to agriculture. However, there is a visible break in the relationship at the nationalisation cut-off: banks just above the cutoff lend substantially more to agriculture than banks, even after accounting for the effect of size. For example, for agriculture in 1992, the estimated break is .084, with a standard error of .029: the difference between nationalised and private banks is quite significant, both economically and statistically. The point estimates of the structural break confirm some of the differences, but suggest that others are merely functions of bank size. In particular, as measured by credit in 1992, nationalisation had a causal effect on agricultural credit and rural credit, increasing each by about 8 percentage points.

These numbers are large, given that the set of all banks lent only 11 percent of credit to agriculture and 12 percent to rural areas. These results are significant at the 1 percent level. Nationalisation appears to have had no effect on the amount of credit banks lend to small scale industry, but caused a nine percentage point decrease in the credit banks issued to trade, transport and finance. Not surprisingly, we see that nationalised banks lend more to government-owned enterprises; the two-percentage point difference is particularly large in light of the fact credit to government borrowers represents only two percent of bank credit. Public sector banks appear to lend at slightly lower interest rates, though the point estimate, seventy basis points, is not statistically significant. We also attempted to measure whether public sector banks gave more credit to industries that had been identified for support in various five-year plans after 1980, but found no evidence that these industries were favoured.

The differences between the nationalised and private banks seem to have decreased over time: in the 2000 data, the point estimate on agricultural lending drops from 8 to 5 points, on rural lending from 7 to 3 points, and on trade and transport and finance from –11 to –6 percentage points. In sum, bank ownership does seem to have had a limited impact on the government's ability to direct credit to specific sectors. Through the early 1990s, the credit environment in India was very tightly regulated.

The government set interest rates, required both public and private banks to issue 40 percent of credit to the priority sector, and to meet specific sub-targets within the priority sector.

Nevertheless, banks controlled by the government provided substantially more credit to agriculture, rural areas, and the government, at the expense of credit to trade, transport, and finance. Though, surprisingly, there was no effect on credit to small scale industry. Lending differences shrunk over the 1990s, and in 2000 were about half of what they were in the early 1990s.

This might reflect the increasing dynamism of the private sector banks in the liberalised environment of the 1990s or the loosening grip of the government on the nationalised banks.

BANK OWNERSHIP AND SPEED OF FINANCIAL DEVELOPMENT

To determine whether public ownership of banks inhibits financial intermediation, we again compare banks just above and just below the 1980 nationalisation cut-off, using data from the Reserve Bank of India, for the period 1969 to 2000. We include the six, which were nationalised, which were not.

Since we have data from both the pre and post period, we adopt a difference-in-differences approach. Specifically, we regress the annual change in bank deposits, credit, and number of bank branches on a dummy for post nationalisation, and a dummy for post-nationalisation in a liberalised environment. We break the post-nationalisation analysis up into two periods because the former period was characterised by continued financial repression, while substantial liberalisation measures were implemented in the beginning of the 1990s. Public and private banks could well behave differently before and after liberalisation. Because larger banks may grow at different rates than small banks, we include bank fixed effects (βi).

The parameters of interest are $\gamma 1$ and $\gamma 2$, which capture the differential behaviour of nationalised banks after the nationalisation. Standard errors are adjusted for auto-correlation within each bank. The results suggest that while the overall rate of growth in deposits and credit slowed substantially in the period 1980-1990 relative to the 1969-1979 period, there was no differential effect for nationalised and private banks. In the nineties, deposit and credit growth slowed further still. In this liberalised environment, deposits and credit of the nationalised banks slowed down more than the private banks: deposits grew 7.3 percent slower, while credit grew 8.8 percent less quickly. These results are significant at the ten and five percent level, respectively. The growth rate in bank branches generally tracked credit and deposits, though the decline after 1980 was more severe. While the growth rates for nationalised banks were slightly lower in both periods, the differences are not statistically significant. To answer the question of whether there was a significant difference between public and private banks prior to nationalisation, were estimate equàtion, replacing the bank fixed effects with a nationalisation dummy, and a control function $(K_{b,80}) = \pi_1 K_{b,80} + \pi_2 K^2_{b,80,}$, which controls for the effect of 1980 log deposits of each bank in 1980 (denoted $K_{b,80}$). (These results are not reported, but are available from the authors).

The control function allows bank growth to depend on bank size, while the nationalisation dummy will pick up any differences between the nationalised and non-nationalised banks that are not related to size. The estimates suggests that credit, deposit and number of branches grew at the same speed between 1969 and 1979 for banks that were going to be nationalised in 1980 and those that were not. The coefficients on the interaction terms remain negative, and are virtually unchanged from the specification. Thus, it is only after the 1980 nationalisation that banks nationalised in 1980 started to grow more slowly.

These results provide some evidence that nationalisation hindered the spread of intermediation in the 1990s, but not earlier. We look for features of public banks, examining both official lending policies, and other incentives faced by employees of public sector banks. Official Lending Policies While public sector banks in India are nominally independent entities, they are subject to intense regulation by the Reserve Bank of India (RBI). This includes rules about how much a bank should lend to individual borrowers–the so-called "maximum permissible bank finance."

Until 1997, the rule was based on the working capital gap, defined as the difference between the current assets of the firm and its total current liabilities excluding bank finance (other current liabilities). The presumption is that the current assets are illiquid in the very short run and therefore the firm needs to finance them. Trade credit is one source of finance, and what the firm cannot finance in this way constitutes the working capital gap. Firms were supposed to cover a part of this financing need, corresponding to no less than 25 percent of the current assets, from equity.

The sum of all loans from the banking system was supposed not to exceed this amount. This definition of the maximum permissible bank finance applied to loans above ₹. 20 million. For loans below ₹.20 million, banks were supposed to calculate the limit based on the projected turnover of the firm.

Projected turnover was to be determined by a loan officer in consultation with the client. The firm's financing need was estimated to be 25 percent of the projected turnover and the bank was allowed to finance up to 80 percent of what the firm needs, *i.e.*, up to 20 percent of the firm's projected turnover. The rest, amounting to at least 5 percent of the projected turnover has again to be financed by long term resources available to the firm. In the middle of 1997, following the recommendation of the committee on financing of the small scale industries (the Nayak committee), the RBI decided to give each bank the flexibility to evolve its own lending policy, under the condition that it be made explicit.

Moreover the Nayak committee recommended that the turnover rule be used to calculate the lending limit for all loans under ₹. 40 millions. Given the freedom to choose the rule, different banks went for slightly different strategies. The bank we studied adopted a policy which was, in effect, a mix between the now recommended turnover-based rule and the older rule based on the firm's asset position. First the limit on turnover basis was calculated as: min (0.20

Projected turnover, 0.25 Projected turnover " available margin). The available margin here is the financing available to the firm from long term sources (such as equity), and is calculated as Current Assets " Current Liabilities from the current balance sheet. In other words the presumption is that the firm has somehow managed to finance this gap in the current period and therefore should be able to do so in the future.

Therefore the bank only needs to finance the remaining amount. Note that if the firm had previously managed to get the bank to follow the turnover based rule exactly, its available margin would be precisely 5 percent of turnover and the two amounts in 6 would be equal. The rule did not stop here. For all loans below ₹.40 million, the loan officer was supposed to use both equation 6 and the older rule represented by 5. The largest permissible limit on the loan was the maximum of these two numbers. Two comments about the nature of this rule are in order. First, this turnover based approach to working capital finance is relatively standard even in the USA.

However the view in the USA is that working capital finance is essentially financing inventories and is therefore backed by the value of the inventories. In India, the inventories do not seem to provide adequate security, as evidenced by the high rates of default. In such cases it may be much more important to pay attention to profitability, since profitable companies are less likely default. Second, in the USA the role of finding promising firms and promoting them is carried out, to a significant extent, by venture capitalists. In India the venture capital industry is still nascent and it will be a while before it can play the role that we expect of its US equivalent.

Therefore banks may have to be more pro-active in promoting promising firms. Following a rule that does not put any weight on profits may not be the way to favour the most promising firms: while the projected turnover calculation does favour faster growing firms, the loan officer is not allowed to project a growth rate greater than 15 percent. This may be enough to meet the needs of a mature firm, but a small firm that is growing fast clearly needs much more than 15 percent. It is important that the rules encourage the loan officers to lend more to companies on the basis of promise.

Actual Lending Policy

The lending policy statements give us the outside limits on what the banks can lend. There is nothing in the policies that stops them from lending less, though bankers are always enjoined to lend as much as possible in official documents. It is also possible, given that it is not clear how these rules are enforced, that the banks sometimes exceed the limits–it is, for example, often alleged that loan officers in public sector banks give out irresponsibly large loans to their friends and business associates. It is not even clear how one would necessarily know that banker had lent too much given that he is given the task of estimating expected turnover. Based on work by Banerjee and Duflo, we therefore look at the actual practice of lending in our sample of loans. We use the same data source that was used in previous work by Banerjee and Duflo to look at what bankers actually do. Since we have data on current assets and other current liabilities, it is trivial to calculate the limit according to the traditional, working capital gap-based method of lending (henceforth LWC). We can also calculate the limit on turnover basis (henceforth LTB). The maximum of LTB and LWC is, according to the rules, the real limit on how much the banker can lend to the firm. Inertia and the fear of prosecution Since public sector banks are owned by the government, employees of the bank are treated by law as public servants, and thus subject to government anti-corruption legislation.

There is an impression among bankers that it is very easy to be charged with corruption, and that the law states that if any government functionary takes a decision which results in direct financial gain to a third party, the individual is prima facie guilty of corruption, and must prove her or his innocence. The executive director of a large public sector bank was quoted saying "Fear of prosecution for corruption hangs over every loan officer's head like the sword of Damocles."

The Economic Times of India has attributed slowdowns in lending directly to vigilance activity. A working group on banking policy set up by the Reserve Bank of India, and chaired by M.S. Verma, noted: The [working group] observed that it has received representations from the managements and the unions of the banks complaining about the diffidence in taking credit decisions with which the banks are beset at present. This is due to investigations by outside agencies on the accountability of staff in respect of some of the Non- Performing Assets. The group also noticed a marked reluctance at various level to take any credit decision."

In response to criticism from bankers, economists, and others, the Central Vigilance Commission (henceforth CVC), which is the body entrusted to investigate potential cases of fraud in the public sector, introduced in 1999 a special chapter of the vigilance manual, on vigilance in public sector banks. The language would probably not reassure anyone with experience working in a western bank. The manual reads, for example, that "every loss caused to the organisation, either in pecuniary or non-pecuniary terms, need not necessarily become the subject matter of a vigilance enquiry... once a vigilance angle is evident, it becomes necessary to determine through an impartial investigation as to what went wrong and who is accountable for the same."

Interviews with public sector bankers revealed widespread concern: the legal proceedings surrounding charges of corruption can drag on for years, leaving individuals charged with corruption in an uncertain state. Even if an individual is exonerated, she may have been relieved of her duties, transferred, or passed over for promotion during the time of investigation. In theory (as well as practice), even one loan gone bad may be sufficient to start vigilance proceedings.

The possible penalties stand in stark contrast to rewards. While banks are constantly urged by the Reserve Bank of India to lend as much as possible, there are no explicit incentives for making good loans, or ways to penalise officers who make conservative decisions. In effect, bankers are accountable to more than one authority –the loan officer's boss is one of them but central vigilance may be another, and the press may be yet another. In such circumstances, it may be very difficult to provide effective incentives. If this were the case, loan officers would prefer not to take new decisions. Simply renewing the loan without changing the amount is one easy way to avoid responsibility, especially if the original decision was someone else's (loan officers are frequently transferred). And when they do take a decision, making sure that they did not deviate enormously from the precedent, is a way of covering themselves against charges of wrong-doing or worse.

Not surprisingly, the Central Vigilance Commission disputes the claim that there is a "fear psychosis," and, to bolster their position, released in 2000 a "critical analysis" of vigilance activity in public sector banks in 1999. The analysis reveals that in 1999, the Central Vigilance Commission received 1916 references, 72 per cent of which were credit-related, recommending punishment in the majority of cases. Their 2000 report states "out of every 100 cases coming before it, the Commission would advice major penalty proceedings in 28 cases, minor penalty proceedings in 32 cases, and administrative warning/exoneration in 40 cases."

The author of the report, a CVC official, argued that this level of activity should not be enough to cause "fear psychoses": "These figures reveal that a person is not damned the moment his case is referred to the Commission... These statistics appear to indicate a very fair and objective approach on the part of the Commission to the cases that were referred to it." Based on work by Cole looks at whether there is any evidence for the so-called fear psychosis. The basic idea is simple: we ask whether bankers who are "close to" bankers who have been subject to CVC action, slow down lending in the aftermath of that particular CVC action.

Monthly credit data, by bank, were provided by the RBI. Data on frauds are naturally very difficult to come by. It is also the policy of the government of India to keep the data on vigilance activity confidential: while some aggregated statistics are published, they are too aggregated to be useful for econometric analysis.

However, in 1998, in an effort increase the penalty for fraud through stigma, the government authorised the CVC to publish the name, position, employing bank, and punishment of individual officers of government agencies charged with major frauds. This list consists of eighty-seven officials in public sector banks between the years 1992 and 2001. While nature of the fraud with which they are charged is not known, we do know that approximately 72 per cent of frauds relate to illegal extension of credit, while the balance is classified as kite-flying or "other." Since our hypothesis is that vigilance results in a decrease in lending activity, the inclusion of spurious non-credit related vigilance activity should bias coefficients towards zero.

The first approach is to use bank level monthly lending data to estimate the effect of vigilance activity on lending, using the following equation,

$$y_{it} = \alpha_i + \beta_t + \sum_{k=0}^{\omega} \gamma_k D_{i,t} - k + \varepsilon_{it}$$

where y_{it} is log credit extended by bank i in month t, α_i is a bank fixed-effect, β_t is a month fixed effect, and $D_{i,t-k}$ is an indicator variable for whether vigilance activity was reported by the CVC for bank $\boldsymbol{i}$ in month $t\text{-}k$.

Standard errors reported are adjusted for serial correlation and heteroscedasticity. The basic idea is to compare the bank that was affected by the vigilance activity with other public sector banks, before and after the vigilance event.

Which event window to use is not immediately clear: the appropriate start date would most likely be the month in which it became known that vigilance proceedings were under way, or perhaps the date bankers learned of the judgement. The data published by the CVC give only the date at which the CVC provided advice on the case, and the date on which action was taken. Nor is it clear how long it should take before an effect appears, or for how long one would accept this effect to last. We therefore let the data decide, by estimating models which allow effects ranging from one month to four years.

Bibliography

A. Poshadri and Aparna Kuna : *A Handbook of Food Techno's*, New India Publishing Agency, Delhi, 2013.

Ashok K Chauhan and Ajit Varma:*Microbes : Health and Environment*, I K International, Delhi, 2007.

B.N. Dash: *Commercial Banking : Risk and Credit Management*, Arise Publication, Delhi, 2011.

Benton E. Gup and James W. Kolari: *Commercial Banking: The Management Of Risk*, Wiley, 2001.

Bijay Kumar Sinha: *Indian Banking and Economic Reforms : Problems and Prospects*, Classical Publication, Delhi, 2007.

Cristobal Noe Aguilar; Juliana Morales Castro; Efren Delgado; Diana Jasso Cantu and Ashok Pandey: *Food Science and Food*

Dalip Kumar and Asmi Raza: *Agriculture and Food Security*: *Contemporary Issues*, Deep and Deep Publications, Delhi, 2011.

G P Kapoor: *Commercial Banking*, APH Publication, Delhi, 2004.

Harbans Lal Sharma: *Commercial Banking Development : A Study*, Rajat Publication, Delhi, 2003.

Harmeet Singh: *Dairy Farming*, APH Publication, Delhi, 2011.

K.R. Gupta: *Economics : For UGC-NET/SLET and Other Competitive Examinations*, Atlantic Publication, Delhi, 2011.

Keshava, S R.: *Economics*, New Age International, Delhi, 2009.

M Lakshmi Narasaiah: *Economic Growth and Food Security*, Discovery Publishing House, Delhi, 2008.

M.S. Gopalan: *Indian Money Market : Structure, Operation and Developments*, Deep & Deep Publication, Delhi, 2000.

Madhulika Bhatnagar.: *Encyclopaedia of Catering Technology, Food Service and Hospitality Management, Vol. I to III*, Delhi, Anmol Publication, 2008.

Manoj Negi: *Career in Dairy Farming*, Abhishek Publication, Delhi, 2010.

N.K. Sharma: *Economics : Theory and Practice*, DND Publications, Delhi, 2015.

P R Gupta:*Dairy India 2007: Serving the Dairy Industry Since 1983*, Dairy India Yearbook, 2007.

Piyush Sharma and Prem Ram : *A Textbook of Food and Beverage Management*, Dominant Publication, Delhi, 2013.

R K Uppal and Rimpi Kaur: *Indian Banking : Transformation Through Information Technology*, Mahamaya Publishing House, Delhi, 2008.

R K Uppal: *Indian Banking Industry and Information Technology*, New Century Publication, Delhi, 2006.

R S Paroda: *Sustaining Our Food Security*, Konark Publication, Delhi, 2003.

R. P. Saxena.: *Hotel Management : Food And Food Services*, Delhi, Centrum Press, 2010.

R.K. Uppal: *Indian Banking : A New Vision*, Mahamaya Publication, Delhi, 2009.

R.K. Uppal: *Indian Banking : Scaling New Heights*, Kunal Books, Delhi, 2009.

R.K. Uppal: *Indian Banking and Contemporary Issues*, Kunal Books, Delhi, 2011.

R.K. Uppal: *Indian Banking in New Global Order*, Sarup Publication, Delhi, 2012.

R.K. Uppal: *Indian Banking in the Globalised World*, New Century Publications, Delhi, 2008.

R.K. Uppal: *Indian Banking Industry : Issues Challenges and Opportunities*, Sarup Publication, Delhi, 2013.

Rajesh Pal: *Indian Banking and Globalization*, Adhyayan Publication, Delhi, 2009.

Ravishankar Kumar Singh: *Indian Banking and Financial Sector Reforms : Realising Global Aspirations (2 Vols-Set)*, Abhijeet Publication, Delhi, 2006.

W.L. Slatter, T. Krishtofferson and D.A. Seiberling: *Manual of Dairy Industry : Training and Development of Personnel for the Dairy Industry*, Asiatic Publication, Delhi, 2012.

Index

A

Abilympics 83
Addiction 79
Adequate 152, 224, 248
Agricultural marketing 42
Agriculture Credit 112
Agriculture credit 106
Allocation 153, 205
Animal Husbandry 68

B

Banking in India 24, 30
Banks 91, 92, 93, 94, 95, 96, 97, 98, 99, 100, 101, 102, 103, 118, 119, 120, 142
Baseline Data 49

C

Commercial Banks 38, 43, 47, 108, 109, 110, 111, 112, 113
Cooperative Management 106
Cost Benefit 41
Credit Flow 5, 6
Crop Production 51, 52, 67

D

Dairy Farming 44
Decentralization 53
Devolution 78
Differential Interest Rate 44

E

Economic Development 118, 119, 122
Entitlement 79
Entrepreneurship 81, 85
Exception 240
Exposure 76, 80, 85, 87
Extended 150, 188, 260

F

Farmers Service Societies 44
Financial Inclusion 94, 101, 102, 120
Financial Institutions 175, 178
Financial Products 102, 103, 143
Foreign Exchange 177, 179

I

Illegitimate 198
Impairment of Governance 111
Incapacitation 243
Indian Banking 22, 31
Initiatives Towards Rural Banking 21
Insemination 87

K

Kisan Credit Card 7, 47
Knitting 83, 85

L

Lead Bank Scheme 43

Literacy 77, 81, 82
Litigation 75, 79, 84
Loan 98, 101, 102, 120, 123

M

Markets 39, 99, 103, 122, 139, 140
Micro Finance Institutions 26
Mobile Banking 25
Money Lenders 2, 5

N

New Rural Economy 119

P

Political Interference 38
Priority 85
Probate 200, 220

R

Ratification 82
Regional Rural Banks 3, 4, 118, 119
Remittances 188, 218, 230, 242
Rural Banks 91, 92, 94, 97, 98, 99
Rural Communication 40, 41
Rural Consumer 40, 91
Rural Credit 91
Rural Credit 96, 101, 120
Rural Development 2, 9, 28, 33
Rural Financial Institutions 1, 2
Rural Marketing 39

S

Sanitation 76, 77, 80, 81
Scrupulously 244, 265
SHG Bank Linkage Model 27
Small Farmers Development Agency 44
State Control 107
Subsequently 227, 253, 269
Sustainability 78, 89
Symposium 79

V

Village Panchayats 102

W

Watershed Development 46, 73
World Bank 14